INVENTING JERRY LEWIS

Inventing
JERRY LEWIS

FRANK KRUTNIK

SMITHSONIAN
INSTITUTION
PRESS
Washington and London

Copy editor: Karin Kaufman
Production editor: Ruth Spiegel
Designer: Janice Wheeler

Library of Congress Cataloging-in-Publication Data
Krutnik, Frank, 1956-
    Inventing Jerry Lewis / Frank Krutnik.
        p.   cm.
    Includes bibliographical reference and index.
    ISBN 1-56098-369-8 (alk. paper)
      1. Lewis, Jerry, 1926—Criticism and interpretation. I. Title.
    PN2287.L435 K78 2000
    791.43'028'092—dc21
    [B]   99-04695

British Library Cataloguing-in-Publication Data available

Manufactured in the United States of America
06 05 04 03 02 01 00   5 4 3 2 1

∞ The paper used in this publication meets the minimum requirements of the
American National Standard for Information Sciences—Permanence of Paper for
Printed Library Materials ANSI Z39.48-1984.

FOR STANISLAW

CONTENTS

7

A BIG NIGHT IN HOLLYWOOD: THE SELF-DIRECTED FILMS   140

8

KID ON THE RUN: THE WANDERING YEARS   165

9

COMING HOME: THE NUTTY NATIONAL TREASURE   191

ACKNOWLEDGMENTS

Writing about Jerry Lewis is an experience that has proved—often at one and the same time—challenging, fascinating, and deeply maddening. One thing is certain: I would not have survived the process without the generous assistance and moral support provided by family, friends, colleagues, and others. I owe a special debt to the following and would like to dedicate the book to them all: Stanislaw, Sheila, Conrad, Alex, Vanda, and Ryan Krutnik; Olga and Chris Tanner; Jan Levine Thal; Robert and Marie King; Steve Cohan; Steve Neale; Steve House; Steve Lines; Ina Rae Hark; Shawn Levy; Mark and Ruth Penner; Henry Jenkins; Gene Martin; Marshall Deutelbaum; Emmanuel Dreux; Luke Gibbons; Anna Davie and Simon Jones; Celestino, Anita, and the Zaragoza crew; Mike Quinn; Charles Musser; Henry Jenkins; Ann Martin; Jeffrey Sconce (for igniting the idea of this book); Corinna Russell and Barry Redhead (for their translation skills); and the students in my comedy classes at the University of Aberdeen. But most of all to Catherine Morris.

I owe an enormous debt of gratitude to the staff at the following institutions: the British Film Institute Library; the British newspaper library at Colindale; the British Library; the New York Public Library; the Memorial Library at the University of Wisconsin, Madison; Roehampton Institute's Learning Resources Centre; the Queen Mother Library at the University of Aberdeen. I would also like to thank the Faculty of Arts and Divinity of the University of Aberdeen for the award of a semester's research leave. I am especially grateful to Mark Hirsch of the Smithsonian Institution Press and to Karin Kaufman for her editing wizardry. Travel grants from the British Academy enabled me to deliver portions of material from this project as a lecture at the Centre Universitaire de Luxembourg in 1991 and as papers at the 1992 *Theory, Culture and Society* conference at Seven Springs, Pennsylvania, and the 1993 Society for Cinema Studies conference in New Orleans. I would also like to thank the audiences who responded to presentations of my work on Lewis at the University of Toronto and the University of East Anglia in 1993.

Material from chapter 6 was initially incorporated in "Jerry Lewis: The Deformation of the Comic," an article published in the Fall 1994 issue of *Film Quarterly* (vol. 48, no. 4). Some of the work from chapter 3 found earlier expression in "The Handsome Man and His Monkey: The Comic Bondage of Dean Martin & Jerry Lewis," published in the spring 1995 *Journal of Popular Film and Television* (vol. 23, no. 1). Snippets from this project also appeared in "A Spanner in the Works? Genre, Narrative and the Hollywood Comedian," a chapter in *Classical Hollywood Comedy;* this AFI Film Reader, edited by Kristine Karnick and Henry Jenkins, was published by Routledge in 1995. In each case the material has been substantially revised.

Permission to quote from "By Myself" by Arthur Schwartz and Howard Dietz in chapter 4 was kindly granted by Paul Schwartz. I would also like to thank Warner Chappell Music, Ltd. for allowing me to quote from "With My Eyes Wide Open I'm Dreaming" by Harry Revel and Mack Gordon in chapter 3, and from "Two Lost Souls" by Richard Adler and Jerry Ross in chapter 2.

INVENTING JERRY LEWIS

AMERICA'S SACRED MONSTER

AN INTRODUCTION

In 1955 Metro-Goldwyn-Mayer released *It's Always Fair Weather,* the third and final musical collaboration between Gene Kelly and Stanley Donen. Playing like a disillusioned rewrite of *On the Town* (1949), the team's earlier triumph, the film deals with three soldier buddies who return from the war to encounter a civilian America that erodes their ideals and their friendship.[1] Ted Riley (Gene Kelly) abandons his ambitions for a legal career in favor of a dissolute life of gambling and womanizing. Angie Valentine (Michael Kidd) hopes for a classy restaurant but ends up with a hamburger joint and an ever-expanding family. Doug Hallerton (Dan Dailey) relinquishes his artistic aspirations in favor of an emotionally destitute marriage and a career as an advertising executive. The reunion of the trio a decade after demobilization provokes them to reconsider and ultimately to repair their lives. Despite the final reconciliation, however, *It's Always Fair Weather* remains an unusually sour and disenchanted Hollywood musical. Lacking the euphoric intensity of *On the Town* and *Singin' in the Rain* (1952), the film sketches a postwar landscape of shattered dreams and unfulfilled promises.

Of the three buddies' stories, it is Hallerton's that connects most keenly with contemporary anxieties. Doug is an upwardly mobile domestic breadwinner, an archetypal "man in a gray flannel suit" whose overidentification with the imperatives of corporate culture requires the sacrifice of his creativity, his masculinity, and his sense of self.[2] While Angie produces copious offspring and Ted loses himself in dames and dice, Doug scales the executive ladder of the advertising industry — and degenerates into a stuffy, self-repressed snob who doesn't smoke, drink, or enjoy himself in any other way. Struck with the realization that his disaffected wife and his wartime buddies regard him with a combination of "boredom, disgust, and pity," Doug gets drunk at a party thrown by his boss — and something snaps. He shaves off the moustache he has cultivated as a badge of maturity and then propels himself into a virtuoso performance of rebellious abandon. Appropriating the stilted argot of the business community ("situation-wise," "saturation-wise," etc.), Doug mangles it into a mélange of nonsense.[3] As he leaps around the room, breaking into frantic bursts of tap dancing and popular song ("I Dream of Jeannie," "Be My Love"), he commandeers household objects and astonished guests, using them as props in a series of extravagant impressions (a flapper, a Scots piper, a cavalryman). Near the end of his exhibition Doug hitches his jacket round his shoulders and lurches over to his boss, Mr. Fielding (Paul Maxey). Prodding Fielding in the chest, he declares, "I'm with you, Jerry Lewis-wise." Doug then staggers toward the dining room in an approximation of Lewis's convulsive lope, hands moronically glued to his head, elbows and knees akimbo. After he sends the tableware cascading to the floor, Doug collapses in a drunken faint.

At the party Doug Hallerton experiences a life-affirming epiphany of crazed exuberance. The staid organization man mounts a carnivalesque assault upon propriety and hierarchy that transforms him from an executive yes-man into a vaudevillian dynamo. By invoking Lewis's name *It's Always Fair Weather* allies Doug's white-collar revolt with the public figure who most clearly opposes the maturity and responsibility expected from 1950s corporate man. To be "Jerry Lewis-wise," Hallerton suggests, is to get wise to an alternative imagining of 1950s America — a transgressive universe of irresponsibility and unruliness.[4] And to enact his dissent, he draws upon the performance strategies for which Lewis was renowned at the peak of his early fame: an unrestrained and childlike enthusiasm, a rapid-fire parade of identities, and an excessive mobility of voice and body. Although he was clearly a product of American culture, Lewis was also assertively and undeniably "other": he was a locus of deviance, a clown prince of disorder, a monster from the id.[5]

Four decades after *It's Always Fair Weather,* the sixty-nine-year-old Jerry Lewis made his Broadway debut as another figuration of 1950s excess. In a much-lauded revival of the 1955 musical comedy *Damn Yankees* he was cast as Applegate, a Mephistophelean devil who conspires against the homely pieties of postwar suburbanism. However, the demonic countercurrents of Doug Hallerton's mutinous dance are absent from this 1990s rendering of Lewis's otherness. Applegate is an engaging prankster rather than a provocative insurgent, the domesticated fixture of a benign past instead of a contending voice of the present. Replacing the anarchistic body comedy of the young Lewis is a controlled and ironical persona that reminded several critics of venerable entertainer Jack Benny. For his triumphant performance in *Damn Yankees* Lewis received an astonishingly warm reception from a critical establishment that had generally reviled him throughout his professional career. He was welcomed, however, not as the insurrectionist id/iot of old but as an elder statesman of American show business. In a sympathetic review of the show carried by the *Washington Post* in 1996, for example, Lloyd Rose acknowledged Lewis's contentious history but proposed that he be cherished as a national asset:

Jerry Lewis makes his appearance in a puff of smoke. It's an altogether appropriate entrance, not only for the character but for Lewis, who brings with him a certain touch of dark magic. Now 70, Lewis has been performing for 65 years: Anyone who's spent that many years in show business knows something about Hell, and a helluva lot about performing. . . . The French have always adored him, so let's describe him with one of their phrases: *monstre sacré,* sacred monster. Behemoth. A unicorn. The last of his kind. (Rose 1996, C1)

This book examines Lewis's career as an entertainer, filmmaker, and celebrity from his early days as a madcap clown to his new eminence as an icon of American entertainment culture. Rose's term "sacred monster" strikes me as a particularly appropriate description of the ambivalent place Lewis has occupied within U.S. culture since he first shot to fame in the 1940s. A public figure for more than half a century, Lewis has received numerous awards for his contributions to comedy, his work as a film director, and his humanitarian activities. But he also has been repeatedly damned as a rampant egomaniac, a talentless vulgarian, and an exploiter of the disabled. It is difficult to think of any other entertainer who has inspired such ferocious extremes of adulation and hostility. The controversy surrounding Lewis intensified in the early 1960s when he began to direct and write his films as well as star in them. Admired by European intellectuals and film critics (especially, though not exclusively, in France) but denounced by their U.S. counterparts, Lewis's self-directed work triggered a war of cultural canons. The fallout from the conflict was to contaminate him for many years.

Although numerous books devoted to his work have been published in Europe since the 1960s, critical discussion of Lewis has been remarkably thin in his home country.[6] Prior to 1995, for example, no U.S. publisher authorized a book-length study of his films.[7] Despite the longevity of his career and the range of his achievements, Lewis has largely been excluded from the explosion of discourse generated over the past three decades as film studies and cultural studies established themselves as academic disciplines.[8] As I discovered soon after beginning this project in the early 1990s, the cultural prejudice against Lewis remains firm among sectors of the U.S. intelligentsia. I initially submitted a proposal for this book to the London office of a respected and prolific academic publisher. It met with an enthusiastic response from the two anonymous readers commissioned to evaluate the project—one of them describing the draft manuscript as "one of the best treatments of a star career I have ever read." Although the London branch was keen to proceed, editors at the New York office vetoed the proposal because they "[did] not feel that they could be confident of the success of a book on Jerry Lewis in their markets."

I encountered a more extreme reaction when, in 1995, I attended the annual conference for the Society for Cinema Studies in New York. Informed that a U.S. publisher had commissioned a biography of Lewis, I approached the publisher's representative in the book hall and asked for more information. Visibly affronted when I mentioned Lewis's name, the agent snapped, "God, I hope not!" To further underline her distaste for this unholy project, she grudgingly suggested that I contact the publisher's trade division. This encounter encapsulates the splitting of consciousness Lewis provokes in the United States: a breach between intellectuals and the public, between mind and body, between "culture" and "trade."[9] Ironically, two blocks away from the conference hotel Lewis had just opened at the Marquis Theater for his highly successful run in *Damn Yankees*. Although Lewis's validity is still actively resisted by many in the U.S. intellectual establishment, the Broadway show—as Tom Shales suggests—confirmed his status as "populist giant" (Shales 1997, D5).[10]

Partly to blame for Lewis's contested reputation, Charles Derry argues, is his "contradictory public persona: egotistical yet insecure, insulting yet sentimental, juvenile yet adult, emotionally naked yet defensive. Were not the real Jerry Lewis apparently so hard to love, the celluloid Lewis might be loved all the more" (Derry 1997, 604). Such paradoxes have been readily exploited by numerous tabloid exposés, which often portray the "real" Jerry Lewis as a monstrous and vulgar egomaniac. The ambivalences of Lewis's public image have also fueled an intensive industry of biographical speculation. For example, he is the subject of book-length studies by Richard Gehman (1964), Arthur Marx (1975), and Shawn Levy (1996a) and features as a key player in the autobiography of film producer Hal Wallis (Wallis and Higham 1980) and in Nick Tosches's monumental account of Dean Martin's life (Tosches 1992). Lewis's

autobiography, co-written with journalist Herb Gluck, appeared in the early
1980s (Lewis and Gluck 1982), and a decade later his former wife Patti followed
suit with her ghosted memoirs (Lewis and Coleman 1993). Representations of
the "real-life" Jerry Lewis have also issued from countless profiles and interviews circulated through newspapers, magazines, and television. These range
from hagiographic publicity materials such as the three-part Martin and Lewis
"autobiography" published by the fan magazine *Picturegoer* in 1953 (Martin and
Lewis 1953a, 1953b, 1953c) to the malevolent character assassinations printed by
the *National Enquirer*.[11]

This book is not a biography. I do not aim to trace the contours of the "real
man" who lies behind the public mask but to examine how "Jerry Lewis" has
operated as a complexly *mediated* subject. With so much of his life lived in the
public eye, it is not feasible to separate Lewis as a private individual from the
vortex of representations and discourses in which he figures. The Faustian pact
he made to achieve mass-media celebrity required him to forfeit his claim to
private selfhood. Like his vaudevillian father, Jerry Lewis was trained in the live
aesthetic of variety performance, but he also adapted to technologically advanced contexts of mass entertainment—films, television, radio, phonographic
recordings—that challenge the unity and authenticity of performance. These
media not only enforce a temporal and spatial separation between artist and audience but also subject artistic expression to the intervention of other hands
(editors, directors, and cinematographers, for example). Moreover, mass production and mass dissemination translate the singular instance of performance
into multitudinous copies that circulate widely and freely within potentially in-
finite economic, cultural, and cross-cultural processes of exchange.

Of the many battles in which Lewis has been engaged throughout his career,
the most intense and sustained has been the struggle to secure authorship of his
public persona. In Hollywood, for example, he set out to attain greater command
over the economic and signifying value of his cinematic self-representation by
boosting his status from star to producer to hyphenate filmmaker (producer-
writer-director-performer). The problem is that the biographical individual
Jerry Lewis can never fully control, contain, or exhaust the plurality of meanings generated by the commodified sign that bears his name.[12] This does not
mean, of course, that he has ever ceased trying. Since he began his career as a
solo entertainer in the mid-1950s Lewis has sustained an extremely combative
relationship with the U.S. press, passionately disputing the right of journalists
and reviewers to make negative assessments of his work and his character.
When called upon to justify himself, Lewis does so with vehement and nakedly
emotional righteousness, in a manner that, as Leslie Bennetts puts it, is "so

hostile and paranoid it seems almost Nixonian" (Bennetts 1993, 33).[13] In 1993, for example, he told Shawn Levy, "The press, of course, are cunts, like they've always been and always will be. They're getting worse. They're not getting better, they're getting worse. They're just absolutely fucking scum" (Levy 1996a, 487).

Levy's biography ends with an extraordinary anecdote that suggests the intensity of Lewis's desire to police his public definition. Lewis initially welcomed Levy's attentions because, the latter speculates, "he saw in the appearance of an interested young writer a means to resurrect his lot in the public eye." Relations between the two grew strained, however, when it became obvious that the book would not elide the murkier aspects of Lewis's life. At their second and final meeting Lewis exploded into rage when Levy asked about his unfinished film *The Day the Clown Cried*—a topic he is notoriously sensitive about. Ranting at the biographer, Lewis accused him of being an "insensitive prick" and the product of a "sick childhood." Levy describes his stunned incomprehension as Lewis continued his tirade and then seized the tape on which it had been recorded— a tape eventually returned to its owner with the outburst removed (Levy 1996a, 484, 489).

I faced a similar though, thankfully, far less extreme rebuff when I tried to arrange a meeting with Lewis in London in July 1997. I sent him a letter via the Adelphi Theatre, where he was playing in *Damn Yankees,* explaining my plans for the book and outlining my credentials as a writer and teacher on film. Two days later I returned from work to find that Lewis had left a message on my answering machine, requesting that I contact him at the Dorchester Hotel.[14] Returning the call, I was extremely nervous at the prospect of a close encounter with the awesome presence I had come across in countless films, television programs, interviews, and articles. When I asked Lewis if he would be prepared to meet me, he let out a wry laugh. It soon became apparent that this was not the reason why the king of comedy had contacted me so swiftly. Instead, I was in for a right royal reproach for my article "Jerry Lewis: The Deformation of the Comic," published in *Film Quarterly* a few years earlier (Krutnik 1994). Reading me the *Webster's Dictionary* definition of the word "deformation," Lewis informed me that the word made him "very uncomfortable."[15] Taken aback by this unexpected lesson in semantics from the grand master of linguistic mutilation, I tried to defend my use of the term, pointing out that like many of his French admirers I was interested in the way his films play with form.[16] But Lewis would have none of it. When I told him that it was a shame he did not want us to meet, he tossed back flippantly, "You're English, you'll get over it." I tried to impress upon him that, no matter what he thought, I genuinely admired his work and believed that my book would contribute significantly to the revival of interest in his achievements. "Have a nice life," he replied, signing off.

The Jerry Lewis who confronted me on the telephone was certainly not the ranting maniac portrayed by Shawn Levy, but he nonetheless exuded a stately authority that made it clear he would take no prisoners if things got nasty. The point of the exchange was to let me know that I had courted the great man's disapproval and would consequently not be granted an audience. For my own part, I was glad that this was the closest I would come to the sacred monster of American show business. The fact that the source of contention was the meaning of a word brought home to me the problems in communication that would inevitably intrude in any interview with Lewis. For decades he has woven a protective smoke screen of myths to shroud his person and, as Levy shows repeatedly, has routinely embellished and reordered his past to suit his own construction of "Jerry Lewis." A face-to-face encounter could never reveal the real Jerry Lewis, only one more of the performances of self in which he is so practiced.

In his homeland Lewis's abrasive personality has proved a substantial obstruction to the critical recognition of his achievements as a comedian and filmmaker. Even more problematic, however, is the grotesque body comedy upon which he built his fame. Lewis's performance style is a mode of expression that challenges the logocentricity of "legitimate" bourgeois culture: "I'm basically a facial and physical mime performer. Because I make noise in this country when I do comedy, that's one thing, but if you come and see concerts that I do in Europe, you wonder how I can do 90 minutes on the stage without talking to the people. The mime and the pathos is what my forte was from the beginning. And I am most comfortable doing that. I am the most comfortable when I'm doing pieces that are clear to an audience without a lot of words to convolute it" (JAS Productions 1992c).

The fervent endorsement of Jerry Lewis by European intellectuals short-circuited the conventional polarization of elite and popular cultures. With little formal education, Lewis was a creature of American show biz: he was schooled in pre–World War II variety traditions, serving his apprenticeship in the Jewish resort hotels of the Catskills, in small-time vaudeville and burlesque, and in nightclubs. Popular entertainment furnished him with an expressive language, and in return he has treated its value and purpose with great seriousness. Unlike Woody Allen, a Jewish comedian-filmmaker much beloved of refined critics, Lewis has never sought legitimacy by invoking such high-cultural icons as William Shakespeare, Ingmar Bergman, and Federico Fellini. Instead, he proclaims his allegiance to populist heroes such as Al Jolson, Charles Chaplin, and Stan Laurel. Allen's precisioned wisecracks are complicit with the intellectual values of elite culture, but Lewis's most characteristic verbal routines subject language to the same kind of convoluted deformations and interruptions that he puts his body through.

Lewis developed an extreme form of physical comedy in which the unruly body overturns its subjugation to the intellect, to the spirit, to speech. As Raymond Durgnat points out, "Like all great expressionists, he thinks with his body, and translates the soul's impulses into a semaphore of spastic acrobacy; he stutters with his feet, trips over his tongue, squints with his kneecaps and turns the simple act of crossing his legs into a bout of cat's cradle" (Durgnat 1969, 234).[17] Through such "frenetic cadenzas" (ibid., 235), Lewis presents the spectacle of a body liberated not just from social and physical constraints but also from the command of the subject who occupies it. At the same time as his grotesque convulsions fragment bodily expression into a collage of misdirected and disconnected gestures, Lewis's performance also enacts a spectacular dissolution of identity. In the grip of hysteria, his body pays host to a multiplicity of personae that collide, compete, and combine with dazzling rapidity: "He doesn't so much emote, as disintegrate into an emotional gamut ranging through Donald Duck, the Frankenstein Monster, Pluto, Cheetah, Alfred E. Neumann, Phlebus, Stan Laurel, Michel Simon in *La Chienne,* and, in *The Nutty Professor* Humphrey Bogart pretending to be the kind of dirty old man who buys pornography in *The Big Sleep. . . .* His emotional gears crash and freewheel from one response to the other" (ibid., 234-35).

In an intriguing 1991 article, "Film Bodies: Gender, Genre, and Excess," Linda Williams examines a group of low-status genres that not only parade bodies caught in the grip of intense sensation or emotion but also elicit a heightened bodily response from the viewer (tears, fear, sexual arousal) (Williams 1991, 4). Williams focuses upon melodrama, horror, and pornography, explicitly excluding comedian-comedy from her discussion on two counts. First, such films do not involve a close imitation of the onscreen action by audiences, and second, unlike the other genres, they do not center on the spectacularized female body:

What may especially mark these body genres as low is the perception that the body of the spectator is caught up in an almost involuntary mimicry of the emotion or sensation of the body on the screen along with the fact that the body displayed is female. Physical clown comedy is another "body" genre concerned with all manner of gross activities and body functions — eating shoes, slipping on banana peels. Nonetheless, it has not been deemed gratuitously excessive, probably because the reaction of the audience does not mimic the sensations experienced by the central clown. Indeed, it is almost a rule that the audience's physical reaction of laughter does not coincide with the often deadpan reactions of the clown. (Williams 1991, 4)

These remarks clearly have little applicability to Lewis's films, which have been condemned repeatedly for their "gratuitous excesses." At a far remove from Williams's conception of the deadpan clown, Lewis's performance is driven by the same kind of ecstasy she identifies in her preferred genres of sensation: "a quality of uncontrollable convulsion or spasm—of the body 'beside itself' with sexual pleasure, fear and terror, or overpowering sadness." Melodramas, horror films, and pornography may locate women as the "primary *embodiments* of pleasure, fear, and pain" (Williams 1991, 4), but Lewis's comedy renders the male body a site for the grotesque disordering of normative protocols of gender, sexuality, and identity. There is evidence, too, that the response of his teenage fans actually did mirror Lewis's bodily paroxysms. For example, in his *New York Times* review of *Jumping Jacks* (1952) Bosley Crowther expressed alarm not simply at what Lewis did on screen but also at the frenzied derangement of a young audience that greeted his comic antics with unseemly bursts of "whooping and hollering" (Crowther 1952, 30). In a discussion of the anarchistic comedian films of the 1930s Henry Jenkins similarly emphasizes the physicality of the audience response to such comedies: "The dominant laughter of the early 1930s was undoubtedly the belly laugh, an intense eruption that shook the entire body, an anarchic laughter that challenged the power of institutions to exercise emotional and social constraint upon individual spontaneity, a nonsensical laughter that was meaningful precisely in the way it transcended narrative meaning. Perhaps most important, it was a popular laughter, which entertained without pretenses of moral education or social reform" (Jenkins 1992, 284).

The gross physicality of Lewis's performance resembles the mode of popular comic activity that literary theorist Mikhail Bakhtin identifies as the "carnivalesque."[18] Bakhtin argues that the carnival festivities of medieval Europe permitted a dynamic popular expression that posed an alternative to the regimentation of official culture: "Carnival celebrated temporary liberation from the prevailing truth and from the established order; it marked the suspension of all hierarchical rank, privileges, norms, and prohibitions. Carnival was the true feast of time, the feast of becoming, change and renewal. It was hostile to all that was immortalized and completed" (Bakhtin 1984, 10).[19] Carnival celebrations enabled an imaginative overthrow of the established power structure, not only turning the social hierarchy upside down but also releasing the human body from its social delimitation. In the peculiar aesthetic regime of medieval carnival culture, coined "grotesque realism" by Bakhtin, the "essential principle . . . is degradation, that is, the lowering of all that is high, spiritual, ideal, abstract; it is a transfer to the material level, to the sphere of earth and body in their indissoluble unity" (ibid., 18-21).

Parading bodies that exceed social definition—through their exaggerated proportions, unquenchable sensuality, and revolting assertiveness—grotesque realism emancipates the lower bodily stratum (belly, genitals, anus) from its subjection to the intellect and the spirit (Bakhtin 1984, 21). But Bakhtin stresses that by celebrating formlessness over fixity (and "becoming" over "being"), carnival grotesquerie serves as a force for social revivification:

The material bodily principle in grotesque realism is offered in its all-popular festive and utopian aspect. . . . In grotesque realism, therefore, the bodily element is deeply positive. It is presented not in a private, egotistic form, severed from the other spheres of life, but as something universal, representing all the people. . . . The body and bodily life have here a cosmic and at the same time an all-people's character; this is not the body and its physiology in the modern sense of these words, because it is not individualized. The material bodily principle is contained not in the biological individual, not in the bourgeois ego, but in the people, a people who are continually growing and renewed. This is why all that is bodily becomes grandiose, exaggerated, immeasurable.

This exaggeration has a positive, assertive character. The leading themes of these images of bodily life are fertility, growth, and a brimming-over of abundance. . . . The grotesque body is not separated from the rest of the world. It is not a closed, completed unit; it is unfinished, outgrows itself, transgresses its own limits. (Bakhtin 1984, 19, 26)[20]

As Bakhtin insists, these observations on the carnivalesque pertain to a historically specific cultural and social regime that shares little in common with the contemporary Western world: "The depth, variety and power of separate grotesque themes can be understood only within the unity of folk and carnival spirit. If examined outside of this unity, they become one-sided, flat, and stripped of their rich content" (1984, 51–52). The grotesque body continues to figure as a potent signifier of the ambivalent relations between the individual and the social community, but twentieth-century popular culture charges it with distinctive meanings (ibid., 33–52; Jenkins 1992, 223). Whereas the medieval carnival was a participatory event that was shaped directly by collective action—the people literally were the entertainment—technologically mediated mass entertainment forms such as film and television enforce a distinction between the professionalized performer and the generalized audience.[21] Thus Jerry Lewis may unify the discrete members of an audience into a community of laughter, but he himself remains apart: no longer *of* the people, he must cater *to* them.

Lewis's physical excesses underscore his singularity as an entertainer and "personality," but they nonetheless communicate broader anxieties regarding the social codifications of the body and its articulations of identity, gender, sexuality, and class. As in the carnival culture of the Middle Ages, the grotesque display is stamped through with the particularities of the milieu that inspires it. For example, the films Lewis made with Dean Martin in the early 1950s associate his carnivalesque deformations with a challenge to the normative parameters of male identity and desire, their homosocial intimacy offering a sly alternative to the heterosexual affirmation prevalent in the postwar years. During this period Lewis was also strongly identified with the young audiences that constituted his most loyal and vociferous fan base. Fifties youth appropriated his insubordinate seizures to voice their own resistance to the constricted options decreed by adults and adulthood. Engaging the hysterical urgings of 1950s teenage culture, Lewis's spasmodic ruptures provoked the same kind of delirium that would later be excited by the libidinal undulations of Elvis Presley or the sexual frenzy of Little Richard.[22] Despite serving as a comedic precursor of rock and roll rebellion, however, Lewis's insurrectionary countercurrents were not reserved exclusively for the kids. The Martin and Lewis films may have been targeted increasingly at the young, but the team also played risqué sets to adult nightclubbers and made television shows aimed at family audiences.

With a language of physical expression inherited from popular variety entertainment, silent slapstick comedy, and animated cartoons, Lewis's extremist performance overturns the hegemony of reason and language to flaunt the body as a site of boundlessness and process. When severed from the cosmic function it served in medieval carnival culture, however, the grotesque body loses its connotations of social renewal, becoming instead a mode of spectacle capable of inciting extremes of laughter and discomfort, joy and disgust, identification and disavowal. In a 1972 interview Lewis produced a striking metaphor of physical rupture to highlight the intimate connection between horror and comedy in his outrageous physical outbursts:[23] "The things that I do, of course, are terribly lowbrow. I'm not talking about reviews now. I'm talking about general consensus, that comedy is lowbrow. But you take someone like Stan Laurel, who had the greatest dignity and the most influence of any man I've ever known. And he was just chucked under the rug. I finally found out the reason for it: most people fear comedy. Because the truth of it is like a bone coming through the skin. Comedy is nothing more than a mirror we hold up to life. And people don't want that" (Meisel 1972, 6).

The bone tearing through the skin induces pain, but it also reveals disturbing "truths" concealed beneath the decorous and orderly surfaces of life. As the reference to Stan Laurel suggests, the comedian must be ready to pay the price for daring to enact such disreputable excesses. Lewis attained his own peculiar status as a bone of contention within American culture by tendering himself as a figurehead of, and a scapegoat for, the unleashing of carnival liberties. Borrowing dialogue from the character he played in the film *Funny Bones,* Lewis confided in a 1995 interview, "You can teach someone to be funny, but you can't teach them 'funny bones.' You're born with that. I could teach someone to say funny things or to delineate a funny notion. But you can't instill timing. You have to have funny bones to feel that beat" (*Iran News* 1995).[24] The funny bones Lewis was born with enabled him to build a dazzling career as an entertainer, filmmaker, and philanthropist. But they have also been his curse. Despite his multifarious ambitions and accomplishments, Lewis has never been able to escape the daunting shadow cast by the grotesque body comedy that brought him fame. Several interviewers have remarked upon Lewis's tendency to use the third person mode of speech when alluding to the comic character he created, which he describes as "Jerry," the "Kid," or the "Idiot."[25] However, Lewis's endeavors to disentangle the performing self from the extremity of that which is performed generally meet with incomprehension. Lewis himself seems unwilling to accept what others take at face value — that he is, incontrovertibly, "Jerry Lewis," in all his magnificence, munificence, and monstrousness.

This book explores the successive phases of Lewis's strange career as a public figure, from the partnership with Dean Martin that first brought him to attention in the 1940s to his Broadway triumph with *Damn Yankees.* Chapters 2 and 3 study the dynamics of the Martin and Lewis team, focusing on their live television performances and films. Launched into the public eye in tandem with Martin's handsome man, Lewis was faced with the task of redefining his image when the professional and highly personal relationship between the two men foundered in 1956. Chapters 4 and 5 examine the work Lewis produced in the crucial period of transition that followed the demise of the team, when he sought to both reconstruct himself as a solo performer and exert increasing control over his public representations. In chapters 6 and 7 I consider how these processes culminated in the self-directed films of the early 1960s, which are especially fascinating for the way they play upon the conflictual potentialities that constitute Lewis's public identity. As Dana Polan notes, the French critics seized upon this feature of Lewis's self-directed movies, perceiving in their "constant obsession with performance and showmanship a kind of meditation on the presentation of self in everyday American life" (Polan 1984a, 46).

Ironically, the peak of Lewis's creative accomplishments as a filmmaker coincided with the beginning of a rapid decline in his popularity as a star of cinema and television. As chapter 8 outlines, although Lewis faced a series of professional crises through the late 1960s and 1970s he also succeeded in shaping the most audacious and contested of Lewisian texts from the annual telethon he hosts for the Muscular Dystrophy Association. While other avenues and opportunities diminished, this high-profile humanitarian venture guaranteed Lewis regular exposure to a mass audience. Chapter 9 examines the slow but steady reclamation of Lewis's reputation that has been building since the early 1980s. Lewis has received critical plaudits for his dramatic performances in *The King of Comedy* (1983) and the television show *Wiseguy* (1988–89), and for his showcasing role in *Damn Yankees*. He has also benefited from the success of Eddie Murphy's version of *The Nutty Professor* in 1996, the first of several planned remakes of his earlier films. As we head toward the millennium, the former bête noire of popular entertainment faces cultural enshrinement as a monument to the glories of twentieth-century American entertainment. As I will suggest, Lewis himself has done much to nurture and direct his late-blooming eminence, by helping to build an empire of remembrance that will long outlast him. Before I begin looking at the progression of Lewis's work and career, however, I will spend some time disentangling the complex causes and repercussions of Lewis's association with "the French."

AN EMBARRASSMENT TO THE ORDER

JERRY LEWIS AND THE FRENCH

It's funny but true, or true because it's funny: the French public rates Jerry Lewis as a classic virtuoso comedian comparable to Charlie Chaplin. The Lewis syndrome . . . is also infectious in West Germany, Spain, the Netherlands and Belgium.

—James F. Clarity

Clarity's use of the term *syndrome* makes explicit an assumption that underlies most discussions of Jerry Lewis's work and its foreign reception by U.S. journalists and critics. Treated as a symptom of disease, disorder, or deviance, enthusiasm for Lewis is displaced onto non-American audiences and pathologized, consigned to a realm of embarrassing otherness. Since the mid-1960s the demonization of Jerry Lewis by U.S. cultural guardians has been so forceful and so unquestioning that it, too, demands to be read as symptomatic. An exchange between novelist William Burroughs and film director David Cronenberg during their 1991 publicity junket for *Naked Lunch* neatly illustrates the persistence of the anti-Lewis syndrome among North American intellectuals. Burroughs deems it appropriate that the French Order of Arts and Letters[1] should include a wife-killing junkie novelist and a maker of visceral horrorfests, but Lewis's presence within such exalted company cannot be tolerated: "There's not much in this world left to horrify Burroughs, but being told that he, Cronenberg, and Jerry Lewis have each been elected members of the French Order of Arts and Letters is nearly enough send him on another heroin jag. 'We need to vote him out, then,' shouts Burroughs. 'Yeah, we can all get together to expel him from the order,' says Cronenberg, 'because everyone always says, "Yeah, but so is Jerry Lewis." It's an embarrassment to the order'" (Snowden 1992, 25).

Knee-jerk responses like this have been astonishingly commonplace since Jerry Lewis's merits as a filmmaker were hotly contested by French and American critics in the mid-1960s.[2] In a favorable account of Lewis in his book *A Biographical Dictionary to Film,* David Thompson (1994) observed that "to live in America is to witness the naked incredulity at Lewis being taken seriously. Few things are held against the whole of France more fiercely than French love of Lewis" (443). Dana Polan (1984a) posits that the most disturbing feature of "the common clichés of American critics and intellectuals toward Lewis is not that they dislike him but that they present that dislike as a natural commonsensical, automatic reaction that is categorically beyond debate. *Rolling Stone* quotes [film critic] John Simon: 'I stay away from his films. It's the kind of low, infantile, witless farce that does not interest me in the least'" (46). One consequence of such casually purposeful denigration is that the very mention of Lewis's name is sufficient to call into question the integrity of "the French," especially the radical theoretical interventions bred by France's intellectual culture (existentialism, deconstruction, poststructuralism, postmodernism, etc.). However, Lewis was not only a favorite of French intellectuals, and of European audiences, but was also one of the most consistently popular film and television stars in the United States itself. His television shows drew high ratings throughout the 1950s, and from 1951 to 1963 he failed only once to make the annual list of the top ten stars at the North American box office (Steinberg 1981, 478-80). The very popularity and cultural visibility of Lewis's grotesque comedy made him a problem for cultural legislators of taste in North America long before the French got their hands on him. And when they did, American critics seized the opportunity to assert the distinctiveness of their tastes over those vulgar consumers who bought into such "witless farce."

This chapter examines the circumstances that made possible Lewis's enthronement as a critical and cultural bête noire. The Pavlovian dismissal of Lewis by U.S. cultural authorities is rooted in the revaluation of mainstream popular cinema forced by the critics of the journal *Cahiers du Cinéma.* But as I will show in chapter 4, the American Lewis syndrome did not begin with this controversy; American film and television reviewers routinely vilified his work before he even directed his first film. However, the lavish praise heaped upon Lewis by French ciné-critics struck home in the wake of the international acclaim for New Wave films, which boosted the profile of auteurist film criticism. In this context prejudices against Lewis took on a new sense of purpose. He was no longer regarded simply the upstart entertainer who brandished an embarrassing form of low comedy. American intellectuals could visit upon Lewis a ritualistic punishment for the body blows delivered against their sensibilities by a guerrilla force of French critics who treated products of the Hollywood assembly line with the reverence accorded works of art. When his French enthusiasts crowned Lewis a carnivalesque *roi du crazy,* they pitched his grotesque body comedy against the refinements of literate cultural experience. The canonization of Lewis implied a wholesale overturning of the civilized values of taste and discrimination that American intellectuals guarded so diligently. Jerry Lewis was not himself a revolutionary, but he had his own distinctive part to play in a revolution of ideas about the significance of popular film as an art form and as a cultural activity. Although many of the principles of the French critics were soon incorporated within mainstream discourses on film, Lewis himself was the designated fall guy, a sacrificial scapegoat who made their acceptance possible.

REIMAGINING HOLLYWOOD

> You badly underrate your films[,] . . . especially those you regard as debased by so-called Hollywood commercialism. Far too often you are offended by the simplifications, so necessary in a mass medium. But we see behind these simplifications—oversimplifications, if you prefer—the style, which can result in a deepening and complication of the material. I think your problem may be that you mistake ordinary, easy-to-achieve realism for meaning. For the French it is more important that cinema possesses imagination.
>
> —Jean Domarchi (Alpert 1966)

In the late 1950s a series of low-budget French films — distinctively styled, assertively modern — attracted considerable attention both within France and on the international art-cinema circuit. These films were Louis Malle's *Les Amants* (*The Lovers*) (1958), Claude Chabrol's *Le beau Serge* and *Les Cousins,* François Truffaut's *Les Quatre cents coups* (*The 400 Blows*), Alain Resnais's *Hiroshima mon amour* (all 1959), and Jean-Luc Godard's *À bout de souffle* (*Breathless*) (1960). Resnais was awarded the International Critics' Award at the 1959 Cannes Film Festival, and Truffaut received both the Cannes prize for direction and the New

York Critics' award for Best Foreign Language Film. Tagged the *nouvelle vague* (New Wave), these filmmakers and the many who followed in their wake were soon being regarded as a modern art-film movement that could rank with the achievements of German Expressionist cinema, the Soviet montage films and Italian Neorealism.

Kristin Thompson and David Bordwell (1994) note that New Wave film-makers were not a unified group sharing a common set of aesthetic and cultural protocols so much as "a brief alliance of varied temperaments" (524). A moment rather than a movement, the New Wave was a diversified response to a period of upheaval within both French cinema and French society (Williams 1992, 327-30).[3] The directors who came to prominence between 1958 and 1962 entered filmmaking by various routes, but most attention was focused upon a group, in itself diverse, who progressed to making films from analyzing them as critics.[4] Truffaut, Godard, and Chabrol wrote for *Cahiers du Cinéma*,[5] the most influential journal to emerge from the revitalized film culture of postwar Paris.[6] The critical discourse of this period, Alan Williams suggests, provided a catalyst for an alternative French film culture: it was "an activist, often theoretical discourse aimed at a new kind of cinema as yet rarely realized in images and sounds" (ibid., 306).[7]

Founded in 1951 by Jacques Doniol-Valcroze, with help from André Bazin, *Cahiers du Cinéma* attracted several rebellious young critics.[8] In January 1954 the journal published François Truffaut's article "Une Certaine Tendance du cinéma français," which called for the overthrow of the prestige cinema of costume dramas and literary adaptations that dominated French cinema after the war (Truffaut 1976). In place of this "Tradition of Quality" Truffaut advocated a cinema of auteurs, ruled by the presence of the director rather than the writer. Although the concept of the auteur was not new to French film criticism, Truffaut and his followers redefined it to locate the visual orchestration of mise-en-scène as the prime criterion of cinematic creativity.[9] Disillusioned with an "official" French cinema that had resisted the postwar creative revolution that had energized the cinemas of Italy and the United States (respectively, neorealism and film noir), the *Cahiers* writers were passionate in their enthusiasm for auteur films and boldly provocative in writing about them. As Jim Hillier (1985) stresses, Truffaut's call to arms "caused ripples, and more, in French film culture and beyond . . . because the idea was used . . . with polemical brio to upset established values and reputations" (7). Although it was not a contentious strategy for dealing with the minority practice of art cinema, the *politique des auteurs* generated intense controversy when applied forcefully and headily to films from the Hollywood "production line." From 1944, with France vulnerable to

American economic and cultural influence, the cinema was an especially visible and symbolic site of contested cultural definitions.[10] Following the liberation, a four-year backlog of Hollywood films was unleashed upon French screens. Audiences flocked to see them, but the domestic industry cried foul because foreign films, largely American, accounted for 60 percent of the French cinema market in early 1945, an increase of 25 percent over the prewar average (Crisp 1993, 74).[11]

The Tradition of Quality was a "heritage" cinema that dealt with issues of national identity at a time when France faced an accelerated process of capitalist modernization and the infiltration of American consumer culture. Even though it aped Hollywood practice by investing in high budgets, lavish production values, and popular stars, the Tradition of Quality looked to the past for visions of the cinema and visions of France (Williams 1992, 278, 283). New Wave films, by contrast, engaged with the cultural contradictions of postwar France, even if they repressed its political controversies. The term *nouvelle vague* was first used by journalist Françoise Giroud in the left-wing weekly *L'Express* to designate "the generation that had been formed culturally and politically after the Liberation" (ibid., 328). New Wave films seemed to capture something of the new mood of 1950s French youth, whose experiences had little in common with the nostalgic nationalism of the quality films.[12] The *nouvelle vague* filmmakers, many of whom were born after 1930, were willing to engage with the seductions of American commercial culture — and they did so playfully, critically, and ambivalently.[13]

The *Cahier*ists directed their films with the same vigorous antiauthoritarianism that infused their writing about cinema. They pursued a freewheeling, improvisational approach to filmmaking that was opposed to the studio mode of quality cinema. Hand-held cameras roamed the city streets, conventions of continuity editing and narrative development were jettisoned in favor of the hedonistic delights of self-reflexivity and intertextuality, direct sound and jagged musical scoring replaced the carefully crafted soundtrack. It was a hip, differentiated, and euphoric rendering of cinema — simultaneously stylized and realist — that worked against not only the formal restraint of the Tradition of Quality but also the self-effacement and classicism of Hollywood.[14] New Wave films repeatedly evoked Hollywood models, but they fractured their stylistic and ideological certainties.[15] By rupturing the representational conventions of mainstream cinema, New Wave films managed to create potent imaginings of the disconnectedness of modern life. The *nouvelle vague* opened new possibilities for French cinema in the late 1950s and early 1960s, and it would also have a long-lasting impact on filmmakers outside France.[16]

Although a faction of *Cahiers* auteurists (nicknamed the MacMahonists) avidly fetishized Hollywood films and directors (Elsaesser 1975, 213), the *politique* cannot easily be dismissed as a perverse desire to elevate "low" over "high" culture. The younger *Cahiers* critics by no means restricted themselves to the consideration of American films, but the particularly close manner in which they embraced Hollywood paraded their lack of faith in the products and priorities of the "official" French cinema.[17] By declaring that a melodrama, a western, or a thriller from the Hollywood assembly line could possess greater merit than a literate quality film, an avant-garde film, or a politically committed film, these critics assaulted traditional evaluative protocols. At the same time, however, they made use of the latter as a means of validating their favored auteurs. The *Cahier*ists were less concerned with the practical contexts of Hollywood film production than with demonstrating the consistency of expression of the films signed by such preferred directors as Alfred Hitchcock, Fritz Lang, Orson Welles, Howard Hawks, Sam Fuller, Nicholas Ray, and Frank Tashlin. No matter what their degree of involvement in the studio system — and regardless of what other factors impinged upon the making of the individual film — the creative personality of the auteur-director was held to be the wellspring of its meaning, a master code to be deciphered across the body of work.

Since achieving its domination of the international film market in the wake of World War I, the American cinema has repeatedly been damned as a vehicle for U.S. cultural and economic imperialism, especially by European nations whose own prosperity derives from centuries of colonial exploitation. In her recent analysis of the American cinema's relations with its foreign markets in the interwar years Ruth Vasey observes that "nationalist" objections to Hollywood's dominance can operate as a cover story for a class-based protectionism:

As in the United States, resistance to American movies abroad was sustained by a cultural elite. The great mass of people in most countries responded very well to the American product, with its action-oriented aesthetics and lavish production values; if the movies had not been popular they would not have constituted a problem. Those most opposed to the free circulation of U.S. films were those who felt they had most to lose — not only the filmmakers and social conservatives but also governments themselves, who feared the erosion of their political and economic prestige through the cinematic equation of American values with glamour and prosperity. (Vasey 1997, 41)

Hollywood cinema may be distinctively American, but like U.S. popular culture in general it does not belong exclusively to the Americans. The intensified Americanization of European screens after World War II was due not solely to the financial and political muscle of the U.S. film industry. It had as much to do with the readiness of audiences to adopt Hollywood films in preference to the "official" national culture.[18] To conceive of these audiences as the mindless dupes of U.S. cultural imperialism is to underestimate how the textual meanings of American films can be rearticulated to serve other goals. Dick Hebdige makes this point in a discussion of debates concerning the "specter of Americanization" in Britain from the mid-1930s to the early 1960s.

Hebdige (1988) notes that for commentators as diverse as Evelyn Waugh, George Orwell, and Richard Hoggart, American styles, products, and values came to symbolize broader shifts within British culture, associated in particular with the "intrusion" of the working class and the young into the sphere of conspicuous consumption. As the supreme world military and economic power, the United States was a ready scapegoat for the multifarious social and economic transformations experienced by a declining, postimperial Britain (73, 52–54). Although "Americanization" soon became a shorthand term for the threats of "homogenization'" and "leveling-down," Hebdige stresses that Britons who embraced U.S. popular culture put it to a productive variety of uses:

There can be no doubt that America, particularly in the post-War period began to exert considerable cultural and economic influence on European culture. . . . But there is little evidence to suggest that the eradication of social and cultural differences imputed to these developments by a generation of cultural critics has taken place at least in the form they predicted. For instance, the sheer plethora of youth cultural options currently available (e.g., the rockabillies, heavy metal enthusiasts, ted revivalists, etc.) most of which are refracted however indirectly through a "mythical America" seems to suggest that the early fears about the homogenizing influence of American culture were unfounded. Rather, American popular culture—Hollywood films, advertising images, packaging, clothes and music—offers a rich iconography, a set of symbols, objects and artifacts which can be assembled and re-assembled by different groups in a literally limitless number of combinations. And the meaning of each selection is transformed as individual objects—jeans, rock records, Tony Curtis hair styles, bobby socks, etc.—are taken out of their original historical and cultural contexts and juxtaposed against other signs from other sources. From this perspective, the style of the teddy boys can be interpreted less as the dull reflex of a group of what Hoggart called "tamed and directionless helots" to a predigested set of norms and values than as an *attribution* of meaning, as an attempt at imposition and control, as a symbolic act of self-removal—a step away from a society which could offer little more than the knowledge that [as Tom Wolfe put it] "the fix is in and all that work does is keep you afloat at the place you were born into." (Hebdige 1988, 73–74)

It may be, as Stuart Hall has suggested, that through the globalization of Hollywood "the world dreams itself to be 'American'" (Corrigan 1991, 4). Hebdige argues, however, that "Americanness" involves identification not so much with the United States itself as with the regime of *difference* it signifies. Hollywood films offer imaginings of alternative possibilities, and as such they can be used by audiences barred from access to social and cultural power as an implicit or explicit strategy of resistance against the limitations of the domestic culture. For elite and middlebrow tastemakers,[19] mass-produced Hollywood films are a problem precisely because they connect so effortlessly with so many diverse audiences.[20]

André Bazin, and the *Cahiers* critics he inspired, welcomed the affective immediacy of Hollywood's popular narrative cinema. Bazin argued that, like the Italian neorealist films of Roberto Rossellini and Vittorio De Sica, Hollywood films possessed an "authentic" or "organic" connection to the society in which and for which they were produced. They displayed a rootedness absent from much contemporary French cinema: "The cinema has been able, in an extraordinarily competent way, to show American society just as it wanted to see itself; but not at all passively, as a simple act of satisfaction and escape, but dynamically, by participating with the means at its disposal in the building of this society. What is so admirable in the American cinema is that it cannot help being spontaneous. Although the fruit of free enterprise and capitalism—and harboring their active or still only virtual defects—it is in a way the truest and most realistic cinema of all because it does not shrink from depicting even the contradictions of that society" (Bazin 1985, 251).[21] Soon after the liberation Bazin warned that French cinema would not be able to counter Hollywood's onslaught of "grandeur, violence, hate, tenderness and hope" unless it too could "set down the deepest roots in the soul of our time—in its angers and its sorrows as well as in its dreams. French cinema will only save itself if it learns how to become even greater by rediscovering an authentic expression of French society" (Williams 1992, 299).

During the studio era, which was beginning its decline in the heyday of French auteurism, the Hollywood style was as highly relaxed as it was intricately choreographed. It was a cinema of formal discipline and stylistic self-effacement that eschewed literary or philosophical values for the construction of an emotional form realized through a dynamic process of mise-en-scène. The impact of the best Hollywood cinema derived from what was not directly expressed in words, from the suggestive power of a cinematic expressiveness. For the *Cahiers* intellectuals, Hollywood's deceptively simple cinema was amenable to a multileveled play of significances. In a characteristically provocative, distinctively ambivalent statement, Jean-Luc Godard proclaimed in 1962 that

Americans, who are much more stupid when it comes to analysis, instinctively bring off very complex scripts. They also have a gift for the kind of simplicity which brings depth—in a little Western like *Ride the High Country,* for instance. If one tries to do something like that in France, one looks like an intellectual.

The Americans are real and natural. But this attitude means something over there. We in France must find something that means something—find the French attitude as they have found the American attitude. (Milne 1972, 193)

Godard's reference to *Ride the High Country* points to some of the problems in the application of the *politique* to Hollywood. Although his remarks clearly evoke Bazin, Godard does not share the latter's interest in the cinema's "sociological" implications. The underlying complexity he discerns in this 1961 film derives not exclusively from the achievements of director Sam Peckinpah but also from the film's engagement with the legacy of conventions that comprises the western as a generic form. Auteurist criticism would open new avenues for the discussion of film, but as Bazin stressed in his cautionary 1957 article "On the *politique des auteurs,*" it could easily degenerate into a "cult of personality." As interested in the cinema's social and cultural functions as he was in its expressive possibilities,[22] Bazin took his younger colleagues to task for slighting the representational conventions their auteurs worked within:

The evolution of Western art towards greater personalization should definitely be considered a step forward, as a refinement of culture, but only as long as this individualization remains only a final perfection and does not claim to *define* culture. At this point, we should remember that irrefutable commonplace we learnt at school: the individual transcends society, but society is also and above all within him. So there can be no definitive criticism of genius or talent which does not first take into consideration the social determinism, the historical combination of circumstances, and the technical background which to a large extent determine it. . . . What makes Hollywood so much better than anything else in the world is not only the quality of certain directors, but also the vitality and, in a certain sense, the excellence of a tradition. Hollywood's superiority is only incidentally technical; it lies much more in what one might call the American cinematic genius, something which should be analyzed, then defined by a sociological approach to its production. (Bazin 1985, 251)

The ideological premises of auteurism were critiqued far more vigorously by the film journal *Positif,* which objected to the "confused and implicitly reactionary" practice of the *Cahiers* writers (Gozlan 1968, 132).[23] In his 1962 article "The King Is Naked," Robert Benayoun attacked the complacent commodification of the New Wave style. He accused the filmmakers of evading the political controversies of Gaullist France, such as the war in Algiers, by retreating into a self-contained formalism that prized cinema at the expense of social engagement. Writing at a time when the success of New Wave films at festivals and in foreign markets had already thrust *Cahiers* into the international spotlight, Benayoun called for modes of film analysis and film practice that were politically activist and interventionist. He regarded the *nouvelle vague* as "a palliative regression, a misuse of analytical and critical activities which tends to limit or discredit the attempts at renewal which film language is undergoing" (Benayoun 1968, 164-78). The kind of politicized approach Benayoun envisaged would gain force through the 1960s, especially after the revolutionary ferment of May 1968. *Cahiers du Cinéma* would itself emerge as one of its principal advocates, helping to shape the direction of film analysis for another generation (Hillier 1986, 12-18, 355-56).[24]

THE SMELL OF A SKUNK

The *politique des auteurs* sparked further controversy in the early 1960s when it was adopted and adapted by the British journal *Oxford Opinion* and *Movie* and by film critic Andrew Sarris in the United States. Despite its ideological opposition to the writers and directors of *Cahiers du Cinéma, Positif* remained committed to the belief that the American cinema merited serious consideration. However, for several established Anglo-American critics the auteurist valuation of popular Hollywood films threatened cinema's potential to match the achievements of literature and theater. Although it would shortly become an orthodox practice within film criticism, reviewing, and marketing, the auteurist approach initially provoked a heated backlash. It is worth considering some of the Anglo-American objections to *Cahier*ist criticism in detail, as they anticipate the arguments later used to dismiss French readings of Jerry Lewis.

In the autumn of 1960 *Sight and Sound,* the institutional voice of quality film criticism in Britain, carried separate articles by Richard Roud and Penelope Houston that indicate the degree to which French auteurism was shaking canonical presuppositions about cinema as an art form (Roud 1960; Houston 1960). Both Houston and Roud maintain clear distinctions between Hollywood movies, which provide narcotic doses of action, spectacle, and cheap emotions, and films fit for higher sensibilities. Reviewing *Cahiers du Cinéma*'s lists of ten best films for 1959, Roud notes the presence of respectable art movies that would be readily acceptable to mainstream British critics—films directed by Sergei Eisenstein, Ingmar Bergman, Kenji Mizoguchi, Alain Resnais, and Truffaut. But these jostle for position with Hollywood films directed by auteurist favorites Howard Hawks (*Rio Bravo,* 1959), Alfred Hitchcock (*Vertigo,* 1958),

Samuel Fuller (*Run of the Arrow*, 1957), Douglas Sirk (*A Time to Love and a Time to Die*, 1958), and Nicholas Ray (*Wind Across the Everglades*, 1959). "One's first reaction," comments Roud, "might be to conclude that these men must be very foolish. And indeed, until a year or two ago, one might have got away with it. But today it would be difficult, I think, to maintain that filmmakers like Alain Resnais, François Truffaut, Claude Chabrol, Jean Luc-Godard, Pierre Kast and Jean-Pierre Melville are fools" (Roud 1960, 167).

As Roud suggests, the success of the New Wave boosted both the profile and the credibility of French auteurism. Established critics in Britain and the United States were set on the defensive: although they could not ignore *Cahiers*, they were not prepared to accept it without a mighty struggle. Roud and Houston berate the French writers for their overly enthusiastic embrace of the "cult of America" and for elevating form over content. Roud laments that "in France the more noble a film's subject the more suspiciously it is regarded" (1960, 167). Houston, especially, is alarmed by the desire to prioritize cinema over the claims of the "real world":

What the young critics mainly admire . . . are films whose relation to the business of living is in itself somewhat precarious. You cannot write, for instance, about a film like *Pather Panchali* (or *Les Quatre cents coups*, or *The Tokyo Story*) without concerning yourself with the way in which certain truths about the relationships between people, and the place of these people in their society, are defined on the screen. The film is not enclosed within its circumference; it is not retreating behind any protective hedge of "art." *The Crimson Kimono*, however, which is pulp literature with (oddly enough) some stabs at social conscience, is a film which can only be admired in terms of its impact. (Houston 1960, 163)[25]

The films Houston cites as worthy of serious attention are all non-American, and she dismisses Hollywood productions — represented by action-director Sam Fuller, much admired by *Cahiers* and the new British critics — because of their vicarious sensationalism. Houston prefers a contemplative cinema that can be illuminated by the discerning eye of a critic whose main qualification is knowledge of "life" not the movies. To underline the authority of her assessment she informs the reader that those, like herself, "who grew up during the war, when violence was perhaps too close to be also a handy stimulant, and whose attitudes to the cinema were being formulated at the time of the neo-realist experiment, of the general outburst of wartime and post-war realism, are not easily inclined to divorce art and morality or art and society in our minds" (1960, 164).

Houston is concerned not so much with the French auteurists as with a threat closer to home — the *Cahiers*-influenced critics of *Oxford Opinion*, which introduced a film section in 1960 (Barr 1985, 6). In its May issue the Oxford journal had declared war on the "pernicious" taste culture of *Sight and Sound* at a time when Houston was its dominant voice (Armitage 1961, 5).[26] The new British critics, she asserts, operate a dangerously irresponsible and morally bankrupt agenda: "There are no good or bad subjects; affirmation is a word for boy scouts; social significance is a bore; don't expect a film to present you with sympathetic characters; don't even, if one takes it far enough, look for character; don't have any truck with anything that smells of literature. Cinema, by this definition, means first and foremost the visual image; and the critic's response is to the excitement it can communicate" (Houston 1960, 163). Cinema, Houston insists, should be "about the human situation, not about 'spatial relationships'" (ibid.). Her objection to the formalist aestheticism of the new critics echoes Bazin's critique of the *politique des auteurs*,[27] but neither she nor Richard Roud shares his conviction that American cinema is worth taking seriously.[28] Whereas Bazin argued that popular Hollywood films require a very different approach from art cinema, Roud and Houston do not to want to dirty their sensibilities with the bargain-basement end of cinematic achievement.[29] As cultural guardians, they set themselves above the barbarous seductions of Hollywood, speaking to and for a constituency of middle-class white liberals. Anxious to impress with their moderation, Roud and Houston are at pains to distinguish an extremist younger faction at *Cahiers,* which includes Fereydoun Hoveyda, Luc Moullet, and Michel Mourlet, from the more readily recuperable François Truffaut. Both regard *Les Quatre cents coups* as a prime example of quality cinema; Roud, for example, describes it as "a fusion of significant form with literary or humanistic content" (Roud 1960, 170).

The British debate over the new French criticism was a battle between competing cinematic canons and contested valuations of the role of film criticism itself. Roud and Houston objected to not just the interest in Hollywood films but also the feverishly intellectual discourse about them.[30] Houston pleads for a film criticism that operates within the protocols of discourse on the traditional arts: "That the cinema is an art is no longer in question; that battle is over and won. But if it is an art on the same plane as literature and the theater, then it is the use of special techniques for the expression of ideas that must make it so. . . . If cinema is the art we think it is, then it is entitled to the kind of critical analysis that has traditionally been devoted to the theater and the novel: and the principles which seem most likely to be constructively used remain the liberal ones" (1960, 164-65). Less myopic than Houston, Roud nonetheless calls for the return of "common sense and intellectual values" in both the subject matter and the style of film criticism: "Unfortunately, when a critic has to quote Hegel and

Kant in reviewing a film by Minnelli, it is not because, as Hoveyda maintains, the cinema is at least as important as literature, painting and the drama. It is because somehow the critics feels he must dignify his liking of the film by the most impeccable intellectual references. It is a curious paradox that those French critics who delight in non-intellectual, irrational films always feel called upon to discuss them in the most pedantic and academic way possible" (1960, 171).

Roud and Houston seem genuinely bewildered that the new critics, French and British, can so willingly squander their intellectual resources on the two-bit whore of Hollywood. Bazin's belief that American popular cinema connects with "the soul of our time" was barely tenable among cultural voices in Britain and the United States, who routinely pilloried the "dream factory" as the antithesis of "authentic" art. In the United States Andrew Sarris's auteurist intervention provoked a more savage response. Sarris began writing on film in 1955 as a reviewer for the newly formed small-circulation journal *Film Culture,* which billed itself as "America's independent motion picture magazine."[31] Sarris himself started out as a "foreign art-film snob" (Sarris 1995, 359), writing, for example, on such films as Ingmar Bergman's *Seventh Seal* (1956) (Sarris 1959), but his outlook changed radically after he encountered the New Wave and the *politique des auteurs* at the 1961 Cannes Film Festival (Cook 1985, 137). Thereafter he set himself in opposition to his colleagues at *Film Culture* who, under the leadership of Jonas Mekas, championed the new American avant-garde film.

Film Culture published Sarris's "Notes on the *Auteur* Theory in 1962" (Sarris 1962–63) and a year later followed it with a special issue devoted to Hollywood directors, most of which was taken up with Sarris's elaborate auteurist mapping of American film history from the silent feature film onward (Sarris 1963b).[32] His influential 1968 book *American Cinema: Directors and Directions, 1929–1968* reworked these earlier articles into an elaborate league table of the American cinema, topped by a pantheon of great directors that included D. W. Griffith, Charles Chaplin, Orson Welles, John Ford, and Alfred Hitchcock. Sarris's reformulation of the *politique* as the "auteur theory" signaled his polemical intention to challenge the priorities of established American film criticism—both the investment in European art cinema by mainstream quality reviewers and the valuation of the avant-garde by *Film Culture* and the *Village Voice.*[33] In his 1962 article Sarris went way beyond the claim that individual Hollywood directors could make distinctive films by declaring the aesthetic preeminence of Hollywood as a whole:

Some critics have advised me that the *auteur* theory only applies to a small number of artists who make personal films, not to the run-of-the-mill Hollywood director who takes whatever assignment is available. Like most Americans who take films seriously, I have always felt a cultural inferiority complex about Hollywood. . . . After years of tortured revaluation, I am now prepared to stake my critical reputation, such as it is, on the proposition that Alfred Hitchcock is artistically superior to Robert Bresson by every criterion of excellence, and, further, that, film for film, director for director, the American cinema has been consistently superior to that of the rest of the world from 1915 through 1962. Consequently, I now regard the *auteur* theory primarily as a critical device for recording the history of the American cinema, the only cinema in the world worth exploring in depth beneath the frosting of a few great directors at the top. (Sarris 1962–63, 5)

Sarris's heretical celebration of Hollywood cinema may have had little consequence were it not for a vituperative attack by Pauline Kael (Sarris 1968, 26). Writing on film from the early 1950s, the prolific, idiosyncratic, and ambitious Kael would establish herself as one of America's preeminent film critics. She wrote reviews for the *New Republic* and the *New Yorker,* from 1968 to 1991, and contributed to journals as diverse as *Film Quarterly, Sight and Sound, Film Culture, Partisan Review,* and *Atlantic Monthly.* In an article first published in *Film Quarterly* in 1963 Kael used her considerable rhetorical battery to blast Sarris's auteurism out of the water (Kael 1966). Some of Kael's objections have validity, especially her refusal of the *Cahier*ist tenet that even the worst film of a genuine auteur necessarily has more going for it than the best film of a mere stylist, a *metteur-en-scène.* However, her fundamental prejudice against Hollywood popular cinema launches the discussion into self-regardingly polished invective that aims to jettison further debate. Kael retreads many of Penelope Houston's complaints, but her tone is far more aggressively performative—she even finds time to castigate *Sight and Sound* for its stuffiness.[34] In the following passage, for example, she takes issue with Sarris's claim that the distinguishable personality of the director is the prime criterion of value: "When Sarris begins to work on his foundation, the entire edifice of civilized standards of taste collapses while he's tacking down his floorboards. Traditionally, in any art, the personalities of all those involved in a production have been a factor in judgment, but that the distinguishability of personality should in itself be a criterion of value completely confuses normal judgment. The smell of a skunk is more distinguishable that the perfume of a rose; does that make it better?" (ibid., 297).

There is much more of the same. As Sarris would later protest, one of Kael's strategies is to characterize the auteurist as a stunted adolescent: "The *auteur* critics are so enthralled with their narcissistic male fantasies . . . that they seem unable to relinquish their schoolboy notions of human experience. . . . Can we conclude that, in England and the United States, the *auteur* theory is an attempt by adult males to just justify staying inside the small range of experience of their boyhood and adolescence — that period when masculinity looked so great and important but art was something talked about by poseurs and phonies and sensitive-feminine types? And is it perhaps also their way of making a comment on our civilization by the suggestion that trash is the true film art? I ask; I do not know" (Kael 1966, 319).[35]

The virilist preferences of the auteurists certainly needs stressing, but Kael goes into overdrive when she implies that any serious discussion of Hollywood films — the preference for "trash" over "art" — is motivated by sexual inadequacy. For cultural connoisseurs such as Houston and Kael, the commercial and industrial nature of the Hollywood film can only permit degraded pleasures, and it is the duty of the critic to patrol the border between legitimate and illegitimate pleasures. In Kael's opinion the best judges of Hollywood trash are not intellectuals but the adolescents who flock to such action pictures as *North to Alaska* (1960); adults like herself demand more rarefied pleasures from the films they patronize. Like Houston, Kael suggests that Hollywood films are base because they rely upon sensation at the expense of contemplation:

These critics work embarrassingly hard trying to give some semblance of intellectual respectability to a preoccupation with mindless, repetitive commercial products — the kind of action movies that the restless, rootless men who wander on Forty-Second Street and in the Tenderloin of all our big cities have always preferred just because they could respond to them without thought. These movies soak up your time. I would suggest that they don't serve a very different function for Sarris or [Peter] Bogdanovich or the young men of *Movie*— even though they devise elaborate theories to justify soaking up their time. An educated man must have to work pretty hard to set his intellectual horizons at the level of *I Was a Male War Bride* (which, incidentally, wasn't even a good commercial movie). (Kael 1966, 307)

Kael is especially annoyed by Sarris's claim that auteurism is a theory, not for its lack of rigor but because the very concept of a systematized intellectual program challenges her own qualifications as a critical voice.[36] She attacks Sarris's valuation of directorial personality for being grounded in "mystical insight" but nonetheless practices her own brand of highly familiar mysticism: the fundamental criterion of the critic, Kael insists, is "discrimination." Like Houston, she asserts that this is based in the experience of life, which "is pitifully absent from the work of the *auteur* critics; they seem to view movies, not merely in isolation from the other arts, but in isolation even from their own experience." Houston and Kael disparage not only the auteurists' credentials as experts on film but also their qualifications as human beings — for Kael, the *Movie* critics are "indistinguishable read-alikes, united by fanaticism in a ludicrous cause" (Kael 1966, 301, 309-10). This cutting portrayal of sad, robotic ciné-anoraks enslaved by Hollywood trash makes plain Kael's own ambivalence about cinema. Her writing is cautionary, warning of the dangerous cinematic seductions that have lured the auteurists from the path of reason and common sense.[37]

Motored by the high profile of French New Wave films, and publicized further by the Kael-Sarris feud and the patronage of such cult voices as Andy Warhol, *Cahiers du Cinéma* and its iconoclastic valuation of Hollywood cinema became de rigueur accessories for hip young cinéastes in the 1960s. In 1965 Eugene Archer claimed in the *New York Times* that "*Cahiers* has become an 'in' term, like 'pop' and 'camp' and 'the *auteur* theory.' It is an in word that means far out" (Archer 1965, 41). Thirty years on, as Thompson and Bordwell (1994) note, "the idea of authorship has become a commonplace in film criticism. Journalistic reviewers now commonly credit a film to its director. Many ordinary moviegoers use a rough *auteurism* as a criterion of taste, applying it not only to art-cinema directors but also to Hollywood filmmakers like Steven Spielberg and Brian De Palma (directors who themselves held auteur assumptions). *Auteur* criticism also helped create film studies as an academic discipline" (494).

Despite its upfront challenge to established principles of film criticism, auteurism was relatively easy to incorporate within mainstream discourse on film because it invested in a number of the key principles of traditional criticism, especially the concept that the creative individual is the essential basis for worthwhile art. In much of 1960s auteurism iconoclasm was somewhat uneasily balanced with a desire for legitimation. The new critics tried to validate Hollywood directors by comparing them to established nonfilmic authors: for example, the 1968 book on Howard Hawks by *Movie* writer Robin Wood (1981) sought to justify him as an artist by invoking high-cultural heavyweights such as Joseph Conrad, Shakespeare, and Mozart. Wood and other auteur critics led a valuable safari into the tangle of meanings and pleasures that comprises the imaginative topography of the Hollywood film, but their inability to shake off high-cultural models of discourse prevented them from engaging in a fully satisfying manner with the popular nature of Hollywood's aesthetic.

Even though the auteurists frequently turned a blind eye to the cultural, institutional, and industrial factors that shape a film's significance, their intervention would spark productive reconsiderations of Hollywood cinema and the principles of film criticism. As Jim Hillier (1985) suggests, by discussing popular genre films as the works of creative individuals with distinctive stylistic signatures, the *Cahiers* writers "raised crucial questions, however unsystematically, about the status and criticism appropriate to film as an art form in which unsystematic divisions were constantly being made between art and commerce" (7). Through auteurism, newer waves of film critics in France, Britain, and the United States were able to confront their own entrenched cultural traditions and open new possibilities for conceptualizing the cinema. For example, from the late 1960s film critics such as Geoffrey Nowell-Smith and Peter Wollen sought to move beyond the auteurist stress upon the expressive individual by conceptualizing the author as a nucleus of structural codes within the text (Caughie 1981, 123-29). Subsequently, the issue of authorship was progressively displaced from vanguard film criticism by theoretical paradigms that critiqued rather than valorized the unified subject (ibid., 1981, 199-207). John Caughie argues that "*Cahiers'* function in the history of film criticism appears as a shaking loose of established modes. Not necessarily progressive in itself, *Cahiers* seemed to enable progress. In so far as there was a 'critical revolution' it was a revolution within bourgeois film criticism, which made other critical revolutions possible and necessary" (ibid., 38).

STRANGE FANCIES: LEWIS AS *AUTEUR*

Question: "How long has this extraordinary popularity you have abroad been going on?"

Lewis: "It's all been in the last seven or eight years [*sic*]. I've had to put three girls on just to handle the international press and mail. As you know, some of the European critics—French and Belgian and Spanish and Italian and German—read stuff into films that I've done that if I took seriously I would have myself committed. Did I indeed have a fat lady syndrome in my life? Was my mother—? All I did was write what I thought was a physically funny joke. It had nothing to do with any hang-ups."

Question: "What do you think of critics closer to home?"

Lewis: "We don't have enough time. I just think they're a bunch of whores, that's all."

—Jerry Lewis (Alpert 1977)

Jerry Lewis first attracted the attention of French critics in the 1950s as a result of his association with Frank Tashlin. Received with great enthusiasm by the rival camps of *Cahiers du Cinéma* and *Positif,* Tashlin comedies such as *Artists and Models* (1955), *Hollywood or Bust* (1956), *The Girl Can't Help It* (1956), and *Will Success Spoil Rock Hunter?* (1957) were appreciated for their distinctive style (garishly modern; inventively parodic; self-reflexive, cartoonlike gags) and their satire of contemporary U.S. consumer culture (advertising, Hollywood, rock and roll, comic books) (Eisenschitz 1994a, 103). Five Tashlin films opened in Paris between July 1956 and October 1957 and drew accolades from Godard, Truffaut, Jacques Rivette, Erich Rohmer, and others (ibid., 103-4). Godard's review of *Hollywood or Bust* in *Cahiers du Cinéma* went so far as to assert that "in fifteen years' time people will realize that *The Girl Can't Help It* served then — today, that is — as a fountain of youth from which the cinema now — in the future, that is — has drawn fresh inspiration" (Milne 1986, 28).

Artists and Models and *Hollywood or Bust* were two of the final comedies Jerry Lewis made in partnership with Dean Martin. In a creative relationship that replaced his intense teaming with Martin, Lewis collaborated with Tashlin on six of his solo comedies (Ehrenstein 1994a, 44). However, it was not until Lewis began directing films in 1960, with *The Bellboy,* that he began to receive extended discussion among French film critics. Dana Polan (1984a) suggests that while Lewis was exclusively a performer, most French critics shared the dismissive attitude of the American reviewers: "Early reviews, both American and French, continually reviled Lewis for a physicality that seemed to them to show the coarsest side of human existence" (44).[38] For example, in a 1957 review of Martin and Lewis's *You're Never Too Young* François Truffaut wrote,[39] "Jerry Lewis's comic persona is based on degeneration; scriptwriters create for him foolish stories that concentrate on character defects, the symptoms of which he mimics all too well. . . . What causes the audience to laugh here are the misadventures of a character who's more stupid than they are. The general public wants to see an exceptional person, but genius, or simply intelligence, bothers their eyes like a cinder would; it annoys them and makes them ashamed" (Truffaut 1993, 66-67).

There were significant exceptions to this line. In a special 1958 issue of *Positif* devoted to Frank Tashlin, Roger Tailleur (1973) spoke of the "extraordinary talent of Jerry Lewis" (24). Robert Benayoun wrote his first appreciation of the performer in 1956, and he would subsequently make Lewis a lifelong obsession (manifested through numerous articles and interviews, a book, and a television series).[40] Jean Domarchi, a philosophy professor and *Cahiers* contributor, informed Hollis Alpert in 1966 that he and several other critics had recognized Lewis as an auteur in the mid-1950s, before he was officially a director: "It was clear to several of us . . . that Jerry Lewis was turning to direction. And that is exactly what happened. When he made *The Bellboy,* he was on his own" (Alpert 1966, 29).

The *Cahiers* critics generally regarded the director as a film's auteur, but there were key exceptions. In a 1957 discussion with his fellow critics Jacques Rivette proposed French performer Jean Gabin to be the author of the films he appeared in:

In fact, Gabin wasn't a actor, he was something else. He wasn't an actor, he was someone who brought a character into French cinema, and it wasn't only scripts that he influenced but *mise-en-scène* as well. I think that Gabin could be regarded as almost more of a director than [Julien] Duvivier or [Jean] Gremillon, to the extent that the French style of *mise-en-scène* was constructed to a large extent on Gabin's style of acting, on his walk, his way of speaking or of looking at a girl. It's also what gives the great American actors their dynamism, actors like Cary Grant, Gary Cooper or James Stewart. (Bazin et al. 1985, 37)

Film comedians are even more worthy of being considered as auteurs because the display of their specialized performance skills — their presentational authorship — is the predominant attraction of their films, no matter who holds the directorial reins. In a 1967 article entitled "A Concise Lexicon of Lewisian Terms" *Cahiers du Cinéma* asserted that "Jerry Lewis is not only the author of the films he has directed, but also, to a greater or lesser extent, of those films he was not merely satisfied to perform in, particularly *You're Never Too Young, Cinderfella* and *The Disorderly Orderly*" (Aumont et al. 1973, 91). As Truffaut suggests, Lewis's extreme performance style certainly qualifies him as a star who goes beyond "just acting": his hyperbolic use of the body results in a comic grotesquerie that cannot easily be subjugated to the demands of narrative and character. Lewis was the first comedian since the silent era to take over the production, direction, and scripting of his films, and long before *The Bellboy* he had also been making significant behind-the-scenes contributions to his starring vehicles.[41]

Directed, scripted, and produced by Lewis, *The Bellboy* shares with the New Wave films a flamboyant, self-reflexive love of cinema and a desire to work against the grain of conventional Hollywood practice. This low-budget location-shot feature is as idiosyncratic, playful, and self-aware as Godard's early films. It opens with a series of satirical stabs at the values of mainstream filmmaking before launching into a virtually plotless series of gag sequences unified by the presence of Lewis's nonspeaking bellboy. His second film, *The Ladies' Man* (1961), confirmed Lewis's distinctiveness as an auteur-director. According to Luc Moullet this elaborately conceived surreal comedy galvanized the interest of the French critics: "Large sections of critical opinion realized we had a filmmaker to reckon with. The comic vision we had glimpsed in *Cinderfella* and *The Bellboy* was now fully apparent. The 'young' critics chose it as the best film of the year" (Alpert 1966, 74). Lewis made the cover of *Cahiers du Cinéma* in June 1962, when the magazine published its first article devoted to his films (Labarthe 1962).

John Russell Taylor claims that with the French release of Lewis's fourth self-directed feature, *The Nutty Professor,* at the end of 1963, "the floodgates opened.

The script was published (as *Docteur Jerry et Monsieur Love*) by *L'Avant Scène du Cinéma,* new tributes appeared in *Positif, Cinéma 64* and even *Midi-Minuit Fantastique,* and by the end of the year Lewis had achieved the twin accolade of an *entretien* (two, as a matter of fact) in *Cahiers* and a retrospective at the Cinémathèque — an event which provoked *Cinémonde,* normally silent as the grave about the Cinémathèque and its activities, to remark that many people thought the whole thing might be a hoax, and was anyway going too far" (Taylor 1965, 82–83).

As Taylor makes clear, Lewis was not unanimously valued in French film culture but he nonetheless received considerable attention from both popular and highbrow critics. Moreover, Lewis's films remained remarkably successful at the box office in European territories after his audience in the United States began to decline: in the mid-1960s his movies were at least twice as profitable as the average American release in the French market (Alpert 1966, 28). When he arrived in Paris in 1965 to shoot scenes for *Boeing Boeing* Lewis was welcomed "by a swarm of wild-eyed fans, a phalanx of photographers, a rout of reporters and a small but select group of France's leading film critics." The Parisian art cinema Le Passy staged a three-week festival to commemorate Lewis's visit, and the eminent Cinémathèque Française also mounted a detailed retrospective of his film work (ibid.).[42] "I knew that I was liked there," Lewis told Hollis Alpert, "but the extent of the thing was a revelation to me. And I was so used to being looked down upon by the American critics" (ibid.).

Investigating the Lewis mania he had first glimpsed in the pages of *Cahiers du Cinéma,* Hollis Alpert visited Paris to canvass the views of leading film critics. In a 1966 article for *New York Times Magazine* entitled "France Is Mad for . . . Jerry Lewis? 'Le Roi du Crazy'" Alpert provides a fascinating insight into both the French critical enthusiasm for Lewis and the bewilderment of "cultured" Americans.[43] "I understand," Jean Domarchi tells him, "that in America Jerry Lewis is both misunderstood and despised by intellectuals. A great pity. I find his films among the best made anywhere — not as flashy, perhaps, as those of Fellini of Italy, but more sincere" (1966, 28, 74). Robert Benayoun proclaims that since the death of Buster Keaton Lewis is

the foremost comic artist of our time. . . . He corresponds to our era, both reflecting and criticizing our civilization. There is also the intensity of his impact over the years. He has appeared in 35 movies and directed seven, coming out anew before the public's eye twice a year, on the average.

Jerry Lewis is a witness to his time by being a satirist, as Chaplin was. His satire is of the American civilization. But, being pertinent, its appeal is universal. . . . Lewis is a philosopher of what's comic, a self-taught thinker who is not an intellectual, and a marvelous technician. (ibid., 74)

Benayoun and Domarchi imply that American intellectuals find it difficult to accept the validity of cultural activities that do not speak in the languages they demand from art. More finely attuned to the distinctiveness of film as a medium for popular expression, the French critics conceive of Lewis as an intuitive artist who bypasses the high-cultural traditions that underpin American film criticism. As Alpert puts it, "Lewis, being seemingly unimpeded by intellectual and dramatic preoccupations, is thus, according to them, able to use the film medium more naturalistically than those whose tendency is to use the screen for basically literary purposes. They thus find Jerry Lewis cinematically aware and intelligent" (1966, 75).[44]

Ultimately Alpert finds it impossible to reconcile the conflicting French and American perceptions of Lewis. Since the success of the New Wave, he proposes, French critical preferences have been a "puzzling phenomenon" to Americans who have stumbled across them:

The French critics miss seeing the subtle humor of *The Ipcress File* and go mad about the much broader *Goldfinger.* They will analyze and "see into" a film so thoroughly that the results approach intellectual arabesques, if not sheer fantasy. For this reason alone, the French regard for Jerry Lewis is mistrusted here. And not only do the French have their own strange fancies about movies; they also have strange fancies about the nature of American life. They will seize upon oddities as characteristic of the whole; they are more attracted to the zany than we are, and they delight in "proving" that what appears to be awesomely bad is really very good. (Certain American film enthusiasts dismiss the Jerry Lewis mystique in France as a snobbish, faddish — and veiled anti-American — conceit or, if not that, as part of current pop art concepts. The French deny this. "We do not think of Jerry Lewis as pop art," Louis Marcolles said categorically. "He is a genuine artist.") (Alpert 1966, 74-75)

As Ephraim Katz (1986) would later observe, for the critics of *Positif* and *Cahiers* Lewis's work revealed "something profound about America which Americans themselves fail to understand" (718). Lewis functioned, Shawn Levy (1994) suggests, as "a kind of Rorschach test, in which Americans saw an embarrassing reflection of themselves, while the French saw a metaphoric embodiment of the postwar United States" (28).

The wrangles over auteurism permitted Lewis's problematic otherness *within* the United States to be recodified as a conflict of intercultural perceptions. The American taste brigade sharpened their axes and used them vigorously, and in turn the French critics went into overdrive in their praise for the controversial comedian-director. Like *Positif, Cahiers du Cinéma* continued to champion each new Lewis film, devoting a special issue to the star-director in 1967.[45] That same year, Jean-Luc Godard proclaimed that "Jerry Lewis . . . [is] the only one in Hollywood doing something different, the only one who isn't falling in with the established categories, the norms, the principles. . . . Lewis is the only one to-day who's making courageous films. And I think he's perfectly well aware of it. He's been able to do it because of his personal genius" (Godard 1986, 295). Faced with such euphoric excesses, Andrew Sarris felt obliged to restore some "sanity" to the proceedings. As editor of *Cahiers du Cinéma in English* he engaged in a critical dialogue with Lewis's French celebrants. The fourth issue of the magazine carried a translation of an interview with Lewis by Axel Madsen and appreciations of his 1965 film *The Family Jewels* by Serge Daney, Sylvain Godet, André Téchiné, and Claude-Jean Phillippe. Sarris devoted the bulk of his editorial to an assault on the Lewis cult, firing off a twelve-pronged salvo against the star-director's value as an artist (Sarris 1966, 64–66). This material was later incorporated into the section on Lewis in his 1968 book, *The American Cinema: Directors and Directions, 1929–1968,* in which he made his allegiances even clearer by declaring that "the French critics often use Lewis as a club against American critics" (Sarris 1968, 243). Attempting to preserve his Americanized brand of auteurism from the scorn meted out to Lewis's continental advocates, Sarris aligned himself with the moderate stance of Hollis Alpert: "It would be presumptuous of Americans to tell the French that Maurice Chevalier represents their national soul. Similarly, it is presumptuous to claim that Lewis's screen experiences represent something profound about America" (Sarris 1966, 64).

SHOW-BIZ MODERNIST

Characterizing Jerry Lewis as a cinematic modernist, the critics of *Cahiers du Cinéma* and *Positif* read his films as critiques of capitalist society and corporate culture. Jean Domarchi, for example, argued, "We can trace in them a theme, a motif. To put it generally, this motif has to do with a little man attempting to cope with the ways of a mechanical civilization about which he understands nothing. It is necessary for him to escape, and this he can manage through dreams and fairy tales" (Alpert 1966, 74).[46] However, Lewis's modernist credentials derive not just from the subject matter of his films but also from the way their style confounds orthodox procedures for storytelling and gag making. Interviewed by Alpert, Luc Moullet extolled the self-reflexive intelligence of Lewis's auteurist movies: "We began to understand several years ago . . . that he was more than a clown, that actually his comical way was very conscious and elaborate, and that in his movies he played too much of the idiot to be idiotic to that degree. The answer was that he had to be, actually, very intelligent. The gags he invented were carried to a point of disintegration. He would go so far as to put us, the audience, behind the camera and make his process visible. There is always the camera as an element in his films" (ibid., 76).

As Dana Polan (1984a) suggests, the French critics were especially excited by the "systematic deconstruction of comedy" in Lewis's work: "Lewis receives analysis as an artist who avoids standard comedic patterns and, most particularly, dismantles the immediate impact of a joke through repetition, derailing, blending of tones, a deliberate subversion of expectation. Where Americans frequently find Lewis's attempts at humor intolerable, many French critics argue that the Lewisian form of humor demands special talents on the part of the viewer: a concern for humor not as punctual moment of hilarity but rather as a kind of deflated duration" (46).

In a more recent assessment, Michael Selig (1990) takes issue with Lewis's reputation as a modernist by arguing that many of the disruptive features valued by the French critics were themselves highly conventional within the Hollywood genre of comedian comedy (46–54). However, Selig underestimates the distinctive spin that Lewis's films give to this familiar material, especially the way they play with his star image and his newfound authorship. Comic performer Danny Kaye, for example, takes on multiple roles in the films *Wonder Man* (1945), *The Secret Life of Walter Mitty* (1947), and *On the Riviera* (1951) as a means of flaunting the fragmented identities of the characters he plays, but when Lewis casts himself as both Julius Kelp and Buddy Love in *The Nutty Professor* the situation is much more complex because of the way these contrasting personae connect with Lewis's high-profile history as a public figure. Buddy Love is commonly interpreted as a commentary on either Lewis's former partner Dean Martin or the Las Vegas incarnation of Lewis himself. As in Kaye's films the divided nature of subjectivity is the principal issue, but in Lewis's case this problem exceeds the textual regime of character to engage with the broader problematic of "Jerry Lewis" as a discursive construct. Buddy Love may be a monster born of Julius Kelp but both are themselves representations of "Jerry Lewis," impersonated by Lewis as a performer and organized by him as director. Nothing like the same dynamic exists with Danny Kaye.

American cultural commentators seized upon Lewis's desire to direct as confirmation that he was an abrasive self-promoter who lacked taste and humility.

"Even within the commercial ramparts of Hollywood," Alpert reports, "Lewis is taken less than seriously. His fondness for assuming total responsibility for making a film — writing, directing, etc. — is often regarded as symptomatic of his egocentricity" (1966, 78). The cocktail of low body comedy and artistic aspiration being too heady for many to imbibe, Lewis was accused of yielding to the seductions of self-aggrandizement that had formerly blighted his self-professed idol Charles Chaplin. French critics, however, recognized that Lewis's work involves a more intricate process of self-definition in which "Jerry Lewis" is located not simply as the man behind the camera, nor the performer in front of it, but as the product of a panoply of competing and conflicting discourses. For the French, Dana Polan argues, Lewis was "someone whose life and films appear to combine the contradictory sides of America, the United States as a clash of attitudes and styles" (1984a, 45):

Even those qualities, like his almost maniacal ambition and his avowed egocentrism, that began to turn off American audiences . . . became for French critics further proof of Lewis's *auteurism*. Central to the *auteurist* idea is a notion of the *auteur* as [a] strong-willed figure desirous, at all costs, of imprinting his or her needs and views on the world. Consistently, French discussions of Lewis turned from the films to the man, enthralled by his admitted desire to order the world into a systematized totality with Lewis in control. Hence, there has been constant reference to the facts of his private life with his fetish for gadgetry, his innumerable projects, his desire to spread his fame everywhere . . . , and his desire to hold his private life in an invulnerably stable order. (Until his divorce, Lewis had one of the longest running Hollywood marriages, a fact well noted by the French critics.) (Polan 1984a, 44–45)

Hollis Alpert is wary of the grand claims made for Lewis's work because his films are aimed primarily at children and adolescents: "Few so-called mature American filmgoers are aware of any real satire or comment on our civilization in the dim-witted simpleton Lewis so often plays" (1966, 78).[47] He also implies that the French adulation for the comedian-director derives from insufficient knowledge of the American scene: like much American popular culture, Lewis seems enticingly exotic when read from afar. But as Polan stresses, this argument cuts both ways: "What the French find in Lewis is an analysis that corresponds to their image of America that may be missed by Americans. Indeed, the Lewis films are almost the only way that French audiences have consistently had a chance to see the Las Vegasy show world side of American life; what may stand out as a particular representation of American entertainment may be more ordinary to American audiences who encounter Lewis's tacky colors and musical groups like Les Brown and his 'Band of Renown' at every turn. The French critics gain, then, a certain distance from what becomes for Americans the fabric of everyday life" (1984a, 46).

Defining Lewis as a modernist is a problematic enterprise because the term implies allegiance to an avant-garde aesthetic that frequently legitimates itself through its opposition to popular commercial culture. Although Lewis's self-directed films resemble modernist experimentation in their sophisticated disruption of inherited forms and conventions, his work is forged unmistakably from the materials of American entertainment culture. He is, if anything, a "show-biz modernist" who collides together these seemingly opposed regimes of meaning and practice. He may not be an intellectual artist, but Lewis is nonetheless a highly self-conscious one, both communicating through show-biz culture and commenting upon its institutions and stratagems. The self-directed films ostentatiously proclaim his ascension from the lowly sphere of comic performance to the elevated ranks of Hollywood auteurs, but they simultaneously grapple with the questions raised by Lewis's very celebrity, offering a convoluted and prismatic account of their subject that is arguably as complex as anything produced within the modernist canon.[48]

THE COMIC BONDAGE OF DEAN MARTIN AND JERRY LEWIS

J erry Lewis was steeped in the heady culture of American entertainment long before he teamed up with Dean Martin.[1]
Throughout the 1920s and 1930s his father, Danny Lewis, plied
his song-and-comedy wares in the marketplace of small-time vaudeville, burlesque, and the "Borscht Belt"—the Jewish resort hotels of New York's
Catskills Mountains and the New Jersey coast. Danny and his wife Rae, who
accompanied him on piano, occasionally took Jerry along on their seasonal engagements.[2] The show-business ambitions of the parents clearly infected their
son: Jerry Lewis made his own precocious debut before an audience in 1932 at
the age of six, when he sang the topical Depression anthem "Brother, Can You
Spare a Dime" at a fireman's benefit in the Catskills (Levy 1996a, 15). Five years
later Lewis had devised the routine that would service his show-biz aspirations
until he met Dean Martin: a "dummy act" in which he acted out outrageously
exaggerated mimes to phonographic records.[3] For several years Lewis honed his
performance during vacations in the Catskills until he could quit school at sixteen to try his luck as a professional.[4] Bookings were intermittent, but Lewis was
able to secure confidence-building gigs at burlesque houses, hospitals, military
dances, and nightclubs.[5] He showed sufficient promise to attract the services of
a sharp Broadway agent, Abner J. Greshler, who would prove one of the principal architects of Martin and Lewis's rise to fame.

Lewis first encountered Dean Martin in August 1944, when they were signed
as individual attractions at New York's Glass Hat club: Martin was the headliner
while Lewis played his record act and served as master of ceremonies.[6] Martin
had been a professional crooner since 1940 and had recently quit Sammy
Watkins's dance band to pursue a solo career.[7] He was nine years older than
Lewis and had led a far more boisterous life—working as a prizefighter and a
croupier in gambling joints, engaging in highjinks and womanizing. Lewis was
immediately entranced by the self-contained masculine cool radiated by the
older man. When they next shared a bill, at Manhattan's Havana-Madrid Club
eighteen months later, the two men demonstrated their rapport by intruding
playfully into one another's sets. As Lewis put it, "He would kibitz while I was
on, and I'd kibitz when he was on, never knowing what we were gonna do ultimately" (Tosches 1992, 84-93, 56-86, 126). These improvisations went down
so well that they developed into a regular spot, which closed the show. In March
1946 Bill Smith wrote a glowing review of one of these performances for the
trade magazine *Billboard:* "Martin and Lewis do an after-piece that has all the
makings of a sock act. Boys play straight for each other, deliberately step on
each other's lines, mug and raise general bedlam. It's a toss-up who walks off
with the biggest mitt. Lewis's double takes, throw-aways, mugging and deliberate over-acting are sensational. Martin's slow takes, ad-libs and under-acting
make him an ideal fall guy. Both got stand-out results from a mob that took dy-
namite to wake up" (ibid., 126-27).

Three months later Dean Martin and Jerry Lewis were reunited at the 500
Club in Atlantic City, New Jersey. They followed their solo specialties with a
variation of the impromptu interventions devised at the Havana-Madrid.[8] The
results were sensational. "After the first night he was on stage with me," Lewis
reminisces, "I knew we had lightning in a bottle" (Soapbox Productions 1996).
Within three days Martin and Lewis were the talk of the town, playing to
packed houses every night—a reception far in excess of anything either had
known alone (Tosches 1992, 140). Sensing a lucrative opportunity, Greshler hijacked Martin from his agent, Lou Perry, and presented the two entertainers as
an official team at Philadelphia's Latin Casino in September 1946 (Levy 1996a,
76).[9] Over the next few months Martin and Lewis found continuous work at
increasingly prestigious nightclubs and theaters in the East and Midwest. Greshler also hired the services of George B. Evans, the renowned publicist who had
choreographed the bobby-sox delirium sparked by Frank Sinatra in 1943
(Tosches 1992, 145).[10] While Martin and Lewis took care of the onstage priorities and Greshler made the business deals, Evans worked on their image—por-

traying them as "freewheeling, fun-loving guys whose act was merely an extension of their everyday personalities and antics" (ibid., 149).[11]

Martin and Lewis's remarkably successful club act caught the interest of Hollywood movie producers; after the team's celebrity-studded West Coast debut at
Slapsie Maxie's Café in Los Angeles, Greshler was shuffling bids from Universal
Pictures, Metro-Goldwyn-Mayer, and Hal Wallis. They eventually signed with
Wallis, who ran an independent production company with Joseph Hazen with
guaranteed distribution through Paramount Pictures (Levy 1996a, 92).[12] The
highly favorable contract committed Martin and Lewis to Wallis for only three
months of the year, enabling them to take a great deal of outside work (ibid.,
94), including several films made for York Pictures Corporation, the production
company they had set up with Greshler.[13] That same year, 1948, Martin and
Lewis also signed a recording contract with Capitol Records and made their first
appearances on radio and prime-time television. Although they were going
places fast, they remained a cult act known mainly through nightclubs and the
occasional slot on the broadcast media (ibid., 102). *My Friend Irma,* the first of
their sixteen Hollywood films movies, exposed Martin and Lewis to much
wider audiences. This low-budget adaptation of a popular radio sitcom drew
extremely high attendances when it opened at Broadway's Paramount Theater
in September 1949, with Martin and Lewis playing live support, and the film
continued to do good business nationwide (ibid., 113).[14] Their stardom was consolidated a year later with the triumphant success of their own prime-time television show.

ALIVE AND HOT: THE HANDSOME MAN AND HIS MONKEY

Show-biz stars of the highest magnitude by the early 1950s, Martin and Lewis
achieved within a few years the kind of cross-media celebrity that major performers such as Bob Hope and Jack Benny had taken decades to build. Their
films, television shows, and live appearances were enormous successes; their
photographs decorated the covers of *Life* and *Look* magazines; and they were
even the subjects of a monthly DC Comics book.[15] In an era of nervous con-
formity Martin and Lewis made it possible for diverse audiences—nightclub
sophisticates, family television viewers, teenagers—to embrace a wild and bewitching liveness.[16] Among their juvenile fans Martin and Lewis inspired an intensity of hysteria usually reserved for pop idols such as the young Frank Sinatra, Johnny Ray, Elvis Presley, and the Beatles. In July 1951, for example, their

record-breaking two-week engagement at the Paramount Theater saw Manhattan streets jammed with thousands of screaming teens. Film director Norman Taurog, a witness to this spectacle of youth untamed, testifies to the rebellious currents of adulation stirred by the two men: "The response was almost orgiastic. Little girls were practically having orgasms every time Dean and Jerry opened their mouths" (Marx 1975, 142). This may have represented the most extreme reaction to Martin and Lewis, but such rebellious sexual abandon was also communicated to more mature audiences. In 1949 Hollywood correspondent Gladwin Hill wrote a piece for the *New York Times* that heralded their forthcoming appearance on motion-picture screens. She praised the team for their "refreshing brand of comic hysteria," which followed "the Catskill formula of just letting themselves go":[17] "Jerry interrupted Dean's songs. They grabbed instruments from the band and clowned with them, smashed plates, and squirted each other and spectators with seltzer—the ensemble being accompanied by a frantic and incessant barrage of gags ranging from kindergarten riddles to the latest wheezes from the midtown sector" (Hill 1949, 2:5).

Reviewing a 1946 set at the Havana-Madrid Club, *Variety* described the Martin and Lewis act as "a bunch of zany routines, apparently following a set format but improvising most of the way along the line" (Tosches 1992, 141). Into the white-collar playground of the contemporary nightclub, Martin and Lewis conjured up a dazzling spectacle of energy, liveness, and abandon, whipping up a vortex of destabilizing delight that beggared description. As Lewis puts it,

People couldn't tell you when they left the Copa what the fuck Martin and Lewis did. They knew one was a singer and one was a monkey. That's it. People used to sit in Lindy's and say, "They tore the fuckin' joint apart." "What did they do?" "Uh . . . uh . . . you gotta see it." No one ever said what we did. No one could ever write what we did. They could try it, and good writers on *The New York Times* attempted it, and Dean and I used to sit and get hysterical. Laughing hysterically because they're trying to be uppity and upscale: "Of course, the straight man, who would come on after the comic, would do a gag or two, and he would sing some songs . . ." Well, Dean and I would say, "They don't fucking get it. They just don't get it." And we would laugh hysterically. We were putting on the whole fucking world. (Levy 1996a, 75)

Their laughter mocked the efforts of professional scribes who grappled to find a language fit to capture the secret of the transcendent fusion that transformed Dean Martin and Jerry Lewis—crooner and comic, Italian and Jew, handsome man and monkey—into the indescribable sensation that was Martin and Lewis. As Bill Davidson observed in 1951, "It is difficult to record just exactly what their act is, for they rank among today's leading masters of the ad lib and the improvised business" (Davidson 1951, 65).

Abbey Greshler claimed that on his own Lewis had been "a scared kid with a high squeaky voice. He was afraid to talk, to express himself, and that was why he had been crazy to do a record act. He didn't have to speak. The record did it for him" (Gehman 1964, 106).[18] Drafting Martin in as a living replacement for these phonographic voices, Lewis latched onto him as both a straight man and a "front man," designing his comic persona as a multiply-accented inversion of everything the handsome man stood for. Against Martin's vocal and bodily control, Lewis pitted his dizzying, dysfunctionalizing specialties: a strangulated voice, a body riven with discoordination, an excessive and directionless energy. Dean Martin's idealized heterosexual male is "verbally or acoustically shanghaied into serving as a hapless foil for the strident and nonsensical but compelling antics of Lewis" (Hill 1949, 2:5). His initial resistance ultimately gives way to an embrace — as he both consents to, and actively participates in, the carnivalesque process of the two-man show.

The distinctiveness of their act derived not from Lewis's comic inventions alone, nor from scripted situations and dialogue, but from the interaction of the men as they "made live." It was a liveness that required the totality of voice and body — neither their phonographic recordings nor the NBC radio series *The Martin and Lewis Show* (1949–52) were particularly successful. Reviewing the latter, *Variety* noted that "potentially, the boys have got it. But bridging the gap from a nitery visual assist into a strictly audio medium still remains a big 'but'" (Tosches 1992, 190). *Time* magazine concurred: "Radio cannot show the half of what Martin & Lewis have; they must be seen, on television or in a nightclub" (Levy 1996a, 106).[19] The rapturous buzz of their liveness together is evoked by Lewis's memories of their television shows:

Once we were alive and hot on the air, the two of us would just *explode* with things that we did, that we knew were minimal in the rehearsals, even though they were growing and nurturing, one off the other. And they became magic on the air. (JAS Productions 1992b).

It was a wonderful period for us . . . and we were at the height of young abandonment. To watch these two guys who were so crazy in love with another, and in love with one another's ability — it's magic, it's absolute magic. (JAS Productions 1992a)

Onstage, the two men engaged in a vertiginous process of exchange and reversal, igniting a dazzlingly singular *jouessance*[20] that dissolved boundaries and differences. Over and again Lewis voices his astonishment at Martin's intuitive capacity to connect with him, his willingness to relinquish self-sufficiency in response to his partner's demands: "See, all I had to do was tell Dean I was gonna do such and such; that during the numbers I was gonna be a busboy in the audience. That's all I had to tell him; he went with me. . . . If I started something, he'd pick up on it like a child goes after milk. . . . We had that certain something that I wish I could say we planned. We didn't plan it. It was innate within us that out of the blue he was doing six, seven, eight minutes of comedy and I was straight for him" (Tosches 1992, 139).

Biographer Nick Tosches speculates that the team's antics provided an escape from the anxieties of the Cold War era. They offered audiences "not laughter in the dark, but a denial of darkness itself, a regression, a transporting to the preternatural bliss of infantile senselessness. It was a catharsis, a celebration of ignorance, absurdity, and stupidity" (Tosches 1992, 204). Lewis likewise stresses that their appeal was rooted in the conditions of the postwar era, but he offers a different reading of this "catharsis." Martin and Lewis were a hit, he suggests, because they provided a celebratory vision of togetherness that helped to exorcise the traumas and divisions of the war: "Remember, you just came out of World War II. And this country was *hurting*. And this country needed a binding of some kind. And to see two people care as much about one another as they did, and get you to laugh on top of it. . . . I don't think that act, or those two people, would have meant one tenth of what they were had it happened 10 years before" (JAS Productions 1992a). But the binding was not as generalized as Lewis makes out. Their act was special because it consisted of and proclaimed the union of two *men*. When the curtains closed on the theater of war, and soldiers were aggressively reinterpellated as husbands, Martin and Lewis were waiting in the wings to transform into laughter the homosocio-eroticism that was an inevitable byproduct of mobilization.

Steve Cohan (1993) posits a similar rationale for the phenomenally successful teaming of Bob Hope and Bing Crosby, whose male friendship was enacted through the series of "*Road*" movies they made for Paramount in the 1940s.[21] Arguing that Hope and Crosby's popularity was fed by "the intensity with which men formed close relationships in the all-male environment of the military," Cohan sees their films as providing "a comic site for renegotiating the homosocial organization of masculinity during and then immediately after WWII" (2–3).[22] Cast as American buddies adrift in a series of foreign spaces, Hope and Crosby would inevitably encounter Dorothy Lamour, Hollywood's incarnation of the exotic but nonthreatening femme.[23] The stage would be set for the playing out of a homosocial scenario akin to those analyzed by literary critic Eve Kosofsky Sedgwick (1985): as Hope and Crosby compete for the glamorous Lamour, their heterosexual rivalry both intensifies and provides a cover story for their own bonding. Cohan (1993) suggests that Lamour's regular presence as their costar "gives assurance of the buddy pair's eventual heterosexualization" while also facilitating such transgressive moments of homoerotic expression as the two gags in *The Road to Morocco* in which Hope and Crosby share a kiss (4-5).[24]

Martin and Lewis went much further along this route, without the need of a regular female costar to alibi the intensified pleasure they derived from one another. Most comedy teams, Andrew Sarris (1968) suggests, "have a certain internal cohesion that unites them against the world outside. That is to say that members of a comedy team have more in common with each other than with anyone else. Martin and Lewis at their best . . . had a marvelous tension between them. The great thing about them was their incomparable incompatibility, the persistent sexual hostility" (142-43). As Lewis likes to point out, the partnership was grounded in "sex and slapstick," in the collision and collusion of a handsome man and a monkey (Lewis and Gluck 1982, 142-43). The team's liveness married together not merely two contrasting performance styles but also two polarized and conflictual figurations of masculinity. Moreover, whereas Hope and Crosby each had separate careers prior to and during their partnership Martin and Lewis were firmly bonded as a "corporate identity." In the public eye each man was defined by the other, incomplete and unimaginable without him.

Capitalizing on the homosocial intensities that were a legacy of wartime, Martin and Lewis served up a charismatic and complexly shaded spectacle of male abandon and male togetherness. Their volatile and protean interaction provided a sly alternative to the heterosexual affirmation that gripped the United States in its return to a civilian order.[25] Explicitly coded as a "marital" union of differences, the partnership showcased a panoply of emotional and guardedly erotic intensities between men.[26] In a 1993 interview Graham Fuller asked Lewis, "What exactly was the formula that made you and Dean Martin click?" Lewis replied, "It was the same chemistry, and this may sound weird— well, I don't know how it's going to sound—that happens when the sperm and egg make contact and can reproduce a magnificent miracle. That's what we had. I don't know of any other chemistry that's as godlike" (Fuller 1993, 93). Lewis frequently makes explicit comparisons between the playing out of his relationship with Martin and the cultural scripts of heterosexual romance. Here, for example, is his description of their disintegrating partnership: "The love affair was so strong. And the break, though we wanted it, must have psychologically shattered us more than we knew. That's the only excuse I have for it. That's the only rational answer I can give you. We wanted to have nothing to do with one another. 'How dare you spoil what I've created!'—is what both men are saying, to one another, who have agreed to part" (Tiger Television/BBC 1992). However, this was no by means strictly a private affair. In the late 1940s and early 1950s audiences looked on longingly as these special friends put on their show, competing playfully against one another, having fun, being together, loving it.

In a discussion of the team's films Ed Sikov (1994) describes Martin and Lewis as the same-sex equivalent of the sparkling screwball romancers of such comedies as *The Awful Truth* (1937) and *Bringing Up Baby* (1939) (186). The screwball romances represented a defiance of the conformism of marriage, offering an idealized vision of heterosexual love as a process of continual gaming (Neale and Krutnik 1990, 149-66). Martin and Lewis similarly generated an enticing atmosphere of fun, spontaneity, and eccentricity in which two individuals were united in conflictual harmony. Sikov suggests that "like the equally homophilic Laurel and Hardy, Martin and Lewis play the sexual side of buddyism for dangerous comic effect, turning a kind of vicarious homosexual panic on the part of audiences into pleasure by way of nervous laughter" (1994, 186-87). But whereas, like the Hope and Crosby movies, such Laurel and Hardy films as *Liberty* (1929) and *Their First Mistake* (1932) feature homoerotic *eruptions,* the dynamics of the male love story were *integral* to Martin and Lewis's work. As Lewis told *The Hollywood Reporter* in 1948, "If you break down our routines, I guess there's very little in them. There's nothing we do that another act couldn't do, and maybe better. But it's the way we feel for each other that nobody can duplicate. The kind of comedy we do, it's our own fun. We do it for laughs, and we have a lot of laughs, and the audience is part of us. So there can never be another two-act like this because there's never going to be two guys who feel this way about each other. There couldn't be two men who are as close to each other as we are" (Marx 1975, 64).

Lewis's strident departures from the norms of heterosexual masculinity occasionally provoked complaints. For example, a *Variety* review of one of the team's 1949 shows at the Paramount Theater in support of *My Friend Irma* warned that "Lewis can get away with the nance stuff in a cafe—but not in a family theater" ("Paramount N.Y." [review], 5 October 1949, 5). In 1953 Robert Kass also expressed alarm at his imitations of "prancing imbeciles and mincing homosexuals" (122). Bosley Crowther's review of the 1954 film *Money from Home* similarly criticized Lewis's distasteful lapses in gender role: "This time we're afraid Mr. Lewis runs too much to effeminacy, which is neither very funny nor very tasteful. Mr. Martin stands discreetly to one side" (Crowther 1954).[27] The spectacle of feminization made Lewis a grotesque doppleganger yoked to

Martin's self-assured, self-consistent masculine ideal. It was not the only card he held in his repertoire of disturbances — he also careered gleefully through a welter of childlike and animalistic deformations — but he certainly dealt it with a flourish.[28]

Sikov (1994) characterizes Lewis as "a jester in a court of sexual panic" whose "anxiety-filled protogay characters" both displayed and displaced the specter of homosexuality: "By incarnating the kind of subversive homosexual desire that could not be overtly expressed let alone fulfilled (hence its sheer repetition), and by doubly subverting this desire by making it seem, as Lewis's character puts it in *Artists and Models,* 'retarded,' Lewis could express the (for want of a better word) homoeroticism that could no longer be denied on the screen but could scarcely be stated forthrightly in this era of officially-sanctioned gay-bashing. . . . He is the hysterical manifestation of his culture's failed repressed — imminent sexual criticism incarnate" (190). In such a climate of tyrannical homosexual prejudice Lewis's grotesquely affirmed return of the repressed enabled fear to be translated into the uneasy embrace of laughter. But what needs to be added to the equation is the degree to which his hysterical assertion-denial of homosexual desire — Lewis's impersonation, as Sikov puts it, of a "gay icon from Hell" (ibid., 185)— coincided with a *celebration* of his relationship with Martin. Lewis may have been grotesque, in other words, but Martin and Lewis were not. The love proclaimed through their live kibitzing simultaneously incorporated and transcended Lewis's stylized figurations of "excessive" homocosmic desire.

MARTIN AND LEWIS GO TUBE

With their act receiving ecstatic reviews and feverishly enthusiastic word of mouth, Martin and Lewis were among the hottest names on the nightclub circuit in the late 1940s. Although this made them seem a sound bet for the blossoming television industry, their transition to the new entertainment medium was a risky proposition. They faced the challenge of submitting themselves to the technical and ideological constraints of broadcast television without sacrificing the anarchistic abandon that made them such a hit. In addition, because television was formalizing its address to the family audience, Martin and Lewis also proved something of a test case for exploring the boundaries within which the medium could operate in its institutional role as a domestic and commercial service. Their nightclub act was premised upon a spectacular dissolution of fixed roles and positions, upon a continual breeching of boundaries. A space of potential excess, the nightclub was an antithetical realm to the hearth-based haven of television: it signified a liberated space beyond the routines of work, home, and domestic consumption. David Marc suggests that

the urban nightclub of the 1950s was, or at least strove to be, a missing link between day-to-day respectability and what Jack Kerouac was calling "the great American night." People came to the clubs to enjoy themselves—to drink, dance, meet other people, and keep up with the latest jazz, both musical and verbal. After a day, a week, a lifetime at the office, they expected, or even demanded, something of the exotic, the naughty, the "adult"; otherwise, why not stay at home and watch TV? Young middle-managers and Ivy League aristocrats could, if but for a weekend's moment, feel a connection to the beatnik America of dark streets, open sex, militant drug use, and racial intercourse that teased them from the pages of *Esquire* and *Playboy* as they toiled in the office towers. Television created no such liberated space. It went directly to the home of whoever turned it on. (Marc 1989, 43)[29]

Regular commercial television broadcasts began in New York city in 1941, but further development was blocked when, a year later, the federal government froze civilian television transmission and the manufacture of television equipment for the duration of World War II (Balio 1990, 14). After a faltering start when it was relaunched after the war, television commenced a period of accelerated growth from 1948. "The number of TV sets in use soared by more than 1,000 percent," notes film historian Tino Balio, "from 14,000 in 1947 to 172,000 a year later. In 1949, the number went up to 1 million, in 1950 to 4 million, and in 1954 to 32 million. By 1955, more than half of all American homes had television" (ibid., 15). By the end of the decade television had almost virtually reached saturation point, penetrating 90 percent of U.S. households (Belton 1994, 258). Building on the achievements of radio broadcasting—which had achieved its preeminence as a domestic, commercial mass medium in the 1930s—television would radically reconfigure American popular entertainment. Although it is traditionally held responsible for the decline in moviegoing from 1946, the rise of television was, as John Belton stresses, "merely a highly visible, superficial symptom of a much more profound change in postwar entertainment patterns" (ibid., 258). After the war the cinema found itself competing with a range of other pursuits for the time and money of American consumers: home-based activities such as DIY, gardening, and outdoor barbecues; participatory recreation such as fishing, hunting, golf, and other sports (Belton 1990, 73). The triumph of television has to be read in relation to a complex series of social transformations experienced by the United States in the postwar decade.[30]

Although it was more an effect than a cause of such transformations, television proved a powerful force in the domestication of consumerism. It played a key participatory and symbolic role in the consolidation of a postwar social regime of domestic affluence in which the ecstasy of consumption was contained within the functional orbit of the suburban home. Elaine Tyler May (1988) has suggested that "purchasing for the home helped alleviate traditional American uneasiness with consumption: the fear that spending would lead to decadence. Family-centered spending reassured Americans that affluence would strengthen the American way of life. The goods purchased by middle-class consumers, like a modern refrigerator or a house in the suburbs, were intended to foster traditional values" (166).

In the days before households were fragmented by multiple TV sets, television provided a central focus for home life, as parents and children gathered around the box to be unified ritualistically in the act of viewing.[31] Occupying a privileged place in the technological armory of the American family home, the television receiver not only was a favored consumer object in itself but also secured the promise of the domestic regime's self-sufficiency, beaming the world straight to the hearthland. Television was especially enticing because once the receiver was purchased the service was free—or, rather, it was provided on condition that audiences submitted themselves to the impeachments of the program sponsors. "The mass-marketing of television," Stuart Ewen (1977) argues, "carried the consumer imagery into the back corners of the home life. . . . Situated in the midst of the American household, TV became a vehicle for a consumerist mentality" (206–8). Television intensified the pacting of the American public to the new consumerist imperatives of the postwar age, with advertisers' messages interwoven into the panoply of entertainment entering the home.

With the sale of receivers continuing to rise through the early 1950s, the broadcasting networks concentrated on boosting their geographic and demographic penetration. They aimed to consolidate the potency of television as a commercial entertainment medium by building a national audience and attracting regional affiliates to the network chain.[32] Live performance—drama, comedy, variety—proved a vital network-building strategy. The National Broadcasting Company (NBC) had been the major force in U.S. television since the late 1930s, and Vance Kepley (1990) notes that from 1949 to 1955 the company[33] "exploited live programs to make affiliates dependent on the Radio City feed and to differentiate television's product from that of a competitor, the film industry. 'Television is not movies,' [program chief Pat] Weaver insisted, 'It is show business in the living room'" (46–47). Liveness served the networks as a tool for defining the identity of broadcast television as a distinctive entertainment form. However, the networks rapidly abandoned the live aesthetic as a broadcasting norm in the mid-1950s, when the U.S. television industry was stabilized as a mature oligopoly that would remain virtually unchanged over the next two decades (Boddy 1993, 57).

Until the mid-1950s the major television networks were centered in New York, which provided a plentiful and diverse supply of theatrical and variety talent from which to draw (Putterman 1995, 10).[34] The live variety-revue show, which drew on forms and performers from vaudeville and cabaret, emerged as an especially important context for differentiating, organizing, and stabilizing commercial television as a mass-entertainment vehicle. In the fledgling days of broadcast television, Timothy Scheurer (1985) stresses, the variety show "provided an anchor for an audience being exposed to a new medium, and, like vaudeville, through its different formats of 'vaudeo' (general variety), musical variety, and comedy variety, it drew on the viewer's past experience to provide entertainment in a new electronic age" (307).[35] The first hour-long program on network TV was NBC's variety show *Hour Glass* (1946), and by the early 1950s such programs constituted a major television genre, accounting for nearly half of all programming in the United States (ibid.). The pioneering success was NBC's *Texaco Star Theater,* a show so popular between 1948 and 1951 that its host — vaudeville and nightclub comedian Milton "Mr. Television" Berle — became the first star of the small screen (Wertheim 1983, 55-56).[36] As television scriptwriter Max Wilk attests, the extraordinarily high ratings of the Berle program inspired a wave of similar shows:

Since imitation is not only the sincerest form of flattery but also a guaranteed way to make a buck, the success of Berle's weekly burlesque spawned a tidal wave of carbon-copies. In the next few years new "personalities" would explode all over the home screen. It was something like the Alaskan gold rush of 1898 as every comic — male or female, high or low, stand-up or fall-down, monologist, quick-change artist, top or second banana, talking woman or straight man, dialect specialist or pantomimist — who'd ever induced the vaguest snicker from an audience was rushed by his eager agent to attend a top-level meeting with equally eager advertising men, sponsors, and network executives. (Wilk 1989, 52-53)

In the early 1950s Martin and Lewis were among the most significant performers on U.S. television, but until recently their fascinating work for the small screen has remained largely unseen since the initial telecasts. In the 1990s the Disney cable channel transmitted a series of documentaries, produced with Lewis's cooperation, which feature extensive material from kinescope recordings of the team's live television shows (JAS Productions 1992a, 1992b, 1992c, 1993a, 1993b).[37] Recordings of entire programs have subsequently been made available through small video companies specializing in the television-nostalgia market.

The following discussion will consider this newly available video material in conjunction with reviews from *Variety* and *Daily Variety*, trade journals of the entertainment business that provide an invaluable insight into Martin and Lewis's role within the institutional and discursive contexts of 1950s television.[38]

TELEKINESIS

Martin and Lewis made their television debut with a six-minute slot on the first edition of Ed Sullivan's *Toast of the Town*, telecast by the Columbia Broadcasting Service (CBS) on 24 June 1948. Like *Texaco Star Theater*, which had premiered twelve days earlier, *Toast of the Town* was a live variety-revue show that simulated and domesticated the atmosphere of big-time vaudeville and cabaret.[39] Reviewing the broadcast, *Variety* predicted correctly that "top vaude and nitery talent available for television is going to be at a premium in the very near future" ("*Toast of the Town*," 23 June 1948). Martin and Lewis capitalized on this demand, doing frequent guest shots over the next two years on programs such as the *Texaco Star Theater*, the *Bob Hope Show*, *Welcome Aboard*, *Saturday Night Revue* (the *Jack Carter Show*), and the rowdy late-night comedy and talk show *Broadway Open House*. Although these early appearances drew highly favorable notices from the trade magazines, reviewers also identified problems besetting the team's attempt to effect a successful transition to television.

As the networks developed their programming and scheduling strategies through the late 1940s and early 1950s, the trade press was not simply concerned with the quality of specific programs and performers but also participated actively in the process through which television was shaped and consolidated as a mainstream entertainment service. With the trade coverage attempting to both define and police the boundaries within which television operated as broad-based familial medium, Martin and Lewis were appraised in relation to a decorum that was itself still in the process of being formulated. The trade reviews of Martin and Lewis's television work, then, were not solely concerned with the team itself but engaged with broader conceptions about what television entertainment was and should be. A good example of this is the *Variety* review of the *Toast of the Town* show, which praised the "zany comedics" of Martin and Lewis but warned that CBS had allowed them "to give out with some blue material, okay for their nitery work but certainly not for tele" ("*Toast of the Town*," 23 June 1948). Similarly, in its review of the team's first appearance on *Welcome Aboard* in October 1948, *Variety* suggested that Martin and Lewis needed to re-jig their club style to suit the technical and domestic constraints of broadcasting:

"The Dean Martin–Jerry Lewis song and comedy patter routine was a little disappointing as TV fare. Somehow, this is one of those acts which gets across beautifully in the intimacy of a nightclub, but loses much of its flavor in televising; the zanyisms don't register the same click in the living room. Act suffered in part from unflattering camera angles. Perhaps the fact that televiewers watch their sets alone or as a family rather than in a crowd with nitery surroundings hurts the TV comedic effect of such acts as this" ("Tele Follow-Up Comment," 13 October 1948).

Subsequent reviews suggest that Martin and Lewis learned quickly. A spot on *Welcome Aboard* two weeks later inspired a rave notice: "Dean Martin and Jerry Lewis, on their third straight repeat, zinged over a sock specialty. On each successive stint the boys unloosened more and to advantage, with result that Martin's tongue-in-cheek crooning and Lewis's madcap humor came through in so resounding a manner as to augur well for their film career under Hal Wallis's aegis" ("Tele Follow-Up Comment," *Variety,* 20 October 1948). Within a few months, the team demonstrated that they could manage a more than workable compromise between the conflictual demands of liveness and domestication, looseness and control. The frisson that Martin and Lewis could deliver as a television attraction is well demonstrated by their astonishing work as guest stars on the Bob Hope and Bing Crosby telethon in June 1952.[40] This fourteen-and-a-half-hour benefit for the U.S. Olympics Fund, a rare collaboration between NBC and CBS, provided Bing Crosby with his much-heralded television debut.[41] *Daily Variety* praised Crosby for deporting himself "with the ease and nonchalance of his radio show and pictures. He matched ad libs with the more experienced Hope and was relaxed all the way. . . . As a TV personality he projected all the attributes and exuded a warm and friendly feeling that must have endeared him to the millions who sat through the show into the late hours across the cable" ("Hope-Crosby Olympics Telethon Doubles Goal, Exceeds $1,000,000," 23 June 1952). But as soon as Martin and Lewis bounced onstage Crosby lost his cool: the "warm and friendly feeling" was ousted by a far different kind of entertainment spectacle as Martin and Lewis extended their scheduled two-minute slot into a manic half-hour.

It begins with Crosby and Hope drooped casually around the central microphone as Hope introduces Martin and Lewis as their next guests. They leap onto the scene in unison: Martin breaks off his stage curtsey to glide into a handshake with Bing, a major professional idol, but Crosby slides away in panic when he sees Lewis lunge at Bob Hope and start to clasp and kiss him frantically. Crosby retreats, off camera and offstage, while Martin playfully but forcefully disentangles his partner from Hope. Though he is clearly in on the gag,

Martin seems amazed at the extremity of Lewis's assault on the older comic. When Martin and Lewis have sole command of the microphone, Hope, clearly furious, paces behind them and takes retaliatory action by swatting the two men with his clipboard. Lewis declares, "It's time for the old-timers to sit down," underscoring the significance of the intrusion as the routing of the show-biz old guard by these frisky, unconstrained newcomers. After celebrating their ascendancy with a brief bit of high-energy improvised dancing Lewis capitalizes upon Crosby's retreat, calling loudly and repeatedly for the crooner to come back onstage:

Lewis: "Uh Bing! Uh—Bing—uh—Crosby! Uh—Bing Crisby! Uh—here, fellow! Boy! Young man! Here, innkeeper, find that boy! Bob—uh—"
　Martin: "—Mr. Hope"
　Lewis: "—Robert. Where's Bing Crosby? Here, fine lad! Up there! Walk him around for an hour!"

Shaken by the taunting of his nervous partner, Hope comes back to the microphone and tries to reclaim what he can from the debacle. A tense expression on his face, Hope slaps Lewis's head with a wad of notes and pulls the microphone stand away from him. "Stop talking about my father that way," he quips, trying to win back the advantage with a characteristic wisecrack that evokes his famous mock feud with Crosby. Lewis does not stop, however, but meets the interruption with one of his own specialties: a grotesque piece of body mime that combines a distorted simian expression and a clawed-hand effect.

　Playing with the rules Lewis has enforced, Hope changes tack and begins to call out to the absent crooner, a ploy enabling Hope to regain control over the microphone, which he pulls close to his body, protectively.[42] Hope has thought of a gag, but Lewis's antics—conducting the orchestra, singing along with a yowling screech—transform his usually slick banter into a peripatetic stuttering more akin to Lewis's own verbal mangling: "When. . . . Listen . . . when did they cut the. . . . *When* did they cut the . . ." Hope then taps Martin on the shoulder with his papers. The handsome man turns round to face him and Hope shrewdly attempts to bring Martin into collusion with him, against Lewis, to create space for the completion of his wisecrack: "Hey, when did they cut the strings off him." The audience laughs, and to trumpet his victory Hope turns to face the audience/camera. But his triumph is short lived. Lewis rapidly shifts gear; he breaks off conducting, spins round, walks toward Hope with an exaggerated lope, and snaps back into the "Hey Bing!" routine. Hope grabs the microphone and turns to face the camera once more: "He's hiding, and I don't blame him," he says seriously.

In this battle of the comics, Lewis's nonstop, rapid-fire shape shifting is a dazzling wonder. Even Martin seems perpetually astonished at how far his partner is prepared to go to get a laugh, and through much of Lewis's performative skirmish with Hope he stands with a hand in his pocket, doing very little apart from just being there. But he does what little he does extremely well—and his being there is crucial. Lewis needs Martin's presence to legitimate his actions, and the audience needs him too, as an alibi and pretext for enjoying Lewis's bewitching excess. As Daniel Farson (1953) has suggested, Martin provided a strategic counterbalance to Lewis's extremism: "Martin, perhaps, is the safety-valve, the keeper; he does not give the impression of being a natural comedian, he seems rather to participate in the gags to placate and at the same time control his partner. On the screen, at least, he is utterly sane; he is calculating where Lewis is hysterically impulsive. Without him, Lewis's infantilism, his destructive mania, might run absolutely wild. Remove the joke from any extreme form of modern American comedy and what is left usually appears rather dangerous. Meantime, Lewis is often extremely funny" (31).

The scintillating telethon performance underlines the differences between Hope and Crosby and Martin and Lewis as male entertainment teams. Hope and Crosby were never this energetic, this unpredictable and explosive. Hope establishes an authoritarian relationship with the audience, seeking to assert order by laying claim to the microphone and buttonholing the camera with his voice and his gaze. Lewis, by contrast, whips up a whirlwind of sheer abandon. He does not need to acknowledge the camera: he *shows* it something instead. As Lewis forces him to play straight man to the gyrating carnivalesque he unleashes, Bob Hope—exemplar of polished, domesticated entertainment—stands no chance. Hope and Crosby were seasoned professionals who adapted themselves over a long period to a variety of media platforms: television was but the latest vehicle for their tried and tested routines. Martin and Lewis, by contrast, were offering something that broke with the decorum of entertainment as a professionalized service: they would nowadays be tagged "alternative" comedians. The heady emotions released in Hope and Crosby during this highly public humiliation imply a near-breakdown of the concept of television that comes from the hearth. Martin and Lewis are manic, edgy, risky, dangerous—and the audience loves them. Instead of simply running through their routines they "make live" with television, producing a devastating comic spectacle that threatens to burst through the confines of small-screen domestication. In their style—the male relationship as a resistance to postwar marriage—Lewis and Martin offered something completely different.

The team began to receive more concentrated televisual exposure from 1950, hosting the first of their twenty-eight contributions to NBC's *Colgate Comedy Hour* in September of that year. Playing against Sullivan in Sunday night prime time, *The Colgate Comedy Hour* was a variety show hosted in turn by a monthly rota of entertainers — initially, Eddie Cantor, Martin and Lewis, Fred Allen, and Bobby Clark.[43] The policy of using rotating hosts permitted greater flexibility and also alleviated the strain felt by performers committed to a weekly show (Wilk 1989, 56).[44] Moreover, it was an arrangement that suited Martin and Lewis's hectic schedule. The team worked on all five seasons of the *Comedy Hour,* although their appearances became less frequent when other work commitments demanded their time — and especially once their partnership began to founder. This more or less regular televisual showcase was extremely successful, with Martin and Lewis frequently beating Sullivan in the ratings and drawing almost half the national audience (Levy 1996a, 138). The pace would flag on occasions, but trade reviews suggest that on the whole Martin and Lewis — referred to fondly as "madcap revelers," "the zanies," "the daffiness boys," and "madmen of the megacycles" — kept to a remarkably high standard in their television work.

Most variety programs featured a serial host and a range of specialist performers — singers, comics, dancers, and so on — but Martin and Lewis did just about everything themselves on their sixty-minute programs. Able to showcase a range of attractions without the need of support from guest stars or lavish production values, they virtually constituted a two-man revue. As *Variety* observed of one of their 1948 nightclub performances, "Theirs is the type of act that throws everything at the audience, from impersonations, low comedy to straight singing" (Tosches 1992, 157).[45] The *Comedy Hour* shows enabled them to display their individual specialties — Martin's songs, Lewis's facial and bodily distortions — but this separateness was premised upon and facilitated by the promise of their dynamic combination, their explosive telekinesis. Their *Comedy Hour* debut was as dynamic and seemingly unmediated as their nightclub performances. *Variety* reports that "the show was almost played as an elongated 'next-to-closing' duo attraction. Too, the show was played strictly for video and to suggest the intimacy of a nitery, for it's under these conditions that M&L can best sock across their distinctive talents" ("*Colgate Comedy Hour,*" 20 September 1950).

Early discourse on broadcast television regarded intimacy as an essential criterion of successful televisual entertainment. In a *New York Times Magazine* article in 1956 television critic Jack Gould wrote that "live television . . . bridges the gap instantly and unites the individual at home with the event afar. The viewer has a chance to be in two places at once. Physically, he may be at his own hearthside but intellectually, and above all, emotionally he is at the cameraman's side. . . . Both the player in the studios and the audience at home have an intrinsic awareness of being in one another's presence" (Boddy 1993, 80). The ability of television to make itself seem at home with the audience was demonstrated most clearly by a mode of variety show that represented a more domesticated alternative to the spectacular show-biz visions of vaudeo. Programs such as *Arthur Godfrey and His Friends* (CBS, 1949–59) were more concerned with the creation of an intimate atmosphere than with the display of performers. Godfrey's program used "a living-room setting, where regulars and guests casually sat around. . . . Godfrey brought to TV no particular genius or comic or musical talent but he did bring a genuineness, a seeming honesty, which came across in his conversations with his guests and with the audience via commercials. Godfrey was, according to CBS chairman William S. Paley, 'the average guy's wistful projection of what he would like to be'" (Scheurer 1985, 309-10). On these "easygoing heartland personality shows," adds Barry Putterman, "the cast was presented as a 'family' of performers who, like papa Godfrey, staked their audience appeal as much on personal rapport as they did on artistic talent" (Putterman 1995, 13-14).

Many champions of live television regarded it as enabling an authenticity denied to the medium of film. In the cinema the presented images are always of the past and thus evoke separation and loss; by contrast television promises immediacy, nowness. For example, William Boddy (1993) cites Gilbert Seldes's 1952 eulogy on the virtues of live television drama: "The essence of television techniques is their contribution to the sense of immediacy. . . . The tension that suffuses the atmosphere of a live production is a special thing to which audiences respond; they feel that what they see and hear is happening in the present and therefore more real than anything taken and cut and dried which has to feel of the past" (80-81). In 1956 Jack Gould similarly propagandized for the raw integrity of live television's "metaphysic of presence" by chastising polished telefilm productions: "In their blind pursuit of artificial perfectionism, the TV film producers compromise the one vital element that endows the home screen with its own intangible excitement: humanness. Their error is to try to tinker with reality, to improve upon it to a point where it is no longer real. In so doing, they break the link between human and human. The viewer loses his sense of being a partner and instead becomes a spectator. It is the difference between being with somebody and looking at somebody" (ibid.). Quality television critics such as Seldes and Gould, elite guardians of cultural priorities, were committed to a vision of television that defined itself against the mainstream populism and spectacle of the Hollywood film. The reviewers of the trade press were oriented more toward television as entertainment, but they nevertheless shared the valuation of immediacy, presence, and intimacy.

Martin and Lewis were repeatedly praised for the skilful manner in which they accommodated their wildness to the demands of the small screen: "The zanies whammed over an hour of entertainment that, if anything, had more punch and hilarity that their teeoff stanza. It was strictly bigtime comedy video. . . . Lewis was particularly in fine fettle, his visual madcaps clicking with all the required TV intimacies" ("Tele Follow-Up Comment," *Variety,* 18 October 1950). Martin and Lewis were veterans of long-term cabaret engagements, and by simulating an intimate club ambience they were able to retain their freshness while appearing before a national audience on a more or less regular basis. Whereas in a nightclub their performance was immediate and localized, on TV Martin and Lewis were immediately *everywhere.* They played to an audience that was expanding rapidly as more television receivers were purchased and more regional stations plugged into the major networks.[46] As the trade reviews testify repeatedly, Martin and Lewis could be as hot, as alive, as liberated, and as fresh on television as they were onstage:

Martin and Lewis worked no differently than they do at the Copa. It's an act that has the appearance of improvisation, but since they're essentially a colorful and zany duo, anything went. ("Tele Follow-Up Comment" [*Broadway Open House*], *Variety,* 7 June 1950)

There probably isn't another comedy team around today with such uninhibited zanyism and the talent to carry it off successfully. Duo was on for virtually the entire hour, piling yocks on top of yocks without overstaying their welcome. ("Tele Follow-Up Comment," *Variety,* 7 February 1951)

Dean Martin & Jerry Lewis have probably reached the topmost level of their development. At this point, it's probable that this team can do no wrong. Call them the funniest twosome extant, and you can't be far wrong. Their periodic video displays on NBC's *Colgate Comedy Theater* [*sic*] series have become landmarks to home viewers. ("Tele Follow-Up Comment," *Variety,* 2 May 1951)

The zany comics demonstrated once more that video is as much their cake as niteries. They paced virtually the entire production at breakneck speed and, if the studio audience is indicative of home viewers' reaction, there must have been an epidemic of laughing sickness on the co-ax. ("Tele Follow-Up Comment," *Variety,* 23 May 1951)

As far as the viewer was concerned, it was M & L all the way, with all other program facets more or less stage waits. . . . If, as the current hue and cry would have us believe, the major comics are going around in a repetitive groove, and the sameness of material and faces have already created a TV crisis, these ominous overtones haven't, at least as yet, caught up with the Martin & Lewis comedics. ("*Dean Martin & Jerry Lewis,*" *Variety,* 7 November 1951)

Unlike other comics who exhaust their stocks-in-trade by overdoses of video, M & L have achieved that rare talent of easing their way through variations of old and familiar business, yet managing to giving [*sic*] it a continuing spark of freshness and comicality. They wear well on TV. ("Tele Follow-Up Comment," *Variety*, 30 April 1952)

One long succession of laughs. Moving like a tornado through Kansas. ("*Martin & Lewis,*" *Daily Variety*, 1 December 1952)

They never worked harder or were more deliriously received by an audience that rocked with the gags and callused their hands with applause. ("*Martin & Lewis,*" *Daily Variety*, 3 May 1954)

The trade reviewers, however, also found frequent cause to berate Martin and Lewis for breaches of decorum. In the new telescapes explored and colonized by the networks certain territories needed to be kept off limits. Not only was "blue material" taboo, but so too was any direct play with the two men's ethnic identities as Italian and Jew: "With the success of their straight comedy, incidentally, it seems needless for the duo to play on their racial backgrounds, something which might not sit too well with a number of their viewers" ("Tele Follow-Up Comment," *Variety*, 7 February 1951). Like vaudeville and radio before it, American television of the 1950s proved a powerful model of cultural assimilation. It was a large-scale popular medium that both showcased diverse ethnic and regional styles (Marc 1990, 24) and channeled differences into an increasingly homogenized framework for mainstream cultural identity. Forging television as an all-purpose mass-entertainment service, the networks were overly cautious about issues of ethnicity and race — especially after the sitcoms *Amos 'n' Andy* and *Beulah* were canceled in 1953 following protests against their derogatory representation of African Americans (Marc 1990, 35; Cripps 1983, 33–54). In the nervous political and social climate of the early 1950s, in which a cold war vigilante logic had supplanted the liberal idealism engendered during World War II, difference of all kinds was rendered a difficult proposition.

Anxiety about Martin and Lewis's ethnic comedy was not restricted to television. In an April 1949 review of a Martin and Lewis performance at the Copacabana *Variety* wrote,

Maybe their best friends won't tell them, or their management seems unable to see it or control it, but the fact is that people are beginning to talk about Dean Martin's and Jerry Lewis's dialectics [*sic*]. The ever-growing accent on Martin's Italian extraction and Lewis's Yiddishisms are annoying and unshowmanly.

The personable singer, furthermore, is evincing his dialectic predilections by throwing in some other Bronx patois and all this tends to make for a needless hurdle for two of the freshest, upcoming comedians extant. And that goes ditto for Lewis. Fact is they are extraordinarily talented, particularly in the visual medium. But when the new things that have been added become increasingly flavored with kosher or antipasto *hors d'oeuvres,* it's time to mention it.

Team has gotten so that their chatter and patter put emphasis on "some of my people are here tonight too," and wheezes like "even the tables go to shul" [synagogue], etc. (Marx 1975, 114)

The "needless hurdle" of ethnicity was identified as a problem on numerous occasions, and the team was keen to respond to such criticism. The *Variety* review of their *My Friend Irma* support in October 1949 suggested that Martin and Lewis had toned down their material for the broader audience sought for the film: "On the plus side — and for the better, of course — is the elimination, at least for the theater, of all those Yiddish and Eye-talian references, which they belabored in the niteries. Here, there's only a fleeting bit of that business, and that's all" ("Paramount, N.Y.," 5 October 1949, 46).

Aligning himself with the familiar stereotype of the Latin lover, Dean Martin capitalized on the exotic connotations of his Italian heritage, but he also colluded with the process by which his ethnicity was mainstreamed and diluted. Before teaming with Lewis, for example, he sought to de-Latinize his appearance by having his nose streamlined through plastic surgery. With Lewis, the situation is rather more complex. Despite his formative years in the Borscht Belt, Lewis was careful not to flaunt his Jewishness in his television shows or films.[47] Shawn Levy (1996a) points out that Lewis's comic persona attests to the repression of his ethnic identity: "Unlike his creator, who liked to indulge in touches of Yiddish onstage and often referred to himself as a 'Jewish movie star,' Jerry's comic character was utterly without ethnicity. True, few Jewish comedians of the era flaunted their religious roots in mainstream entertainment; but beyond that, Jerry's very position as half of a team required he sublimate his ethnic background. Jerry's partner was highly regarded for his way with Italian songs, and the contrast between the virile and confident singer and his skinny-shouldered, nebbishy friend could easily have been loaded with ugly implications had the little guy's ethnicity been allowed to surface" (74).

When he set out on his public career, the young Joey Levitch followed a commonplace practice in U.S. show-biz culture by adopting a de-Semitized name to disguise his ethnic origins. Within the safe haven of the Borscht Belt, performers such as Danny and Jerry Lewis could express their Jewish cultural identity with ease, but the increasingly homogenized entertainment business — big-time vaudeville, Hollywood, radio, television — required the assimilationist embrace of ethnically effaced Americanism.[48] Even after the team split Lewis refrained from portraying explicitly Jewish characters along the lines of such later comedians as Lenny Bruce, Mel Brooks, and Woody Allen (Levy 1996a, 74).[49] Nevertheless, his Jewishness could be said not simply to disappear but to take on the character of a fugitive ethnicity that speaks through other voices and other guises.[50] It was a standard feature of their act, for example, that around Dean Martin's totemic straight guy Lewis would weave a range of alternative identities — including grotesquely inflated impressions of Frenchmen, Germans, and Japanese.[51] By comparison with Martin, Lewis was the conductor of a polyphony of differences: he was otherness incarnate. Moreover, his racial impersonations — like his gendered deformations — affirm an identity that is based in fluidity and heterogeneity, an identity that exists in the very slippage between established cultural categories.[52]

PLUG-HAPPY

Another area that drew consistent reproaches from the trade reviewers was Martin and Lewis's ambiguous relationship with the apparatus of commercial promotion that motored U.S. network television — itself the subject of a great deal of public debate through the early 1950s. As had been common in radio, commercial sponsors and their advertising agencies controlled programming and scheduling in the early years of broadcast television: "The companies bought a block of time on a given night and from year to year they would decide what kind of program featuring which artists would be presented. The program was calculated to appeal to the sponsor's market and the show's stars were often so closely identified with the sponsor's product that they appeared in advertising both in and beyond the show itself" (Putterman 1995, 9).[53]

William Boddy (1993) suggests, however, that although the networks "encouraged advertising agencies to move into the new medium, they were also fearful of repeating the pattern of network radio of the 1930s, when the agencies gained substantial control over network prime-time programming." During the early 1950s the two major networks, CBS and NBC, mobilized an economic and discursive campaign to wrest programming control from commercial sponsors in order to secure a greater share of advertising revenues.[54] Portraying themselves as sensible mediators between self-serving advertisers and the television audience, the networks mouthed a rhetoric of public service that simultaneously justified their oligopolistic agenda (94–96, 159–60).

The entertainment trade journals made an important contribution to this debate about the contested relations between programming and advertising, devoting substantial space in their scrutiny of individual programs to the way that commercials were handled. On their radio shows seasoned entertainers such as Jack Benny and Bob Hope managed to make the delivery of the commercial message a part of the act, naturalizing their service to the sponsor within their broadcast personas. So long as they furthered the domestication rather than the alienation of the audience's relationship with the product, performers were allowed to wring humorous capital from their obligation. Radio's much-noted aura of intimacy made it easier to bridge the roles of entertainer and commercial spokesperson.[55] However, the networks adopted a different strategy for the television variety-revue shows, enforcing a sharp differentiation between the provision of entertainment and the process of selling.[56] Although it was an expected and accepted part of the show, the commercial was located at a greater distance from the performer's general relationship with the audience; instead of delivering the plug themselves, the hosts of these shows merely introduced filmed commercial inserts or handed over to a specialized announcer (Putterman 1995, 14). Selling is calculated and manipulative in its seductions, an anxiety the networks cannily exploited as a means of consolidating their hegemony. By contrast, the utopian sensibility of American popular entertainment idealizes performance as auratic: it connotes genuineness, spontaneity, the integrity of presence.[57] Because the aura of entertainment can be compromised by making the alliance with the corporate sponsor too overt, the entertainment trade press was acutely troubled by the way the alternative comedy of Martin and Lewis interacted with the commercial agenda of broadcast television.

Like many other shows of the time — the *Ford Television Theater, Texaco Star Theater, Kraft Television Theater*—Martin and Lewis's regular television showcase bore the name of its commercial sponsor. But instead of holding to the decorous dividing lines the networks had erected between promotion and performance, Martin and Lewis repeatedly went plug-crazy, pitching promos for their live engagements, movie appearances, and favored charities.[58] *Daily Variety* complained that on some shows the plugs "seemed to saturate" ("*Colgate Comedy Hour,*" 28 April 1952). A few weeks earlier *Variety* had launched a lengthy attack on an episode of the *Comedy Hour* for its frenzy of promotional excess:

What the public saw were a couple of funny kids, the hottest comedy act in show business today, waxing so overly generous in their we-love-everybody plugs as to border on the ridiculous.

They're just cuh-razy for some Boston beanery boniface who ministered to their inner manhood when they played the Hub, and so the first commercial was for him because he's such a fast man with the groceries. In a photography studio scene Lewis plugged Revere Cameras like he was Tex Briskin's partner. Themselves w.k. within the trade as pretty fast with a buck—not to mention that $2,000,000 in wages they will knock off in 1952—this certainly couldn't be a "promosh" but it sounded that way and the tongue-in-cheek "when you gonna send it like you said?" must have struck a false note.

Then it seemed that an April 22 issue ("but it comes out April 8"), of *Look* has "a very fine story on us," said Lewis, and the close-up on the weekly, with the comics' kissers on the cover, certainly paid off the mag in spades.

Then followed two laudable commercials—one for the Red Cross, part of an emergency pitch on all networks by all programs, keyed to the current Midwest tornado catastrophe; the other for their pet Muscular Dystrophy charity, with a flash of the box-office and the New York address.

The buildup to Danny Lewis, Jerry's dad, was another kind of commercial—an affectionate salutation wherein Dean Martin saluted him as his "partner-in-law." ("Tele Follow-Up Comment," *Variety*, 26 March 1952)

Martin and Lewis, the reviewer intimates, are violating the compact of intimacy that television makes with its audiences. Unrestrained plugging of this order threatened to unravel that intimacy, exposing it as a ruse, a strategy of the television institution's machinery of consumer seduction. In a telling precursor of Lewis's later demonization the *Variety* reviewer seems especially affronted by the team's flamboyant *self*-publicity. Their stardom assured by 1952, Martin and Lewis eagerly flaunted their phenomenal and prolific success, showing that they were fully aware of the "mythic" status their stardom had purchased in postwar U.S. culture. One of their *Comedy Hour* shows, telecast on 2 May 1954, was even structured as a pseudo autobiography to commemorate the 8th anniversary of their teaming. Uneasy with such lack of restraint, the trade reviewers intimated that at times Martin and Lewis seemed more interested in pleasing themselves than their audiences. Even though they recognize that "making live" is the team's prime attraction, several reviews evangelize the script as a tool for discipline and containment:[59]

If anything, Sunday night's seasonal teeoff was as frantic as anything they've done. But there was little else to accompany the frenzy. . . . The attempts to "laugh it up" at forgotten lines, miscues and unoriginal material that inevitably dissolved into slapstick of the bedlam variety, at times made the viewer forget what an excruciatingly funny fella The Jerry can be.

There was nothing the boys did here that they hadn't done before—but with a difference. That M & L are "repeat artists" with the ability to pyramid their laughs and popularity with each successive reprise of the same trademarked zanyisms has been more of a virtue than a detriment in their fabulous career — but only when they're getting an adequate assist from their writers. Last Sunday, neither the spark nor the script assist were in evidence. It was one of the rare occasions on TV when the duo rode along on "we-can-do-no-wrong" kite. ("*Martin & Lewis Show,*" *Variety*, 24 September 1952)

Martin and Lewis hit the spot because of their provocative play with boundaries, their testing of limits. As is made clear by the trade reviewers' nervousness about the team's handling of the sensitive issues such as ethnicity and commercial promotion, the zanyisms registered because Martin and Lewis trod the narrow and nervous line that separates entertainment and transgression. Whipping up dynamic tensions between order and disorder, regularity and chaos, structure and spontaneity, their liveness was always a risky proposition. "Martin and Lewis on TV were brilliantly anarchic," Shawn Levy (1996a) claims, "teetering on the edge of improvisation while never straying too far from written structures" (133). The trade reviewers, though, were not convinced. Their calls for scriptual discipline highlighted the need to banish nervousness by making Martin and Lewis more regulated, more domesticated, more *accountable*. "The casual air that they assume is fine," commented *Variety* of their *My Friend Irma* support, "but sometimes there is a strong suspicion that the casualness is not all it's supposed to be. The boys will engage in pieces of business of which they, and possibly the bandsmen, may be only aware, leaving the audience wondering what it's all about" ("Paramount, N.Y.," 1 October 1949, 46). Their performance on a 1955 *Comedy Hour* show was similarly chastised for it's "sloppiness and what-do-we-care attitude" ("Tele Follow-Up Comment," *Variety*, 16 February 1955).

A furiously busy schedule — films, regular TV, gigs at clubs and theaters — required Martin and Lewis to rely increasingly upon material supplied by writers. The team of Norman Lear and Ed Simmons were hired for the *Comedy Hour* shows but left in 1954 after a major falling-out with Lewis, who had suggested hiring them in the first place.[60] Bitter feelings still rankle: the writers accuse Lewis of an obsessional desire for control (Levy 1990, 172), and Lewis protests that the writers were not sufficiently attuned to the team's enticing liveness: "There isn't any of that stuff that's as funny as the stuff we did together, or that I wrote for us. I'm not putting down the writers — we had very good writers — but, compared to what Dean and I brought to one another, spontaneously, far outweighed anything they ever could write. Because the written material came off as written material. . . . Writers were never ever capable of really writing for Dino and I, except giving us a frame, go . . . put them in that frame and then, bang! They're exploding" (JAS Productions 1992a). The script did not count in itself; it was nothing more than a springboard for the performative interaction of the two men: "We always left it loose," Lewis claims. "We called most of the writing we did blueprint" (JAS Productions 1992b). As *Variety* noted of one of their TV shows, "The team reaches its apex when they use their own devices as the major peg for comedy, and the script is used as a general outline or as a guide to general procedure" ("Tele Follow-Up Comment," 5 May 1954).

Other reviews were less enthusiastic about the prospect of Martin and Lewis unbounded. "Perhaps it's significant—and even newsworthy—" runs the write-up of one of the 1955 shows, "that M&L hit their best moments when they were exercising some restraint and willing to concede that the novelty of their buffoonery has long since worn off and that some concession must be made to the writers and the kind of material they're provided with" ("Tele Follow-Up Comment," *Variety*, 16 February 1955).[61] The reviewer cites a hoary old sketch idea involving a patient in a doctor's surgery who needs quiet: instead of ending up with the characteristic Martin and Lewis bedlam, "the boys managed to check themselves and permit a couple of real scripting cuties to take over." By contrast an earlier sketch was not so funny because it relied on "Lewis mugging to the degree that every movement was telegraphed." The *Variety* scribe concludes that "the two skits were a revelation in terms of a then-and-now transition of the comedy team into a more—let's hope—composed duo. The 'now' part seems to fit them better these days—at least on tv" (ibid.).

A prison sketch featured in the *Comedy Hour* show of 4 November 1951 provides a clear illustration of the potential friction between script and performance. Lewis's mincingly nervous neophyte is introduced into a cell shared by Martin and another hardened con. The playlet opens to a good reaction from the in-studio audience, with Lewis confronting the tough guys with a high-energy impression of James Cagney's gangster character. But it hits a slow spot in a dialogue-heavy routine in which the inmates test the kid's knowledge of underworld vernacular. The stars become captives of the script, concentrating too hard on delivering their lines instead of generating a spark. At one point Lewis even fluffs a line: "Give the chance a kid." It gets a laugh, but he is clearly annoyed at his mistake. The sketch struggles along until an obviously bored Martin tosses off an impromptu comic hand grenade, a consciously nonsensical line that sounds something like "Did ya ever take it on the lam with a shamus who had the croaker beside the cree?" This is not simply an ad lib, but an ad lib with a purpose: it signals a rejection of the scripted roles and dialogue that are constraining the team. Lewis and the other inmate break up at Martin's casually willful diversion, and Lewis turns to the camera. Smiling broadly and shrugging his shoulders, he confesses with gleeful wonder: "He ad-libbed—I don't know where I am now." The sketch has been turned around; the two men are no longer going through the motions and doing what they've been told. Martin's exquisitely cunning quip has detonated a laugh-grabbing explosion of liveness, which clears space for their liberated interaction.

On the *Comedy Hour* broadcasts Martin and Lewis were constantly on the lookout for opportunities to break away from and work against the script. Writer and performer Carl Reiner, a regular on the highly successful ninety-minute NBC comedy-variety program *Your Show of Shows* (1950–54), claims that the early days of broadcast television "had a vitality that's completely gone. I mean, if you were out there in front of the audience and you goofed, or something misfired, well, you just stood there and improvised, and sometimes what emerged was funnier than anything you could have thought of in a month of rehearsals" (Wilk 1989, 57). Martin and Lewis became experts at milking technical glitches for laughter. One *Comedy Hour* gag called for Lewis to pull a wishbone from a turkey; he accidentally dropped the turkey onto the floor, but he and Martin amply demonstrated "their ability to capitalize on production snafus. They lost the payoff prop in the skit, a turkey wishbone, but ad libbed their way to more yocks" ("*The Colgate Comedy Hour*," *Variety,* 23 May 1951).[62] Martin and Lewis also asserted their freedom from constriction by flaunting an irreverent attitude to television's technical and organizational machinery. The *Comedy Hour* telecast of 20 May 1951, for example, runs faster than expected, leaving them with 5 minutes to fill; Lewis vents his frustration by rushing offstage to lay hold of the studio timekeeper, whom he thrusts before the camera (JAS Productions 1992a). On the *Comedy Hour* of 10 January 1954 Lewis goes further than simply bringing the apparatus into the picture by transforming it into an instrument of oppression. As Martin tries to make it through a version of "That's Amore," Lewis pushes the cameras in around him, eventually surrounding the crooner and subjecting him to their unflattering and aggressive gaze (huge, distorted close-ups of the singer fill the screen) (JAS Productions 1992a).

Many of the *Comedy Hour* sketches develop through the gradual unleashing of a process of creative disruption. The two men start out divided but overcome their differences to become united against an external world of constraints, the process of fusion generating a joyously destructive energy. A good example is a sketch in their final Colgate show, when the team itself was on the verge of disintegration (*Colgate Variety Hour,* 13 November 1955). Martin is a guest at a garden party held to commemorate his engagement to an extremely rich, upper-crust woman. Sydney/Lewis, his gormless and casually attired friend, arrives on his bicycle and unknowingly triggers a series of disturbances that cause the formal occasion to degenerate into chaos: he interrupts a violin recital, drops the engagement ring into a bowl of punch, picks fights with the guests. Martin is held to blame for these disorderly transgressions, and his fiancée calls off the engagement. The sketch concludes with Martin and Lewis stepping out of the situational frame to perform a musical number that reasserts the superiority of their buddy relationship to the divisions of heterosexuality and class and to the demands of their scripted identities. After the fiancée dumps Martin he is left alone with Lewis on the set. Music starts and two men move into a performance of "Two Lost Souls"—a song from the then-current show *Damn Yankees*—in which they profess that no matter what else, "we got each other."[63] They walk forward and the stage curtain closes behind them, signaling the transition to a space of untrammeled performance:

> *Martin:* "It's Jerry and Dean"
> *Lewis:* "Go now!"
> *Martin:* "And no-one in between"
> *Lewis:* "Like, let's say, Gallagher and, let's say, Shean"
> *Martin:* "Of course, we complain, we fuss and strain"
> *Lewis:* "But after the fussin' there's always us, an'—"
> *Martin:* "Two lost souls, each wedded to each"
> *Lewis:* "We go hand in hand in all kinds of weather."[64]

The most resonant moments on the *Comedy Hour* programs, however, come not from the sketches but from more open contexts designed to spark their spontaneous combustion. Reminiscent of their nightclub act, the finale sequences were described by *Variety* as "probably the highlight of all their shows[,] . . . when lots of time is left open for them to do virtually as they wish" ("Tele Follow-Up Comment," 24 June 1951). These loosely scripted endpieces provide a strategic reassertion of the team's "pure" liveness after sketches in which they are attired, however skimpily at times, in the garbs of character identity and situation. Lewis generally conducts the orchestra while Martin sings his final song, but his increasing interruption of the performance sparks a mock skirmish between the two.[65] In the *Comedy Hour* show of 15 October 1950 Martin tries to sing one of his stage favorites, the easygoing Italian ballad "Oh, Marie," in the face of an inappropriately classical-styled arrangement that Lewis encourages from the pianist. The song is constantly broken off as the two men take turns to launch humorous assaults upon one another; at one point Lewis sticks his fingers in Martin's mouth and pulls it wide, to which Martin's responds, "This wasn't in the script, buddy." Several other finales build toward a similar escalation of disorder. On one show, for example, Martin's rendition of "Singin' in the Rain" ends with the two men throwing buckets of water at one another and then slipping around on a sodden stage (*Colgate Comedy Hour,* 12 November 1950). On another Lewis packs the stage with the massed ranks of a male choir who drown the crooner beneath their raucous backing on "Sometimes I'm Happy" (*Colgate Variety Hour,* 13 November 1955). These sequences work so well because they have no rationale apart from showing two guys going crazy, having fun together, generating sparks. It is a comedy of reverent irreverence, which thrusts two fingers at a world of regularity and constraint while simultaneously asserting the positive force of a very special relationship.

PHOTOCHEMISTRY

MARTIN AND LEWIS ONSCREEN

With the exception of *Artists and Models* and *Hollywood or Bust,* directed by cult Frank Tashlin, the sixteen films Martin and Lewis made between 1949 and 1956 have received very little serious attention. Although the films, as many critics have noted, fail to capture the electric liveness of Martin and Lewis's cabaret and television work, their use of extended fictional contexts generates some intriguing possibilities. Martin and Lewis's movies also merit reconsideration because they were among the most popular and successful films made in the 1950s. Film exhibitors in the United States regularly voted the team among the top ten box-office attractions from 1951 to 1956, and eight of their films figured among the annual top twenty commercial hits (three in 1953 alone) (Steinberg 1981, 435–36, 479).[1]

The Martin and Lewis films were lucrative enterprises for Hal Wallis: for example, their most profitable vehicle, *Sailor Beware,* was made for less than $750,000 but took in $27 million worldwide (Tosches 1990, 272). Wallis had a mercenary attitude toward his comic cash cows, warning Ed Simmons that "a Martin and Lewis picture costs a half-million, and it's guaranteed to make three million with a simple formula: Jerry's an idiot, Dean is a straight leading man who sings a couple of songs and gets the girl. That's it, don't fuck with it, go back to the typewriter" (Levy 1996a, 104). Dean Martin was the most notable casualty of Wallis's formulaic production regime. In live performance and on television Martin was never exclusively a straight man to the madcap clown, but frequently joined in with Lewis's disruptions. The films, however, established a much more straightforward division of labor between crooner and comedian, handsome man and monkey. Simmons says that when he and Norman Lear were called in for rewrites on *Scared Stiff*, Wallis flamboyantly rejected scenes that would stretch Martin beyond his functional role as Lewis's foil (ibid.). The story material chosen for the team reveals Wallis's opportunism. A large proportion of the Martin and Lewis films derived from preexisting properties made over to fit the team: *My Friend Irma* and its sequel *My Friend Irma Goes West* were based on a radio program, *Scared Stiff* was a remake of Bob Hope's *The Ghost Breakers* (1940), and *Sailor Beware* and *Artists and Models* were both based on Broadway plays. It is misguided, however, to blame Wallis alone for the lack of ambition of the Martin and Lewis films.[2] Since the late 1930s the comedian-centered film had been entrenched as a standardized Hollywood format, a blend of fiction and entertainment spectacle that could accommodate such diverse talents as Danny Kaye, Bob Hope, Red Skelton, Abbott and Costello or Martin and Lewis.[3]

All star-centered films negotiate tensions between the specific requirements of the fictional role and the signifying effects of the star image, but the comedian comedy was a highly specialized form of star vehicle that had the display of the performer as the prime rationale.[4] In Hollywood comedian films produced from the late 1930s to the late 1950s the representational paradigm motivates the scenes of performance, establishing both a context and a register for disordering process set in motion by the comic performer.[5] The frame story provides an overtly conventional narrative problematic, with ostentatiously clichéd intrigues, goals, and characters. Thrown into this orderly fictional regime, the comedian proceeds to deform the rules and logical procedures that sustain it. One of the most common ways of organizing this dynamic is to situate the comic performer in the midst of a highly coded genre, and like many others before them Martin and Lewis served time in a haunted house (*Scared Stiff*), at the circus (*Three Ring Circus*), out West (*Pardners*), at the racetrack (*Money from Home*), on the road (*Hollywood or Bust*), and in the armed services (*At War with the Army, Sailor Beware, Jumping Jacks*). The comedian is never fully bound by the frame story—indeed, much of the comic play comes from maintaining a *fluctuating* gap between performer and character identity, between presentation and representation. While the fiction maneuvers to subjugate deviance and disruption to the demands of stability and coherence, the performative impetus aims to transform the film into a stage upon which to mount a denarrativizing entertainment spectacle. In the Martin and Lewis comedies the dialectic between the two processes is articulated and resolved in different ways.

At one extreme *That's My Boy* reveals a relatively serious treatment of the problems faced by the Lewis figure in establishing his identity as a male subject.[6] With a story reminiscent of such contemporary melodramas of masculine crisis as *Rebel Without a Cause* (1955), *Tea and Sympathy* (1956), and *Home from the Hill* (1960), *That's My Boy* organizes its scenes of comic disruption within a dramatically articulated Oedipal paradigm. Lewis plays Junior Jackson, the neurotically frail offspring of an overbearing football hero, "Jarring" Jack Jackson (Eddie Mayehoff). Jarring Jack desires a son who will reflect the sporting glory of his youth, but Junior is unable to fulfill his expectations. His psychosomatic infirmity provides a means by which he can challenge the father's hypermasculine success ethic by adopting a position of rebelliously "feminized" maleness.[7] Dean Martin's Bill Baker steps into this Oedipal impasse as a mediator. The superathletic son of a weak and impoverished father, Bill is a reverse-image of Junior — and can thus stand in as idealized son for Jarring Jack and an idealized buddy for Junior. Under his guidance Junior is ultimately able to attain legitimacy in his father's eyes: taking Bill's place in a crucial football game for the Jackson alma mater, Ridgeville University, he leads the team to victory. Martin and Lewis's service comedies — *At War with the Army, Sailor Beware,* and *Jumping Jacks* — represent a contrasting tendency. These films offer a different conceptualization of the identity thematic, in which "finding a place" for the Lewis figure involves defining the self in relation to a hierarchically structured masculine institution. More important, the narratives of these films are elaborated far more loosely than is the case in *That's My Boy*. The principal function of the frame story is to provide a legitimate linking structure for a variety of entertainment attractions: compressed plot sequences, solo comic spots by Lewis, Martin-Lewis duo performances, Martin's songs, and other musical numbers.

Even though the Martin and Lewis movies privilege the comedian as the center of attention, the handsome man plays a crucial role in contextualizing the Lewisian spectacle of disorder and dysfunctionalism. Martin's very straightness serves to accentuate the edginess that was an integral feature of the team's liveness — the intermingling of affection and hostility, togetherness and difference, independence and interdependence. The specific narrative intrigues of the Martin and Lewis films are less important in themselves than for the manner in which they move the two men through a range of emotional intensities and relational permutations. Overriding the flow and ebb of the characters they play is the extrafictional familiarity of Martin and Lewis's distinctive buddy relationship. This is most clearly expressed at the start of *The Caddy:* to document the appearance of popular entertainers Joe Anthony (Martin) and Harvey Miller (Lewis) at New York's Paramount Theater, the film incorporates footage of the teenage fans who jammed the streets when Martin and Lewis played there in 1951.

The Caddy is a flashback-fiction about two men who overcome their differences to emerge as a supreme entertainment team. The first scene, set in their dressing room, portrays Anthony and Miller as wild and crazy guys who engage in continual play and cross-talk. Like Martin and Lewis's own publicity, the film suggests that the act is an extension of their real selves.[8] Anthony and Miller then take the stage for a rendition of "What Would You Do Without Me (When I'm Gone)," one of numerous partnership songs performed by Martin and Lewis throughout their career. The lyrics playfully mock the ties that bind the two together, with each man expressing his desire to have the other removed. However, these sentiments are vibrantly contradicted by the sizzling marriage of their bodies in motion. Proclaiming and celebrating their sublime togetherness, scenes like this recur in the team's films — but rarely so near the start. Such performative collusions generally mark the ultimate triumph of the characters played by Martin and Lewis over the narrative obstructions that have impeded their union.

The most dramatically sustained account of the conflictual relationship between the male partners can be found in *The Stooge,* a film that gives Dean Martin an unusually prominent role. Martin's Bill Miller is a swell-headed crooner who breaks up his successful partnership with comedian Ben Bailey (Richard Erdman) "because I want to play the big time on my own, as a single." Miller's new act lays a resounding egg until his agent, Leo (Eddie Mayehoff), suggests hiring a stooge to work as his offstage foil. Lewis's fragile outsider, Ted Rogers, takes this role and the act is an immediate hit. Although Miller surpasses the success he knew with Bailey, he is unwilling to accept Ted as a partner instead of a mere hireling. His desire for self-sufficiency disrupts all his sustaining relationships: his agent and his wife leave him, and he sacks the devoted Ted in a fit of drunken and egotistical pique after a gig at New York's Palace Theater. When he hits the skids on his first show without Ted, Miller delivers a repentant speech to the audience: "Ladies and gentlemen, I want to apologize. This is the Sutherland Revue, which is supposed to bring you the finest entertainment that can be offered. You've heard of an act, 'Bill Miller.' Bill Miller is me. But I'm only half an act. The fella that made the act work is a little guy by the name of Ted Rogers, and he isn't here tonight. I can play an accordion and sing a song, but I need that spark, that something, the chemistry that makes two men a successful team. I've bored you, and I've imposed upon you. I've done an injustice to an audience. This is the biggest sin in show business, to be a ham. I humbly apologize." From his box by the stage, Ted calls out, "Who's your little Whozis"—the cue for a song. He clambers down onto the stage and the two men glide into a trademark routine to commemorate their reconciliation: Martin follows Lewis's lead; Lewis breaks into a manic solo dance, and then they close the number in harmony.

With the entertainment team of Miller and Rogers, as with Martin and Lewis, neither man can attain fulfillment on his own. *Variety* described Ted Rogers as "a wistful ugly duckling who adores the man who gave him a chance in show business" (*"The Stooge,"* 8 October 1952). Such adoration is typical not only of Lewis's screen roles but also of his accounts of the offscreen relationship he shared with Dean Martin.[9] The diffident and separatist Martin figure finds the other's demand for love problematic, and from film to film the handsome man expresses his discomfort by trying to exploit and to discard the monkey who clings so fervently to his very straight back. The more Lewis cleaves to Martin, the more Martin seeks to cleave the bonds that bind them together. Despite the multiaccented grotesquerie of Lewis's embrace, however, Martin must ultimately accept that they are destined to be, as the theme song of *Pardners* (1956) expresses, "the greatest pardners, buddies and pals."

The Stooge is unusual in the way it gives a sustained melodramatic spin to the male partnership, explicitly narrativizing its driving instability. Most of the Martin and Lewis film vehicles articulate similar conflicts in a more compressed and intense form, through individual scenes and sequences that are motivated, yet not exhausted, by the narrative.

SCARED STIFF

A scene early in *Scared Stiff*, the eighth Martin and Lewis film, invokes their early club act.[10] Incompetent busboy Myron Mertz (Lewis) disrupts the nightclub act of Larry Todd (Martin) when he accidentally drops a plate of spaghetti onto a customer's head. Myron is overcome with emotion when Larry asks him to participate in the show, but the handsome man is actually setting him up for a smoothly calculated public humiliation. The performance consists of a comic sketch in which a husband discovers his wife's infidelity, a routine that is played out three times. Larry first casts Myron as the lover and himself as the husband. Myron puckers his lips in anticipation when Larry's glamorous assistant Rosie (Dorothy Malone) comes onstage, but Larry himself enters the scene and assaults the luckless lover. Myron complains, and Larry allows him play the husband in a second enactment. This time, however, it is Larry the surprised lover who turns on Myron the husband. Larry then lets Myron select whatever role he wishes to play in a third version of the scenario. He chooses the part of the wife, hitherto the safest option. This time around Larry the husband and Rosie the lover decide that the wife is the cause of all trouble between them, and they set upon Myron in unison. In the end "husband" and "lover" walk away arm-in-arm, leaving Myron prone on the floor.

This nightclub routine taps into a vein of violence and exploitation that is latent in many of the characters played by Martin: Larry launches a devastatingly extended punishment on Myron for daring to get in his face. But the scene is also fascinating for the way it specifies what is at stake in the mesh of conflicts between the men. Myron is the only player to occupy *all* three possible roles within the scenario; in each instance he is the butt of the gag, the outsider punished repeatedly by the other performers for a sexual transgression from which he is not allowed to derive pleasure. When the rules and the roles keep shifting, Myron fails to secure a position of control or stability. The woman and the Lewisian misfit both occupy transsexual positions, but the sexuality and identity of the handsome man remain fixed, unquestioned. Rosie only shifts roles once, however, whereas Myron does so continually. The nightclub routine crystallizes how the grotesquerie of the Lewis figure derives not so much from a simple inversion of Martin's idealized handsome man as from a more chaotic process and mobility.

The public hostility of the show is followed by a crucial backstage scene, where it is made clear for the first time that Myron and Larry are longtime friends. In a private moment of reconsolidation Larry seeks to raise the spirits of the younger man. Speaking softly to Myron, he clasps him with tender affection and then sings of his devotion ("What Have You Done for Me Lately"). In the films Dean Martin carries the burden of the "straight" romantic plot, and as a necessary bulwark against homosexuality he is assertively — even aggressively — heterosexual. But as the juxtaposition of these scenes suggests, it is the relationship between the men that provides the central emotional focus. Martin's singing is associated with romantic expression; his voice is a tool that enables him to attract women, not simply by making plain his own desire but also by expressing a sensitivity that is not apparent from his character's brash demeanor. When he sings to Lewis's Myron in the backstage scene in *Scared Stiff,* the erotic connotations of his voice are displaced by the sentimental rhetoric of partnership — but they do not simply disappear.

THE STOOGE

In several other films Martin's romantic vocalizing is similarly redirected from its conventional female addressee to Lewis. I will consider below an instance from *Living It Up,* but first it is worth citing an especially resonant example from *The Stooge,* the only film in which the Martin figure is married.[11] The entry of the Lewis figure into the story triangulates the heterosexual relationship; or, more accurately, from the start the marriage of Mary Turner (Polly Bergen) and Bill Miller constitutes a local narrative triangulation of the anticipated Martin and Lewis showcase. Ted Rogers volunteers himself as mediator in the troubled relationship between Mary and the insensitive crooner, transforming a brusque telegram written by Bill into an impressively devotional billet doux and writing lyrics with which the laconic crooner can serenade his wife ("A Girl Named Mary and a Boy Named Bill"). Through Ted's intervention Bill and Mary are able to secure their marriage, but his service to the couple also legitimates his own emotional and physical proximity to the handsome man. A further alibi for the male love story is provided by Lewis's eccentric heterosexual love interest, Frecklehead (Marion Marshall), an infantilized woman whose like can also be found in *Sailor Beware* and *Jumping Jacks.*

At the beginning of their show-biz career, Bill and Ted take an overnight train journey to an engagement, providing an opportunity for one of the many bed scenes that litter the Martin and Lewis films (a major instance from *Pardners* is discussed later). It is Ted's first night away from New York, and from his over-doting mother (whose lap he crawls into a couple of scenes earlier). In their private sleeping compartment Miller beds down in the lower bunk while Ted battles with the compact technology of the ensuite washroom. When Ted comes back into the room, the gauche kid crawls across Bill to snuggle up against him in the bunk. Bill sternly commands him to go to the other bed, but Ted is unable to sleep because of homesickness. He tells Bill that his mother always sings him to sleep—and to shut him up Bill obliges. He picks up a photograph of Mary and croons to it the ballad "With My Eyes Wide Open I'm Dreaming."

As soon as Martin starts to sing the film cuts from a long shot of the men in their separate bunks to a series of softly spotlit views of Martin. These close shots emphasize Bill's sturdy gaze at Mary's portrait. But although the voice of romantic desire speaks to a (distanced) heterosexual object, it is nonetheless a private performance requested by the other man. Mary provides the means by which Ted can communicate his adoration for Bill, facilitating the simultaneous expression and containment of an erotically tinged male bonding. Martin sings "Can it be true / I'm holding you / Close to my heart," and with the final plosive *t* he casts his eyes upward. As if in answer to the handsome man's look, the film cuts immediately to a close view of Lewis in the upper bunk — insinuating momentarily that he is the "you" the other man dreams of embracing. However, almost immediately the shot is made to have another purpose — it becomes the first of two cutaways from Martin that detail the comic disruption of Ted's serenity by the noisy juddering of the train. Even so, when the film moves back to Lewis in his bunk for a third time, it once more teasingly implies that he could be the object of the song. Martin concludes his performance with the lines

> With my eyes wide open, I'm dreaming,
> Do I deserve such a break?
> Pinch me to prove I'm awake,
> I can't believe that you're really mine

The final word inspires the camera to pan up swiftly, fixing on Lewis. Asleep at last, smiling beatifically, it looks like Ted has received the message.

LIVING IT UP

The team's eleventh film features an intriguing negotiation of the threats posed to the male partnership by competing heterosexual attachments. *Living It Up* is a lavish remake of the 1937 satiric screwball romance *Nothing Sacred,* in which Carole Lombard plays Hazel, a small-town girl mistakenly assumed to have contracted a fatal dose of radiation poisoning.[12] To realize her dream of visiting New York Hazel exploits the diagnostic error at the expense of a big-city newspaper, which hopes to wring every drop of public sympathy from her predicament. *Living It Up* retains the basic components of this subterfuge plot — in which a hick outscams the professional scammers — but it substantially reworks the intertwined romantic story line. *Nothing Sacred* centers on an abrasive love affair between Hazel and Wally Cook (Frederic March), the reporter who chaperones her during her newsworthy "final days." In *Living It Up* Lewis is cast as the central figure, *Homer* Flagg,[13] while a *female* Wally Cook (Janet Leigh) carries the amorous narrative with Homer's incompetent doctor and coconspirator Steve Harris (Dean Martin).

However, the film also weaves a web of emotional entanglements between Homer and the other two major players. Steve finds himself facing competition for Wally's affections when Homer's "illness" draws out her maternalistic sympathies. Frustrated by the woman's refusal to submit to his persistent advances, Steve asks Homer to plead his case for him. Instead, Homer blurts out his own love for her, and Wally is so moved by the plight of the imaginary invalid that she proposes marriage. The woman's wish to give Homer a glorious send-off is potentially an intriguing scenario—mobilizing desires that are simultaneously selfless and self-fulfilling—but the film is concerned exclusively with Homer's stake in the mesh of desire. Although he adores the mothering attention she lavishes upon him, it is evident that Homer has a crush on Wally because she is the woman his buddy wants (and to underline the invalidity of Homer's heterosexual desire, the film has him collapse in a faint when they kiss).

Homer's emotional quandary is dramatized in an especially resonant scene. As he prepares for the wedding, in the bedroom of the suite he shares with the handsome man, Homer looks down at mounted photographs of Wally and Steve that sit side by side on the dressing table. Covering the eyes of Steve's picture, Homer picks up Wally's photograph and sings to it, dances round the room with it and kisses it. The song—"How Do You Speak to an Angel?"—makes clear the idealization that characterizes Homer's feelings for Wally. However, it is also the song that Steve serenaded her with earlier.[14] On the one hand Homer's love scene with the photograph accentuates the Lewis figure's predilection for fantasy and his difficulty in addressing female sexuality; on the other hand the film specifically contextualizes the scene in terms of his relationship with the handsome man: his access to women takes the form of a fantasy inspired by his buddy's desire. When Steve first appears in the film Homer catches him singing to a photograph of movie star Audrey Hepburn. Steve merely waits for a flesh-and-blood female, but Homer invests the distanced and unattainable image of the woman, desired by another, with serious romantic purpose.

Steve arrives in the bedroom as Homer finishes serenading Wally's picture. A hostile exchange erupts between them, concluding with Steve's decision to move out. As he leaves, though, he meets Wally, dressed in her bridal grown. They go into the apartment looking for Homer, just as he has crawled under the bed in search of a dropped cufflink. In the bedroom Steve clasps Wally and they kiss. The camera, at floor level, registers Homer's agonized expression as he sees Wally's heels lift from the floor in sexual excitement. But just as the film introduces this melodramatic scenario of thwarted desire—with Homer in danger of losing both the woman and the handsome man—it rapidly shifts gear. Plagued by the memory of this "primal-scene" kiss, Homer is unable to proceed with the wedding: he rushes from the altar, declaring that his illness is nothing more than a sinus condition. To offset suspicion Steve snaps into action by persuading Homer to feign insanity. The "invalid" climbs onto a chandelier and does an impersonation of a crazed bomber pilot, pitching light bulbs at the concerned wedding guests. This typical moment of heavy Lewisian performance siphons off the dramatic tensions generated by the preceding scenario of triangulated desires. The film never returns to these tortuous emotional intrigues. Frustration is transformed into the externally directed energy of broad comedy as Homer successfully reinstates himself as the center of attention.

JUMPING JACKS

The ending of *Jumping Jacks* (1952) provides a good illustration of the way the Martin and Lewis movies juggle the competing demands of presentation and representation with the opposing attractions of heterosexuality and the homosocial. Like *That's My Boy, Living it Up,* and *The Stooge, Jumping Jacks* delays the onscreen teaming of the partners. Cast adrift from his normal context, Lewis plays stooge to a woman in an onstage performance routine that serves up a comically aggressive articulation of female desire. Declaring in song that she "can't resist a man in a uniform," Betsy Carver (Mona Freeman) throws Hap Smith (Lewis) round the stage and tears the sleeves from his army tunic. As she mocks his unmanly figure, while embracing other, more likely soldiers behind his back, it is clear that the hapless Hap is not the ideal male the song calls for. The narrative's principal concern is to maneuver Lewis away from this aberrant heterosexual act, back to the sheltering arms of his regular buddy. The team is reconsolidated when Hap's erstwhile partner, paratrooper Chick Allen (Martin), tricks him into a one-shot performance for his army revue.

The revue climaxes with a spectacularly overstated testosterone anthem, "Do the Parachute Jump," which counters the opening number's display of female assertion and male subjugation. Backed by a chorus line of burly uniformed men, Chick takes the lead with suave confidence while Hap comically punctuates the set piece masculine display. In a Harpo Marx-style routine he transforms the strings of a parachute into a musical instrument and then dances around the stage with a mop (woman reduced to a prop). Unlike the "Boy in a Uniform" number, Hap has a more central, active, and independent role, integrating him within the male regimentation of the army but allowing him to occupy a place of privilege as the troop's "special baby." After the show various circumstances, but largely the manipulations of Chick, prevent Hap from returning to Betsy. Trapped in a false identity as a soldier (Private "Dogface" Dolan), Hap moves from the female-centered regime of civilian life to the homosocial world of the armed forces.[15] The film generates comedy from Hap's collision with the regimented procedures of military training, as he cannot or will not play by the rules. Among the men, Hap's special skills as an entertainer enable him to maintain a measure of difference from the more traditional model of adult masculinity signified by Chick: he is not subjected to the same expectation of being-a-man, and being-a-man-among-men.[16]

Jumping Jacks also incorporates a subplot of triangulated desires in which Chick and Betsy fall for one another. As in *Living It Up,* the Lewis figure is caught up in a potentially melodramatic scenario: as well as being alienated from both civilian and army life, he also faces exclusion from his two partners. The Chick-Betsy relationship is clinched at the Servicemen's Club in New York City: Chick ties Hap to a large dog, which leaves him free to dance with — more important, to sing to — the pliant Betsy. Serenading her with "I Know a Dream When I See One," Chick installs himself as the metteur-en-scène of desire. The taming of Betsy is followed by the film's sole, and unusually brief, Martin-Lewis duet. Chick begins an Al Jolson-style rendition of "Keep a Little Dream Handy," with Hap accompanying and interrupting him in equal measure. This characteristic performance reinscribes the familiar terms of the Martin-Lewis male partnership, just as it is threatened narratively by the heterosexual romance. After the duet Hap looks on disconsolately as Chick kisses Betsy, but the film conjures up a girlfriend for Hap, an adoring young fan called Julie (Jody Gilbert). Once they have been established, however, these two sets of heterosexual relationships are exhausted: Julie and Betsy disappear from the film. Evoking Bob Hope's *Caught in the Draft* (1941) and Danny Kaye's *Up in Arms* (1944), the film concludes with a war-games exercise that pits the paratroopers against the army's tank division.[17] Through sheer ineptitude Hap manages to both rescue his pals and capture the enemy commander. When General Timmons (Ray Teal) offers him the choice of enlisting for real or rejoining civilian life — to face imprisonment — Hap allows himself to be legitimized as a corporal.

The Lewis figure's success in combat represents a deformation of the rules of acceptable masculine achievement decreed by the army, a carnivalesque scenario that is perfectly conventional in Hollywood comedian comedy. The sequence at the Servicemen's Club raises the promise of a resolution through heterosexual union, which, no matter how casually it is motivated, tends formally to signify social integration through marriage and the possible termination of the comedian figure's difference. Like the football match in *That's My Boy,* the war-games sequence is a trial by fire that permits the Lewis figure to gain recognition by the father figure, the general, and to consolidate his identity as a man. But the film moves beyond these two integrative scenarios, offering an emblematic coda that dislocates their principles of narrative resolution and triumphantly promotes the film as a Martin and Lewis showcase. On a training exercise, Corporal Smith falls out of the aircraft without a parachute. He manages to land on top of Chick's parachute and crawls down its side, to grasp hold of his buddy's body. This is the payoff: Martin and Lewis unified as star team and male couple, their physical embrace displacing the preceding Oedipal scenarios of narrative integration. The multiplication of resolving scenarios that wraps up *Jumping Jacks* works as a structural joke leveled against the procedural decorum of narrative resolution, but it also enables this spectacle of physical intimacy between the men. The clinch may be motivated by comic incompetence, but it nonetheless substitutes for the conventional sexual embrace that wraps up many films.

A closing gag both shifts away from this display of bodily unification and makes it permissible. When the parachute touches down Hap and Chick land on a motorcycle and sidecar. "After what we've been through, nothing can separate us," Hap says, and the men ride off together. However, a fork in the road pulls them apart: Hap and the motorcycle take one path, Chick and the sidecar the other. For Martin and Lewis to function successfully as a team across a range of films, the tension between them—and the homoerotic circuitry that underlies it—must be maintained, not resolved in any permanent fashion (as either total union or separation). When Hap Smith loses Chick Allen at the end of the film, it is an act that restores the very instability and lack of balance that is fundamental to the teaming of Martin and Lewis. The two men are separated so that they can be reunited once more as a team, working through its internal conflicts, in their next film—where the process will begin anew.

PARDNERS?

In *Pardners,* their penultimate release, Martin and Lewis play, respectively, Slim Mosely and Wade Kingsley, the sons of two legendary Wild West buddies shot dead twenty-five years earlier. Where Slim is raised in the muscular world of the West, Wade grows up in New York under the dominance of his powerful mother, Matilda (Agnes Moorehead), head of an industrial empire. Weakened by her influence, and by the trappings of luxury, Wade Jr. is a henpecked wimp who daydreams of the rough, tough, adventurous West of his dead father. This lost world is embodied in Martin's burly ranch hand, who travels East for a rodeo contest in order to win a prize bull. Wade purchases the bull and gives it to Slim. When Matilda arranges a socially correct marriage for her weakling son, Wade flees to join Slim on his journey back West. The gift of the bull puts the handsome man under obligation to the rich kid, and he reluctantly agrees to take Wade under his wing. Wade strives continually to gain the cowboy's acceptance, and their friendship is consolidated in a ten-minute sequence that is structured around the film's theme song.

As they pitch camp Slim tries to educate Wade in such macho rituals of the West as building a fire, gunplay, roping skills, and horse riding. Undeterred by the persistent failures of his enthusiastic yet incompetent admirer, the handsome man sings the praises of "pardnership." When Slim eventually gives up and suggests they turn in for the night, a dejected Wade refuses to join him. As the rich kid slopes away, Slim tugs at the rope he carries in his hand: a sign of attention that inspires Wade to twist round, his face lit with a pleading, expectant smile. Slim then throws his arms open wide and sings the refrain, "You and me will be the greatest pardners, buddies and pals." Incapacitated with joy, Wade staggers over and sings the refrain back. As Slim makes room between the blankets, the two men are joined in song. Slim then offers a hand in friendship and they embrace—Wade clasps the hand eagerly, Slim puts his other hand on the kid's shoulder. In this moment of rapture they look into each other's faces and finish the song in harmony. Having reached this pinnacle of togetherness, Slim says they should get some sleep. Wade ecstatically pats the top blanket around the handsome man before he eventually slips beneath the cover himself. The teasingly overplayed scene fades out on a minor gag: as Wade turns over into sleep, he robs Slim of the blanket he has spent so much care arranging.

As in the train-compartment scene in *The Stooge,* the homoerotic spectacle of the two men bedding down together is made acceptable through the Lewis figure's naïveté about adult sexuality, especially the homosexual connotations his overeager responses may provoke. Lewis's playing of Wade bears his characteristically hyperinflated mannerisms—jack-knife legs, facial distortions, interruptive and interrupted responses to stimuli—that render the ascription of directed desire a questionable proposition. The scene's narrative function provides a further legitimation for this presentation of male intimacy: getting close to Slim is the means by Wade can liberate himself from the disabling influence of the oppressive mother, a common scapegoat for various forms of masculine dysfunction in the postwar decade. In 1953 Robert Kass offered an explanation for Lewis's appeal that was couched in the tenets of contemporary "Momism":[18]

Much of Lewis's comedy derives from the sentimentalized concept that, when we are in trouble, Mom can set anything right. . . . Lewis capitalizes on this character of the Jewish lad under feminine domination who has never been taught to grow up. Away from Mom, he screeches and stamps for the attention he gets at home, and cannot command in the world of men. A woman has nurtured this misfit who, away from her emasculating influence, might have learned to become an individual. Lewis's comic character is an exaggeration of what feminist [*sic*] domination can do to the male.

Further, the twisted youths — and girls — who think of Dad only as the stern provider whom Mom uses as a threat over them, love Lewis, because he dares to be uninhibited away from the influence of Mom. Lewis is the spokesman of a generation of mama's boys. (Kass 1953, 122–23)

In Kass's view, Lewis offers a regressive fantasy of revolt against the responsibilities of adulthood: the Lewis figure is a fixated mama's boy who refuses to make the transition to self-determining adult masculinity. Like many other commentators of the period Kass neglects to take Dean Martin into account; his fashionable accusation of sinister, emasculating "feminist" subversion is complicated by Martin's complex, protean relationship with Lewis in these films. The Martin figure may, as Kass suggests, take on the role of restraining "keeper" but the sequence in *Pardners* illustrates that he also serves the Lewis figure in other ways. Slim not only provides Wade with an opportunity to escape his domineering mother but also allows him to *maintain* his lack of "correct" masculine values, his feminized and regressive behavior. The sequence implies that Martin's performance as the "straight," self-consistent handsome man — exemplified by the nightclub act in *Scared Stiff* — may operate as a cover story that allows the safe slippage of roles his characters tend to experience through most of the films. In the campsite sequence, for example, Slim services Wade as an identificatory ideal ("father"), a nurturing and protective force ("mother"), and also as an object of desire ("lover").

QUEER ROMANCE

The erotic intensities displayed at the *Pardners* campsite reverberate throughout Martin and Lewis's enactment of the male partnership, manifested most clearly in those moments such as the parachute scene in *Jumping Jacks* in which the two men are thrown into a bodily embrace.[19] Despite being interwoven with homoeroticism, this multifaceted male union can never reveal itself as a fully patterned homosexuality. The love Lewis expresses for the handsome man can only speak its name if the insulatory disavowals of comic absurdity are guaranteed.[20] But there are numerous instances that resonate with nuances and longings that poke through the fabric of insulation, and many of these involve the Lewis figure's intense, self-abnegating idolatry of Martin. In the central section of *The Caddy* Harvey Miller (Lewis) trains Joe Anthony (Martin) in the golfing skills he is himself too neurotically afflicted to display to the public (as in *That's My*

Boy, the Lewis figure's impairment is down to an overbearing father). Anthony becomes Miller's front man, but as with the Martin figure in *The Stooge,* success goes to his head, leading him to neglect both Harvey and what he teaches him. After winning a tournament Joe Anthony returns to their cabin to find Harvey working at the stove, preparing a celebratory dinner for two. With Harvey dressed in his apron, cooking a meal his mother taught him, the scenario deliberately evokes heterodomestic norms. But Joe forsakes Harvey's selfless, wifely devotion to attend a party at the golf club with socialite Kathy Taylor (Donna Reed). To the accompaniment of a lonely violin theme, the scene closes with Lewis alone at the table, gazing wistfully at the pots steaming away on the stove. Cast in an explicitly feminized melodramatic role, as the loyal lover whose worth is not recognized by the man he adores, Lewis here inhabits the emotional wastelands explored by the women of *Only Yesterday* (1933), *Stella Dallas* (1937) and *Letter from an Unknown Woman* (1948).[21]

Within the framework of the comedian-comedy genre, Martin and Lewis inaugurated a play of disruption and containment that assaulted the conformist options of male identity, sexuality, and responsibility. Because women are aligned with the demands of marital and social integration, however, they must ultimately be eliminated so that the comedian figure can maintain his position of resistance and difference. The endings of Martin and Lewis's films frequently make this plain: women are removed from the screen to provide the men with a "final bow" that asserts their distinctive buddy relationship over all other attachments. *Sailor Beware* finishes with perhaps the most blatant instance, showing the two men retreating from demanding women, back to the all-male haven of their waiting submarine. The finale of *Living It Up* outlines a similar set of priorities: Wally and Steve have married but the film makes their union marginal, restricting it to a throwaway dialogue remark. As Wally departs for work the two men are left free to close the film with a reprisal their earlier set-piece song, "Ev'ry Street's a Boulevard (in Old New York)." Finally, *The Stooge* concludes with an especially telling instance, accomplished in a single shot. After Miller and Rogers are reunited at the Sutherland Revue the film cuts backstage to show Bill and Mary kissing. Bill pulls away from the embrace to look over his shoulder, and the camera pans right to fix on Ted and Frecklehead wrapped in an intense clinch. The camera pulls back to incorporate both couples in the shot, and as Ted pulls away from Frecklehead's lips, she collapses to the floor in a faint. Bill slaps Ted on the back and shakes his hand to congratulate him on his sexual prowess. The camera then dollies forward for a closer shot of Bill and Ted, which excludes Mary (Frecklehead remains out of view, lying on the floor). Ted/Lewis signals his own pleasure to the camera and immediately throws his head onto the shoulder of the handsome man. The scene fades out with Bill clasping Ted to him, his face lit with a broad smile.

The flight from heterosexual and maternal bonds may seem to align Martin and Lewis with the "male rebellion" that Barbara Ehrenreich (1982) identifies as a powerful current within American culture through the postwar decade (14–51). It is not sufficient to note the exclusion of women, however, without considering what they are excluded for and replaced with. As the closing embrace of *The Stooge* intimates, the Martin and Lewis comedies provided a disorderly rewrite of gender scripts. The homocomic play of the team overturned the conventional polarization of sexual difference, replacing it with a range of distinctions existing between men. In the process their movies opened onto conflictual currents within male subjectivity and sexuality. As Mark Simpson (1994) has cautioned, male comedy duos are remarkable not because they permit a codified representation of male "homosexuality" but because they initiate a more intriguing process of "queer romance": "Reading them as 'gay'—either as part of a laudable attempt to raise the visibility of homosexuality or as part of an execrable attempt to protect the nation's youth from unwholesome influences—diminishes the subversive potential of queer comedy romance, offering as it does a queerness everyone can aspire to" (68). Serving an era in which the normalization of gender identities and sexual roles was a particularly pressing obsession (May 1988, 98–113), Martin and Lewis set in motion a complex *queering* of gender, a process of queer romance analogous to the negotiation of differences found in heterosexual amorous comedy.

The key to Martin and Lewis's success was their persistent and multileveled attention to the dynamics of the male love story. The promise of their union, however, coexisted with an awareness that the competition between them, and between their distinctive talents, always threatened to rend the partnership asunder. The homocomic process through which their differences were displayed, negotiated, and transcended drew much of its impact from the high degree of personal feeling that was felt to exist between the two men, always an integral feature of the team's publicity. The show was authenticated as an expression of a genuine dynamic between the two players. As *Sight and Sound* critic Daniel Farson put it in 1952, "One has the feeling that their success as a comedy team mirrors the success of an important personal relationship" (Farson 1952, 31). Years of reported schisms and hostilities gradually eroded the sense that the relationship was based on authentic feeling, and the disintegration of their partnership lent new resonance to the play of unity and division, togetherness and separation they enacted. The dynamic state of tension that had fueled their success gave rise to another, more potentially melodramatic scenario. Bosley Crowther's review of their 1953 film *The Caddy* suggested that "Mr. Martin, for his pretty singing and his romancing, rates the usual nod. But Mr. Lewis is slowly taking over. Just give him a couple more years" (Crowther 1953, 16). This was to prove true. When the end came in 1956, with Martin's inevitable revolt, the masquerade was over.

ONE MAN ALONE

A STAR IS REBORN

**The two worst things that happened to Jerry were taking a good picture
with a Brownie and reading a book about Chaplin.**

—Dean Martin, 1957

In his partnership with Dean Martin, Lewis not only took charge of
the creative responsibilities but also drew the lion's share of public
attention. Growing increasingly disenchanted with the supporting
role he played to the careering monkey, Martin's restlessness came to a head during the production of *Three Ring Circus* in early 1954.[1] As Lewis puts it, "During the filming Dean kept blowing his top at me and everyone else, saying he
was fed up to the ears playing a stooge. It got pretty hairy. There were days
when I thought Dean would ditch the whole package. . . . It developed into
psychological warfare for the balance of the picture" (Lewis and Gluck 1982,
185–86).

The two men resolved their differences on this occasion, but there were further wrangles over the next two years. On the set of *You're Never Too Young* in
1955, for example, Martin snapped at Norman Taurog, "Why the hell should I
come in on time? There's not a damn' thing for me to do" (Gehman 1964, 146).

The cooling of Martin's personal and professional regard for his partner is often blamed on Lewis's desire to monopolize the corporate identity, but the crooner's discontent was also fueled by the independent success he was enjoying as a recording artist. His numerous releases on Capitol Records since 1948 had yielded some moderate hits, but Martin struck gold with his 1953 waxing "That's Amore," a massive popular hit in both the United States and Britain (Tosches 1992, 233).

As their relationship disintegrated, the instability endemic to the team acquired a new significance, a new sense of danger. Repeated schisms and excited rumormongering made it difficult for audiences to perceive them as the freewheeling, fun-loving guys of old. In June 1955 Martin withdrew from a special premiere of *You're Never Too Young* that Lewis had arranged in his old stomping ground, the Catskills. Forced to go it alone at short notice, the comedian broke down in tears onstage and spoke emotively of his disappointment (Marx 1975, 192; Levy 1996a, 195–96).[2] The two men did not communicate with one another for four months afterward, choosing instead to articulate their grievances through public channels. In August 1955 Martin told a reporter, "To me, this isn't a love affair. This is big business. I think it's ridiculous for the boy to brush aside such beautiful contracts" (Tosches 1992, 280). Financial incentives encouraged them to continue working together, but offstage the two men avoided one another as much as possible (JAS Productions 1992c). Despite attempts to present a unified front, the in-fighting was directly acknowledged during a *Comedy Hour* program in September 1955. In a sketch satirizing the manipulative tactics of the popular television show *The $64,000 Question* (CBS, 1955–58) quizmaster Dean Martin forces contestant Jerry Lewis to answer questions while submerged in a tank of water.[3] As Martin pushes Lewis's head down for the jackpot question, a familiar moment of comic aggression and humiliation is charged with uncharacteristic resonance. Coming up for air, Lewis shrieks, "Haven't you heard—the feud is over," an ad lib that draws an impressive howl of laughter from the studio audience.[4]

In May 1956 on the set of their last film together, *Hollywood or Bust,* Martin gave a savage twist to his earlier denigration of the bonds that held them together. "You can talk about love all you want," he told Lewis. "To me, you're nothing but a dollar sign" (Lewis and Gluck 1984, 203).[5] Within a few weeks the partners had finally agreed to go their separate ways, after seeing out whatever contractual obligations they could not escape. In June 1956 Martin and Lewis appeared on NBC's news magazine *Today* in an item, broadcast from the 500 Club in Atlantic City, celebrating their tenth anniversary as a team. The *Variety* reviewer was dismayed by the personal animosity on show:

There have been teams on the books that would fly into a rage at the sight of each other, and yet, some were quite successful. Take Gilbert and Sullivan, Abbott and Costello, the Dorsey Bros. and a few others who harbored personal animus — yet they could all work together.

However, the bulk of these teams was based on the fact that the combos were formed primarily on the basis of respect for each other's talent. Starting from that basis, they can survive personal splits. In the case of Martin and Lewis it seems to have been born on the basis of personal regard. In their early years, they laughed at and with each other, each gave the other a lift that communicated itself to the audience. Now that the personal warmth is gone the base of the team is gone, as reflected in their *Today* contribs. They are now two talented performers and nothing else. It seemed a pity to sport their coolness for each other on a network show. ("M&L: Miffed & Lousy," *Variety*, 27 June 1956)

Their final television performance came a few days later, when they hosted a twenty-four-hour telethon for the Muscular Dystrophy Association. *Variety* commented that despite an effort to conceal their feuding it was obvious that "the bond that makes them a big team is uncertain and tenuous. There were moments of fusion, and there were times when they spoke around and over each other" ("*Martin & Lewis Telethon,*" 4 July 1956).

The acrimonious fall-out, which began before the partnership was officially terminated, would continue to haunt them through subsequent years as each man struggled to escape the shadow of their shared past.[6] Martin's solo career had a faltering start with the misfire of his first solo film, *Ten Thousand Bedrooms* (1957). However, he eventually proved his mettle both as an entertainer and as a dramatic actor, with heavyweight character parts in films like *The Young Lions* (1958), *Rio Bravo* (1959), and *Career* (1959). Only after he had parted from Lewis was Martin able to realize his potential as an iconic handsome man. Such Hollywood sex comedies as *Who Was That Lady?* (1960), *All in a Night's Work* (1961), and *Who's Been Sleeping in My Bed?* exploited Martin's suave allure, and his Rat Pack frolics with new buddy Frank Sinatra ensured him a niche in the headlines.[7] NBC's highly popular *Dean Martin Show* ran for nine seasons, from 1965 to 1973, and he simultaneously meandered through a series of throwaway cinematic adventures as Donald Hamilton's playboy spy Matt Helm.[8] Through the 1960s Martin limited himself progressively to an extremely lucrative persona as a casually inebriated swinger. But even though his solo work relied increasingly upon a self-parody of his image as the handsome man, at least it was the organ grinder rather than the monkey who now ran the show.

ONE-MAN CAVALCADE OF SHOW BUSINESS

A mere two weeks after ending his partnership with Dean Martin, Lewis made his debut outing as a solo artist.[9] When a bout of laryngitis prevented Judy Garland from performing at the Frontier Casino in Las Vegas, she asked Lewis to take her place. His hour-long set was received with great enthusiasm, especially the finale — a version of the old Al Jolson song "Rock-a-Bye Your Baby (With a Dixie Melody)" (Lewis and Gluck 1982, 208-9). This was a propitious moment for Lewis, as Shawn Levy (1996a) speculates: "It was as if his whole life, the decade with Dean included, had been leading him to that stage, that crowd, that song" (213). Al Jolson was the greatest Jewish stage entertainer of the century and the professional idol of Danny Lewis; like Charles Chaplin, he proved an influential template for Lewis's inspirations and aspirations through the late 1950s. Within weeks of the Garland gig Lewis recorded the Jolson song and several other numbers at his own expense and sold the material to Decca Records. In November 1956 Decca released the album *Jerry Lewis Just Sings,* with "Rock-a-Bye Your Baby" as the single. Both discs charted: the single reached the top ten and stayed in the top forty for fifteen weeks, amassing sales of almost one and a half million. The LP peaked at number three on the album charts and sold strongly for a further five months, outperforming all of Dean Martin's previous releases (ibid., 216).

Together with Dean Martin, Lewis had signed to Capitol Records in August 1948. As well the occasional sides he cut with Martin, Lewis also recorded thirty-two solo numbers between 1949 and 1954 — none of them successful.[10] Most of Lewis's Capitol sides — for example, "Are You for Real" (1949), "I've Had a Very Merry Christmas" (1952), and "The Book Was So Much Better than the Picture" (1952) — are comic novelties in which he adopts the voice of a whiny, adenoidal adolescent.[11] On "Rock-a-Bye Your Baby," however, he essays a more mature vocal delivery that offers a very close approximation of Jolson's dramatic emotional technique. Accompanied by a stabbing, brass-driven arrangement, he delivers a performance of showful ebullience that is strikingly similar to the high-kicking Las Vegas tricks of Frank Sinatra's 1970s anthem "New York, New York." After his success with "Rock-a-Bye Your Baby" Lewis continued to draw upon his earlier record act in live performances and television shows, but his publicly legitimized validity as a singer added a new dimension to his solo work. He could now use his own voice instead of relying on Dean Martin or phonographic support. Although Lewis's Jolsenesque voice differed considerably from Martin's self-possessed and technically proficient instrument of seduction, his success as a straight singer did more than add to his existing accomplishments—it also signaled his bid to annex the territory formerly occupied by the handsome man.

Rather than finding another straight man to play against, Lewis sought to erase the absence left by his significant other through a compulsive process of self-proliferation. As one *Variety* TV reviewer put it, it seemed that Lewis's dream was to become "a one-man cavalcade of show biz—one who has inherited the mantle of Al Jolson, Danny Kaye, Charlie Chaplin and some of the greats who have preceded him" ("*The Jerry Lewis Show,*" 13 November 1957). It was a dream he worked furiously to realize, by energetically reconstructing himself as a multifaceted solo entertainer. In the final months of 1956, for example, Lewis not only made his first self-produced solo film, *The Delicate Delinquent,* but he also performed on numerous charity benefits and made several guest appearances on such popular TV programs as *What's My Line* and *The Steve Allen Show.*[12] In November Lewis began a three-week engagement in Las Vegas, headlining a lavish revue at the Sands Hotel. *Variety* warned that the new Lewis unveiled at the Sands was by no means the much-loved Jerry of old: "Those who see him here will be seeing a much different Lewis, now more the suave comedian than the goof; a straight singer rather than the off-key, screeching zany; a more often dignified entertainer rather than the most often mugging, eccentric bouncing clown. It takes some doing to get used to the new Lewis, just as obviously it will take some doing on Lewis' part before he himself becomes accustomed to his 'new' stage personality and finds the best in it" ("Jerry Lewis," 5 December 1956, 73).

Lewis continued his tireless pursuit of self-legitimation. In January 1957 he launched the first of his NBC television specials as well as playing residencies at the Chicago's Chez Paree nightclub and the Fontainebleau Hotel in Miami Beach. These engagements laid the groundwork for an enormously successful four-week showcase at the most prestigious vaudeville house in North America, New York's Palace Theater. Lewis's set, which included tap dancing, songs, gags, mime comedy, his familiar Japanese routine, and impressions of Elvis Presley and Al Jolson (Green 1957, 14), received appreciative notices from critics who had been expecting an embarrassing shambles (Levy 1996a, 222). In a lengthy review, *Variety* editor Abel Green (1957) wrote approvingly of Lewis's debut show: "That Lewis had first-night jitters is incidental because, despite the somewhat uphill struggle, the sum total can't be denied that he has nothing but talent and is as potent a comic as there is to be found in front of a mike—electronic, saloon or podium. . . . From the kickoff the young comic is a poised and polished performer. . . . Some 90 minutes of Lewis as a one-man talent of great versatility does make this Palace excursion worthwhile." Green's enthusiasm, however, was not unqualified. He suggested that Lewis was trying a little too hard to prove himself a major-league show-business presence: "Barely 30, he may still be a year ahead of himself as a Palace or Palladium single entertainer. This is a special type of prowess. It's one thing for a Sinatra or other pash balladeers of the moment, but it's another thing in the single comedian sweepstakes to assert his grip on an audience" (14).

The more apparent Lewis's drive for success, the more he was to alienate critics, reviewers, and other cultural observers. The new Lewis who rose with such untimely haste from the ashes of the beloved entertainment team met with a remarkably hostile reception. Attacks on his aspirations and abilities were to become commonplace in the U.S. press long before the French staked their claim to his genius. A comment made by an anonymous "friend" to *TV Guide* in 1957 neatly condenses the suspicion provoked by Lewis's new agenda: "Whether he knows it or not—and I think he knows it—Jerry had dedicated himself to become the great institutional American entertainer. The pattern is there—heading up charity drives, doing benefits at the drop of a hat and, consciously or unconsciously, pouring his heart into the old Al Jolson songs. It's pure and simple ego drive" (Levy 1996a, 220). The opposition grew more vocal as Lewis began to colonize territories of expression barred to the simple funnyman of old. By the end of the decade he was not just one of the best loved of American entertainers, he was also just about the most reviled. Nowhere is this better illustrated than in the trade coverage of the fifteen one-hour television specials he made for NBC from 1957 to 1960.[13]

BÊTE NOIRE

The Palace Theater gigs may have demonstrated Lewis's authority as a live solo performer, just as the triumphant box office of *The Delicate Delinquent* secured his viability as a movie comic. On television, however, he was not permitted to exorcise the ghost of Dean Martin so easily. Compared to their enthusiasm for the Martin and Lewis programs, the trade reviewers savaged Lewis's television specials, which nonetheless continued to draw high ratings. Whether he tried out new ideas or recycled material from his past, Lewis could do nothing right in the eyes of the professional scrutineers of the small screen. They protest repeatedly that there is *too much* Lewis in these shows: he hogs the limelight, he tries excessively hard, he is too concerned with winning approval.[14] For example, in June 1957 *Daily Variety* complained that "there was a maximum of

Jerry Lewis but, unfortunately, a minimum of laughs. . . . There were overlong, lackluster routines and on the whole it was not an auspicious outing for the comic" ("*The Jerry Lewis Show*," 10 June 1957). In January 1957 *Variety* acknowledged that Lewis was "probably one of the most ambitious performers extant" but suggested that his aspirations exceeded his abilities: "Since he went into business for himself, he seemingly thinks he has to prove a lot of things, mainly his virtuosity. There seems to be a prevailing belief that he's trying to become the world's youngest elder statesman in the realm of entertainment. . . . Lewis needs to sharpen his sights. Perhaps his attempts at versatility and the unwarranted plugs that creep into his script at every opportunity should be eliminated. Lewis can be funny, and that's why he continues to get king-sized ratings. The superfluities in his show bring him down several pegs" ("*The Jerry Lewis Show*," 1 January 1958).

The trade reviewers consistently attacked Lewis for his disorderly excesses. *Daily Variety* described his performance on one 1960 special as "an undisciplined binge of crossed-eyes, crooked-teeth, puckered lips and tasteless asides such as 'I'm nauseous already,' hardly a rewarding observation for a star of Jerry Lewis' caliber to be making to millions of tviewers [*sic*]" ("*The Jerry Lewis Show*," 18 April 1960). A few weeks later the same journal blasted Lewis for his disorganization and tastelessness: "It seemed almost incredible that one man could make such a shambles of an hour spec. But Jerry Lewis did it Friday night with all the diabolic devices of a wrecking crew . . . Rhymeless, reasonless and too forced to be funny. . . . Lewis's bad taste reared its ugly innuendo in many places" ("*The Jerry Lewis Show*," 23 May 1960). One of his guest appearances on *The Eddie Fisher Show* in 1958 spurred particularly hostile criticism, with *Variety* chastising Lewis for his unbounded self-promotion: "At the finish it became a shambles when Jerry Lewis broke up Fisher and everybody else by his physical contortions that even had him rolling on the floor. Fisher tried to salvage something out of the close-off but Lewis was not to be denied the red-lighted camera. . . . Professional courtesy to the star of the show went out the window. The audience screamed at Lewis's break-up antics to the total disregard of Fisher, who seemed annoyed at such unsporting intrusion" ("*The Eddie Fisher Show*," 22 October 1958).

Despite scoring a huge triumph with the audience, Lewis must nonetheless be censured for "professional misconduct," even though, from this account, his interruptive antics seem remarkably similar to his acclaimed invasion of the Hope and Crosby telethon six years earlier.[15] Clearly, it is not *what* Lewis is doing that strikes alarm so much as the new significance his performance attains when he is no longer shielded by the presence of a straight man. Thus there are persistent calls for Lewis to devolve more responsibility to his costars. "There's a need for Lewis to take it easier in his telesessions," *Variety* argued in June 1957. "He doesn't have to be on camera nearly all the time, and there are some capable performers around, who, if used properly, could serve a valuable function in framing Lewis's efforts to better advantage" ("*The Jerry Lewis Show*," 12 June 1957). A few months later, *Daily Variety* commented that "on his initial outing of the season, Jerry Lewis displayed boundless energy, but much of it was misdirected. Lewis worked hard—too hard, perhaps. . . . As he goes into his second season, it becomes increasingly evident that Lewis needs as a foil someone off whom he can bounce his zany type of humor. Standing up there alone, he seems to depend chiefly on mugging to cue the laughs" ("*The Jerry Lewis Show*," 7 November 1957).

The television specials are also condemned for displaying *too many* Lewises: the infantile comic grotesque, the pathetic Kid, the earnest singer, the flagrant sentimentalist. The trade reviewers find an alarming lack of cohesion in his work: "Lewis's humor lacks consistency. At times he tries for the pathos of a Chaplin; other times he's as broad as Wilshire Blvd. But at no time is there an intelligent cohesion between all this" ("*The Jerry Lewis Show*," *Daily Variety*, 19 May 1958). Another critic asserts, "Jerry Lewis was a study in disorganization. . . . It was a mixed up affair that had no strand of continuity or meaning and all his efforts displayed more sweat than satisfaction" ("*The Jerry Lewis Timex Show*," *Variety*, 20 January 1960). With the proliferation of personae spinning out from the ambitious entertainer, the center that holds them together seems progressively displaced. Lewis remains curiously elusive despite his persistent overpresence, offering himself only through a bewildering succession of masks and guises. In a critique of one of his 1957 specials *Daily Variety* charged that "Lewis emerged as a composite of a number of top bananas rather than a personality in his own right" ("*The Jerry Lewis Show*," 10 June 1957). A 1960 review takes up the same theme: "Apparently, he feels the mantle of Jolson, the hand of Chaplin, and a seriousness in his make-up that makes him forget he is capable of a style of his own. Lewis seems to want to impress with his wide range of talent as well as his comedy creation" ("*The Jerry Lewis Show*," *Variety*, 20 April 1960).

There is too much Lewis. There are too many Lewises. There is not enough of the "real" Jerry Lewis. His distasteful otherness is exemplified most clearly by his persistent and outrageous mugging: "Lewis, when displaying his talent for neat spills and agile body movements, was fine. But, unfortunately, he restricted his displays of mobility mostly to the facial variety—the idiotically puerile eye and mouth postures that have become his trademark — and, more recently, his enigma" ("*The Jerry Lewis Show,*" *Daily Variety,* 18 April 1960). Through his facial contortions Lewis channeled into the world an ever-shifting parade of identities and unseemly gestures. The overtelegraphed reactions, the spasms and seizures of bodily hysteria seemed like messages from some realm of repressed psychic and social forces. Without the reassuring stability promised by Dean Martin, the "superfluities" present in Lewis's work from the start of his career seemed more exposed, more perplexing, more ugly. Without Martin to rein him in Lewis became a conundrum, a series of propositions that refused to add up to a comprehensible and acceptable whole. The discomfort was intensified by the way the gross physical comedy coexisted with Lewis's ambition to enthrone himself as an American show-biz institution, a classic all-around entertainer.

For the critical voices of both the trade journals and the quality press, Lewis's extreme comedy bodied forth the excesses and degradations of the popular body. Writing about the Martin and Lewis film *Jumping Jacks* in the *New York Times,* for example, Bosley Crowther was disturbed not just by the comedian's performance but also by the hysterical manner in which the audience responded to it:

The spectacle of the gawky Mr. Lewis jerking fearsomely in the shrouds of a dangling parachute-trainer as a tyro at a paratrooper camp may be mildly and tolerably amusing, by the standards of cinema farce, but it scarcely seems cause for anybody to laugh so hard that they split a vein. . . . However, the whooping and hollering of the audience at the Paramount yesterday was such as to make these demonstrations seem the crowning achievement of comic art. These and other exercises of Mr. Lewis in the film . . . were greeted with such enthusiasm that one can only inquire what has happened to the standards of humor, even those of Jerry Lewis fans. (Crowther 1952, 30)

The demonization of Jerry Lewis intensified with his phenomenal pervasiveness and with the seemingly unstoppable success he enjoyed through his films, TV shows, phonographic records, and live appearances. Because of the very seriousness with which he personified his mission to entertain, Lewis proved an especially appropriate whipping boy for cultural taste-makers who were determined to establish their distance from the vulgarizations of mass commercial culture.

FEARS OF A CLOWN

Another big area of conflict was in our concepts of comedy. Dean wanted wild, crazy noise without rhyme or reason. On the other hand, I felt that af-

ter years of such meaningless, nonsensical humor, we had just about run the gamut of things we could do. I firmly believe that you cannot "sustain" with a pie in the face as well as you can with a puppy on your lap—that the best comedian is a man in trouble, a tragic figure, as Charlie Chaplin was.

—Jerry Lewis

After his divorce from Martin, Lewis was frequently reproached for the prominence of sentimentality in his work.[16] However, as early as 1951, in an article on the team published in *Colliers* magazine, Bill Davidson had suggested that comedy and pathos were integrally related in Lewis's performance: "Lewis . . . is the misfit, the lout, the boy with ten thumbs, the wrong-doer. He is kicked about by Martin and by Fate, and he builds up such a store of pathos for himself that when he explodes into wild and tumultuous revenge, all his impishness seems justified and doubly funny to the audience. This basically has been the formula of all the great Low Comedians since Shakespeare's time—and no one uses it more effectively than Lewis does today." Films such as *The Caddy, Scared Stiff, The Stooge,* and *Living It Up* teased with the Lewis figure's status as a harassed misfit, but the poignancy had always been trammeled. As Davidson makes plain, the sentimentalizing of the Lewisian outsider threatened the dynamic of the male partnership by rendering Martin as "the handsome, self-possessed oppressor of the Chaplinesque waif" (Davidson 1951, 65). Repelled by this prospect, the crooner savagely and sarcastically derided his partner's obsession with "Chaplin shit" (Levy 1996a, 160).[17]

Lewis's role in *Three Ring Circus,* the film that ignited Martin's dissent, was modeled on the reluctant clown of *The Circus.* In his autobiography Lewis claims that Charles Chaplin's 1928 comedy provided his introduction to the magic of motion pictures: "He's a riot! He does all sorts of things with his face and body. He stands like a mechanical doll, twists his can while walking the tightrope, dashes out of the lion's cage and up a pole—there's nobody funnier than Chaplin. And I'm falling out of my seat laughing at a scene in which he's trapped among hundreds of distorted mirrors, showing him in hundreds of different poses. But even then, I sense the sad reality of my own life. I feel that I'd rather live in a world of make-believe, where I can be anyone I wish—soldier, sailor, doctor, lawyer—anyone. Sure . . . I can be a clown! I can do it. I know that" (Lewis and Gluck 1982, 16–17). It soon became a cliché for critics to ridicule Lewis's Chaplinesque pretensions, but this reminiscence suggests the multifarious meanings he saw in the famous clown. The Chaplin conjured here knots together the key elements of Lewis's own work: the bodily distortion, the fantasy, the "sad reality" of the outsider, the multiple imagings of self.

Unshackled from his quarrelsome partner, Lewis was free to use his familiar Idiot/Kid figure to develop a more serious and extended treatment of the comic misfit as a beleaguered outcast striving for recognition and acceptance. It was a mode of self-representation that was by no means restricted to the regime of performance. Lewis began to disseminate his own biographical narrative of "Jerry Lewis," portraying him as a man impelled to win the love of others as a means of compensating for personal traumas, for his fear of love withdrawn. During the post-Martin era he adopted as his signature song an Arthur Schwartz–Howard Dietz number that Fred Astaire had performed in the 1953 MGM musical *The Band Wagon*.[18] Astaire plays Tony Hunter, a washed-up star of Hollywood musical comedies who is offered a chance to rekindle his Broadway career. At the start of the film a fragile and self-doubting Hunter lacks confidence that he has what it takes to reclaim the limelight. When he arrives at New York's Grand Central Station, movie star Ava Gardner entices the reporters away from him and Hunter walks down the platform alone, crooning softly to himself:

> I'll go my way by myself,
> Like walking under a cloud,
> I'll go my way by myself,
> All alone in a crowd.
>
> I'll try to apply myself
> And teach my heart how to sing,
> I'll go my way by myself,
> Like a bird on the wing.
>
> I'll face the unknown,
> I'll build a world of my own.
> No one knows better than I myself,
> I'm by myself . . . alone.

Lewis co-opted this fragile lament as a manifesto for his reconstruction as a solo artist: he included the song on his first album and also used it in his cabaret and television shows, as well as in *The Delicate Delinquent* (Levy 1996a, 216).[19] Replacing the partnership anthems of the Martin and Lewis years, "By Myself" captures perfectly the emotional register of Lewis's sentimentalized self-representation as a man alone who conceals his anguish beneath the garbs of self-assertion. Fearing that fans would blame him for alienating the handsome man's affections (JAS Productions 1992c), Lewis strategically rearticulated his star image in a manner that skillfully accommodated and transcended the past he shared with Dean Martin. The traumatic breakup of Martin and Lewis was contextualized within a bio-narrative of abandonment that stretched back to the lonely childhood he experienced while his parents pursued their show-biz dreams.

This biographical alibi was fleshed out in an article Lewis wrote with journalist Bill Davidson shortly after the partnership folded.[20] Published as a nine-page cover feature in the February 1957 issue of the glossy magazine *Look*, "I've Always Been Scared" exposes a bruised sensitivity cowering in the shadow of the manic clown. "All my life," Lewis declares, "I've been afraid of being alone." In a story he would repeat with ever more emotive embellishment, Lewis portrays himself as a pathetic outsider who deploys the mask of comedy as a protective shield.[21] Questing for love and acceptance through the show-biz success his father never attained, Lewis is compelled to win the substitute gratifications of applause and laughter: "If I could make people laugh, I thought, they'd like me and let me be with them" (Lewis and Davidson 1957, 51, 54).

Through his childhood Lewis formed an intense bond with his maternal grandmother, Sarah Rothberg, who cared for him while his parents were absent. The "hopeless terror" experienced by the eleven-year-old Lewis when his grandmother died came back to haunt him when he faced the prospect of life without Dean Martin (Davidson 1957, 54, 58). "When we finished the last show together, I went back to my dressing room," Lewis wrote. "I was numb with fright and shaking all over. My clothes were drenched with perspiration. I sat in my dressing room, crying. I thought I'd never be able to get up before an audience again. I thought it would be impossible for me to work without Dean" (ibid. 51). Lewis's 1982 autobiography embellishes the dressing room scene into a startlingly dramatic portrayal of the traumatized man alone as he faces an abyss of uncertainty:[22]

I got up and went to my dressing room suite above the Copa and flopped on the bed. I had no idea what I would be doing the next day or any day after that. There was only a foreboding sense of failure, of my life emptying away and becoming an absolute blank.

I closed my eyes. I felt myself falling, tumbling over and over in space like a feather — down into a trackless desert. . . . *No sign of life anywhere. Not a solitary bird crosses the sky. Even the stars are gone. I struggle forward, engulfed in a wide river of sand.*

Suddenly the desert spreads open. A highway shimmers before me. I'm walking on it — to where? Then the movie marquee! — It straddles the highway; ornate, gilded, the lights flashing round and round.

There, appearing in bulging, silvery brightness is the most enormous word I have ever seen:
A L O N E
I stagger, sink to my knees. I'm screaming at the top of my lungs:
"ONE! ONE! ONE ALONE!" (Lewis and Gluck 1982, 5)

The biographical back story of hurt and rejection represented Lewis's rebirth from the ashes of the blistering partnership as an attempt to eradicate the nagging absence at the heart of his being rather than a triumphant act of self-assertion. A year after the Davidson article *Look* carried another profile of Lewis, by Isabella Taves, which similarly depicted him as an insecure man driven to heroic accomplishments: "Jerry Lewis is a man who is always in a crowd, yet always alone, a man who clowns and gags because he wants to please, to make people like him. At 32, he is rich and successful, by anybody's standards. He's attractive, well co-ordinated, well built. . . . Yet he is driven; driven to succeed, to do half a dozen jobs as well as be an actor; driven to be a good husband, a good father; driven, above all, to please people, to make strangers as well as friends like him" (Taves 1958, 83–84). The new Mr. Lewis displayed in these articles is not the handsome crooner's carefree sidekick but a responsible and devoted family man.[23] Many of the photographs accompanying the Taves feature show Lewis at home with his wife, children, and pets, and the writer also confides that "when Jerry goes on stage, he carries nothing in his pockets except pictures of his family. Twice in his career, he forgot the pictures, and both times he had bad luck. . . . Jerry isn't superstitious about anything else, but he is sure that these family pictures are talismans" (ibid., 91).

The magic formerly associated with the two-man team is transferred to the more normative regime of the family. In the Davidson article Lewis presents an explicitly psychoanalytic reading of the break from Martin, rendering his solo career as a move toward a heterocentric maturity. Lewis claims that after talking with a psychiatrist friend he was prompted to shift his emotional allegiances from his male partner to his wife: "I began to realize that my strength was coming from Patti, and not from Dean or anyone else. It dawned on me that *she* was the one who kept me going, soothing me, building my ego; and that she was my grandmother all over again, representing the home, the stability, the full life I never had as a child" (Lewis and Davidson 1957, 58). From the mid-1950s the flaunting of familial dedication became increasingly important to Lewis's public image. For example, in *Rock-a-Bye Baby* Lewis cast his first child, Gary, as a younger version of the character he plays, and a quasi-flashback scene allows father and son to duet together on "Love Is a Lonely Thing." Gary was also featured on two of Lewis's NBC specials: in a 1957 Father's Day tribute Jerry, Gary, and Danny Lewis teamed up for a version of the Jolson song "Sonny Boy" ("*The Jerry Lewis Show*," *Variety,* 12 June 1957); a year later the familial threesome were reunited for a rendition of "Rock-a-Bye Baby" ("*The Jerry Lewis Show*," *Variety,* 23 April 1958).[24]

Shawn Levy's biography of Lewis questions the veracity of the Davidson interview, gleefully exposing alleged factual inaccuracies and inconsistencies in Lewis's account of his past (Levy 1996a, 2). But what is at issue here is not truth but myth. Like any star or celebrity, "Jerry Lewis" is more than simply a person—he constitutes a publicly circulated aggregation of signs that bears a shifting and unstable relationship to the private individual who embodies them. As a discursive construct, "Jerry Lewis" exceeds the control of Jerry Lewis (né J. Levitch). The dramatic ending of Martin and Lewis's much-loved partnership inevitably generated a proliferation of competing and contending representations of Lewis and his motives. The warmly receptive public relations exercises by Davidson and Taves provided him with a chance to stake his own claim to the meaning of his star image and offer his own rationale for "Jerry Lewis." The psychological narrative articulated by these articles highlighted the degree to which Lewis's star image constituted a very different constellation from the carefree zany of old.[25] Whereas earlier publicity stressed the congruence between the onstage and offstage selves of Martin and Lewis, Lewis's solo career instituted a strategic opposition between the real man alone and the onscreen comic misfit. "It may be," offered Taves, "that audiences are drawn to him because they see or sense the real Jerry, the lonely man of many complexes" (Taves 1958, 83–84).

Eager to show that he had more to offer than comic Id/iocy Lewis sought out vehicles that enabled him to demonstrate his new maturity. In November 1956, for example, he deputized for Ed Murrow as host of CBS's celebrity-interview program *Person to Person*. *Variety*'s response was characteristic of the carping reception often accorded the performer when he sought to deviate from "straightforward" comedy: "Jerry Lewis couldn't make up his mind whether to play straight-man or funny-man. . . . When he was serious, Lewis registered as a parody of Murrow even unto the somewhat ponderous questions, the crossed legs and those ever-going cigarets [*sic*]. When Lewis played for laughs via some facial twitching, it clashed with everything else on the show" ("*Person to Person*," *Variety*, 14 November 1956).

Lewis's appearances on the NBC program *Youth Wants to Know* met with greater approval. In July 1957 *Variety* applauded his ability to communicate with the young: "Clown Lewis surprised by showing the good judgement to take his young interrogators seriously. Obviously nervous at beginning of show, Lewis warmed up mid-way, and soon relaxed enough to toss in a few typical gags, albeit retaining good taste throughout and giving thoughtful, serious answers to a barrage of canny questions. Lewis did himself a great deal of good by displaying the gentle side of his frequently frenetic personality. . . . Lewis must have won over many of his severest critics by his straight, sincere approach on show"

(*"Youth Wants to Know," Variety,* 31 June 1957). When he returned to the show in October 1959, *Variety* noted that "Lewis enacted the role of a mature and adult person who sometimes talked down to the youngsters and sometimes became genuinely enlightening" (*"Youth Wants to Know," Variety,* 7 October 1959).[26]

The most headily symbolic vehicle for the new-look Jerry Lewis, however, was his starring role in NBC's updated dramatization of *The Jazz Singer,* broadcast as part of the *Ford Startime* series on 13 October 1959. Based on a short story and play by Samuel Raphaelson, Al Jolson's original 1927 film was a landmark part-talking picture.[27] The NBC teleplay not only cemented Lewis's identification with the legendary Jewish American celebrity, but he also appropriated it for his own biographical legend. *The Jazz Singer* is concerned with the conflictual cultural and emotional allegiances tugging at a Jewish entertainer as he moves from his traditionalist ethnic and religious subculture into the popular mainstream. The NBC version gives the narrative a Lewisian makeover, transforming the protagonist from a singer to a clown and providing him with Lewis's original first name, Joey (Levy 1996a, 241).[28] The play received a generally negative reception from critics and trade reviewers, many of whom read it as an especially loathsome manifestation of Lewis's unchecked self-regard.[29] Arguing that "no amount of modernization can actually update the story," *Variety* suggested that it was not an appropriate showcase for Lewis: "It's a difficult yarn to bring up to date and still retain the drama of the original, and it's also a role which today would be a tremendous problem for any actor. Lewis, who has been a comedian for all his adult life, is hardly the figure to swing between the double masks of comedy and tragedy with any degree of ease, and there were times when the demands of the role were just too much for him" (*"The Jazz Singer," Variety,* 21 October 1959). *Daily Variety* concurred, claiming that *The Jazz Singer* "looks awkward, almost satirical, in modern dress, and becomes a spectacle misplaced in time instead of a touching, pertinent conflict." The drama "also had to reckon with the difficulty of containing Jerry Lewis in its pivotal role. Lewis gave a sincere performance and attained fleeting moments of strength in the serious portions of his portrayal. It was hard to forget he was Jerry Lewis, for he had trouble submerging his personality in the part, and that's one of the things the role required of him" (*"The Jazz Singer,"* 15 October 1959).[30]

Lewis would have to wait until 1983 before achieving recognition as a "serious" performer—for his remarkably joyless enactment of the man alone in *The King of Comedy.* He complained that the production of *The Jazz Singer* was hampered by NBC's interference: the network insisted on taping the play rather than mounting it live, and they also compressed it into a lean sixty minutes (Levy 1996a, 242). Nevertheless, Lewis also acknowledges flaws within his own contribution to the project, admitting in 1995, "I was too young to play the role. A leading character who looks less than 30 years old wrestling with deep problems of life comes off looking silly" (Neibaur and Okuda 1995, 262). Although Lewis keeps a copy of *The Jazz Singer* in his archive, it remains one of the few items from his back catalogue that he has kept from public view (ibid.).[31]

DELICATE/DELINQUENT

THE TRANSITIONAL FILMS

After all the running around dealing with studio people who were saying and doing things I didn't understand, by the fourth picture I began to feel like a streetwalker on Saturday night.

They'd place me in front of a camera—"OK, Jerry, make your little funny faces"—and after they were finished and had walked away, I would be left standing, of no further interest to them until the next setup. I wasn't going to have that. I wanted to know how things worked.

—Jerry Lewis

Swept to Hollywood by the whirlwind success he whipped up in cabaret with Dean Martin, Jerry Lewis began to exhibit an almost obsessional fascination with movie making. But his hunger for cinematic creativity did not sit well with studio contract personnel, who regarded filmmaking as a collaborative enterprise in which everyone had their own specialized roles to perform. Veteran director Norman Taurog, who helmed six Martin and Lewis pictures and two of Lewis's solo films, told Arthur Marx,

In the beginning, he was a doll. He listened, did what I told him to do, and didn't bother anyone. Then one day I noticed him looking through the camera between takes and starting to make suggestions to Lyle Gregg, our cameraman, on things he had no business making suggestions about: how high a crane to put the camera on, for example, or what kind of lens to use. . . . I used to tell him, "For God's sake, Jerry, why do you want to waste your energy doing things other people are getting paid for? Nobody goes to a Martin and Lewis movie because you directed a scene or because you told the cameraman what to do. They go because it says on the marquee—Jerry Lewis in so and so; not Jerry Lewis, cameraman. Save your energy for acting." (Marx 1975, 172)

Refusing to heed such advice, Lewis set about learning as much as he could about the mechanics and the business of film production. His fascination with image making was evident as early as 1949, when he opened his own camera shop in Hollywood, the "Jerry Lewis Camera Exchange" (Marx 1975, 110-11). Lewis also furnished his home with film equipment and spent a great deal of his spare time fooling around with it. In the early 1950s he made a series of 16mm movies with his Hollywood cronies. Janet Leigh recalls:

We made these films at Jerry's house; he was the cameraman, the director, everything. His place was loaded with movie equipment: 16mm cameras, lights, reflectors, tripods and anything else you can think of. Dick Stabile, who was Dean and Jerry's bandleader, and Mack David supplied the music; Danny Arnold, who wrote material for the Martin and Lewis movies and TV shows, worked on the scripts; and Jerry cast Dean, my (then) husband Tony Curtis, and myself and others—sometimes even himself—in the lead roles. The results were often hilarious. . . . We did the pictures for fun, but you could see that Jerry was learning all the time—how to direct actors, how to set up a scene, etc. (Neibaur and Okuda 1995, 9)

Lewis's first home production, *How to Smuggle a Hernia across the Border,* was an army satire in which he played a gay recruiting officer. He followed it with a series of movie spoofs featuring such Hollywood actors as Leigh, Curtis, Martin, Shelley Winters, Van Johnson, and Jeff Chandler.[1] Lewis held lavish black-tie premieres at a playhouse specially constructed in his home, to which he invited movie stars, studio executives, and Hollywood columnists (Marx 1975, 156, 157).

As Leigh suggests, Lewis's amateur films provided him with an important training ground in such basic movie-making skills as writing, direction, photography, and editing. These experiences fueled his dissatisfaction with Hal Wallis's production-line attitude to the Martin and Lewis films. In particular he felt that Wallis had little understanding of what made comedy work in the cinema. "I had great respect for him till I saw him cut comedy," Lewis said. "Wallis didn't know how to make fucking comedy. He was a butcher. He cut anywhere. He was a complete butcher. If the film got released, I was in complete shock. Even in my beginning, when I didn't understand what film was" (Levy 1996a, 103).[2]

Annoyed at the uppity star's persistent interference, Wallis used his 1980 autobiography to mount a scathing assault on Lewis's aspirations:

Jerry developed an ego as tall as the Empire State Building, talking to Paramount
executives as if he were running the studio, demanding more scenes alone, trying to
push Dino into the background. He began to write his own dialogue, argued with
directors, and tried to take over their work. He suggested musical themes to the
composers and wanted to edit. I fought this constantly and we had many arguments.
The more he screamed and threw his arms about, the quieter I got. It was all very
difficult. . . . Later, Jerry got the autonomy he sought from the beginning. He produced, directed, wrote, starred in, edited, and supervised the music of his pictures.
There is no need to comment on their quality. (Wallis and Higham 1980, 142, 146)

Despite his antipathy to Lewis's ambitions, Wallis made numerous concessions.
He allowed Lewis to write the boxing sequences for *Sailor Beware,* styled after
similar routines performed by his heroes Chaplin and Stan Laurel, and also gave
him a screen credit for his contribution to the musical numbers in *Money from
Home* (Tosches 1992, 240, 268). Lewis was also permitted a say in the choice of
production personnel; at his suggestion Walter Scharf was hired as the musical
director for *Living It Up* and Joseph Pevney as the director of *Three Ring Circus*
(ibid., 268-70). It was only after he finished with Dean Martin, however, that
Lewis was in a position to have more concerted input into his films. His first
solo venture, *The Delicate Delinquent,* demonstrated that Lewis meant business.
He not only starred in the film but also produced it for York Pictures (Levy
1996a, 209), completing it on a tight five-week shooting schedule for the astonishingly low budget of $460,000 (Marx 1975, 205). The film eventually grossed
more than $7 million, confirming not only Lewis's viability as a solo star but also
his acumen as a creative entrepreneur.[3] The subsequent year he produced both
Rock-a-Bye Baby and *The Geisha Boy.* As I will consider, all three films foreground the thematic of self-redefinition that is characteristic of Lewis's output
in the transitional phase of the late 1950s.

   This was also a period of transition for Hollywood cinema. Geared toward
the manufacture of a large number of films for a mass heterogeneous audience,
the studio system became less viable after World War II. Added to the drastic
decline in cinema attendances was the 1948 ruling, at the conclusion of a
lengthy Supreme Court antitrust action, that the five major vertically integrated
film companies must divest themselves of their theater chains. The majors em-
barked on an extensive process of rationalization to meet the new economic climate — shedding, for example, their huge rosters of technical staff and contract
players. Instead of taking responsibility for a large volume of regular produc-

tions, they began to rely increasingly upon independent companies (such as the Wallis-Hazen firm) for the supply of films, offering financing and distribution deals in return.[4] After World War II the Hollywood studios moved from a system in which several producers took responsibility for an annual roster of films to a more flexible package-unit system in which films were assembled as specialized combinations of saleable elements such as story, stars, director, and spectacular effects (Bordwell, Staiger, and Thompson 1988, 330-35).[5]

Lewis's entire career as a popular film star spans this transitional era, which saw the classical studio system superseded gradually by a more diffuse organization of production. Writing in the *New York Times* in 1958, Thomas M. Pryor noted that "in a large sense, the big studios today are financiers of movies, having taken over the role formerly performed by banks and private loan companies. The studios are obliged to put up most or all of the risk capital in order to get the stars, directors, writers and producers to work for them. Thus there is in the movie industry perhaps the strangest conglomeration of corporate structures within corporate structures that exist in the nation's business world" (Pryor 1958, 121).

Pryor's article is concerned with one particular manifestation of postclassical Hollywood practice — the altered relations between star and studio. During the classical era the major film companies sought to control the exchange value of their stars with long-term contracts granting the studio copyright over the star's public image (and, through morality clauses, their private lives). By such means the studio aimed to both protect its economic investment in the manufacture of the star (costs of training and publicity, etc.) and exert monopolistic control over the star's value as a box-office enticement.[6] After the war, however, it was increasingly common for major stars to broker their talents through their own production organizations. In the late 1950s Lewis joined the growing band of incorporated Hollywood performers that included Cary Grant, Burt Lancaster, John Wayne, Kirk Douglas, Alan Ladd, Frank Sinatra, Bing Crosby, Bob Hope, and Gregory Peck. Incorporation provided strong financial incentives — highearning performers could make tax savings of up to 40 percent by registering themselves as corporations — and permitted them to arrange coproduction deals with the majors that guaranteed them a percentage of the film's gross income (Pryor 1958, 121).

Besides such financial advantages, Lewis found incorporation attractive because it allowed him a greater measure of control over the exchange value of his star image and, hence, over his films. Once more it seemed to be the example set by Charles Chaplin that steered Lewis toward his new horizons. Chaplin had not merely achieved commercial and critical success within the "low" medium of performative comedy, but he was also the supreme example of the hyphen-ate filmmaker: an actor, writer, director, producer and even composer. A few months after starting his celluloid career with Mack Sennett's Keystone Film Company in 1913 Chaplin was a phenomenally successful international star. He shrewdly exploited his immense popularity to secure independence from the in-creasingly regimented studio system. A million-dollar contract with the First National Exhibitor's Circuit in 1918 enabled Chaplin to set up his own studio in Los Angeles. The following year he joined star-performers Mary Pickford and Douglas Fairbanks and star-director D. W. Griffith in the formation of United Artists, a distribution company that would fund their individual projects. By serving as his own boss Chaplin could escape the constraints of institutional filmmaking, particularly the specialized division of labor that was established in the major studios from the mid-1910s. Chaplin's working methods ran counter to standard Hollywood practice: instead of using a precosted continuity script, he derived much of the material for his films from on-set rehearsals.[7]

At the start of his solo career Lewis did not enjoy such a secure position. Paramount initially had doubts about his viability as a box-office attraction without Dean Martin. Y. Frank Freeman, the studio's vice president in charge of production, told the *New York Times* in 1956, "At least we'll try it for one picture . . . and I'll see if it works out" (Marx 1975, 203). The success of *The Delicate Delinquent,* however, proved that Lewis was still one of company's major as-sets — and one of the few surefire stars at the U.S. box office. His films also did phenomenally good business abroad, at a time when the overseas box office ac-counted for up to 50 percent of the revenues of the major film companies (Balio 1990, 6). By 1958 Lewis was the only major star remaining under exclu-sive contract to Paramount (Eames 1985, 225), and they were unwilling to risk losing their hot property to a competitor.[8] In June 1959 the studio offered Lewis a contract that guaranteed him $10 million for fourteen films over a seven-year period (Schumach 1959, 32). As the Paramount publicity office keenly an-nounced, it was the largest price a Hollywood company had ever paid for a per-former's services. The deal may have gone against the prevailing trend of stars avoiding long-term commitments to studios (ibid.), but it guaranteed Lewis the creative autonomy he desired. Half the films were to be owned by Lewis, the other half by a combined interest of the newly formed Jerry Lewis Productions and Paramount Pictures, which would distribute the films (Levy 1996a, 239).[9] The contract granted Lewis the power to choose his producers and directors, paving the way for the self-directed films that were to provoke so much contro-versy in the 1960s.

HAMLET TO CLOWN

Before the release of his first self-directed project Lewis starred in six films, half of which were contractual obligations he owed Hal Wallis (Levy 1996a, 209). Lewis's performance is unusually restrained in the three Wallis movies: as James Neibaur and Ted Okuda (1995) suggest, he "plays it straight . . . in an effort to get laughs out of the material" (141). *The Sad Sack* (1957) and *Don't Give Up the Ship* (1959) returned the comedian to the safe territory of the armed services, a context he had milked dry with Dean Martin in the early 1950s. The former is a loose adaptation of George Baker's popular comic strip, the latter a straight-forward farce of sexual frustration. *Visit to a Small Planet,* his third Wallis film, also subjugates Lewis to the script, but this reworking of Gore Vidal's satirical Broadway play delivers a more productive setting for the Lewis figure's charac-teristic otherness. Cast as an explicitly alien presence, Lewis plays the extrater-restrial Kreton, who visits small-town America for a vacation. Kreton's immu-nity to such human feelings as love, jealousy, and pain prevents *Visit to a Small Planet* from engaging with the delirious complexities of emotion and identity explored by *Rock-a-Bye Baby* and *The Geisha Boy.* Instead the comedy derives from the spaced-out misfit's inability to read the physical and cultural codes of the world into which he intrudes: for example, Kreton attempts to converse with a dog, he believes that a TV cigarette commercial is speaking directly to him, and he takes idioms such as "I'm pulling your leg" literally.

Anticipating many of the strategies of his self-directed films, Lewis's own productions are more ambitious. *The Delicate Delinquent,* like *The Sad Sack,* was initially conceived as a Martin and Lewis project.[10] In the final months of the partnership Lewis was eager to make a film based on the classical legend of Da-mon and Pythias, hoping that this story of self-sacrificing male friendship would help reconsolidate his relations with the handsome man (Marx 1975, 196-97).[11] Martin took exception to the idea of playing a cop, however, and refused to make the film. Written and directed by Lewis's friend Don McGuire, who had also scripted *Three Ring Circus* and *How to Smuggle a Hernia across the Border, The Delicate Delinquent* was subjected to a strategic makeover to showcase Lewis as a solo attraction. Although Darren McGavin deputizes for the absent Martin, he is a less demanding straight man because he lacks the complex history Lewis shared with the crooner. The film also differentiates itself from the lavish pro-duction values of such Martin and Lewis entertainment spectaculars as *Living It Up* and *Artists and Models,* opting instead for the gritty black-and-white styling of the 1955 juvenile-delinquency problem picture *The Blackboard Jungle.*

At the height of Lewis's success with Dean Martin, Robert Kass attempted to fathom the comedian's phenomenal appeal in an article published by *Films in Review*. Lewis's antics, Kass (1953) suggested, were "reflections of some of the untoward aspects of our time." For Kass, Lewis was a signifier of the otherness of 1950s youth, a symbol of "young America gone berserk" (119, 123). From a more celebratory perspective, J. Hoberman (1988) proposes that in the early 1950s "the young Jerry was America's id. His every cute outburst threatened to escalate into loss of control; the sight of his big mouth promised a kind of ecstatic self-annihilation" (47). The uncontrolled eruptions of Lewis's body connected with the rebellious stirrings of a nascent youth culture, which would itself erupt into national and international consciousness with the primal beat of rock and roll. As Karal Ann Marling argues, Lewis's manic gyrations prefigured the shock of Elvis Presley:

Until the advent of Martin and Lewis, the comedy team that virtually owned the airwaves in the early 1950s, TV remained little more than radio accompanied by black-and-white photographs. But Jerry Lewis helped to change the aesthetic of television. While Martin . . . stood still, in the prescribed manner, Jerry Lewis stomped around him, arms and legs akimbo, shouting, aping, and mugging the camera with mad abandon. Established chiefly by erratic movement, Lewis's emotional intensity was sometimes compared with method acting. More remarkable than the histrionics was the effect of his physical movements on an audience that howled in transports of unrestrained delight as Lewis circled his suave and motionless partner. Like Elvis, Jerry Lewis seemed rebellious because he wouldn't stand still; he both projected and aroused strong emotion through motion. (Marling 1994, 176-777)

Capitalizing upon the recent success of juvenile dramas such as *The Blackboard Jungle* and *Rebel Without a Cause* (1955), *The Delicate Delinquent* flaunts Lewis's allegiance to the youth audience.[12] But at the same time the film distances Lewis from the uncontainable energy and rebellious excess that characterized his earlier comic performances. Lewis's redefinition as an all-round entertainer required him to renegotiate the terms of his relationship to the adolescent constituency. The *Youth Wants to Know* programs, for example, offered an image of the comedian that was more in keeping with his new ambitions, displaying a Jerry Lewis eager to impress with his thoughtfulness and moral purpose. The anarchic spectacle of motion celebrated in Lewis's earlier work relied as much upon a continual shifting of identities as it did upon physical movement: in both spheres flux and mobility were prized at the expense of decorum and stability. However, Lewis's delicate delinquent Sydney Pythias does not abandon himself to the delights of sheer abandon; he is instead searching (literally) for direction.

After a street rumble Sydney is mistaken for a gang member and taken to the neighborhood precinct house, where he encounters patrolman Mike Damon (McGavin). A reformed juvenile offender with a self-appointed mission to save slum kids from criminal temptations, Damon befriends Sydney to test out his theory of benevolent rehabilitation. Sydney himself is a no-hoper from a slum environment who lacks social and familial ties or any other external context of self-definition. "How does a guy know what he wants to be?" he asks Damon. "Especially somebody like me? I'll tell you what I am—I'm a nowhere." The sentimentalizing of the good-hearted misfit anticipates later films like *Cinderfella, The Errand Boy,* and *The Patsy,* which similarly define the Lewis figure as a "nowhere" or a "nothing." But this example is charged acutely by the star's post-Martin crisis of self-representation. Sydney not only performs Lewis's theme song, "By Myself," but the articulation of his dream to be somebody also evokes a passage from his 1957 *Look* article "I've Always Been Scared": "Grandma Sarah was the only one who understood my loneliness. . . . She was the only one who thought I was anything. I used to say to her, 'The trouble with me is that I'm nothing.' She would say, 'Well, you're a human being.' I'd answer, 'But I want to be *something*. I want to be respected.' She knew what I meant" (Lewis and Davidson 1957, 52).[13]

Melodramatic scenarios frequently underpin the narrative maneuvers of the Martin and Lewis movies, but the male partnership remains the key definitional context for the Lewisian outsider. Darren McGavin, however, lacks the long-term resonance of Lewis's former partner, and he is cast in a role that further diminishes the homocosmic dynamic: by playing a law officer he serves as an agent of the broader social order. Whereas Martin and Lewis films such as *Jumping Jacks* conclude with the two men rejecting social and narrative obligations to be with one another, *The Delicate Delinquent* closes with Sydney Pythias achieving a licit social identity by joining the police force. He becomes "somebody" by becoming, like Mike Damon, a cop who can reconcile the conscience of society with its heart. With Damon's help Sydney manages to pass through the police academy's rigorous training procedures without ever properly following the rules. Reminiscent of the training sequences in *Jumping Jacks* and *Sailor Beware,* these scenes offer a tried and tested format for generating comic effects by setting Lewis in conflict with systematized procedures of masculine testing. Sydney's success suggests that a "good heart" will eventually triumph over any degree of ineptitude, and it also inspires a highly schematic change of heart by Monk (Robert Ivers), the leader of the juvenile gang that both plagues and rejects him. Sydney begins his career as a law officer by encouraging Monk and the gang away from their delinquent ways, dispensing the very advice Damon had tendered him earlier.

For Bosley Crowther of the *New York Times* Sydney's characteristically Lewisian eccentricities sat rather uncomfortably with the position of idealized authority he is allowed at the end of this "serious-message comedy":

If there appears in this presentiment a certain sobriety that was not a detectable feature in the old Dean Martin–Jerry Lewis films, it may respectfully be acknowledged as a purpose of the new Mr. Lewis. But it must also be discovered as the cause of an unevenness in this film. Mr. Lewis, as the star of his own picture, runs a gamut from Hamlet to clown. . . . Mr. Lewis warding off a judo wrestler or trying to fit odd-shaped blocks into odd-shaped holes is a delirious comedian. Mr. Lewis trying to act hard like a man, with a policeman's hat planted on his noggin is a mite incredible and absurd. The good intention of his message may be missed in this eccentricity. (Crowther 1957, 16)

Echoing the complaints of the television reviewers, Crowther identified the problem of the film as its failure "to concentrate the actor's comic talents. It lacks consistency. Mr. Lewis is not yet a Charlie Chaplin, though he may aim to be" (Crowther 1957, 16). Others critics also remarked upon the film's uncertainty of tone and its lack of integration. The *Los Angeles Times* concluded that "the spectator may find himself confused, to say the least" (Levy 1996a, 226), and *Variety* charged that this "sometimes-funny comedy-drama . . . is neither fish nor fowl. . . . Slapstick is blended with pathos and some straight melodrama tossed in. . . . Screenplay by McGuire endeavors to play Lewis straight, in a pathetic character, but the next moment he's off on a robust comedy tangent which dissipates characterization attempt" ("*The Delicate Delinquent*," *Variety*, 29 May 1957).

The Delicate Delinquent signals a significantly altered role for Lewis within his films, with the polarization formerly inscribed within the two-man team replaced by divisions existing within the self. The new Mr. Lewis continues to work with and through his familiar Idiot-Kid persona, but as Crowther notes, he is clearly using his comic creation with a different sense of purpose. Nevertheless, the resolving stabilization that concludes the film hints at the paradoxes that were already beginning to manifest themselves in Lewis's unabashed self-parturition. By making the grade as a law officer, Sydney becomes more than simply an ordinary member of society; he sets himself up as a mediator between social institutions and the socially disadvantaged. *The Delicate Delinquent* shows Lewis (as Sydney) becoming a respected figure who can use his new position to improve the lives of others, passing on to them what he has gained through his own process of self-realization. With the ejection of Dean Martin, Lewis took upon himself increasing responsibility not only for expressing comic disruption but also for containing it. Hence the new Sydney Pythias who surfaces at the end of the film does not just learn from Mike Damon but also displaces and internalizes him.

THREE BABIES AND A MA(N)

Lewis's first solo feature is a relatively straightforward comedian-comedy that uses the framework of the contemporary juvenile-delinquent film as a vehicle for articulating the comic misfit's quest for identity. The two films Lewis made with director Frank Tashlin in 1958 subject the comic outsider to a more expressly nonconformist process of identity formation. As a gag man, writer, and director, Tashlin was one of the distinctive creative forces in American screen comedy. Lewis has frequently acknowledged the profound influence Tashlin exerted on his own style as a filmmaker: "His knowledge of comedy far surpassed that of any director I had ever worked with. What I learned from him couldn't be bought at any price" (Lewis and Gluck 1982, 200).[14] In the mid-1930s Tashlin made animated shorts for Leon Schlesinger's unit at Warner Brothers, where he helped nurture the career of his first comic star, Porky Pig (Prouty 1994, 198-201).[15] He worked with flesh-and-blood comedians from the mid-1940s, devising gags for films starring the Marx Brothers and Bob Hope. After writing and directing a substantial portion of Hope's 1951 comedy *The Lemon Drop Kid* Tashlin was subsequently allowed to make feature films in his own right (ibid., 212). He worked with Hope again on *Son of Paleface* (1952), which set the comedian's trademark verbal routines amidst a glittering landscape of cartoon-style gags. But it was in Jerry Lewis that Tashlin stumbled upon the nearest possible human approximation of a cartoon figure—a point made explicitly at the end of *The Geisha Boy*, when Lewis does an impression of former Tashlin protégé Bugs Bunny.

Tashlin and Lewis began their association when the Martin and Lewis relationship was in decline. Impressed by Tashlin's work on *Artists and Models* and *Hollywood or Bust*, Lewis wanted him to direct *The Delicate Delinquent*. After a bitter disagreement with Hal Wallis during the production of *Hollywood or Bust*, however, Tashlin escaped to Twentieth Century Fox, where he made his two highly regarded Jayne Mansfield films *The Girl Can't Help It* (1956) and *Will Success Spoil Rock Hunter?* (1956). Lewis managed to entice him back to Paramount for *Rock-a-Bye Baby* and they worked together on five more comedies until 1964. The title of the first Tashlin-Lewis collaboration was clearly an attempt to capitalize on the star's recent success as a recording artist. Although the film does not include the Al Jolson song, it features six new numbers provided by Sammy

Cahn and Harry Warren. It further seeks to broaden Lewis's appeal by according unusual prominence to familial relationships. Even so, as a family film *Rock-a-Bye Baby* is remarkably strange because it slyly disorders the functional myths underpinning the familial ordering of identity and desire within 1950s America.

Like *You're Never too Young* and *Living it Up, Rock-a-Bye Baby* is a very free adaptation of a Hollywood screwball comedy. *The Miracle of Morgan's Creek,* written and directed by Preston Sturges in 1944, was a notoriously savage satire of wartime sexual morals, its farcical narrative propelled by a scandalous scenario of unwed motherhood. After a spree of drinking and dancing—and via a marriage of immediate convenience—small-town girl Trudy Kockenlocker (Betty Hutton) finds herself pregnant by a serviceman whose name she cannot remember. She tries to extricate herself from her plight by persuading her hyper-neurotic boyfriend Norval Jones (Eddie Bracken) to dress as a soldier and marry her under an assumed name, but the subterfuge is exposed and Norval is arrested before the ceremony is complete. Further complications ensue: Trudy's father springs Norval from jail, and the Kockenlocker family is forced into hiding to avoid scandal. The narrative wraps up with a cynically "miraculous" resolution in which Trudy gives birth to sextuplets. Her prodigious fertility provides an escape from all predicaments because it makes her a national and international celebrity. As news of the miraculous birth wipes even the war off the front pages, Trudy's problematic motherhood is reappropriated as an American triumph. The state governor sees to it that the marriage is legitimated, and that Norval is transformed from criminal to town hero with startling rapidity.

Lewis's Clayton Poole is a composite of the roles played in the original by Hutton and Bracken. But whereas Norval has fatherhood thrust upon him in the final scene of *The Miracle of Morgan's Creek, Rock-a-Bye Baby* offers the male misfit a more extended engagement with parenthood. Clayton is infatuated with his former childhood sweetheart, the movie star Carla Naples (Marilyn Maxwell). Like Anita Ekberg in *Hollywood or Bust* and Jayne Mansfield in *Will Success Spoil Rock Hunter?* Carla embodies the gaudy excesses of Hollywood glamour. Her success in such films as *The Creature from the Lower Tarpit* derives exclusively from her display as an eroticized image, a sign of desire. In many of Tashlin's films the male protagonist negotiates a chaotic pathway through a phantasmic landscape that is alive with the absurd, and absurdly alluring, enticements of commercial culture (Madison Avenue, Hollywood, the record business, comic book publishing).[16] The Tashlinesque movie queen is a feverishly and fetishistically overstated embodiment of commodified desire, a desire that is driven by the illusory plenitude of the image.[17] Although her inflated breasts and pouting orality connote the promise of maternal abundance, her allure is always flamboyantly artificial. Clayton's longing for Carla is framed constantly as a desire for the image of woman — or, rather, for contradictory images. In a flashback sequence he nostalgically visualizes Carla as an icon of presexual innocence, yet he also packs his suitcase with glamour shots of Carla the movie star.[18]

The beguiling lure of images is a recurring source of fascination in Tashlin's films. For example, in *Artists and Models* and *Hollywood or Bust* Lewis is in thrall, body and soul, to consumerist mania. Addicted, respectively, to comic books and movies, the Lewisian misfit pursues his obsessive yearning for the mass-produced images of perfection generated by modern America's industries of consumer seduction. Tashlin's films, J. Hoberman (1994) argues, "have less to do with the production of cultural forms than with their packaging and consumption. His America is a nation of robotic image junkies whose minds have been colonized by the media" (92). Clayton Poole's elderly neighbor Miss Bessie (Ida Moore) is the most startling illustration of this thesis. A mass-culture zombie, Miss Bessie responds hypnotically and ritualistically to every commercial interpellation: swilling coffee, lighting up cigarettes, gulping down Burparex stomach tablets. "I believe in loyalty to the sponsor," she tells Clayton. "That's what's wrong with the world today. Not enough loyalty." Miss Bessie recognizes Clayton as a kindred spirit because he, too, manifests an intense loyalty to the sponsor. But in his case it is Carla, not television, who delivers the seductive promises that make possible his imaginative escape from the confinements of Midvale. Carla, however, emerges as an unusually complex incarnation of woman as object of desire because of the proliferation of imaged roles through which she is presented — she is childhood sweetheart, movie star, maiden in distress, mother. Moreover, her considerable accomplishments inspire the awestruck Clayton to embark on his own voyage into the uncharted seas of multiplicity.

Finding herself pregnant after a short-lived marriage to a Mexican bullfighter who dies in the arena, Carla aims to preserve her viability as a sign of desire by rejecting the sacrifice of motherhood. Before production commences on the ironically titled *White Virgin of the Nile* Carla retreats from the public gaze and gives birth to triplets. She then persuades the doting Clayton to take care of them for her, and in exchange he is granted an opportunity to realize his fantasies. As he makes his secret pact with Carla at the lake-side rendezvous of their youth, Clayton confesses, "I can't sleep just dreaming about you, Carla. Matter of fact, I dream about you every night. Same silly dream. I'm Sir Galahad in shining armor and you're always in trouble and you need me. . . . And in the very same dream I always come up charging on the white horse."

Clayton is able to pursue his adventurous wish by offering service to Carla, but he does not follow the conventional masculine pathway outlined in the dream. Instead he takes upon himself the domestic role Carla spurned by devoting himself tirelessly to raising the children of the woman he adores. When the Midvale court challenges his right to keep the triplets—because children, the judge pronounces, need a mother—Clayton enrolls at the university to obtain a diploma in child care. The only male on the course, he comes top of the class. When Clayton presents his certificate to the court he asserts his credentials as an exemplary "mother": "I did everything every other woman can do."[19] Lucy Fischer (1991) has criticized comedies such as Laurel and Hardy's *Their First Mistake* and Chaplin's *The Kid* (1921) because, in substituting the clown for the mother, they "sustain female absence while positioning maternity at center stage." Arguing that the devaluation of the maternal is ubiquitous in comedy, Fischer suggests that "the male absorption of women" is a stratagem that consigns them further to the regime of lack (67, 60). But she underestimates the degree to which the clown figure can disarrange established gender roles and hierarchies.[20] Clayton Poole is a case in point: his pact with Carla not only enables him to come to her rescue but also provides him with a chance to experience a hermaphroditic transcendence. Through his parenting skills Clayton expresses a comingling of conventional gender roles, a copresence of identities traditionally held to be mutually exclusive. As he tends to the triplets Clayton is their breadwinner, their entertainer, their nurturer, their nursemaid. Instead of replacing the mother, then, the Lewis figure confuses and short-circuits established masculine and feminine protocols.[21]

Clayton Poole is defined not simply as a divided self but also as a figure who encompasses a bewildering range of identities. *Rock-a-Bye Baby* is the first of the solo films fully to exploit the multiplicity that was already a key feature of Lewis's public image. A montage sequence showing Clayton's efforts to provide for the children displays him in variety of roles in quick succession: cutting a lawn, working in a Chinese laundry, bell ringing, performing a rock and roll song on a TV amateur hour. In an earlier scene Carla's teenage sister Sandy (Connie Stevens)—as besotted with Clayton as he is with Carla—invites him home on the pretext of fixing the television. When Sandy's overly protective father (Salvatore Baccaloni) turns up, drunk and belligerent, Clayton is forced to take refuge inside the empty television receiver. Papa Naples insists on watching TV, and Clayton improvises a series of quick-fire impressions to entertain him: a cowboy, a continuity announcer, a derby-hatted politician, an opera singer, an oriental weatherman, and a children's TV host (who is a forerunner of *The Nutty Professor*'s Julius Kelp). This sequence is remarkable not only because of its parade of personae but also for the way that the obsessed Lewisian misfit invades the televisual machinery of image making.

Both Clayton and Miss Bessie immerse themselves in the substitute gratifications of mass-culture images, a willed self-obliteration motivated by the limited options allowed them within the prim and proper confines of Midvale. Clayton's discontent with this archetypal mid-American small town is articulated through the extravagant suite of gags that introduces him into the film. Working as a TV repairman, Clayton attempts to fix an antenna on the roof of the inordinately orderly house of Mrs. van Cleeve (Isobel Elsom). Sandy appears in the street below and tells him that Carla has sent him a package—containing, significantly enough, an autographed glamour still. Clayton looks down from the high roof and suffers an attack of vertigo (cue instant pastiche of Alfred Hitchcock's recently released thriller). Momentarily destabilized, he grasps hold of the antenna—which begins to spin on its axis, taking Clayton with it. As he whirls around, his feet dislodge bricks from the chimney and send them hurtling into the street. One of the bricks knocks out Mr. Newland (Hank Mann), an engineer working on a fire hydrant. Clayton stumbles down the ladder and through the house, to help Sandy tend to the injured man. But as he tries to raise Mr. Newland to his feet Clayton bumps into a wrench that is fixed to the hydrant, causing an awesomely powerful jet of water to spurt from the attached hosepipe. Clayton rushes after the tip of the swollen hose as it snakes its way along the street: he straddles it, grasps it between his hands, and points it into the air. In a parodic spectacle of unbridled sexual force the phallic water hose gushes uncontrollably from between his legs. The outrageous sexual hyperbole continues as the jet of water smashes windows, demolishes a fence, and hurls three people to the ground. Clayton seeks to resolve the problem by inserting the hose into a manhole (penetration gag number one). Clayton rushes back up to Mrs. van Cleeve's roof, and the hose works itself free just as he reaches the chimney. Sandy takes action by grabbing the hosepipe, but as she lifts it into the air the water hurls Clayton down the chimney (penetration gag number two). The sequence of gags concludes with the violation of the pristine whiteness of the van Cleeve home by clouds of black soot.

This chain of disastrous consequences, which is similar to the havoc provoked by Jayne Mansfield's body in *The Girl Can't Help It,* is set in motion by the arousal of Clayton's desire when he hears Sandy speak Carla's name. His bodily discoordination unleashes an overstated spectacle of phallic aggressivity directed at Midvale's placid frustrations.[22] The sexualized excess demonstrated in the hosepipe scene is subsequently channeled and defused through Clayton's adventure into parenting. The babies bring a sense of purpose previously lacking in his life, enabling Clayton to move beyond his unrequited imaginings of perfection. Like *The Miracle of Morgan's Creek, Rock-a-Bye Baby* speeds through a suc-

cession of narrative complications to resolve its scenario of skewed familial relations. The Midvale court decides to award custody of the triplets to Mrs. van
Cleeve, who regards children as a diversion on a par with watching Art Linklet-
ter on television. To bring the babies back to their rightful family Clayton is
forced to marry Sandy, who declares that she is their mother. At the same time,
however, Carla decides to abandon stardom for motherhood and announces to
the press that Clayton is *her* husband. He is subsequently hounded as a bigamist,
another figure of excessive masculine potency. The accelerating complications
are resolved when Carla regains her children after marrying her long-suffering
agent. Clayton, having been associated at different junctures with extremes of
phallic potency and maternal abundance, romps into the bushes with Sandy to
make babies of his own.

Rock-a-Bye Baby ends with the revelation that Clayton has sired five children.
As a result of this extraordinary act of fatherhood, which outdoes the achievements of the macho bullfighter, Clayton is lauded as the town hero. The final
shot of the film shows a statue of Clayton Poole, erected in the center of Midvale, which depicts him holding the quintuplets. Although the statue signifies
that he has finally achieved his wish to become the town hero, the fact that it replaces the monument to an unknown warrior underlines the peculiar redefinition of male heroism sustained by the film. In conventional comedian comedies
the deviations of the comic misfit are measured in relation to an Oedipal trajectory of male subjectivity, but *Rock-a-Bye Baby* articulates and sanctions a more
disorderly perspective on American manhood. Like *The Delicate Delinquent,* the
film presents a story in which the Lewis figure triumphs over adversity and rejection. But whereas the first solo film manifests an uneasy tension between the
eccentricity of the comic outsider and the goal-oriented narrative of masculine
success, *Rock-a-Bye Baby* delivers a more confidently purposeful disorientation
of the conformist scripts of achievement and cultural integration. The next
Tashlin-Lewis collaboration, *The Geisha Boy,* is similarly concerned with the
comic outsider's quest to realize his desire to "be" and to "belong." As in *Rock-
a-Bye Baby* the Lewis figure is subjected to a highly wrought succession of dis-
placements and desiring potentialities, but *The Geisha Boy* adds to the earlier
film's destabilizing of gender roles an intriguing negotiation across cultures.

GEISHA/BOY

Apart from *The Sad Sack* and sequences in *Sailor Beware* and *Scared Stiff,* Lewis's
films had always restricted him within the mainland boundaries of the United

States. By contrast, *The Geisha Boy* casts the Lewis figure as a refugee from home. Magician Gilbert Wooley enlists on a USO tour of Japan because he can find neither acceptance nor employment in the United States. Japanese impersonations were a long-established feature of Lewis's act, their exaggerated stylization of otherness providing him with a conduit for his excesses in gesture and language. But as Bernard Eisenschitz (1994b) notes, *The Geisha Boy*'s representation of Japan is remarkable because, by Hollywood standards, it is "neither racist nor patronizing" (170). With the exception of travelogue sequences comprising stock footage, the film was shot exclusively in Los Angeles. However, the only part of homeland America shown onscreen is the drably functional space of the airport—whereas Japan is tendered as a seductive kaleidoscope of color and spectacle. Moreover, *The Geisha Boy*'s vision of the East is assertively and distinctively cinematic: the film is packed with the kind of self-reflexive ciné-gags beloved of both its director and its star. At one point Bob Hope appears on television dubbed into Japanese. In another scene Wooley asks a Japanese gardener for directions to Mr. Sikita's house but is unable to understand what he says because "the subtitles are all mixed up": English-language titles accompany Wooley's speech and Japanese script supplements the gardener's words.[23] In similar vein is a gag, lifted from the Hope and Crosby film *Road to Utopia,* that transforms Mount Fujiyama into Paramount's mountain logo.

These gags simultaneously expose and celebrate the artificiality of the film's rendering of the East. They are cinematic conjuring tricks that give an unusual spin to the familiar Western representation of the Orient as a domain of exotic and enticing otherness, as what Edward Said (1978) has termed "a sort of surrogate and even underground self" to Occidental culture (83). *The Geisha Boy*'s orientalist vision pits Japan as a utopian realm of creative and emotional realization against the constraints and deficiencies of the United States. In America Wooley is himself an "internal other" or "underground self," but when forced out to the alien otherness of Japan he discovers a landscape of surrealistic transfigurations that offers new possibilities for being and belonging. The first of Lewis's solo films to place him as a professional entertainer, *The Geisha Boy* makes the East a positive counterbalance to 1950s America by characterizing it as a zone of creativity, imagination, and the joys of the cartoon aesthetic.

As in many of Tashlin films, the values of 1950s American culture are satirized with the aid of a parodically overstated movie queen. Lola Livingston (Marie McDonald), the headliner of the USO tour, exemplifies the manipulative gratifications of institutional show business. A clone of Monroe and Mansfield, Lola is a platinum blonde sex goddess whose physical assets provide her passport to fame while the good-hearted, genuinely talented Wooley languishes.

Lola is a vision of manufactured allure, a bleached embodiment of consumer-ized desire (her dress, hat, gloves, bag, and fur wrap are all pristine white). Lola's whiteness is set in opposition both to the Orient and to Wooley's magical white rabbit, Harry, who is the magician's partner and only friend.[24] Wooley's devo-tion to Harry leads him to risk his own comfort and safety when he smuggles the animal on board the plane to Japan. Harry escapes from the baggage hold and sneaks into Lola's bunk, plunging Wooley into an embarrassing encounter with the imperious movie star. Awakening just as Wooley attempts to rescue his rabbit, Lola assumes that someone is out to molest her, and in the confusion Major Ridgely (Barton MacLane) is blamed for the assault. Wooley seeks to apologize to Lola when they disembark at Tokyo airport, but he catches his foot in the extravagant train of her dress, tearing the clothes from the movie star and sending her tumbling down the gangway in full view of the massed paparazzi. The humiliation concludes with a panic-stricken Wooley rolling Lola up in the red carpet that is intended to welcome her arrival.

Like the devastation of the Midvale street in *Rock-a-Bye Baby,* the collisions between Wooley and Lola articulate the Lewis figure's unconscious revolt against the restrictions of modern America, where he is denied an opportunity to feel at home. Another principal source of frustration for Wooley is the U.S. Army, which, like Midvale, serves as a homegrown zone of restriction and regu-lation. Expelled from the USO tour after his escapades with Lola, Wooley pleads for a second chance and is eventually allowed to take Harry on a tour of the front line in Korea. The magician's presence in the combat zone is both incon-gruous and dangerous: dodging bombs and gunfire, he performs to small groups of demoralized American soldiers. The most enthusiastic response to the show comes from a hungry soldier whose eyes light up at the thought of eating Harry. The war-front scenes serve as a comically grotesque reminder of America's militaristic hegemony in Asia after World War II: in Japan there is little sign of a U.S. civilian presence, but its armed forces are overwhelmingly dominant.

Wooley's problems with the army are most clearly conveyed through his rela-tionship with WAF sergeant Pearson (Suzanne Pleshette). On the plane to Tokyo Pearson provides a positive counterbalance to Lola Livingston's narcis-sism, revealing a sympathetic concern for Wooley's welfare. It is also Pearson who convinces Ridgely to entrust him with the Korean tour. But the sergeant's feelings are more than strictly "maternal," and on the flight back to the United States near the end of the film she intimates that she wishes to develop sexual relations with Wooley. He remains immune to Pearson's charms, however, be-cause the uniform she wears compromises her femininity—as he tells her ear-lier, "soldiers can't be sexy." Wooley's other heterosexual option is provided by

Kimi Sikita (Nobu McCarthy). Whereas Pearson is a demanding American, Kimi is both exotically Oriental and, as her eagerness to take off his shoes illustrates, a model of submissive femininity.

However, the film is markedly reticent about developing intimacy between the two, not because of a problem with miscegenation but because of a more fundamental difficulty with adult heterosexuality. Neither Pearson nor Kimi can compete with the central emotional relationship in the film — between Wooley and Mitsuo Watanabe (Robert Hirano), Kimi's six-year-old nephew. As in *Rock-a-Bye Baby,* a scenario of parental surrogacy provides the Lewis figure with a means by which can transcend his initial insufficiency. When he sees Lola toppling down the gangway at the airport the solemn Mitsuo is inspired to laugh for the first time in his life. He immediately idolizes Wooley and wants him to be his "father," and in return Wooley confesses, "I wish I were your father." *The Geisha Boy* clearly evokes Chaplin's first feature film, *The Kid,* in which the comic outsider similarly achieves a new sense of purpose when he "adopts" a young boy. Wooley's main goal after he arrives in Japan is to win and maintain Mitsuo's respect. As he tells Major Ridgely, he needs to succeed in this new world because he has found "a little boy who thinks I'm something. He thinks I'm something special. This is the first time in my life that anybody thought I was something. And I would love to prove to him that he's right."

The relationship between the man and the boy is much more headily sentimentalized than Clayton Poole's adventures with the triplets, but the pathos operates through a tangled circuitry of emotional resonances.[25] As in *The Kid,* the boy is not merely an external object, an other, but also functions as a mirror for the self: Wooley's own past, as an orphan raised by an aunt, directly parallels Mitsuo's situation. Moreover, the significance the boy holds for Wooley is determined by the way he represents an alternative to the other definitional objects the magician encounters through the film — Harry, Sergeant Pearson, and Kimi Sikita. This point is made explicitly in the scene in which Pearson tries to articulate her feelings to Wooley. Believing that she is competing with Kimi for his affections, she confides that her last boyfriend deserted her for a Japanese woman: "So I guess I'm very touchy as far as Orientals are concerned." Wooley's response shows the extent to which he is both resistant to the sergeant's attractions and oblivious to her desires: "Yeah, they're wonderful people. Especially when they're about six, going on seven."

In its concentrated emotionalism the Wooley-Mitsuo dyad directly substitutes for the heterosexual possibilities indicated by Pearson and Kimi. Just before he boards the plane that will take him back to America, Wooley shares a tearful parting scene with Mitsuo. As man and boy openly avow their love for one another, the intensity of emotion supplants that conventionally found in hetero-sexual love stories.[26] Mitsuo is an alien other who serves Wooley as a double, as a projection of his own otherness within U.S. culture. The Japanese boy pro-vides the motivation, and the alibi, for a narcissistic economy of desire wherein the Lewis figure can be protected from sexual object relations and other exter-nal definitional contexts. Mitsuo is affirmed as the one whose love is most worth having, whose love endows the greatest meaning. Of necessity this scenario pro-duces a reversal of the logic of Oedipal narrative, which is concerned with the progress from child to (male) adult. The clown-hero is valued for his courageous determination—despite the risk of cultural disapproval and exclusion—to re-main a child, or to be a child once more. This openly sentimentalized project of reversed self-definition harbors an active fantasy of displacing cultural priorities. Establishing his own meaning primarily through the affinity with a child who is the projected image of himself, Wooley is able to reject the authority invested in U.S. culture, in the army, in women (Sergeant Pearson, of course, embodies all three contexts).

The Geisha Boy's concluding maneuvers foreground the dispersal of the Oedi-pal paradigm, confounding narrative linearity via a series of circular movements between East and West. When Wooley is forced to go back to the United States to take up a job offer, Mitsuo stows away on board the plane—as Harry had done on the trip to Tokyo. The boy is discovered on arrival in the United States, and Wooley vows, "They'll never separate us this time, Mitsuo." He then smuggles himself and Harry onto the flight back to Japan. Such repetitive moves draw attention to the persistent doublings, substitutions, and condensa-tions that constitute *The Geisha Boy*. Wooley eventually escapes the cyclical vac-illations between the two worlds to settle in Japan, united with Harry, Mitsuo, and Kimi. The final scene presents a stage performance by "The Great Wooley and Co.," a scene that unifies the surrogate family, show biz, magic and Eastern promise. Within the familial grouping, however, there is no suggestion that Wooley and Kimi are sexually united. Instead the film conjures a displacement of customary sexual and familial possibilities. Like *Rock-a-Bye Baby*, *The Geisha Boy* wraps up with a last-minute multiple birth, but here it is Harry (more cor-rectly, Harriet) who is responsible for the miraculous act of motherhood. As Wooley pulls a profusion of little white rabbits from his magician's hat, procrea-tion is flamboyantly displaced from the human to the animal.

The group that Wooley gathers around him thus permits his escape from adult sexual obligations. In the "childlike" vision of life celebrated at the end of the film procreation is a magical rather than a sexual act. *The Geisha Boy* reworks the geographical and cultural otherness of the East to construct an idealized world in which adult heterosexuality is othered—and denied a determinate role. The rabbit's shift of gender illustrates that "Japan" is a place where "anything is possible," where the (Western) ordering of identity and sexuality can be transcended. To disavow the seriousness of this thematic play with otherness, identity, and cultural allegiance—and as a further tribute to the joys of metamorphosis—*The Geisha Boy* finishes with a cartoon-style gag in which Lewis himself "becomes" a rabbit. He looks into the camera, chews on a carrot, and declares, Bugs Bunny style, "That's all folks."

MAN WITH A MOVIE CAMERA

THE TOTAL FILMMAKER

I think I love films and those who love them better than just about anything else in the world.

—Jerry Lewis

After finishing work on *Cinderfella* in January 1960 Lewis had a disagreement with Paramount over the film's release date. The studio wanted this lavish fairy-tale comedy in cinemas for the summer holiday season, but Lewis argued that a Christmas release would be more appropriate.[1] He proposed an outrageous compromise: if Paramount held back *Cinderfella* until December, he would present them with a new Jerry Lewis movie before July. Studio president Barney Balaban was understandably skeptical; such a rapid production schedule, for a film that had not even been scripted, flew in the face of accepted Hollywood practice. Balaban relented, however, when the star-producer volunteered to fund the movie himself. Lewis worked out the concept of *The Bellboy,* which he had decided to direct, as he flew to Miami for a two-week stint at the Fontainebleau Hotel. After persuading the owner to let him use the resort hotel for his new film Lewis set to work at a furious pace:

I wrote the script, staying up eight days and eight nights. Not one wink of sleep. I turned out 165 pages like some kind of drugged madman, alternately writing and hallucinating scene after scene. As my own director, I had the added advantage of hiring actors. Fortunately, Milton Berle happened to be available, so I wrote him into the picture. Also, from bygone Catskill days, Jimmy and Tillie Girard, Eddie Schaeffer, Herkie Styles, Sonny Sands, Harvey Stone[,] . . . my sidekicks Lou Brown and Jack Keller in it, too, and half the population of Miami Beach had applied as extras.

On February 8 we started shooting. A month later the picture was wrapped. Then, during an engagement at the Sands Hotel, from March 10 into the middle of April, I cut the picture, scored it, dubbed it and shipped it in May to Paramount for distribution. (Lewis and Gluck 1982, 226)[2]

The gamble paid off. *The Bellboy,* which cost $1.34 million, grossed about $5 million during its initial release in North America (Levy 1996a, 255). The film's triumphant success secured Lewis a degree of creative autonomy that no Hollywood comedian had experienced since the 1920s "Golden Age" of silent slapstick.[3] From 1960 to 1970 he directed half of the eighteen feature films he starred in, and was frequently their producer and writer as well.

This chapter will explore the general issues raised by this crucial phase of Lewis's Hollywood career, beginning with a consideration of how the move from performer to performer-director enabled Lewis to exploit the representational potentialities of the film medium. Attracted by film's ability to reorder the world, rather than simply to reflect it, Lewis seized the opportunity to make movies that were multiply self-directed. What renders these films especially fascinating — or, to some tastes, infuriating — is their persistent and multileveled attention to Lewis himself. These movies not only display the ever-proliferating signs that define "Jerry Lewis," but also enact a struggle for their meaning and authorship. Lewis's directorial force is exhibited through the self-conscious treatment of his own star image and through a filmic and comic style that disassembles conventional Hollywood practice. Especially provocative is the way that their frustration of comic pleasure (as it is commonly understood) opens onto alternative voicings of embarrassment and abasement that generate some of the most deliriously compromised of all cinematic experiences.

LICKING EMULSION

Lewis's show-biz dreams were nurtured during the period in which Hollywood cinema was triumphantly establishing itself as the supreme form of American entertainment. The innovation and standardization of the synchronized sound film made cinema a totalizing form that could replicate the full panoply of existing popular entertainments.[4] To secure the hegemony of the sound film in the late 1920s and early 1930s, the Hollywood studios invested heavily in top-flight Broadway and vaudeville talent and showcased such performers as Eddie Cantor, the Marx Brothers, Wheeler and Woolsey, Mae West, and Joe E. Brown in tailor-made movies. "Ambitious studio executives," Henry Jenkins (1992) argues, "saw sound as a means of broadening their entertainment empire and bringing Broadway and vaudeville under their corporate control" (159).[5] Vaudeville survived competition from the silent film because it provided attractions not found within the cinema's parade of spectacle and narrative. By the mid-1930s, however, it was a spent force, laid low by competition from the silver screen's extravaganza of musical and comic performance. During the same period Broadway was also hit by the popularity of the synchronized sound film: Frederick Nolan (1994) reports that by 1934 "luxurious movie palaces like Radio City Music Hall and the Roxy—'The Most Magnificent Motion Picture House in Any City, or Any Country, Anywhere!'—offered patrons not only a movie but also a lavish stage show for less than the price of a balcony seat in the theater" (195).[6]

Because films were no longer restricted to the realm of pure mime, Hollywood could also compete with Broadway as the horizon of aspiration for adventurous entertainers. The glamorous allure of the Hollywood film was bolstered by its ability to play everywhere, to reach national and international audiences. But the cinema differs significantly from live entertainment because of the gap it inscribes between the moment the performance is rendered and the moment it is delivered to the public. Liveness promises an authenticity of rapport by offering the copresence of actor and audience, but film—as a medium of recording and reproduction—inevitably produces a more complex dynamic between the two. Actors are separated spatially and temporally from the audiences they eventually perform to. In his influential 1935 essay "The Work of Art in the Age of Mechanical Reproduction" cultural critic Walter Benjamin (1935) suggested that film substantially fractures the bonds between performance and self because "for the first time—and this is the effect of film—man has to operate with his whole living person, yet forgoing its aura. For aura is tied to his presence; there can be no replica of it. The aura which, on the stage, emanates from Macbeth, cannot be separated for the spectators from that of the actor. However, the singularity of the shot in the studio is that the camera is substituted for the public. Consequently, the aura that envelops the actor vanishes, and with it the aura of the figure he portrays" (672–73).

For Benjamin, the movie actor of Western cinema exemplifies the alienated subjectivity produced by modern capitalism. In the process of submitting themselves to the economic and signifying industries of commercial culture, film stars sell not only their labor but also the authority over their representation. The performances they give are shot out of sequence and delivered across multiple takes that will be assembled by other hands into an imaginary totality. The actor generally has little say over what is done with the likeness he or she sells to the cinematic machine, an image that will be reduplicated through multiple prints and projected onto screens across the world. In an age of mechanical reproduction "the work of art reproduced becomes the work of art designed for reproducibility" (Benjamin 1935, 669). What is destroyed is not simply the singularity of the artwork but also the auratic certainties of performance and self — their unity, their wholeness, the validity of their very presence. Under such conditions, Benjamin suggests, the player is transformed into a commodified sign:

The feeling of strangeness that overcomes the actor before the camera . . . is basically the same as the estrangement felt before one's own image in the mirror. But now the reflected image has become separable, transportable. And where is it transported? Before the public. Never for a moment does the screen actor cease to be conscious of this fact. While facing the camera he knows that ultimately he will face the public, the consumers who constitute the market. This market, where he offers not only his labor but also his whole self, his heart and soul, is beyond his reach. During the shooting he has as little contact with it as any article made in a factory. This may contribute to that oppression, that new anxiety which, according to Pirandello,[7] grips the actor before the camera. The film responds to the shriveling of the aura with an artificial build-up of the "personality" outside the studio. The cult of the movie star, fostered by the money of the film industry, preserves not the unique aura of the person but the "spell of the personality," the phony spell of a commodity. (Benjamin 1935, 673)[8]

Lewis started out in Hollywood as precisely the kind of "alienated laborer" portrayed by Benjamin. But twelve years after arriving in Los Angeles, as a performer paid to submit himself to the faceless gaze of the camera, he was directing that gaze himself and delivering to the screen images of Jerry Lewis that were no longer mediated by other writers, directors, or producers. The trajectory of his film career from the late 1940s to the early 1960s shows Lewis attempting to overturn his subordination by learning the business and the techniques of filmmaking — and by seizing every opportunity to secure executive and creative control. As a major star of cabaret, cinema, and television, he was amply rewarded for the sacrifices he made to the postwar industries of popular culture, and he used his resources to procure greater dominion over his cinematic self-exposure. With the Garron movies Lewis discovered possibilities for celluloid expression denied him within the regulated milieu of the major studio: "I began to understand that I wasn't doing what they [studio professionals] did *right*. I was just doing it *differently*. And I approached it from a different standpoint; and I found myself terribly involved with it, with a dedication. I found myself involved with understanding the twenty-four frames and every time that shutter opened I was being exposed to the French-, English-, German-, Italian-, Spanish-speaking countries plus many more — and I got myself religious every time a director said 'Roll that camera.' And I found out what I was thinking of. And how could I best do something" (Kantor, Blacker, and Kramer 1970, 270).

The allure of moving pictures rests upon what John Ellis (1992) describes as "a particular half-magic feat" (58). Filming breaks reality down into a series of still photographic images, which are then reanimated during the course of projection into an imaginary continuum of vitality and plenitude:

Cinema as a photographic medium instantly poses its images and sounds as recorded phenomena, whose construction occurred in another time and another place. Yet though the figures, objects and places represented are absent from the space in which the viewing takes place, they are also (and astoundingly) present. . . . The moment shown on the screen is passed and gone when it is called back into being as illusion. The figures and places shown are not present in the same space as the viewer. The cinema makes present the absent: this is the irreducible separation that cinema maintains (and attempts to abolish), the fact that objects and people are conjured up yet known not to be present. (Ellis 1992 38, 58)

The mainstream film is enticing precisely because it promises a masking of divisions, an illusionary obliteration of absence.[9] Within the voyeuristic paradigm that organizes cinema exhibition, spectators are offered a rapport with the flow of sounds and images that is both intense and intensely individuated. Coming live through its performance in the cinema, the film invites the spectator to traverse the boundary between the real-life space of the auditorium and the realm of projected illusion. This is the magic of the movies.

As his memory of watching *The Circus* testifies, from an early age Lewis identified with film's potential for imaginative and transformative self-representations. The young Joey Levitch loses himself in a larger-than-life realm of shimmering perfection, a dream screen presenting images of magical abundance that can compensate for, and transfigure, the "sad reality" of life. As "Jerry Lewis," he was able to make the movie dreams his own, not simply by inhabiting the dream screen but by determining the images projected onto it. Lewis restated his passion for the transcendental promise of film in the prologue to his book *The Total Film-Maker,* an incantatory poem to the joys of the medium that reads, as Shawn Levy (1996a) aptly remarks, "like some weird Las Vegas incarnation of

Allen Ginsberg" (375).[10] Lewis depicts his cinephilia as an obsession that is both overwhelming and erotically charged:

The total film-maker is a man who gives of himself through emulsion, which in turn acts as a mirror. What he gives he gets back. . . .
    I have a confession. Crazy. I have perched in a cutting room and licked emulsion. Maybe I thought more of me would get on to that film. I don't know. I do know that plumbers don't lick their pipes. With emulsion, it's easy to get turned on. (Lewis 1973, 15, 17)

When asked to expand on the creative satisfactions he derives from celluloid, Lewis most often speaks of the solitary pleasure of editing. In 1977, several years after retiring from filmmaking, he told an audience at the American Film Institute, "I get a strange kind of satisfaction sitting in the cutting room, forgetting the clock, not realizing that I haven't seen my family in sixty-five hours, that's unlike anything else. Last night, I closed at a theater outside Boston, and you couldn't get a credit card between the people. That's a different kind of satisfaction. Now, you can't compare that to the aloneness in the cutting room. When you're in the cutting room you're opening the eye to God knows how many people. You don't know if you're going to be playing to twenty-eight million people or close to half a billion people. It's very heavy" (Alpert 1977, 36–37). Editing is a process of combinations and substitutions through which Lewis can reshape and deform pro-filmic reality, organizing the discrete shots into a totality that obeys his dictates. By controlling the assembly of sounds and images he can design his vision of the film that will be performed in the cinema — and also the performance of himself within it.[11] The heaviness he feels is the weight of the audience, the pressure of expectation, the demands of the other. Despite his painstaking efforts to control the mechanisms of self-exposure, Lewis knows that he cannot ultimately determine how his efforts will be received.

    Unlike many performers trained in live entertainment contexts, Lewis did not mourn the loss of spontaneity, immediacy, and interactivity that filmmaking decrees.[12] He quickly grasped the new possibilities enabled by the medium's temporal and spatial dislocations. Not only would the movie play to more people in more places than any live performance, but Lewis would also not have to be there in person. The cinema screen serves as both a surface onto which the actor's image is projected and a defensive barrier that shields the performer from the audience. Where liveness bares the entertainer to a public whose tangible presence is felt at every moment, the exposing to the film negative leads eventually to an exposure to others who are unseen, unknown, and elsewhere. With film, Lewis could conceal himself from the world to labor painstakingly over the self-fabrications that would be projected back into it.

CAPTAIN OF THE SHIP?

> **When you make a film yourself, write it, produce it, direct it, perhaps star in it; a piece of your heart enters the emulsion. It stays there the rest of your life, good film or bad. . . . Also, as a total film-maker, I'm convinced that there is a greater chance of inconsistency when the four separate minds of writer, producer, director and actor collaborate.**
>
> —Jerry Lewis

Lewis sought to *authorize* his filmic representation by taking control over all stages of production.[13] The series of movies he directed in the 1960s do not just display the traces of their author at all levels but are also explicitly concerned with the multiple and conflicting meanings encompassed by Jerry Lewis. Instead of narrowing the gap between the self and its imaging, they amplify it. Rather than tearing through the veils of illusion to reveal a unified and auratic subject, they flaunt an "I" that is formed from a plurality of identities played out on countless public stages. The total filmmaker may champion self-direction (and self-directedness) as affirmations of the integrity of personal expression, but the self that is performed by these films is too chaotic and schismatic to allow a direct or uniform representation. Most evident is the gulf separating the total filmmaker from the Lewisian misfit. Luc Moullet argues that Lewis is "a most unusual film comedian in that, unlike other comic directors—Chaplin, Keaton, Tati—he does not serve his own acting with his direction. It is almost masochistic of him, I might say" (Alpert 1966, 74). In a 1969 interview with Fergus Cashin of the British *Daily Sketch* Lewis suggests that the relationship between director and performer is grounded in a process of domination and subjugation:[14]

As a director I've limited myself to directing an odd genius—Jerry Lewis. He's a cross-eyed, prattling, yelping, spastic lunatic with a vocabulary that has no relationship whatsoever with the Oxford Dictionary.

I don't like him. He has this ego bit, like an id (take this down: ID means the instinctive impulses of the individual) but in Jerry's case it means the instinctive impulses of the idiot. . . . He is an actor I can manipulate. I like the look of the man's track record. But he is nutty. As a director, I sit in the cutting room and crucify him. I can take liberties with myself.

But he is not really me. I am the director. I am the captain of the ship. I cannot stand subordination from people like Lewis. He is a clown — he thinks he can do everything as well as I can. He can't. (Cashin 1969, 8)[15]

The performer's subjection to the authority of the director was facilitated by the use of video monitoring, a standardized feature of movie making since the 1960s that Lewis pioneered, using it on all his films.[16] During the production of *The Bellboy* he had a small video camera fixed onto the motion-picture camera, which he then hooked up to closed-circuit monitors distributed around the set. While Lewis the performer offered his body to the camera, the video monitors provided Lewis the director with a controlling view from within the scene. This system of video surveillance, later bolstered by the addition of playback facilities, proved a valuable asset for a director who spent so much of his time in front of the camera. It enabled him to retain control of many creative decisions that would ordinarily be ceded to the cinematographer (Neibaur and Okuda 1996, 273). In a 1967 interview with Paul Mayersberg, filmed for the BBC series *The Movies,* Lewis elaborated upon his use of the video assist:

It's very difficult to be on both sides of the camera at the same time. And when I'm setting up a shot I live on the camera literally. I spend most of my time composing the shot, the joke, or the gag or the scene, and marking it and setting it and timing it. When I'm in the scene and have other people involved, and if I am to make an entrance, I would never know if the scene is working right. So I established a closed-circuit electronic system of monitoring, where I'd have eight or ten monitors all over the set, and I would be behind the door watching the monitor. If the performers are doing as I indicated and the pace is right, if they're functioning well, I'll make the entrance. If not, from behind that door I'll yell cut and let's rehearse it again, or try it again. Once I come through that door that means I'm satisfied with what has happened up to that time. Now to depend on another individual for . . . what looked okay to me, no. I shan't do that. I don't trust anybody. To pass judgement on how a scene is going. I know that's a — a crass remark to make, that I don't trust anybody, but I don't. I'm . . . the only one that I trust. My heart tells me it's right or it's wrong. (Mayersberg 1967, 2:2)

The video assist permits the exertion of control not just over others but also over competing tendencies within the self. The controlling eye of the director monitors every move the performer makes, an eye consistently aligned with the "I" of the total filmmaker. The dynamic of the Lewis's auteurist films is echoed by the intriguing slippage between positions of self-definition in the following extract from the Mayersberg interview. The "I" who speaks starts out as a neutral observer but subsequently splinters into the warring factions of actor and director:

When I watch Jerry on the screen, if he's funny I really enjoy him. And I laugh. And he can make me laugh when he's good. And I find myself being no different than any — any other human being. When he's forcing I feel it as an audience does, but I feel it even a little more strongly because I've lived there. And it's a recollection of my discomfort. . . . As an actor I've tried to lie, or cheat. Or the day wasn't what it should be, and we do have moods. As the director when I see it on the screen, I'll turn to my cutter and I'll say, lift that piece out of there. I've cut Jerry out of the film more than anyone else. . . . I have sent notes to my secretary, to my cutting department, be sure I get a retake on the comedian. He wasn't very good. I will get that note as a director in the morning which I had sent out from my office earlier that morning, and I will then say to my assistant, let's be sure to pick up the Idiot in this particular scene. Now when it comes time in the afternoon to do that, and I am the actor being told to get dressed for that retake I rebel terribly. I'm very hostile and very angry that I have to do something over because anything I do is marvelous. Well, according to the director everything I do is not marvelous. And it better be better or we'll get someone else. And I would easily get someone else in any role. I can be very, very . . . smug about this because I really can't replace Jerry. Cause that's what they're buying and I got it. I'm stuck with him, you know. (Mayersberg 1967, 2:5–6)

Lewis clearly relishes such identity games. In a 1993 *New York Times* profile, for example, he declared, "I am a dichotomy. I am for progress, yet I hate change. Try living with that problem. . . . I am *the* dichotomy" (Wolff 1993, C1). But the man who speaks so readily of his paradoxical nature clearly wants us to believe that he exerts full command over the contradictions. Thus whereas the Lewisian misfit mangles words and disintegrates in the force of authority, the self-possessed and self-confessed authoritarian who addresses Fergus Cashin is "frighteningly serious, very schoolmasterly" (Cashin 1969, 8). The trouble is that although Lewis may steadfastly assert his authority as captain of the ship, the vessel under his charge sails through vortiginous seas of discourse that make the tacking of a direct course impossible. The fantasy of totalization expresses a craving for domination of both the process of filmic creation and the process of self-definition. However, the biographical individual Joseph Levitch can neither possess nor delimit the identity "Jerry Lewis" because it is formed from an ever-shifting array of public utterances.

Lewis's self-directed movies hijack the Hollywood comedian film and transform it into an insistently nontraditional vehicle for the construction of a discourse of the self. Although the concept of control may be crucial to this project, the films offer a tantalizing and radical splitting of Lewis that exceeds the opposition between performer and auteur. The more evident Lewis's totalizing presence as author, the more he multiplies and the more he divides. As he increased the roles he performed behind the camera Lewis began, to an obsessive degree, to expand his presence within the films. He plays dual roles in *The Bellboy, The Ladies' Man, The Errand Boy, The Nutty Professor,* and *The Patsy* (in which Lewis also plays all three members of a female backing group). He has seven roles in *The Family Jewels,* five in *Three on a Couch,* and three in *The Big Mouth.* In the self-directed films the personae that comprise Lewis's public image—the Idiot/Kid figure, the Las Vegas showman, the Hollywood director, the sentimental didacticist—jostle against and compete with one another. In *The Nutty Professor,* for example, the Lewisian misfit Julius Kelp transforms himself into his desired alter ego, a manipulative and self-obsessed nightclub entertainer who, besides evoking Dean Martin, is also a monstrous incarnation of "Las Vegas Jerry" (Stern 1975, 10). *The Nutty Professor* pinpoints with remarkable clarity how Lewis's self-directed projects engage in a strategic rescripting of the subject who gives them meaning.

Multiplicity emerged as a recurring trope in Lewis's work long before he began to direct films. Ed Sikov (1994) describes how in a scene in *Scared Stiff:* "Lewis walks past a mirror and out pops another version of Lewis, one who speaks with an even dumber inflection as he leans out of the mirror and addresses his twin; the two Lewises then proceed to have an entire conversation with themselves in which the mirror image gives the 'real' Jerry helpful advice" (192). Lewis would frequently counter the coherence of straight man Dean Martin with a dizzying series of protean shifts in his vocal and bodily direction. Set-piece moments of Lewisian performance, such as the chandelier scene in *Living It Up,* present him fragmenting (and figmenting) into multiple identities. "Lewis's is a personality," Sikov comments, "that ceaselessly unravels; its most consistent aspect is the constant dissolution to which it subjects itself" (192). When Lewis's Fella (in *Cinderfella*) tells his fairy godfather (Ed Wynn) that he wants to be accepted as "a person not a people," it is tempting to read this not only as a wish to gain respect for his qualities as a human being but also as a desire for subjective unity and coherence.

Joe Dante, director of *The Howling* (1980) and the two *Gremlins* movies (1984, 1990), proposes that by comparison with Tashlin's comedies Lewis's films present "a different kind of surrealism. . . . Freudian surrealism" (Krohn 1994, 136). The Tashlin-Lewis films deal with the conflict between the Lewisian misfit and social norms, revealing—as Michael Stern (1975) puts it—a "linear and socially-oriented approach" that casts the Lewis figure as an innocent in order to satirize the "plastic culture" of the United States (5). In *Rock-a-Bye Baby* and *The Geisha Boy* the fluidity of the Lewis figure's identity may provoke an unraveling of the cultural texture of Oedipal narrative, but the films do not displace the authority invested in it. The self-directed films, however, free the Lewis figure from the conventional scripts of masculine social and sexual success by making Lewis himself "the center of interest and the *raison d'être*" (ibid.). As star, comedian, and enunciator, he battles to hold together the conflictual potentialities that define "Jerry Lewis" as a subject. Scott Bukatman (1988) suggests that "if . . . this proliferation of Jerrys is evidence of a narcissism, as so many of his critics contend, then it is hardly the passive scene of a Narcissus poised gracefully above a limpid, reflecting pool; it is instead a scene set in a Wellesian hall of mirrors, each glass reflecting back a different image. Beneath the struggle to control body, speech and desire, there exists in Lewis's work an ongoing, but finally failing struggle to control identity itself" (204).

Several interviewers comment upon the extremity of Lewis's determination to retain control over his public representation. Fergus Cashin (1968) reports that he "frowns at your notebook, makes sure you're poised to take down every word and then switches on a tape recorder (just to make sure)" (8). In 1975 journalist Judith Simons claimed that "for 25 years Lewis has been recording his own life with the diligence of a one-man C.I.A" (Simons 1975, 8). Lewis also informed Bart Mills of the *Guardian* that he makes audio tapes of all his interviews, "to impress on my wife and others that I really didn't say what the newspapers say I said" (Mills 1975, 8). Mills portrays Lewis as an obsessive archivist who keeps everything on file, maintaining a constant and "authoritative" chronicle of his life (ibid.).[17] The fear of misrepresentation may be motivated by the hostile treatment Lewis has received at the hands of the journalists, but it also amounts to a great deal more. For fifty years he has sustained an astonishingly public visibility, reinventing himself continually to accommodate the shifting mediascapes of popular entertainment. By keeping his own personal archive of a life lived *in* public and *through* the public, Lewis aims to guarantee the integrity of a private truth that both escapes and contains the flow of discourses that construct his public identity.

A small but telling sign of Lewis's resistance to the mediated determination of self is the refusal to remove his wedding ring when playing characters who are unmarried. Shawn Levy (1996a) remarks of *The Delicate Delinquent:* "Again, Jerry is unable to stay wholly in character: His voice shifts not in comic ways but in a way that reveals the actor behind the fictional character. Sydney Pythias is surprisingly capable of sober, considered thought, and when he indulges in it, his voices [*sic*] takes on a gravity and self-import utterly at odds with the rest of his behavior. Moreover, he's wearing the inevitable wedding band and pinky ring, and he's got a picture of Patti, Gary and Ronnie Lewis in his basement flat—so he's obviously not as much of a nobody as he appears" (227). Levy views the wedding ring and the family photographs as evidence of a generally slapdash attitude toward characterization, but they can also be read as totemic signifiers of a personal life, and a real person, that lie beyond and behind the figure Lewis is playing. Rather than submitting to the authority of the character Sydney Pythias, Lewis mobilizes these private signifiers to enact a resistant subjectivity. Another example of this process is the scene in *The Family Jewels* in which Willard (Lewis) sits down to listen to a record of "This Diamond Ring." The point to what would otherwise be a strange digression is that the song is performed by Gary Lewis's band the Playboys.[18]

Lewis did not just incorporate affirmations of his family within the movies, he also used movies as affirmations of family. Anthony Lewis recalls that "holidays, especially Christmastime, were certainly not your average undertaking in our house. Most folks in those days did just fine photographing Christmas festivities with a silent Super 8 movie camera. We had a miniature sound stage set up in the living room. Dad set up his 16-mm sound-on-film camera with floodlights, shotgun microphones, and even live playback with holiday music" (Lewis and Coleman 1993, 67).[19] In a rather perverse application of the concept of the video assist, the Bel Air mansion the family moved to in 1964 was equipped with an elaborate surveillance system of microphones and cameras that enabled Lewis to monitor activity in any part of the house (Gehman 1964, 46-47; Levy 1996a, 309-10). An anonymous "friend" told Harry Shearer (1979) that Lewis used intercoms as a means of keeping tabs on his family: "'His children are asked to keep their intercoms on at night so he can hear clearly what's going on in their rooms. It was his way,' the friend says half-apologetically, 'of showing his kids that he loved them'" (39).

Such anecdotes characterize the real life Jerry Lewis as a man driven by a paranoid compulsion to order and contain the world through apparatuses of recording and surveillance. Whereas his films incorporate personal signifiers such as the ring and the family photographs, Lewis's personal life is itself interfused with, and validated by, the same technology that renders him as an image to the world. Having pacted himself to stardom's industry of desire, the man who was Joey Levitch must spend his life in pursuit of the increasingly diminishing possibilities for a self that escapes public definition. But these tantalizing avenues of biographical speculation constitute a diversion from the aim of this present book, which is to examine Lewis's work and his self-representation within it. With the auteurist films Lewis signaled a shift in his status from a cinematic product to a producer of signs, forms, and meanings. Taking responsibility for the direction of his highly marketable comic persona, he made a series of films that pushed the Hollywood comedian comedy beyond the bounds of its conventional practice. The next section explores the distinctive features of Lewis's self-directed movies—focusing, in particular, upon their idiosyncratic rendition of gag comedy.

THE DEFORMATION OF THE COMIC

It ought to be stressed that Jerry Lewis, along with Arthur Penn, is the only auteur to have emerged in the American cinema in the last five years. . . . It's because he has created new forms.

—Claude Ollier, 1965

It had always been difficult to contain Lewis within the acceptable province of the comedian as jester, but his move behind the camera gave critics the ammunition they needed to mount a more sustained attack on his comic endeavors.[20] With the widening gulf between the spasticity of the Idiot-Kid and Lewis's flamboyant aspirations as a creative presence, reviewers reproached him for a betrayal of "comic innocence." Leonard Maltin echoed these complaints in a 1978 book on movie comedians, berating Lewis for his failure to make films that were "simply entertaining":

Jerry Lewis decided that he wanted to write and direct his own films, to become "the total film maker." The difference in his films was obvious: they were ponderous where once they had been light and airy, pretentious where once they had been so unassuming. Although Lewis was concerned with his characterization, he no longer supported it with a strong story line, preferring black-out gags instead. Worst of all, especially to a young and nonanalytical viewer, his films were simply not as funny as those that others had written and directed for him. . . . There was no longer anyone to veto an idea, so Jerry indulged his every whim, allowed Jerry the comedian to milk gags far beyond endurance, and discarded conventional notions of good taste, modesty, continuity, and—oddly enough—humor. (Maltin 1978, 217–18)

Maltin's diagnosis of the "Lewis problem" conveniently ignores the fact that such excesses were already a hallmark of his work as a performer. *Newsweek*'s lacerating review of *The Geisha Boy* in 1958 bears a remarkable resemblance to later criticism of the self-directed films: "As in all Lewis movies, the trouble with this one is that the star seems not to know when to stop. Instead of building a bit of funny dialogue to a climax and then leaving it there to simmer, too often he messily lets the pot boil over. He does not allow himself a simple, artful double take; he has to make it a triple take or even a quadruple take" (Marx 1975, 210).

Even though he would later prove one of Lewis's most tenacious detractors, Bosley Crowther (1949) offered a more enthusiastic account of the comedian's antics when discussing his first screen appearance in *My Friend Irma:* "The swift eccentricity of his movements, the harrowing features of his face and the squeak of his vocal protestations, which are many and varied, have flair. His idiocy constitutes a burlesque of an idiot, which is something else again" (39). Crowther intimates that through his hyperbolic rendering of comic "idiocy," Lewis establishes a strange and strangely disordering relationship with both the figure of the comic misfit and the conventions of comic performance. American reviewers of the 1950s routinely acknowledged the peculiarity and difference of Lewis's work, but they were more anxious to distance themselves from his disorderly comic spectacle than to investigate its methods.

Like much of the negative reception of Lewis's work, *Newsweek*'s take on *The Geisha Boy* valorizes restraint as an essential requirement of acceptable comedy.[21] In an integrated film narrative gags interrupt, and throw into momentary disarray, procedures of logic, decorum, communication, and bodily function. However, the rupturous effect tends to be trammeled because the gag's familiar strategies of elaboration and containment enable potentially disturbing events to be disavowed. The gag is defined not by the disruptive event that triggers it but by the mechanisms through which disorder is controlled. When the delivery is restrained and precisioned, the spectator is allowed to escape the potentially disconcerting ramifications of the comic spectacle. But Lewis's work destabilizes the balance between exposure and closure: the eruptions of his unruly body frequently turn the gag against itself, stripping away the insulatory casing to lay bare the pain and embarrassment it conceals. The wide-ranging deformations of the self-directed films thus compromise the joking process, damming its ready yield of safe pleasure.

By comparison with other comedians, Lewis's disorderly performance flaunts an intensively dysfunctional relationship between body and self. Harpo Marx is another performer who communicates through the signifying surface of the body, but unlike the Lewis figure, he does so as an active rebellion against the regime of conventional speech. The difference between the two performers can be illustrated with representative gags from their films. The Marx Brothers' political satire *Duck Soup* (1933) features a scene in which Rufus T. Firefly (Groucho Marx), president of Freedonia, asks Brownie (Harpo) for his address. Harpo pulls open his shirt to reveal the picture of a dog kennel tattooed on his chest; as Groucho looks at the kennel a real dog's head comes out of it and barks. This gag signals Harpo's liberation from the constraints of everyday corporeality, identifying his body as a site for magical transformations. We know the surrealistic effects of this cartoon body are fully under his command because of the exhibitionist glee with which he flaunts the kennel and its inhabitant.

Whereas Harpo's controlling display of the magical body surprises and overpowers his audience (Groucho), Lewis's gags deny such authority to the misfit figure he impersonates. Harpo Marx is a metteur-en-scène of the disruptive body, but Lewis parades a spectacle of the body in disruption, a body that is othered from the self. A good example is the scene from *Sailor Beware* in which Lewis's hypochondriac weakling Melvyn Jones is forced to provide a sample of his blood for a medical test. Navy medics repeatedly puncture his body with their syringes but draw only water from him (he has already donated a pint to the blood bank). The sequence concludes with two gags: first, Melvyn drinks a glass of water and the liquid spurts out through the holes in his arms;[22] second, he faints when he sees a sailor enter the room carrying a power drill. Melvyn is as surprised as the medics when the water sprinkles from him, and his fear that the navy intends to subject him to the drill further illustrates a lack of reasonable awareness of the body he occupies.[23]

The self-directed films articulate the comic spectacle of the unruly body in a far less straightforward manner because Lewis applies to the "body" of the film itself the techniques developed for his performance. Like Frank Tashlin, he favored an episodic and digressive storytelling method that rejects the economy of classical Hollywood narrative.[24] As Jonathan Rosenbaum (1973) describes it, "The cavalier attitude often conveyed in a Tashlin film was that the director might interject whatever he wanted, at any given moment, for whatever reason: a rock number, a fantasy interlude, an editorial aside, a change in the size of the screen, an abrupt shift in the soundtrack. Such a capacity to bounce about a narrative at will was undoubtedly the principal lesson that Godard learned from Tashlin; and one could say that, *mutatis mutandis,* Lewis has benefited from the same instruction" (4).[25] But the Tashlin and Lewis films differ significantly in the uses to which they put such narrative fragmentation. Although *Variety* described *Rock-a-Bye-Baby* as "a series of situations, rather than a substantial story" ("*Rock-a-Bye Baby*," 4 June 1958), these situations nevertheless riff continually off the story of Clayton Poole's search for a meaningful identity. The narrative may proceed more through juxtapositions than linear development, but it retains its importance as a structural backbone.

By contrast Lewis's films operate, in Raymond Durgnat's (1969) terms, as "experiments in plotlessness" in which "the storyline lapses, or disappears, to liberate the gag, which, in turn, becomes rococo, in the sense of a fanciful lingering over offbeat detail" (238, 235). Just as Lewis's reactions as an actor are so over-elaborated that they outstrip the motivating context of the gag, so too his directorial performance persistently foregrounds structural "inarticulacy." As Scott Bukatman (1988) observes, "The carefully delineated narrative situations and conflicts which constitute the logic of the syntagmatic chain inevitably fall victim to a degeneration into a series of isolated sketches unrelated to the main narrative. The discursive operations of these films are dominated by digression and repetition, rather than by causal logic and narrative closure" (197). The films Lewis directed go beyond the *dislocations* familiar from Tashlin, exhibiting strategies of *deformation* that deny both narrative processes and the procedures of gag making their conventional structures and articulations.

Whereas American critics such as Leonard Maltin regard Lewis as failing to provide the conventional pleasures of gag-based comedy, French critics discern in Lewis's work an aesthetic agenda that allies him with the formal experimentation of the avant-garde. In 1970 Jean-Pierre Coursodon wrote that "underneath the clown's makeup there lay, well concealed, not a broken heart — although that is a possibility too — but a sturdy comic mind, a long-frustrated master of film form. . . . As we watch his films we are not reminded of Chaplin or Keaton or any other director-comedian but rather of a [Robert] Bresson (dedramatization, ellipses) or a Godard (filmic fiction redefined through its own destruction). Like today's most advanced film makers, Lewis questions the traditional relationship of audience to film" (Coursodon 1983, 189–90).[26] As a director-performer Lewis repeatedly diverts gags from their sign-posted pathways, luring them down strange byways of wonder and abasement. A common tendency is to lock the gag within an interminable cycle of repetition through which forward motion is frustrated; examples include the hatbox episode from *The Bellboy* and the scene in which Lewis dispenses jelly beans in *The Errand Boy* (both of which are discussed below). Such gag sequences refuse to build to satisfying conclusions, either lacking a conventional payoff climax or finishing in an expressly deflationary mode.[27]

Coursodon (1983) suggests that Lewis specializes in "eluded" or "eliminated" gags that provide not the expected mechanism of disruption/reordering but a process of deformation through which, paradoxically, the gag is itself dissipated and gagged. "These fascinating films are not always very funny," he remarks. "But their originality lies precisely in the fact that, while nominally slapstick comedies, they so transcend categories that laughter in their case ceases to be the test of success or failure" (197, 190). Raymond Durgnat (1969) makes a similar point in his appreciative account of *The Ladies' Man:* "The lapses in, or disappearance of storyline, create a strange osmosis between gag and build-up. . . . But also the absence of continuous dramatic thread piles a special intensity of audience attention on to a gag, and on to its build-up, which permit more so-phisticated forms. . . . What's very funny is that we catch ourselves unsure whether or not they're funny. . . . There's a kind of 'Tickle me or am I dream-ing?' vacillation" (236-37). Claude-Jean Philippe asserts that these comic defor-mations are so extensive that "to be entirely logical with himself, Lewis should eliminate gags from his comedy. That's what he's already done in part. Since *The Patsy,* he has constructed his gags in utter disdain for effectiveness. He barely sketches in the gags or, quite the contrary, he prolongs them, dilates them in di-luting them. Laughter gives way to the lyricism of derision" (Polan 1984a, 46).

The comic process is impelled by the disruption of rules, procedures, and dis-cursive registers, but Lewis's gags frequently take as their raw material the forms through which this process customarily operates. As Coursodon, Durgnat, and Philippe imply, the result is a strange variety of "second order" gagging that rearticulates recognizable gags or gag situations to construct "meta-gags" that are concerned with their own operational procedures. Coursodon (1983) discusses a notable example: "In *The Errand Boy,* Lewis has a routine on a ladder with a huge glass jar which, against all expectations, he never drops. The scene is a varia-tion on an old joke: in a candy store, one kid after another asks for a penny's worth of [jelly beans]; after each purchase, the storekeeper returns the jar to its top shelf, only to have to take it down again for the next kid in line. The audi-ence knows exactly how the routine is supposed to unfold. The only surprise lies in the absence of a punch line, either verbal or visual. Nothing happens, and *that,* the Lewis fans argue, is the gag, as who needs to be told—or shown—what one already knows" (197).[28]

The deformation of the gag finds its most symptomatic articulation when Lewis's body serves as its primary vehicle. A characteristic example occurs near the beginning of *The Patsy.* The entourage of recently deceased star comedian Wally Brandford hit upon the idea of training "some nobody" to take his place. Lewis's bellboy Stanley Belt then bursts into the hotel room, bearing a tray of drinks. Subjected to intensive scrutiny from the Brandford group, Stanley is seized by a fit of stuttering inarticulacy: "The bellboy . . . I . . . um . . . cr—er. The—we—ye—say. Who? Ahm. I mean. . . . See, when I—er. . . . I had it-m-all my clothes . . . were *wet.* So I changed my clothes because when I. . . . That's why I was *long.* Should I pu-pu . . . or not? Just stand? I'll close the door." Squirming in agonized embarrassment, Stanley drops the tray and then crouches to clear up the mess. The ostensible point of the scene is that the inept bellboy is the inverse of Wally Brandford's slick professionalism. But this point is made as soon as Stanley appears, and as the sequence continues it produces a fixation upon the spectacle of maladjustment and discomfort. With painful slowness, the film cuts between long shots of the black-clad Brandford retinue, who remain transfixed at the sight of the incompetent intruder, and closer views of Stanley as he withers beneath the authority of their gaze.

Such masochistic orgies of abasement and abjection proliferate in the self-directed films, pinpointing Lewis's difference from a well-oiled gag comedian such as Bob Hope, whose controlled wisecracks operate as distancing commentaries upon the cowardice and ineptitude he renders. Addressed directly to the audience/camera, Hope's verbal gags establish the supremacy the ego by differentiating performer from character, and mind from body. When the Lewis figure faces an intimidating situation, however, he generates a disconcerting spectacle of linguistic breakdown. Hope is able to overcome the intimidating situation quickly and efficiently, but the Lewis figure seems *branded* by it, his fits of stuttering, stammering, and physical contortion signifying the loss of control over body and language. Lewis's performance disconnects the mouth from the mind, transforming the speech act into an expressive vehicle for the unruly body. This is all the more excruciating for the spectator when, as in *The Patsy,* the situation is not inherently threatening.

Lewis's comedy is remarkable, then, for the way that it mines the riches of embarrassment. As Steve Shaviro (1993) considers in his book *The Cinematic Body,* scenes such as Stanley Belt's first appearance in *The Patsy* replace the cathartic structure expected from physical comedy with the discomfiting presentation of a body writhing in subjugation (120).[29] Whereas anarchistic comedians such as the Marx Brothers provoke disorder by actively rebelling against rules, norms, and institutional constriction, the Lewisian misfit generates chaos because he is an unconscious anarchist who "is not seeking to singularize himself, not trying to legitimate his own deviant pleasures; his only wish is to coincide with what others define as 'normal'" (110).[30] Through chain-reactions of unraveling detonated by his drive to be what others demand of him, the Lewis figure loses control over his voice, his body, and his relationship to the outside world (111).[31] He is not the only one to suffer the consequences of such excessive zeal, however. As a sequence from *The Bellboy* illustrates, the disorderly intensity of the Lewisian misfit's hyperconformist desire also destabilizes the logistics of hegemonic power.

Bob the bell captain wants bellboy Stanley (Lewis) to fetch him a hat box that rests on a steamer trunk across the lobby. Before Bob can finish his request ("Stanley, you see that steamer trunk over—get me—"), the bellboy has bolted over to the heavy trunk and is manhandling it across the floor to the reception desk. Bob chastises him and Stanley then pushes the trunk back across the lobby; he eventually returns, exhausted, with the hat box. The bellboy's spectacularly misdirected energy so hypnotizes Bob that it renders him immobile. Through most of the scene the camera remains behind and to one side of the bell captain, registering his frozen passivity as Lewis scampers frantically from foreground to background and back again. Bob's outstretched arm points toward the luggage, a commanding gesture that has been reduced to a limp signifier of both his own disempowerment and the ineffectualness of any attempt to impose authority upon Stanley. The bellboy's Pavlovian dash for the steamer trunk demonstrates that he is so locked within his slavish compulsion that in a very real sense the actual authority he serves is stripped of relevance. Robbed of his power to direct Stanley's subjection, Bob is himself interrupted and made impotent.[32] This sequence illustrates a key feature of Lewis's self-directed films, which Shaviro (1993) describes as "a movement that is very different from that of carnivalesque transgression, [in which] order collapses as a result of being fulfilled even to excess" (110–11).

In his attention to the dynamics of domination and subjugation Shaviro identifies a crucial feature of Lewis's self-directed comedy. But although he usefully moves the debate beyond the formalist concerns of earlier critics such as Coursodon and Durgnat, the predominant focus on Lewis's protagonists disregards the complex currents that flow among director, performer, and character within the Lewisian text. The Idiot/Kid must contend not only with external authorities but also with the imperious power of the filmmaker/enunciator who asserts sovereignty over him, both within and outside the films. Moreover, the forms of abjection and abasement discussed by Shaviro may be a distinctive feature of the self-directed films but they do not typify all of Lewis's work. The comedy of Martin and Lewis, especially on the *Colgate Comedy Hour,* betrays an insurrectionist agenda that operates more clearly within the conventional parameters of carnivalesque transgression. Not only do the two men repeatedly assault conformist protocols governing identity, gender, and same-sex relations but—by contrast with the convoluted process of self-definition that marks the totalizing projects—Lewis's very slippage of identity tends to be "presented in a joyous and liberating expression" (Bukatman 1988, 204). The auteurist films reveal substantial changes in the meaning and "direction" of Lewis's self-reflexive comedy, a topic that the next chapter will explore further.

A BIG NIGHT IN HOLLYWOOD

THE SELF-DIRECTED FILMS

This is Hollywood—land of the real and the unreal. The unreal are the actors. And the reel is nothing more than a thing to put film on. . . . This is a town where dedicated people spend their every working hour applying their varied talents to the making of a product, the only purpose of which is to take you away from the harsh realities of life into the wondrous land of make-believe.

—Voice-over in *The Errand Boy*

Taking over the directorial reins after twelve years as a movie star, Lewis made a series of strikingly distinctive Hollywood comedies. The five films he directed between 1960 and 1964—*The Bellboy, The Ladies' Man, The Errand Boy, The Nutty Professor,* and *The Patsy*—provided a glorious and audacious culmination to his adventures in the land of the reel. These films engage playfully and polemically with the values of the entertainment business, and with the intricacies of stardom, comedy, and the phenomenon of "Jerry Lewis" itself. To highlight the progression of a self-directed project that climaxes with *The Patsy,* the most complexly realized of Lewis's cinematic dissertations, this chapter examines these films in sequence. Although Lewis continued to impersonate a well-meaning bumbler onscreen, he simultaneously flaunted his ambitions and accomplishments as a filmmaker. While proselytizing for an ethical entertainment that "comes from the heart," these movies dazzle with their formal experimentation, their extrafictional and self-referential ruptures, their markedly eccentric second-order gags. It becomes increasingly less easy to reconcile such contradictions as Lewis moves from the carefree gaming of *The Bellboy* to the agonies of embarrassment expressed through *The Patsy.*

The unraveling that was a hallmark of Lewis's performance also typifies the films he directed. These multiply schismatic texts dismantle the regulated dialectic that conventionally organizes the Hollywood comedian comedy. Instead of focusing on conflicts between the eccentric comic performer and the social machineries of identity, gender, and narrative, they grapple with the dilemmas "Jerry Lewis" faces as both victim to and manipulator of his fame. The Lewis figure is generally a subservient laborer (a bellboy, a domestic, an errand boy, a browbeaten chemistry professor) whose traumas interconnect repeatedly with the narrative of Lewis's own rise in status from hireling to creator. With his newly attained power as a cinematic author Lewis could proclaim his liberation from the subordination he had experienced in Hollywood—as an employee, as an economic and signifying *commodity.* But although they celebrate his ascension from product to producer, these films delineate "Jerry Lewis" not as a coherent and autonomous self but as an atomized subject. Within the carnivalesque autobiography of the Lewisian text, identity is framed as a ceaseless play of signifiers—a vertiginous maelstrom of publicly circulated discourses, representations, and self-imaginings.

BOY IN A UNIFORM

Lewis's first film as a director opens with a teasing declaration of intent. In a pre-credits sequence Jack Emulsion (Jack Kruschen), fictitious production chief of Paramount Pictures, addresses the following warning to the camera:

The motion picture you are about to see isn't the run-of-the-mill film fare that has been presented to the movie-going public of late. [Walks over to a sketch of a man and woman kissing.] Now, it's quite easy making this type of picture—filled with love, emotion and tears. [Turns over other sketches.] And, of course, we could easily make the space, violence and horror films that are enjoyed by many peoples of the world. But we chose to make what you're about to see. A film based on fun. And it's just a little different—insofar as there is no story, and no plot. . . . It is actually a series of silly sequences. Or, you might say, it is a visual diary of a few weeks in the life of a real nut. [Laughs hysterically.] It's real silly. Oh, put it on! Show it to them.

As Christian Zimmer (1962) argues, the pleasurability of Lewis's debut derives from the way it invites "abandon to the delights of absolute arbitrariness" (4). Discarding the narrative formalization characteristic of Hollywood comedian comedy since the late 1930s,[1] the film presents a series of loosely connected blackout sketches that show Stanley the bellboy (Lewis) disrupting the orderly regimen of the luxurious Hotel Fontainebleau.[2] Clearly influenced by the modular gag-based organization of early slapstick comedy, Lewis pays homage to the silent clowns by centering the film on a character who, until the final scene, communicates exclusively through mime.[3] Bill Richmond also makes several appearances as a similarly voiceless impersonation of Stan Laurel.[4]

Jettisoning the structural imperatives of classical Hollywood narrative, *The Bellboy* achieves a free-form style that resembles the modernist European art films of the late 1950s and 1960s: J. Hoberman (1993), for example, describes it as Lewis's "*La Dolce Vita,* his *L'Avventura,* his *Last Year at Marienbad*" (111). Instead of operating from a tightly plotted continuity script Lewis emulated Chaplin by devising scenes for the film as the shooting progressed (Levy 1996a, 247).[5] The production's geographical distance from Los Angeles also guaranteed that Lewis faced minimal interference from the studio, enabling him to reprise the freewheeling atmosphere of the Garron movies (ibid.). Even so, *The Bellboy* is more than a random collection of comic episodes because it is unified by a central theme that it riffs off in various ways. Lewis claims in his autobiography that he was first attracted him to the project by "the vision of a bellboy, the entire role played in pantomime, the character a symbol of protest against people who regard bellboys, elevator operators and, indeed, all other uniformed workers as faceless dummies" (Lewis and Gluck 1982, 225–26).

From the Martin and Lewis period onward Lewis's films frequently cast him in the socially subjugated role of "an unskilled laborer and/or a naive consumer in the American service economy" (Shaviro 1993, 119). The very titles of *The Caddy, The Stooge,* and *The Delicate Delinquent* identify the Lewis figure generically, as a comic type rather than an individual. *The Bellboy* similarly locates Stanley as a servile *Untermensch,* a point made explicitly by Walter Winchell's voice-over narration during the montage sequence that follows the Jack Emulsion scene. As the film presents a series of touristic views of Miami, Winchell's voice intones, "Miami Beach . . . is just waking up, rubbing the sand out of its palms, ready for another 'let's be pretty for the tourists' day. A day that couldn't ever get started without the people who provide the services that are required in order that the visitor is satisfied. The people who serve are the real backbone. The people who serve, and work, in order that you might pay—that is, play." The bellboys differ from the other hotel staff because, Winchell suggests, they have no "real direction." They are all-purpose dogsbodies who must provide service "above and beyond the call of duty."

The aimlessness of Stanley's labor is mirrored by the film's episodic structure, which charts the range of menial tasks he is called upon to perform: delivering messages, manning the reception desk, fetching luggage, and walking dogs.[6] Like the other self-directed films, *The Bellboy* explores "the direct consequence of subordination: of being assigned a low position in the social hierarchy and being compelled to take orders" (Shaviro 1993, 108). The nearest thing to a sustained plot line emerges when the bellboys take strike action to protest against the management's attempt to exert control over their private lives. During one of his military-style addresses to the parade of bellboys Bob the bell captain (Bob Clayton) tells them, "What you do *during* working hours is *our* business. And what you do after working hours is *our* business." The hotel's manager, Mr. Novak (Alex Garry), instructs Bob to ensure that at all times the bellboys conduct themselves in a manner befitting a man wearing the Fontainebleau uniform. As employees of the hotel the bellboys are expected to relinquish their rights as free agents. The film's final scene renders Stanley's voicelessness an explicit signifier of his lack of social power. Novak calls him into his office because he mistakenly assumes that Stanley has instigated the industrial action. Frustrated when his accusations meet with no response, the manager snaps, "How is it we never heard you talk before?" Stanley replies, "Because no-one ever asked me."[7]

Besides playing Stanley, Lewis also takes another, far more personal role in *The Bellboy.* In one of the autobiographical interventions that would crop up with increasing frequency in Lewis's films, he appears as the Hollywood celebrity "Jerry Lewis"—a special guest shot credited to "Joe Levitch"! When "Jerry Lewis" arrives at the Fontainebleau, twenty-seven people clad in sunglasses step out of the limousine ahead of him. The faceless retinue follows wherever he goes, prompting him to repeated shrieks of "Hold it!" in a vain attempt to keep them at bay. Just as nobody wants to hear what Stanley has to say, no one actually listens to "Jerry Lewis": every word he utters is greeted with raucous laughter, no matter how serious the intent. This Pirandellian cameo suggests that, unlike Stanley, Jerry Lewis can never rid himself of the uniform of service. He is fated to remain a prisoner of the public visibility his stardom has purchased.

THE VERY FANTASY

Lewis's second film cost more than $3.4 million, more than three times the budget of *The Bellboy* (Levy 1996a, 266). Just as Orson Welles was able to run wild and free with RKO's studio facilities for the production of *Citizen Kane* (1941), *The Ladies' Man* allowed Lewis an opportunity to experiment with the amenities of high-resource filmmaking, and he came up with a cinematic show-case that, in its own way, rivals Welles's film in terms of ambition and playful-ness. *The Ladies' Man* is a lavishly orchestrated feast of color and movement that celebrates the magical artifice of studio production.[8] Most of the film was shot on a massive set, the largest ever constructed at Paramount, which is lovingly explored through elaborate crane shots and long, fluid takes.[9] The set depicts the interior of a boarding home for actresses, models, and musicians run by the ma-tronly Helen Wellenmellen (Helen Traubel). For the Lewis figure, Herbert H. Heebert, the Wellenmellen house operates as a realm of strangeness and won-der that permits him to discover new possibilities for creative expression. More-over, as Michael Stern (1975) suggests, Herbert's encounter with this imagina-tive space reads like a metaphorical commentary upon Lewis's own adventures in the movie factory: "*The Ladies' Man* occurs clearly on a Hollywood set. Were this a populist film, we would expect to find in the cross-sectioned set a repre-sentative sample of humanity. But this cross section is uniquely 'Lewisian' in its being a glossy, plastic house full of aspiring performers. . . . Herbert Heebert compulsively remains on this set with these Hollywood people. . . . He is, in short, a prisoner of his own fascination with this extraordinary make-believe world" (7).

Whereas *The Bellboy* dispenses with a narrative pretext from the start, *The Ladies' Man* initiates a clearly signaled story of masculine crisis that it subse-quently dissipates. The film's opening sequence recalls the hosepipe scene in *Rock-a-Bye Baby* (the placidity of an archetypal American small town is demol-ished through a series of cumulative disruptions), but in this instance the havoc wreaked in the streets of Milltown is not instigated by the Lewis figure. Con-trary to expectations, Herbert starts out on a trajectory of achievement and con-formity. Lauded as the boy most likely to succeed, Herbert rushes from the graduation ceremony at Milltown Junior College to meet Faith, his childhood sweetheart and future bride. He finds her sitting alone in the park and stops to peer at her through the bushes. But as he gazes on, savoring what lies ahead, a very tall young man approaches Faith and kisses her passionately. Overwhelmed, Herbert collapses to the floor and writhes in a grotesquely inflated spasm of agonized heartbreak. Retreating from this primal scene of emotional treachery, he vows to his mother (also played by Lewis) that he will remain a bachelor forever because he has lost all faith (!) in women. A traumatized Herbert then leaves Milltown to seek his fortune in Hollywood.

Although the stage seems set for a comic tale that will trace Herbert's regaining of faith in women and in himself, the film allows this narrative design to fragment and disperse once Mrs. Wellenmellen employs him as a houseboy. *Variety* objected: "Primarily the plot is little more than a limp excuse for a series of anything-goes slapstick sequences and sight gags punctuated by an occasional song or dance, an occasional romantic interlude, and a lethal dose of the star's homely philosophy. Lewis will try anything for a laugh" (*"The Ladies' Man,"* 7 June 1961). Many of these episodes do not provoke laughter so much as they excite a sense of amazement. In one sequence, for example, Herbert is instructed to dust a display case containing mounted butterflies. As he opens the case to take a closer look, the butterflies escape. At Herbert's whistle, however, the creatures fly back into position as rapidly as they had left. Numerous scenes in the film function in a similar surreal manner, exploiting the fantastical effects that are possible with cinema.

Within the stylized Wellenmellen world Herbert is able to liberate himself from the conformist protocols of gender and desire. Looking for work in Hollywood, he is besieged by attractive women with immediate designs upon him. Herbert accepts employment in the Wellenmellen house because he believes it to be free of sexual danger, but on awakening the next morning he realizes that he is the only male amid a multitude of young women: a scenario that recalls the lascivious fantasies of erotic plenty found in such contemporary playboy comedies as *Pillow Talk* (1959), *Under the Yum Yum Tree* (1963), *What's New Pussycat?* (1965), and *Boeing Boeing* (1965). Beholding the pulchritudinous ranks assembled in the dining room, Herbert is overwhelmed with horror, and he races back to the security of his room.[10] After the hysteria subsides he gradually comes to appreciate that this house of women makes it possible for him to escape the oppressive demands of conventional heterosexuality.

Joanna Rapf (1993) claims Lewis as an "involuntary feminist" because "far from presenting idealized masculine images, Lewis and other male comics often present parodies of such images; in this light they may be seen as critiquing the patriarchy, not exalting it" (195). Rapf discusses two scenes from *The Ladies' Man* that are explicitly constructed as deflations of tough masculinity. In the first William C. Gainsborough (Buddy Lester), a sharply dressed macho bully, visits the house to see his girlfriend and reduces Herbert to "a victimized state of inarticulate stammering drivel" (ibid.). Herbert reverses his subordination when he accidentally sits on the hat Gainsborough fetishizes as a phallic prop; as the hat is crushed, so too is the tough guy's masculine self-confidence. As Herbert nervously fusses about him, trying to squish the hat into some semblance of its former shape, Gainsborough disintegrates until he resembles "a whimpering female" (ibid., 196). The sequence concludes with a gag that exposes the self-contained masculine ideal as little more than a dress code: Herbert pulls on a loose thread from Gainsborough's suit and further unravels the fabric of his manhood.

The second scene features another well-tailored man's man, the former dancer and Hollywood gangster actor George Raft (who also makes a guest appearance in *The Patsy*). Encountering Raft in the lobby, Herbert refuses to believe that he is actually the famous movie star, so he asks him to reprise his coin-tossing routine from the 1932 gangster film *Scarface*.[11] Raft fumbles the demonstration by dropping the coin, and then, seeking to quell Herbert's mockery with a display of his famous dancing skills, puts a record on the phonograph and leads Herbert into a sultry, spotlit tango around the lobby. Although Herbert is forced to take the female role, the scene nonetheless parodies Raft's macho image by showing him dancing intimately with another man. Herbert not only sabotages and compromises the phallic narcissism of the two tough guys, subjecting them to a process of "feminization," but also circulates through the film as a locus of gender confusion — as a ladies' man (sensitive, domesticated) who refuses to be a "lady's man." The film's paradoxical title simultaneously invokes an image of self-assured heterosexual masculinity and yokes together conventionally opposed gender codifications — as do the similarly oxymoronic *Delicate Delinquent, Geisha Boy,* and *Cinderfella* (Rapf 1993).[12]

When Herbert first enters the Wellenmellen house — invited by a sign that reads "Young Bachelor Wanted" — he is so relieved that Katie (Kathleen Freeman) the housekeeper is not a glamorous manhunter that he leaps into her sheltering arms.[13] The film persistently evokes the concept of the mother as a means of differentiating Herbert's trajectory from the masculine regime of Oedipal narrative. Whenever things get too hot to handle, he shrieks "Maaaaaa!" and rushes from the scene. Like Katie, Mrs. Wellenmellen is a protective maternal force who takes Herbert to her heart no matter how much damage he causes through his earnest but misguided efforts to please. Within the maternalized Wellenmellen realm the nubile, often scantily clad ladies serve Herbert not as objects of heterosexual desire but as part of the texture of surreal delights. Fay, the aspiring but self-doubting actress with whom Herbert builds his closest relationship, convinces the other Wellenmellen girls to respond to Herbert as a "human being," that is, not as a *man*. All he wants, she tells them, is to be "really needed." "We need you because you're a nice person," she assures Herbert. "And nice persons are needed everywhere." In *Cinderfella* Lewis's downtrodden servant boy yearns to be accepted by the world for his humanity rather than his social status (as a "person" rather than a "people"). In *The Ladies' Man* being a "nice person" essentially requires the transcendence of heterosexual desire — and in his wish to be "honestly needed," Herbert longs for a relationship with women that eschews sexual claims.

Fay may a supportive woman who helps Herbert to exorcise the memory of the faithlessly sexual Faith, but the film rejects the option of replacing sexual betrayal with romantic union. *The Ladies' Man* reverses the Oedipal narrative's drive toward an ordered, stable, and differentiated regime of sexual identity. Herbert may start out at the point of entry into adulthood and marriage, but by the end he has become an eternal child with an idealized multiplicity of surrogate mothers. After striking out from the small town to find his destiny he is detoured from the traditional avenues of success and adventure that lead to the consolidation of manhood. And he ultimately finds his place within a stylized fantasy realm in which women are transformed from bearers of sexual promise into (non-*Playboy*) playmates. Within this pre-Oedipal paradise of maternal plenitude, a world in which men are unmanned, Herbert can regress without complication. As the scenes with the two tough guys make plain, Lewis's film rewrites the phallic regime of identity in favor of a polymorphic fluidity. The film's progressive dismantling of narrative structure, and of the procedures of acculturation it symbolizes and sustains, mirrors the dispersal of the Oedipal paradigm of sexuality and identity. Not only does *The Ladies' Man* unfold as a succession of varied routines, magic tricks, sketches, and playful non sequiturs, but it is also marked by constant digressions into the imaginative domain of fantasy. Joanna Rapf (1993) argues that there is a strong link between Lewis's "involuntary feminism" and an "involuntary surrealism" because the devices that create sexual ambiguity "are techniques that disorient us, destroying the illusion of reality that film so persistently evokes. . . . True to surrealist tenets, what Lewis gives us is inner reality, the world of dreams, the world of imagination, the world that throws a wet rag in the face of culturally determined norms and expectations" (197, 199).

The most striking surrealistic sequence in the film details Herbert's visit to the room of Miss Cartilidge (Sylvia Lewis), which exists as a segregated zone of excess and sexual danger within the pre-Oedipal playhouse. Katie warns Herbert several times that he must never enter this room, but curiosity eventually gets the better of him and he sneaks in to take a look. Everything inside the massive chamber — the bed, the walls, the floor, the furnishings, the flowers — is a radiant white, except for the extraordinary spectacle of Miss Cartilidge herself. Clad in a black sweater, pencil skirt, and high heels, she hangs batlike from the ceiling, her face a white-painted mask, her mouth a gash of scarlet lipstick. She descends to the floor with a black whip in her hands, and Herbert withdraws silently. As he does so a white curtain raises magically to the ceiling, opening onto another room with walls painted like the sky. The camera follows Miss Cartilidge as she walks over to a phonograph and puts on a record. When Herbert reenters the shot a slick gray suit has replaced his casual clothing, and Miss Cartilidge's skirt has also vanished. All of a sudden Harry James and his band appear in the sky room and blast into a brassy jazz arrangement as Miss Cartilidge strides rhythmically toward Herbert, to lead him into a strange dance modeled on the Gene Kelly and Cyd Charisse ballet from in *Singin' in the Rain* (1952).[14] Herbert attempts to steal away while Miss Cartilidge admires James's trumpet playing, but he finds her waiting for him outside when he reaches the doorway. Shortly afterward the music ends. Herbert's clothes revert back to normal. The band disappears. Miss Cartilidge moves silently to her veiled bed and lies down. Herbert exits the rooms, remarking, "Boy, what imagination can do for you."

Even though Lewis is not working with an awareness of the avant-garde surrealist tradition, the style of *The Ladies' Man* resembles surrealism in the way it destabilizes reality and narrative. Rapf (1993) points out that the Miss Cartilidge sequence offers "no cinematic clue that what we've witnessed is imagined. Indeed, the whole film is so surreal that it perfectly embodies what [Paul] Hammond sees as the crux of that aesthetic: 'the contamination of reality by the imaginary'" (200). As *Variety* noted in its review of *The Ladies' Man,* Lewis's comic fantasia is fed by a different tradition, a distinctively American style of absurdist comedy that was nurtured in vaudeville entertainment, silent slapstick, and, especially, the animated cartoon: "The odd characteristic of this picture, and of many of Lewis's pictures, is its close resemblance to the style of an animated cartoon. It can be found in the technique of absurd facial exaggeration, the repetition, the insane body gyrations, the incongruous relationships of sight and sound, the trick effects, the abundance and short duration of the scenes, the very fantasy of the thing" ("*The Ladies' Man,*" 7 June 1961).[15] Pregnant with signifying cues that can be activated to construct plural readings, the Miss Cartilidge sequence is far from a random collection of strange and meaningless events. The phonograph and dance echo the earlier scene with George Raft, and Herbert's failed attempt to leave the room recalls several moments where the Wellenmellen girls block his escape from the house. Such connections operate through an associational logic that resembles the Freudian dreamwork, a great influence upon the surrealist art movement.

The Ladies' Man ostentatiously proclaims Lewis's versatility and individuality as an auteur. Shawn Levy complains, however, that his directorial ambitions were beginning to have a deleterious effect on his performance:

Jerry the performer leaves a gaping hole in the center of the film that no amount of technical wizardry can fill. Jerry never for a moment looks the part of a juvenile; his body is thick (he has love handles and a potbelly), and he looks like he's grown out of his clothes. People keep calling him "kid," but it's a thin masquerade; he keeps yelling "Maaaaaaaa!" when he's afraid, but it sounds more like a generic squeal than the voice of someone who's recently left his mother's home. His voice won't find a consistent characterization; at times, it's deep or swishy or Jewish or plain. Herbert isn't the Kid, but he isn't anyone else, either. Jerry invents an idiosyncratic physical bit for him—his eyeglasses are forever misapplied on his face—but he doesn't create a character. In the middle of a thrilling, exotic film, the central role is woefully underrealized. (Levy 1996a, 269–70)

Levy repeatedly berates Lewis for the carelessness of his characterization, but to expect a psychologically consistent character role from a film so devoted to magical stylization seems misguided. Instead of subordinating himself to the part, Lewis renders Herbert a vehicle for the display of a multiplicity of identities. Joanna Rapf suggests that "through continual devices of self-referentiality, it is impossible to view the character with any sense of realism. Although he plays 'a kid,' he makes no effort to hide the fact that he is really Jerry Lewis. In *The Ladies' Man,* he continues to wear his wedding ring, constantly reminding us of the performer playing the part" (1993, 196). Moreover, the issue of role playing is explicitly signaled by the film's credits sequence, in which a series of glossy black and white stills—styled after the magazine *Look*—presents Lewis in a plurality of guises (unshaven bum, Roman Emperor, gladiator, medieval baron, Napoleon, Romeo, Samson, an Arab, a Russian).

REEL TIME

As *The Ladies' Man* suggests, Lewis invaded the dream factory and made the dreams his own through movies that explicitly resemble dreams in their disassembly of narrative coherence (Bukatman 1988, 197). Like the earlier self-directed films, *The Errand Boy* consists of a string of episodes in which the unruly Lewisian misfit collides with an orderly environment. In this instance, however, the process is especially fascinating because Lewis makes Hollywood itself the focus of the action. Filmed on the Paramount lot, *The Errand Boy* details the adventures of a movie-struck poster hanger, Morty P. Tashman (Lewis), who is hired by Paramutual Pictures Incorporated as an all-purpose gofer. For the most part, Morty's experiences within the factory of make-believe provide a grim contrast to Herbert's wondrous escapades in the Wellenmellen house.[16] *The Errand Boy* exposes the shabby machinations that lie behind the onscreen plenitude of Hollywood illusion. The movie studio is portrayed as a corporate regime ruled by the whims of a nepotistic elite, the Paramutual family, who control the filmmaking process through an intensive bureaucracy that administers to a segmented and alienated labor force.

As he wanders from scene to scene and from department to department, Morty Tashman collides repeatedly with the regimentation of the film factory. A monkey wrench thrown into the precisioned machinery of Hollywood production, Morty spreads disorder wherever he goes: he mixes together pages from separate scripts, he walks into scenes as they are being filmed, he throws a dubbing session into disarray. In one early episode Morty is herded onto the set of a quality picture under the control of a dictatorial European director. In a 1920s nightclub scene jazz-baby Miss Bubbles Rothschild performs a bouncy crowd-pleaser called "That's the Way." Unlike the other extras, Morty is unfamiliar with the routine and joins in spontaneously with the chorus—his loud, grating voice tossing out vo-de-oh-dohs in all the wrong places. Morty responds to the illusion of the scene, acting as if he really were in a nightclub rather than on a film set. When he eventually realizes that he is making a spectacle of himself, he stumbles away, embarrassed.

Morty's honest and intuitive response is out of place because mainstream filmmaking is presented as a business in which the individual must know and respect his delimited place. Morty's presence within the studio lacks a secure foundation because he has, unknowingly, been employed as a company spy to identify economic inefficiencies. The unsuspecting informer has a sinister double in the thoroughly institutionalized Dexter Sneak (Howard McNear), a corporate yes-man whose furious drive to mould himself to the demands of authority has led to the evaporation of a sense of self. He hovers frantically about studio head Tom Paramutual (Brian Donlevy), hanging on his every word, desirous of his every commanding gesture. Sneak's fawning inarticulacy serves as a parodically overstated warning about the consequences of overidentifying with the corporate order—he is the subordinated Lewisian misfit in extremis. Whereas Sneak clings with rabid overenthusiasm to his servile role within the company, Morty roams through the studio as a displaced person. Like Stanley the bellboy, his employment is characterized by its apparent aimlessness (or, rather, by a functionality he is unable to perceive).

In *The Errand Boy* the Lewisian Kid's capacity for disruption is counterbalanced by a blatantly sentimental attention to his sensitivity and worth. Morty discovers a costume storeroom where he finds refuge from the hostile studio environment. On his first visit he encounters a glove puppet, a Little Clown, with which he plays out a charming scene of make-believe — a closeup mime performance in which the clown makes its bed and lies down to sleep.[17] Visiting the storeroom a second time, Morty discovers another puppet, Magnolia the ostrich. But whereas Morty had himself manipulated the clown's movements, Magnolia is a truly magical entity who moves and speaks independently. Morty opens his heart to the ostrich to express the dreams and disappointments inspired by Hollywood: "I guess for as long as I can remember I always wanted to go to Hollywood and see the movie-stars. And the studios and all the peoples who made the pictures, and how they made 'em. And I guess it wasn't uncommon with me like with a lot of other guys my age that like movies. So I saved up some money, and one day I got on a bus. And here I was in Hollywood. So when I got here I realized I wasn't any closer to it than when I was in New Jersey. And, as you know, when you're far away from something and you can't get to it, that's not quite half as bad as when you're close to that something and you can't get to it — right?"

Through Magnolia the film delivers one of the fairytale homilies that pop up with increasing frequency in Lewis's solo work. In a lilting southern accent she tells Morty to have faith in the power of his own illusions: "Can you remember when you were a little boy, and your parents took you to a puppet show? How you think: 'why, they're almost live!' or 'they made me believe they're live!'? . . . Well, it isn't any different now — especially when you want to believe what you see and hear. So you see, Morty, you actually liked the Little Clown enough to take him at face value. You didn't stop to analyze him, you just liked what you saw, and you believed what you liked." The cutesy surrealism of the Magnolia scene pits the integrity of individual belief against the cynical manipulations of Hollywood's mass-produced dream making. Magnolia's sentimental oration is a self-conscious justification of Lewis's own endeavors as a filmmaker, a schematic apologia for his own worth and work. It is significant, for example, that Morty hails from New Jersey, Lewis's home state. Portraying Hollywood's old guard as a force that crushes intuition, individualism, and honesty, *The Errand Boy* propagandizes for a new order that is modeled closely upon Lewis's cinematic trajectory.

Following the Magnolia episode is a scene in which the studio throws a birthday party for its venerable star Anastasia Anastasia (Iris Adrian). Anastasia makes the mistake of asking Morty to open a bottle of champagne. In a reprise of the hosepipe sequence from *Rock-a-Bye Baby* Morty pops the cork and unleashes a powerful and seemingly unstoppable torrent of liquid that decimates the studio's orderly ritual of self-congratulation. When footage of the party is later projected in a studio screening room, a member of the audience describes Morty's actions as "the best comedy performance I've seen on the screen for years." Tom Paramutual is dumfounded, but a hot young method director (Robert Ivers) rallies to Morty's defense. Representing the voice of youth, Hollywood's new blood, the director delivers a lengthy monologue praising the expressive integrity of the errand boy's talent:

Yes, Mr. Paramutual . . . and just who are *you?* Just who are you, one of those "I've been making pictures for thirty years" kinda guys? That's not enough of a criterion for me. You could of been making those pictures wrong. Let me tell you something—and it might be wise for you to remember it. Anyone in the world would give anything to do a performance. Because . . . because performing is nothing more than a form of expression. But not everyone is capable of expressing themselves openly and . . . and freely. And therefore, only a few, only a very few are chosen, chosen to communicate and express for the millions that—that either can't, don't know how, or would never get the opportunity to do so. And those few that are chosen are called actors. But they're still people. I might add, a very special kind of people. Yes, Mr. Paramutual—that *was* a performance. And given by one who can express what he feels, whether it be dramatic or comic. Because he communicates. Yes, he communicates. And that's the vitally important substance that makes great stars. With this kid, Mr. Paramutual, you've not only got a potential great star and comedy find, you've got a goldmine.

The skepticism of the Paramutual boss soon gives way to an appreciation of Morty's box-office potential. The film cuts from the screening room to a scene in which the errand boy, now a major Hollywood star, rides through the studio lot in a huge open-top limousine. He spies a "kid" having difficulty pasting up a billboard poster that announces the appearance of Morty S. Tashman in the film *It Could Happen To You.* The erstwhile poster hanger climbs the ladder to teach the kid how to do the job properly, and they shake hands as Morty pulls down a banner carrying the words "The End." This conclusion serves as an answer to the mock-documentary sequence with which the film opens, where a hearty voice-over introduces the Hollywood setting with a series of typical images from the films it produces. These sample scenes—which depict Hollywood values of adventure, sex, suspense, violence, and romance—are subsequently debunked when *The Errand Boy* exposes the studio fabrications that have produced them. A cowboy actor rides an artificial horse because he is afraid of the real thing, a brutalized woman is in actuality played by screen heavy Mike Mazurki, the tender screen lovers are really a bickering and snarling married couple. The ending of *The Errand Boy* rejects Hollywood convention to assert its integrally Lewisian determination. It comes as no surprise, then, that Jerry Lewis also plays the kid who has taken Morty's old job.[18] The process will continue: Lewis will both reduplicate himself and reproduce Hollywood in his own image.

BE SOMEBODY, BE ANYBODY

The Nutty Professor (1963), Lewis's fourth self-directed film, marked a return to the lavish mise-en-scène of *The Ladies' Man*. But it also represented something of a departure from the earlier films because, as Jean-Pierre Coursodon (1983) notes, "In contrast to the episodic structure that had become the Lewis trademark, each sequence in *The Nutty Professor* performs a specific narrative function" (192). The most known, the most discussed, and the most acceptable of Lewis's films, *The Nutty Professor* is readily acknowledged as his "masterpiece." Borrowing liberally from the dual-personality story of Dr. Jekyll and Mr. Hyde, the film presents two opposed Lewisian personae: the painfully introverted academic Julius Kelp and his chemically induced alter ego Buddy Love.

A chaotic Lewisian misfit, Kelp lacks a comfortable rapport with his own body and finds it impossible to assert himself in the face of authority. For example, when the dean, Dr. Warfield (Del Moore), reprimands him for causing an explosion, Kelp shrinks submissively into an extremely low armchair. For an agonizingly long time, and in virtual silence, the professor withers and deflates before the disapproving gaze of his superior. Kelp subsequently attempts to assert his professional authority in the classroom but is publicly humiliated by a burly football player, Warshevsky (Richard Kiel), who lifts him from the ground and bundles him into a cupboard. Kelp is rescued from the cupboard by Stella Purdy (Stella Stevens), the glamorous student whom he secretly adores. Stella tries to raise his spirits by disparaging Warshevsky as "a typical bully that loves picking on a small man," but instead of taking satisfaction from her words, the professor is impelled to sign up at a Vic Tanny gym in an effort to build up his body. Leafing through a magazine Stella leaves behind in the classroom, Kelp discovers a Charles Atlas–style advertisement for the gym that seems to speak directly to his imperiled manhood: "Why Be Bullied By the Bigger Guy? Be a Muscle Man *Yourself*."

Seduced by this fantasy of musculinity, Kelp embarks on an intensive training program.[19] The gym provides the setting for a series of gags that demonstrate his inability to conform to the prescriptions of muscular perfection. Kelp is so shortsighted that at the bowling alley he mistakes a group of white-clad by-standers for a set of pins — and bowls them over. The elaboration of the professor's physical ineptitude is capped by a cartoon-style gag in which his arms stretch down to the ground when he drops a heavy dumbbell. With the six-month exercise regimen producing no discernible improvement, Kelp turns to his mind for a solution. In a book entitled *Man, Muscles, What They Are, and How to Get Them,* he encounters the following advice: "A man's mind from childhood right through old age never stops growing, not in size or by measure but by constant learning and knowledge. On the other hand, man's body does stop at a precise point, that of completion in the structure of the anatomy. Yet, we have learned through chemistry, man can grow further with the aid of additional elements."

Inspired by these words, Kelp determines to draw upon his knowledge of chemistry to effect his metamorphosis from geek to superman. The transformation is handled like a scene from a horror film, with Kelp experiencing a series of grotesque changes in his hair, his teeth, and his physical posture. The film then cuts to a tracking shot that represents the point of view of the reconfigured professor as he walks through the street. As soon as he enters the Purple Pit nightspot, the music halts and everyone in the club turns around to stare at him. It is only then that the film allows a glimpse of Kelp's new persona: a reverse-angle zoom on Lewis reveals that he is not a physical monster but a handsome, self-possessed swinger in a dazzling blue suit. Whereas Julius Kelp disintegrates beneath the gaze of others, his alter ego — Buddy Love — solicits and dominates their admiring looks. Born of the professor's desire for social and sexual success, Love radiates a self-contained masculine cool. But although he possesses all the external features absent in Kelp, he has none of the latter's humanizing qualities. The film soon makes apparent the monstrous flip side to this image of idealized masculinity, suggesting that Buddy Love's hipster chic is little more than preening narcissism (Stella tags him a "rude, discourteous ego-maniac"). Buddy is so corrupted by his charisma that it is impossible for him to develop an open relationship with anyone.

Moreover, whereas Julius Kelp is continually intimidated by men with a physical or institutional advantage, Buddy Love wastes no time in taking the offensive (Camper 1971, 32), sadistically haranguing the barman of the Purple Pit and then punching a customer who tries to intervene. Although Stella is repelled by the emotional void at the core of Love's being, she is also captivated by his perfect body, his voice, his poise. She is affronted when this monster of self-absorption brusquely commands her to dance with him but nevertheless melts into submission when he croons a jazzy rendition of "That Old Black

Magic." As Dana Polan (1984a) suggests, the film itself shares Stella's dialectic of attraction-repulsion toward Kelp's alter ego: "Buddy Love, a Dean Martin-type figure, simultaneously encapsulates the hidden desires and dreams of the klutzy, chaos-causing Professor Julius Kelp *and* reveals a horrific dimension to those dreams—in the desperate machismo that drives Love on, making him a night-club hit but simultaneously alienating him from his fans on a personal level. Love's nightclub banter only inadequately conceals a self-doubt and anxiety that, for the film, is self-reflexively not only a comment on the Martin-Lewis team but also on the whole psychology and fate of the American popular performer" (334).

And, of course, "Jerry Lewis" is an especially suitable vehicle for this disser-tation on the perils of stardom. Polan follows many other critics in viewing Buddy Love as a satirical swipe at former partner Dean Martin, who was, simi-larly, a charismatic crooner, boozer, and womanizer. However, Lewis emphati-cally disputes this reading whenever he discusses the film: "A lot of people, then and now, think I patterned Buddy Love after Dean Martin. That's ludicrous—absolutely ludicrous. Buddy Love is a cruel monster, the ultimate bastard; he's a composite of all the hateful schmucks in the world. He's an unfeeling putz, and for people to think that's the way I feel about Dean shocks me. I've always loved Dean, and I know him better than just about anyone. He's a sweet, sensitive guy—the complete opposite of Buddy Love" (Neibaur and Okuda 1995, 171). Given that he chose to name the character *Buddy* Love, Lewis does seem more than a little disingenuous on this count. Even so, to fixate upon Love's superfi-cial resemblance to Martin is to delimit the compound significance he carries in this story of schismatic identity. As Michael Stern (1975) suggests, "The Buddy Love who emerges from the depths of Julius Kelp's personality is a complex fig-ure—partly Dean Martin, partly Jerry Lewis the ultimate nightclub personal-ity; a character invested with a confusing mixture of ambivalent feeling" (10).[20]

Shawn Levy (1996a) reads Buddy Love as a more direct expression of the anxieties propelling the real-life Jerry Lewis: "Jerry saw himself as a bright man with strong empathetic feelings who suffered slights in childhood and desper-ately wanted to be loved. Like Kelp, he transformed himself into a performer to receive affection and attention; like Kelp, he suffered nagging doubts about whether the public loved the real man or the mask. *The Nutty Professor* is, in ef-fect, a confessional about Jerry's neurotic compulsion to perform and the perils of succeeding in the public arena. It's not explicitly a showbusiness story . . . but it's Jerry's most meaningful statement about the heart of the entertainer: Kelp's climactic confession takes place, after all, on a stage" (293).[21] As an extreme in-carnation of Las Vegas Jerry, the slick show-biz star, Buddy Love serves as a warning against the lure of heartless success. Lewis repeatedly promotes a psychobiographical reading of the conflict between Kelp and Love, characterizing the latter as an inner demon he feared to let loose:

He's Buddy Love, infinitely for himself and disliking all other humans. I made him a glaringly destructive force, despicable to the core, as a balance against the loving professor. Creating the role had me in a sweat, especially when I saw images of Buddy Love creeping out from inside me onto the page. A crying horror!

It got even worse during the actual filming. I kept pushing the Buddy Love sequences to the end, procrastinating my ass off, dreading to see him come alive on the screen. I remember shooting the scene where Buddy squatted in a corner facing the laboratory like a terrified animal, feeling an inconceivable loneliness, oblivious to the camera and crew until, finally, I said "Cut!" (Lewis and Gluck 1982, 233)

Through the persona of Buddy Love, the gauche and repressed Kelp can experience the attention and command denied him in his own life: as Stern (1975) notes, Buddy is "every average guy's power trip, the ultimate Hollywood star" (9). With Love, every social encounter is translated into a "staged" moment of self-display. In the Purple Pit he seizes the spotlight with a series of snazzy and jazzy song performances that make it clear that he is concerned less with serving others than with dominating them. Having tasted the power he can wield over people as Buddy Love, Kelp becomes increasingly addicted to the guise and, at the same time, loses the ability to keep his two personalities distinct. Kelp's academic discourse is contaminated by hip Love-isms: he calls Stella "honey," and his voice shifts register halfway through the sentence "Carbon dioxide . . . *has always been a gas!*" Buddy Love also loses stability, generally at critical moments when is required to reveal something of the inner man: his voice changes back to Kelp's nasal twang, forcing him to make a quick escape.

The imposture unravels at the senior prom, an event both Kelp and Love are scheduled to attend. After dancing with Stella, Kelp disappears to take a dose of the potion. Taking the stage in a sparkling gold suit, Buddy Love sits down at the piano for a snappy vocal workout on "We've Got a World that Swings." He then tries to follow it with "That Old Black Magic," but Love's voice is hijacked by Kelp's stuttering, high-pitched whine. In front of a bewildered crowd, the cool swinger dissolves into the disorderly academic from which he sprang, and in an act of public confession Kelp apologizes for his deception. He tells the audience that he has learned his lesson: "I don't want to be something that I'm not. . . . You might as well like yourself. Just think about all the time you're gonna have to spend with you. If you don't think too much of yourself, how do you expect others to?"[22]

Michael Stern (1975) suggests that this scene of exposure and humiliation enables the intrusion into the film of a Lewisian persona that is distinguished from both Kelp and Love. It is a voice that is not embarrassed to "speak from the heart": "At this moment we are watching a film and seeing not 'some Jerry Lewis character' but, rather, a man—Jerry Lewis—talking directly to the audience in the cinema. This is as 'anti-Hollywood' a moment as one could find in a Hollywood film. The real Jerry Lewis bursts through his image to talk to the audience; and when he does so his words are simple, clear and ordinary. Lewis had broken the 'rules' by stepping out of the picture; creating a moment in each viewer's life when we are forced to confront Jerry Lewis—not Julius Kelp or Buddy Love—but Jerry Lewis" (9). To read this sentimental sermon as evidence of the real Jerry Lewis is as problematic as Levy's argument that the Lewis lurking behind the public mask is actually Buddy Love. The scene introduces yet one more Lewisian voice, a voice that, as Levy points out, is also framed within a performative context (as a speech from the stage). Although the film grants a degree of relative authority to this voice, it nevertheless remains only a single strand within the panoply of utterances that speaks the name Jerry Lewis.

It is significant that the film does not conclude with this monologue—and also that it refuses to end with an unequivocal rejection of Buddy Love. Stella visits Julius backstage after his shriving ordeal and assures him that "just being one person is more than enough for one human being to handle." She then proposes marriage, and they kiss. But this scene of heterosexual reconciliation is followed by an epilogue that undercuts the moral lesson delivered at the prom.[23] Julius's father, Elmer Kelp (Howard Shore), has taken a dose of the potion and been transformed from a henpecked squirt into a self-confident powerhouse who physically and verbally dominates his wife, Edwina (Elvira Allman). Bursting into the classroom, with Edwina in tow, Elmer offers to sell "Kelp's Cool Tonic" for a dollar a bottle. As the students clamor to purchase the wonder drug Stella drags the perturbed professor away. The film reveals, however, that two bottles of the potion are stuffed into the back pockets of her jeans—suggesting that Buddy Love will once more be called into service (Stern 1975, 10).[24]

This proliferation of resolving scenarios recalls the Martin and Lewis film *Jumping Jacks*. Whereas that film refuses a definitive ending to assert the preeminence of the male partnership, *The Nutty Professor* uses the same strategy to thwart a stabilization of identity. Despite the dangers posed by the Buddy Love persona, he is an integral component not just of Julius Kelp but also of "Jerry Lewis." As Stern considers, "Buddy is the entertainer that people love (and pay) to see, the kind of star upon which Hollywood has been built. . . . Buddy Love is part of Julius, as Julius is part of Buddy—and both facets of Jerry Lewis are far more inseparably one than Jekyll and Hyde or ego and alter ego" (1975, 10). *The Nutty Professor* not only "tackles the problem of Jerry Lewis's troublesome image" (ibid., 11) but also blocks the presentation of a unified and coherent selfhood by revealing a tantalizing multiplicity of Lewisian personae (Bukatman 1988, 201). The epilogue is of further interest for its qualification of the Lewisian dictum concerning the need to be recognized as a somebody. The placard Elmer displays when he makes his sales pitch hints at a new agenda: "Be Somebody . . . Be Anybody!"

SON OF BELLBOY

Lewis followed *The Nutty Professor* with *The Patsy,* the most sustained and polemical dissertation on his art and career.[25] The film deals explicitly, and sometimes savagely, with the values and practices of a corporate entertainment machine that regards individual talent as the least important component of show-biz success. After famed comedian Wally Brandford dies in a plane crash his backup team—press agent, writer, producer, director, secretary, and valet— decide to manufacture a successor. They propose to replace the singularity of the gifted individual with the pooled expertise of an executive committee, applying the specialized skills they learned from Brandford to fabricate a star who obeys their collective dictates.[26] The narrative premise of *The Patsy* combines a male reworking of the *Pygmalion* story with a show-biz variant of the *Frankenstein* creation myth—Brandford's staff assembling their star from the dismembered experiences inherited from the dead comedian. For these managerial minds, well versed in the business of stardom, Stanley Belt (Lewis) is an attractive proposition precisely because he offers such unpromising raw material. They expressly demand "some nobody" they can train and manipulate, a blank screen upon which they can project their carefully scripted designs. Stanley is a suitable candidate for this undertaking not only because of his personal deficiencies but also because, as a servant, he lacks social power. Throughout his instruction by the Brandford team, Stanley has no say in what he does or what is made of him. Chic Wyman (Everett Sloane), the leader of the team, announces, "This kid can and will be whatever we want him to be" and informs Stanley, "We know all we need to know, and all you need to find out is what we tell you." Within this corporate paradigm, the star is nothing but a designed personality whose distinguishing traits are the well-worn tricks of show-biz experts.

The processing of Stanley Belt begins with the transformation of his appearance: he is equipped with a slick haircut, a manicure, a pedicure, a shoe-shine, and a flash wardrobe that render him a dead ringer for Buddy Love. Following the makeover of his image, Stanley undergoes a crash course in voice training so he can record the teenage pop song that will first bring him to public attention. An exquisite parody of the mechanized chart music of the early 1960s, "I Lost my Heart in the Drive-in Movie" is an instant hit. But when Stanley performs the number on a TV show, *Teenage Dance Time,* he finds it impossible to comply with the orderly rhythm. The Brandford team strives assiduously to mold Stanley into an all-around entertainer, but their carefully plotted routines stand little chance against the eruptions of his unruly body. All the same, the fabrication of the superstar entertainer proceeds mercilessly. Publicity chief Harry Silver (Keenan Wynn) arranges a party to introduce Stanley to the Hollywood in crowd, but the erstwhile bellboy makes an extremely late appearance, compounding the felony by exploding into hysterical laughter when he sees the ornate umbrella hat sported by columnist Hedda Hopper. Hopper rallies to Stanley's defense and, in a speech echoing the monologue of *The Errand Boy*'s method director, she praises Silver for coming across as "someone who hasn't learned to be phony. He thought something, and he said it—which was real and honest. And now if you apply that to his performance, you've got a great success."

The Brandford team disregard Hopper's advice and drill Stanley relentlessly for a stand-up comedy act, a performance mode to which neither he nor Lewis are suited. Stanley is overwhelmed with panic when he meets a formidably unreceptive audience at the Copa Café. Stumbling onto the stage, he knocks the microphone off its stand and then proceeds to decimate the polished routines that have taught to him. He delivers his jokes in the wrong order, turns them inside out, and destroys them through his lack of timing. Instead of firing off a barrage of prepackaged verbal gags, Stanley presents a spectacle of maladjustment that is both characteristically Lewisian and uncommonly discomfiting. Undermined by his disorderly body, a body all too aware of the *pressure* of rules, Stanley's act disintegrates into a succession of gagged gags. The climax of the performance evokes the act that kick-started Lewis's career. Stanley produces a record player so that he can lip sync along to his song, but his nervousness prevents him from getting the machine to operate. He then decides to perform the song unaccompanied, with even more disastrous results. The extent to which this sequence cannibalizes and warps a familiar performance mode qualifies it as the most extended and self-reflexive example of comic deformation in Lewis's films. Simultaneously, the sequence offers both the gagging of a conventional process of gag delivery and also a persuasive representation of the character's pain.[27] It is difficult for either the club audience or the film spectator to accept this as "funny" in anything like a conventional sense.

After a further disastrous show at the Copa the Brandford team is finally persuaded to drop their misbegotten star. Stanley is notified of their decision by telegram, shortly before he is to take the stage for the *Ed Sullivan Show*. When the terror begins to subside, he determines to go ahead with the gig. To show his puppet-masters what he can achieve on his own he abandons the stand-up routine in favor of an elaborate sketch entitled "A Big Night in Hollywood," a sketch that both articulates Stanley's ideal of stardom and functions as an allegory of Lewis's own rise to power. He plays a movie-struck youth, like the characters Lewis portrayed in *Hollywood or Bust* and *The Errand Boy*, who is enraptured by the parade of stars attending a swank Hollywood premiere. The kid sees a pathway into the playground of fantasy when a bickering couple discards two one-hundred-dollar tickets. But there is a further obstruction to overcome: the doorman refuses to admit Stanley because the event requires formal attire. Out of his humble street clothes — and with the aid of a knife, a can of black paint and some fast-motion cinematography — the kid fashions a top hat, cane, black tie, and dress suit. Looking the part, he is able to strut jauntily into the theater.

As a revelation of Stanley's intuitive, untrained talent, the "Big Night" sequence is mighty peculiar. Jean-Pierre Coursodon complains that its incongruities interfere with the film's stress upon being true to oneself:

Another source of puzzlement — if we take the routine for what it is, *i.e.* a
performance — is that Stanley's pantomime is so polished, so perfectly timed and executed, whereas he had proved a complete flop at each preceding rehearsal and performance. Of course, this is the very point Lewis wants to make: Stanley becomes successful once he gets a chance to "be himself." But there is an essential difference between the unintentional funniness of Stanley the bellboy — a typical Jerry Lewis "idiot" with his hopeless clumsiness — and the highly professional, graceful funniness of the television routine. If Stanley were really to be "himself," he would never be able to perform such an act. The sequence is a tangle of ambiguities, obscurities, and inconsistencies that work as jamming devices to distort Lewis's modest message, just as they deactivate his comedy. (Coursodon 1983, 198)

The idiosyncrasies of the "Big Night" sketch become particularly apparent when it is compared with a scene from another film that deals with the subject of star making. The 1954 version of *A Star Is Born* casts Judy Garland as Esther Blodgett, a band singer who finds fame and heartbreak as a Hollywood star. Esther is discovered by the actor Norman Maine (James Mason) as she performs a soulful jazz rendition of "The Man that Got Away" in an after-hours nightclub. Richard Dyer (1991) points out that the scene marks a crucial moment in the authentification of Esther's "star quality" (138). Filmed in one long, continuous take, the scene captures the wholeness of Garland's performance and her "un-scripted" interaction with the band. Dyer comments: "The authenticity the number is after really has nothing to do with what Esther/Garland is singing about—it is the authenticity of her capacity to sing that is at stake. We must know that her star quality has nothing to do with recording techniques, with mechanical reproduction (even though what we are watching is perforce a recording), but is grounded in her own immediate (= not controlled), sponta-neous (= unpremeditated) and essential (= private) self. That guarantees that her stardom is not a con, because an authenticated individual is acting as the guar-antor of the truth of the discourse of her stardom" (ibid., 139).

Ostensibly, "A Big Night in Hollywood" has a similar rationale—to authen-ticate Stanley's talents as a comic performer—but whereas the scene from *A Star Is Born* obliterates the constructedness of the star image and star perfor-mance, the sequence from *The Patsy* fractures the processes of effacement. As Coursodon notes, the sketch is a carefully crafted, skillfully edited, painstaking scored, and assertively *filmic* presentation.[28] Instead of presenting a one-man show of laugh-grabbing integrity, it is an explicitly *constructed* representation that defines Stanley's talent through an all-pervasive *mediation*.[29]

As Coursodon points out, if Stanley were creating comedy spontaneously he would not come up with such a calculated and artificial routine. But Stanley is denied the opportunity to be himself because he is destined to play out his role as part of the discursive assemblage that comprises "Jerry Lewis." In "A Big Night in Hollywood," as in *The Errand Boy*, Lewis depicts himself as an eternal fan who gains admittance to the magical world of Hollywood. He may have to conform outwardly, but inside he retains the integrity of the Kid. Everything in the sketch—and ultimately within the film itself—attains its significance in re-lation to the ubiquitous textual and intertextual presence "Jerry Lewis."[30] In the circuit of subjective overdetermination revealed through "A Big Night in Hol-lywood," Lewis the director uses Lewis the performer to play Stanley Belt, a character who achieves fame (like Lewis himself) by impersonating the familiar Lewisian Kid. Moreover, "A Big Night in Hollywood" is itself an extended ver-sion of a sketch Lewis had performed on one of his TV specials in 1957,[31] while he was attempting to consolidate his solo career after the traumatic divorce from Dean Martin.

Stanley Belt is an overnight sensation after his appearance on the Sullivan show. Like Lewis himself, he capitalizes on his success, exchanging his lowly sta-tus as a manipulated performer for a position of totalizing power. Gathering the Brandford crew in the hotel room where he had first encountered them, Stan-ley reappoints them to their former positions—making it clear that he now calls the shots.[32] But a different tactic is required for Ellen Betts (Ina Balin), the sole woman in the group. Ellen and Hedda Hopper are the only characters in the film to recognize and encourage Stanley's natural talent. From the start Ellen is sharply differentiated from her male partners in star making because she is not guided by mercenary motives but by an idealistic vision of family. When the plan to replace Wally Brandford is first formulated, Ellen beseeches, "Let's have an understanding as to *why* we're going to do this—if it's at all feasible. Are we going to do this because we're spoiled—and used to a comfortable, well-oiled machine? Or is it simply because we've been happy working as a family, and we hate the thought of breaking up?"

Success enables Stanley not simply to be *incorporated* within the familial ideal but to serve as its defining term. The control he secures over the professional entertainment machine also forces a staggering self-transformation. Stanley fires instructions to his staff with the polished self-assurance (and implicit self-regard) of Buddy Love, a similarity bolstered when he brusquely commands Ellen to marry him. But once the danger of corruptive egomania is raised as a possible consequence of stardom, Stanley Belt is terminated immediately. As Ellen advances toward him after his brash proposal, Stanley backs away nervously. He retreats across the patio and comes up against the balcony wall, which he then topples over. Ellen turns to face the camera in sorrow, but Lewis reenters from the side of the frame. Addressing actress Ina Balin by her real name, rather than as Ellen, Lewis announces that they are standing on a studio set rather than a real hotel patio. Stepping out of the fictional guise of Stanley Belt, he declares himself as "Jerry Lewis," the film's director, and commands the crew to break for lunch. The end credits roll.

Stanley's assassination rhymes with the scene of his first appearance. When the Brandford staff choose him as the nobody they will turn into a star, they close in upon Stanley with menacing stealth. Spluttering and squirming, the hapless bellboy withdraws across the hotel suite until he finds himself against an open window, which he falls out of. As his persecutors peer through the window, the film cuts to a view of the hotel's exterior that shows a still photographic image of Stanley as he begins his descent. The bellboy's frozen image is then pushed over to one side of the screen by the appearance of large blue letters that proclaim the name "Jerry Lewis," inaugurating the opening credits. Stanley survives his first fall by bouncing off an awning, but at the end of the film he does not reappear but is instead consumed by "Jerry Lewis." The demise of the fictional character (and fictional star) generates the birth of the total filmmaker. Jerry Lewis, Hollywood director, kills off the fictional obligations that constrain him so that he can order the film's conclusion in his own image.

This is not the only foreclosure involved here: Stanley's brisk removal also blocks the consummation of his relationship with Ellen. The total filmmaker is not of woman born, for the process of creating Jerry Lewis out of the misfit Stanley Belt directly substitutes for heterosexual procreation. The most acutely self-mythologizing of Lewis's films, *The Patsy* postulates that identity can be destroyed and reformulated at will — that the creative self is responsible for the authoring of self. Thus when the story moves toward an inevitably more active role for the woman — as sexual partner, as procreator — she is jettisoned. Ellen Betts is exposed as a controlled and contained component of a filmic masquerade that is fully under Lewis's command. For most of *The Patsy* Ellen serves Stanley as a maternalistic presence who nurtures his fragile ego when he faces dejection and exploitation. When Stanley proves that he can make it on his own, the need for such external support is eliminated. His forced exit from the film is followed swiftly by Ellen's own eradication. But whereas Stanley disappears from the screen for a miraculous rebirth as Jerry Lewis, the mask of Ellen is stripped from Ina Balin onscreen — at the bequest of her director. As Lewis leads her out through the studio in the final scene, Ina Balin becomes but one of numerous personnel over whom he exerts authority.

As the ending of *The Patsy* makes explicit, Lewis's project requires an insistent reformulation of difference: along with more general distinctions between self and other, sexual divisions are subjugated to the immanent potentialities of selfhood. Lewis's strange comedies simultaneously exploit and recodify Hollywood's capacity for illusionism — the magic of cinema that makes possible the reordering of the world, of the self, and of the traditional relations existing between the two. They celebrate the nonconformist desires of the child who, through fantasy, can reshape the world in accordance with its wishes. By giving expression to the kid within him, Stanley Belt is able to prove his superiority to the manipulative adults who try to make him conform to their dictates. Lewis's films repeatedly enact such fantasies of revolt against the demands of the adult realm, the sexual realm, the realm of differences. Writing in *Cahiers du Cinéma* in 1965 Jean-Louis Noames suggested that "if there ever existed a film about conquering the world, it must be *The Patsy*. . . . Lewis attempts to play all the characters, and to resolve in himself the spectacle he provides, and so also the world" (Noames 1965, 146–47).

A self-willed metaphor for Lewis's career, *The Patsy* presents his ascendancy as a comic star and then moves rapidly beyond this to declare his apotheosis as a total filmmaker. Through its calculated deformations of narrative, performance, and comedy, the film asserts Lewis's unique position within the Hollywood system. This is more than a simplistic case of self-promotion, however, because of the extent to which the film lays bare the unresolved contradictions that shape "Jerry Lewis" as a subjective and discursive construct. Michael Stern (1975) argues that the self-directed films seek to come to terms with "the conflicting concepts of Jerry the ordinary guy—or extraordinary genius" (6), but the "Lewis problem" far outstrips this straightforward dualism. In rapid succession, the final sequences of *The Patsy* unfurl a bewildering range of paradoxical Lewisian personae. For example, the film continues to champion the honesty and simplicity of the Kid while nevertheless displaying Lewis as a shrewd and knowing master of cinematic illusion. Between these two polarized figurations is the brief eruption of superstar Stanley Belt, an incarnation of Lewis in his slick Las Vegas guise. Stanley may be eliminated because he has abandoned the integrity of the Kid, but the knowing director Jerry Lewis is clearly at an even further remove from such ingenuousness.

KID ON THE RUN

THE WANDERING YEARS

Jerry Lewis was one of the top ten draws at the U.S. box office from 1957 to 1959 and from 1961 to 1963 (Steinberg 1981, 479-80). By the mid-1960s his long run as a popular star of film and television was over. Even though his movies continued to perform well abroad, especially in Germany and France, they did poorly in home territories. Lewis's diminishing commercial potency threatened his security as an independent filmmaker and provoked a swift deterioration of his long-running partnership with Paramount. Like Hollywood's other major studios, Paramount Pictures Incorporated faced an insecure market from the late 1940s, when cinema attendances began a dramatic decline that would continue for the next two decades. At the same time as audiences began to shrink, the company also had to deal with the consequences of the 1948 antitrust ruling that aimed to dismantle the vertically integrated structures that had dominated the film industry since the mid-1910s (Eames 1985, 115). The first of Hollywood's Big Five companies to effect the divorcement of exhibition from production and distribution, Paramount had sold off its lucrative theater holdings by the end of 1949. The following year the studio registered a 70 percent drop in annual profits, from $20 to $6 million (ibid.).

As profits continued to dwindle through the 1950s Lewis proved one of Paramount's most valuable assets. When he signed his record-breaking $10 million deal with them in 1959 the company was buoyed by the promise of an upswing in its fortunes: in the previous year Paramount reported its largest annual profit ($12.5 million) for nine years (Eames 1985, 224). This proved to be a false dawn, however, and audiences once more proceeded to decrease. Until the early 1960s Paramount's upper management, which had ruled the company since before World War II, sought to maintain a brand identity for its productions by resisting the package-unit system adopted by most of the other major studios (Archer 1964, 41). Y. Frank Freeman retired in 1959 after a twenty-one-year stint as head of production, and five years later Barney Balaban, studio president for thirty years, was bumped upstairs to the less proactive post of company chairman (Eames 1985, 114).[1] In a speech at New York's Hemisphere Club in June 1964 Balaban's successor, George Weltner, himself a loyal company man since the early 1920s, announced a shift in Paramount's production strategies. Acknowledging that the old studio system was dead, Weltner declared that the studio would henceforth focus more on "packages" put together by producers such as Otto Preminger, Joseph E. Levine, and Edward Lewis (Archer 1964, 41). At the same time he also underscored his allegiance to such high-earning Paramount staples as the Elvis Presley musicals produced by Hal Wallis and the comedies made by Jerry Lewis (ibid.).

Weltner expressed great hopes for the forthcoming Lewis release *The Patsy* (ibid.), but when the film did poorly at the U.S. box office, especially in comparison with *The Nutty Professor,* Lewis's standing with the studio was inevitably weakened. Lewis subsequently spoke with some bitterness of the corporate climate that prevailed at Paramount in the mid-1960s: "The politics were harsher. There were a lot of incompetents in the front office, and their politics began to affect me directly" (Lewis and Gluck 1982, 250). Lewis was not the only one dissatisfied with the new Paramount regime. In 1965 board directors Ernest Martin, Cy Feuer, and Herbert Siegel plotted a putsch to unseat Weltner at the same time as the studio faced a takeover bid from Gulf and Western Industries—a corporation with interests in such diversified ventures as real estate, mining, and manufacturing (Eames 1985, 224). When the deal with Gulf and Western was completed, in October 1966, Paramount became the first of several Hollywood majors to pass into the hands of a multinational conglomerate.[2]

Lewis's reminiscences of this period of turmoil vary substantially in detail, but they all reverberate with accusations of betrayal and abandonment. In 1972 he told Charles Higham that he decided to leave the company because "they promised to send a print of one of my pictures to a boys' home. The day it was due for delivery, they changed their minds. I walked out of Paramount and I never went back" (Higham 1972, 9). A decade later his autobiography claims that he was prompted to quit when he discovered that Paramount's creative accounting policies were draining resources from his own production company (Lewis and Gluck 1982, 250). What embittered him most was the undermining of his position, the devaluation of the long years of profitable service he had devoted to the studio. One source of contention was Paramount's policy of cashing in on his back catalogue by rereleasing his old movies as double-feature programs, which Lewis saw as competing unfairly with his current films in the cinema marketplace (Levy 1996a, 325).[3] A more serious problem was Paramount's growing hostility to Lewis's ambitions as a director. With the exception of *The Bellboy* and *The Nutty Professor,* his more personal films generated disappointing returns by comparison with his other comedies.[4] In 1965 the studio went so far as to block his proposal to direct *Three on a Couch,* insisting that he concentrate on acting (ibid.). Shawn Levy suggests that the troubles Lewis experienced in his final months at Paramount were in all likelihood part of a concerted campaign to encourage the star-director to withdraw his services: "Industry speculation was that Paramount . . . had decided he wasn't worth banking any longer. They had been giving him between $1.8 million and $2 million per picture, and as long as those films made over $3 million or so on their initial release, they didn't mind indulging Jerry's desires to be completely autonomous. But when receipts for his films began to thin out and their cost increased, Paramount executives grew balky. And when Jerry refused to let someone else direct him and started creating brouhahas on other people's sets [on *Boeing Boeing*], they chose to wash their hands of him altogether" (ibid., 325–26).

Lewis completed his acting chores on *Boeing Boeing,* the final contractual obligation he owed to Hal Wallis, and walked away from Paramount in July 1965. In a recent interview he declared that

leaving Paramount was a sad affair; I had been there seventeen years. Y. Frank Freeman . . . would do anything for me, and Barney Balaban . . . once said that if I wanted to burn down the studio, he'd give me the match. We had a handshake deal for all those years, the most unheard of deal in Hollywood history. I never lost a nickel on any of my films for them; they always produced a profit. When Gulf and Western took over the studio, they didn't know from handshakes. So they sent me papers, and lawyers, and meetings, and I said fuck you, and you, and you. Go make your belt buckles, and shove 'em up your ass, I'm outta here! (Neibaur and Okuda 1995, 191)[5]

He moved Jerry Lewis Productions and *Three on a Couch* to Columbia, which would distribute an additional three of his movies in the late 1960s.[6] Lewis's departure from Paramount did not reverse his luck at the box office. Ironically, his critique of the mainstream entertainment business in *The Errand Boy* and *The*

Patsy was itself dependent upon the financial and organizational protection of an old-style Hollywood major. At the same time as he attacked the system, he could not escape it—and when that system collapsed, Lewis foundered with it.

UNCONNECTED

Lewis was one of a large number of established movie stars who found themselves out of favor in the hip new Hollywood age of *Bonnie and Clyde* (1967), *The Graduate* (1967), and *Easy Rider* (1969).[7] He was a casualty of what Dennis Bingham (1994) describes as "a massive generational turnover, the likes of which had not been since the coming of sound, [which] took place in only a few years—roughly 1967-71." As Bingham suggests, by the early 1970s the veteran Hollywood performers were "discards, aging remnants of a studio system whose outmoded genres and icons were unwelcome in a polarized society in which everything seemed to have changed overnight. In the wake of near bankruptcies at the end of the 1960s, the studios—what was left of them—out of some degree of desperation turned to new faces" (6-7).[8] Dana Polan (1984a) makes a similar point about Lewis's dilemma, arguing that "the falling off of audiences for Lewis's films by the 1970s may be as much a symptom of Hollywood's fate as a whole—a demographic shift to younger audiences not interested in paying to see a now middle-aged nebbish" (43).

Lewis's reputation was dealt an especially severe blow by the calamitous television series he made for the ABC network in 1963. A hybrid of talk show and variety spectacle, *The Jerry Lewis Show* was broadcast live for two hours in Saturday night prime time. The contract Lewis signed with ABC, which was the biggest deal yet offered to a performer on the television medium, guaranteed him full control over the show (Levy 1996a, 284). Launched on a phenomenal wave of publicity and expectation, Lewis's debut program in September 1963 drew a huge audience—and was an immediate and resounding flop. *Variety* commented: "Considering the months of preparation that went into the 'designing' and formatting of the show . . . it's truly amazing that so much could have gone awry. What was billed as 'an informal two hours of fun, entertainment, discussion and interviews in a spontaneous atmosphere' came off as disjointed, disorganized, tasteless, which, for all its four writers, 'played' as though nobody had bothered to read the script, including the engineers. It just got away from everybody. . . . It was, in truth, an unimaginative, uninspired, unfunny show. Seldom, if ever, did it spark" ("*Jerry Lewis Show,*" 25 September 1963).

The series struggled on, but to little avail. As the ratings nose-dived critics continued to blast away, and Lewis's titanic mistake sank beneath the waves. *Variety* complained that on the 5 October broadcast, "Lewis was still indulging in meaningless palaver from hernias to Sen. McClelland; the show had little pace or direction. . . . Lewis works hard, but too much of the time he works aimlessly" (*"Jerry Lewis Show,"* 9 October 1963). The only favorable reviews came the following week, when Lewis was partnered for almost the entire show with Sammy Davis Jr., whose presence, *Variety* suggested, brought "a cohesiveness previously lacking" (*"Jerry Lewis Show,"* 16 October 1963). Initially contracted to run for forty weeks, the series terminated after thirteen broadcasts, with ABC buying Lewis's contract for $2 million. According to *Variety,* Lewis was not exactly in a gracious mood on the final program: "Jerry Lewis went off his ABC-TV show . . . not with a bang but a whine. He took the closing moments of his 13th and last two-hour variety show for a swan song that tried to pin the rap for his failure on the network and the sponsors. He told the studio audience and whatever viewers might have been left after the one of the longest two-hours in medium history that he was a nonconformist and therefore didn't adhere to certain 'rules and regulations.' The sponsors and the affiliates were running a business, and this, he said, made their standards different from his. 'I don't like to do like I'm suppose [*sic*] to,' he said laughingly" ("Jerry Lewis in TV Swan Song Blames 'Conformism' of Networks," 25 December 1963).

Although he blamed the fiasco on external pressures and obstructions, the consensus among professional commentators was that the major problem with the ABC show was Lewis himself.[9] On this occasion the familiar complaint was given much more force because the series had been such an unequivocal failure with audiences. Dick Cavett, one of the writing staff, told Neibaur and Okuda (1995) that "the show was an ill-conceived idea from start to early finish. Because of Jerry's ability as a guest on other shows, to break things up, somebody had thought it would be a great idea to give him his own show. The point everyone overlooked was that Jerry had been hilarious on those other shows because he was a guest. It was funny to see him tear up someone else's place, but it was embarrassing to see him tear up his own" (262). The show's publicity promised a daring experiment in the history of television entertainment, but despite Lewis's claim that he was a radical nonconformist it turned out to be a very old-fashioned celebrity indulgence. Lewis took the stage not as a manic insurgent but as an established all-around entertainer who peddled routines that were well past their sell-by date: "The comedian's patter throughout," *Variety* complained, "should have been buried 30 years ago in the Catskills" ("Jerry Lewis in TV Swan Song Blames 'Conformism' of Networks").[10]

Lewis's generational displacement was underscored by a television appearance two years later in which he tried to connect with the new youth culture. At the height of his fame with the Playboys, Gary Lewis was invited to host the NBC pop show *Hullabaloo*. He brought his dad along for the ride, just as Jerry had provided exposure for Danny Lewis on many of his past TV programs.[11] On a 1954 episode of the *Colgate Comedy Hour,* just before rock and roll exploded into American consciousness, Jerry Lewis had participated gleefully in the un-inhibited performance of rhythm and blues group the Treniers.[12] As J. Hober-man (1988) reports: "While Dean stiffly tries to groove, Jerry creates his own spastic movement—humping the beat like some sort of strobe—then, having preempted Dino's final song, leading the combo in five minutes of jive babbling to use up the remaining time" (61). In general, however, Lewis had resisted the raucous enticements of the new youth-oriented music, parading his allegiance to the popular music of an earlier era—the big band swing styling of Harry James or the Count Basie Orchestra and the sentimental melodramatics of Al Jolson.

Whenever rock and roll rears its head in Lewis's films it is treated parodi-cally—as in his performances of "Rock-a-Bye Baby" in the film of the same name and *The Patsy's* dumb pop classic "I Lost My Heart at the Drive-in Movie."[13] The *Hullabaloo* show forces him into a more serious embrace with youth music. Jerry not only duets with Gary on versions of the Beatles' "Help!" and the Playboys' "Everybody Loves a Clown" but also performs an unnamed solo number that Shawn Levy describes as "a kind of bad Dylan pastiche, with vaguely poetic lyrics and a brooding undertone. Though he was playing it straight, the very sight of him singing this material was so incongruous that it seemed like a joke." Levy notes that Lewis also sings a number written by Roger Miller, best known for "King of the Road" and "England Swings": "In a red V-necked sweater, he embarrassedly walked through a chorus of the song, shrugging dismissively as he concluded, a man completely unconnected to the scene he was making." In the final segment of the show Lewis invades a perfor-mance by Paul Revere and the Raiders: "Jerry grabbed lead singer Mark Lind-say's tricorner hat and a spare (unplugged) guitar and began mugging with the dancers on the *Hullabaloo* malt shop set" (Levy 1996a, 336). Whereas Lewis's in-cursion into the Hope and Crosby telethon in 1952 signified the assault of youth upon the old guard, in the context of the *Hullabaloo* show his familiar shtick strikes a very different resonance. The man who had begun his career as an ir-repressible Kid now embodied an alienated and outmoded entertainment ethos that sought desperately to stake its claim to the elixir of youth culture.

In his own time Lewis had been an important transitional figure, an enter-tainer who modernized the prewar variety tradition in which he was schooled to suit the mediascapes of postwar America. Lewis's comedy had been unpredictable and transgressive, overturning the norms and protocols of conformist identity. In contrast, by the mid-1960s he was an ambassador of an establishment show-biz culture against which the rebellious voice of "youth" defined itself. On the one hand Lewis's name signaled the complacent values of Las Vegas — the slick, adult-oriented refuge of variety and nightclub entertainment; on the other hand he was regarded as a harmless big-screen babysitter. In 1960 *Variety* noted that "the name Jerry Lewis on a marquee represents the kind of product parents aren't afraid to send their kiddies off to see" ("*Cinderfella*," 23 November 1960). And the following year the trade journal declared him to be "the king of the lucrative Little League legions, a funnyman whom parents are willing to entrust with the chore of keeping their charges entertained" ("*The Ladies Man*," 7 June 1961).

Too old to play the Kid without self-consciousness, Lewis also found that his heritage disqualified him in many eyes as an acceptably adult entertainer. During this era of intense generational self-awareness Lewis faced the crisis of not knowing exactly which audience he was or ought to be playing to. Once before in his professional career he had squared up to the daunting task of remaking himself, but the mid-1960s presented an altered cultural landscape that he was not able to navigate so easily. The clown prince of multiplicity now encountered an audience that was itself splintered and fragmented, and Lewis found it increasingly difficult to package himself effectively for his different constituencies. He was quick to ascribe his increasingly marginalized role in contemporary cinema to the declining moral standards of screen entertainment. Thus he reacted with vehement indignation when offered a role in the film adaptation of Philip Roth's sex-obsessed novel *Portnoy's Complaint* (1969) (Levy 1996a, 361), despite the fact that, as Charles Higham (1972) notes, Lewis's Las Vegas act showed him "tux-clad and tough, making 'Portnoy's Complaint' jokes about toilets and masturbation" (9).[14]

UNCLE JERRY

As the market for his films began to shrink Lewis attempted to redefine his screen image. Trying to shake off both the shackles of the Kid and the child audience associated with it, he appeared in a succession of more adult roles. *Boeing Boeing* is an innuendo-driven sex farce that casts him as a lecherous foil to Tony Curtis's quintessential playboy bachelor.[15] Lewis acknowledges that by making *Three on a Couch*—another sex-grounded comedy, and the first film he directed from someone else's script—he hoped to capture "different audiences—adults who were not ashamed of something that was a little more sophisticated than the idiocy they never admitted to laughing at" (Neibaur and Okuda 1995, 195). For Levy (1996a), *Three on a Couch* "evinces the commercial bind in which Jerry found himself at forty-one—impelled to appeal to an adult audience, yet best equipped for family comedies and even children's entertainment. Mature audiences weren't necessarily going to see a new Jerry Lewis movie in the first place; for the kids, the film had to have been a bore" (344). In his final Columbia release, *Hook, Line and Sinker,* Lewis plays a forty-year-old insurance salesman and family man who must contend with a midlife crisis and an adulterous wife.

The reorientation of Lewis's screen persona is as dramatic as the restraint he must offer in performing it. The point is to lay to rest the spirit of the Kid, to find a place for an adult Jerry Lewis in a world of constricting cinematic options. His films of the late sixties manifest a palpable embarrassment with the comic persona upon which his fame was based. The strangely contorted child-man of Lewis's earlier work gives way to an adult who is displaced and directionless, denuded of purpose. In 1966 Lewis told columnist Earl Wilson that he was thinking of retiring from acting altogether: "I'm waiting to find some young idiot to do what I did, and I'll retire behind the camera, which is where I believe my real field lies" (Levy 1996a, 339).[16] With the exception of the 1970 film *One More Time* Lewis was not able to realize this ambition because, as Norman Taurog had told him years before, he was only a saleable prospect when his name was on the marquee (Marx 1975, 172).[17]

In retrospect Lewis's decision to court an adult audience rather than maintaining his youthful constituencies reads like a miscalculation of cinematic trends. The twelve-to-twenty age group was emerging as an increasingly important sector of Hollywood's domestic market, accounting for almost half of all cinema consumers by the early 1970s (Belton 1994, 296). Nevertheless, as a man in his forties Lewis would clearly have experienced some difficulty in sustaining an acceptable impersonation of the youthful misfit. *The Patsy* and *The Disorderly Orderly* achieve a dark pathos because Lewis is patently too old to pass convincingly for the young man he impersonates. The disappointing commercial returns for *The Patsy* may have persuaded Lewis to abandon the Kid figure in his subsequent movies. The next film he directed seems like an attempt both to relocate the figure of the Kid and to renegotiate the terms of his earlier self-directed project.

The Family Jewels centers upon an actual child, ten-year-old Donna Peyton (Donna Butterworth). Inheriting the mantle of the Lewisian orphans of *The*

Delicate Delinquent, The Geisha Boy, and *Cinderfella,* Donna provides the film with a foundation upon which Lewis can build his most extravagant display of multiple personae. After the death of her millionaire father Donna is given the power to decide which of her uncles she would like as her new "father," a selection rendered explicitly as a choice between contrasting figurations of "Jerry Lewis." Lewis enacts a polyphony of identities, playing Donna's six eccentric uncles—a fashion photographer, a private detective, a ship's captain, a pilot, a gangster, and a clown—as well as her chauffeur Willard Woodward. Each uncle initially seems a glamorous option who will permit Donna access to a life of adventure. She discovers, however, that they are all so obsessively and incompetently dedicated to themselves, and to their particular manias, that they can find no space for her to occupy in their lives (Philippe 1966, 39). Instead of these wild, occasionally deranged blood relatives, Donna chooses the unassuming chauffeur.

For his characterization of the uncles Lewis drew upon his back catalogue of comic masks. The gangster Bugs is a throwback to his well-honed impersonation of boxer "Slapsy" Maxie Rosenbloom (Neibaur and Okuda 1995, 185),[18] and the photographer Julius bears the costume, voice, and facial expression of his namesake, the nutty professor.[19] The most resonant of these roles is the miserly and misanthropic clown Everett Peyton, who decides to abscond from both the circus and America to live in exile in Switzerland. After she overhears Everett's embittered rant about the "squealing brats" he must entertain Donna retreats without meeting him. The clown figure so revered by Lewis is corrupted by the corrosive narcissism and negativity that Lewis had earlier presented through Buddy Love (ibid., 187).

As is implied by Donna's centrality as the film's desiring subject, *The Family Jewels* registers a tactical withdrawal from the tortuous struggle for self-representation articulated through Lewis's films from 1960 to 1964. Michael Stern (1975) argues that "*The Patsy* is the last Jerry Lewis film to deal so directly with the director-star's ambivalent feelings about his relationship as an ordinary man to his alternately or concurrently idiotic and gargantuan screen image. In *The Family Jewels, Three on a Couch, The Big Mouth* and *Which Way to the Front,* there is always a constant Jerry Lewis character. Even when the other roles must be played, never again does the director allow the 'other characters' to vie for center stage, as they did in *The Patsy* and *The Nutty Professor*" (12). Flamboyantly promoting a multitude of Lewises, *The Family Jewels* also rewrites the significance that this pluralized self-imagining holds within the Lewisian text. As Stern argues, the film lacks the "sense of alienation from one's self that characterizes the compulsively played-out myth of rising to fame and Hollywood-style omnipotence" (ibid.). Lewis is split into a variety of roles, but Willard remains whole and undivided. As a register of normality he is carefully distinguished from the grotesque eccentricities of the uncles, making the connection between his sanity and the craziness of the Peytons but virtual and inactivated.[20] Moreover, the thread that links the discrete identities and separate places of the Peyton uncles is not the chauffeur but the little orphan girl, who empowers Lewis to withdraw from the battleground of self-contestation that had climaxed with *The Patsy.*[21]

The "family romance" fantasy staged by *The Family Jewels* situates Donna as the ostensible locus of coherence, but ultimately it operates as a vehicle through which Lewis the filmmaker can reimagine his relationship to the audience.[22] The decision to use a female child in *The Family Jewels* means that a greater distance can be established between Lewis and the orphan, whereas in *The Geisha Boy* Mitsuo Watanabe serves as a mirror of Gilbert Wooley's desires. Donna remains a talismanic incarnation of purity and simplicity, but she also plays a key role in regard to the Lewisian parade of identities—as spectator, as judge. Donna is an idealized personification of Lewis's child audience who is granted the power to decide which version of Lewis she most prefers. As Serge Daney (1966) elaborated in *Cahiers du Cinéma,* "One proposes to the audience different versions of one same man, and one asks it to choose, reminding it that this choice, decisive, carries along all the future. . . . But one has underestimated the audience in presenting only monsters, full of good will, certainly, but too preoccupied with themselves to think really about this very audience. [The film] makes no mistake about that, and chooses the only man who does not wear a mask and who, for that very reason, was out of competition" (33).

Lewis pays court to Donna in multiple guises, and she finally accepts him as the humble man who, by existing simply to serve another, is liberated from the burden of masquerade and performance. But as Daney observes, although *The Family Jewels* announces the "return of Lewis to the land of men, no longer in front of them but among them[,] . . . Willard wins his audience only on condition of denying himself, at least one minute (but that minute is essential), the putting on the make-up of a clown" (1966, 33).[23] In the film's concluding scene Willard claims Donna as his "daughter" by concealing his identity beneath Everett Peyton's costume and grease paint. The disguise is an act of purification that enables Willard to redeem comedy from the contaminations of the selfish clown. At the same time, however, the presence of the mask implies that even as an "ordinary man" Lewis cannot escape the "artifice, make-up, [and] magic" of public performance (ibid.).

THE LOST CLOWN

As Lewis abandoned the Kid, he was drawn increasingly toward the figure of the clown as a symbolic trope of self-representation. In a revealing, if characteristically performative, anecdote Lewis told Charles Higham how the clowns of the Ringling Brothers and Barnum and Bailey circuses invited him to join them for a show at the Shrine Auditorium, Los Angeles, in 1965. Donning his makeup, Lewis played incognito to twenty-five thousand people: "When I left the auditorium, I pulled off the wig and took off the make-up and I burst into tears. Oh, did I cry! I experienced a shocking revelation—that when a clown is through with a performance, he's nothing, nobody. The people had laughed and wept and applauded. But if I wasn't Jerry Lewis, I could have walked through them afterward and they wouldn't have known who the hell I was. I trembled so much when I thought about it that I couldn't sleep that night. Next day, I went to a typewriter and wrote a 12-page screen treatment, 'Two-Faced Clown.' One day I'll make it. When I'm ready" (Higham 1972, 9). Through the resonant image of the clown Lewis addresses the relationship between private self and public representation: the clown costume, like the suit of the bellboy, is a uniform of service. To win applause, tears, and laughter from the audience the comic performer must sacrifice his private anxieties to the demands of the painted smile. But where the clown actor can escape from his public role when he strips off the makeup, it is impossible for Lewis to erase his mask of renown because it is permanently welded to his face.

In Lewis's earlier work, such as his portrayal of Jerrico the Wonder Clown in *Three Ring Circus* and the scene with the Little Clown puppet in *The Errand Boy,* the clown symbolizes the healing joys of laughter and wonder. In *The Family Jewels,* however, the clown disguise is worn by two diametrically opposed figurations of Lewis: Everett Peyton manipulates comic service for selfish ends, whereas Willard's only aim is to please another.[24] Not only is the meaning of the clown contested, but in Lewis's hands it is rendered a signifier of self-contestation. Seven years later he made a film that presents a far more desperate vision of the compromised clown. In *The Day the Clown Cried,* a film that has never been released, Lewis is cast in an uncharacteristically serious role as seventy-eight-year-old Helmut Doork, a German circus clown who sinks into alcohol-fueled self-pity. "A despondent, degraded and broken-hearted reject consigned to the scrap heap" (Lewis and Gluck 1982, 279), Helmut ends up in Auschwitz, where he is appointed the task of entertaining children as they are led into the gas chamber.

Written by Joan O'Brien and Charles Denton in the early 1960s, the script had been circulating in Hollywood for several years and had already been considered by Dick Van Dyke, Milton Berle, and Joseph Schildkraut.[25] Lewis signed on to direct and star in the French-Swedish coproduction when independent Belgian producer Nathan Wachsberger pitched the script to him in 1971. After extensive research on the film's holocaust background Lewis began shooting in 1972 at the Europa Studios in Sweden. The precariousness of the film's financial backing became apparent soon after shooting commenced, and a bitter feud between Lewis and the recalcitrant Wachsberger resulted in the director having to bankroll the final weeks of the production himself. Lewis spent several months editing the film, but its completion was interrupted by a hornet's nest of legal wrangling. Lewis prepared a case against Wachsberger, who began proceedings to sue Lewis for breach of contract. Europa Studios seized the negative, claiming that they were owed substantial production costs.[26] The scriptwriters ultimately blocked the film's release because Wachsberger's option on the property had expired before shooting commenced.

The Day the Clown Cried obviously appealed to Lewis as a weightily significant drama that he could mobilize as another ciné-dissertation on the dilemma of being Jerry Lewis.[27] In the original script by O'Brien and Denton the clown is not only a gentile but also a professional failure: in Lewis's hands the blighted protagonist is Jewish and, in his day, a famous comic star (Levy 1996a, 377; Lewis and Gluck 1982, 279). Lewis's description of the film in a 1972 *New York Times* profile makes explicit its role as a Lewisian text:

The suffering, the hell I went through with Wachsberger had one advantage. . . . I put all the pain on the screen. If it had been my first picture, the suffering would have destroyed me. But I have had the experience to know how to *use* suffering. I think it's given new depth to my playing of the clown, Helmut, whose agony is the center of the picture. . . . Helmut, the clown, had once been internationally famous. But because of his egotistical thinking, his callous attitude, he destroys his own career. He makes a public statement maligning the state and he is put in a labor farm. Behind a fence are 40 children—all Jews. The Germans use Helmut to perform for the children—to keep them quiet. . . . In *The Day The Clown Cried,* I've tried to show by example how selfish we are all becoming, and that we must get back to being kind to each other. I've shown it through the central figure of the clown. Here is this selfish, thoughtless man, who has lived all of his life making people laugh, but who is at heart a cold egotist. These children in the prison camp, he says to himself, who are they? Why should he descend to entertain them? But as he looks into their eyes, he sees the love they have for him, and he becomes a human being. Their love overwhelms him. Now he is theirs. (Higham 1972, 9)

Forced into a reckoning with the obligations he owes to others, Helmut is wracked with the pain of discovering in an inhuman climate the love he has always shielded himself against. The entertainer realizes that he belongs not to himself but to his audience. Although Lewis begins this emotive justification by distinguishing himself from the "selfish, thoughtless man" he plays, his highly charged account of the film's ending eradicates the gap between them:

I was terrified of directing that last scene. I had been 113 days on the picture, with only three hours of sleep a night. I had been without my family. I was exhausted, beaten. When I thought of doing that scene, I was paralyzed. I couldn't move. I stood there in my clown's costume, with the cameras ready. Suddenly the children were all around me, unasked, undirected, and they clung to my arms and legs, they looked up at me so trustingly. I felt love pouring out of me. I thought, "This is what my whole life has been leading to." I thought what the clown thought. I forgot about trying to direct. I had the camera turn and I began to walk, with the children clinging to me, singing into the gas ovens. And the door closed behind us. (Higham 1972, 9)[28]

When Joan O'Brien saw footage from the movie she was horrified, telling her agent that Lewis's rendering of her script was "so bad I wish they'd burn it" (Marx 1975, 276). Shawn Levy (1996a) contends that Lewis's version of *The Day the Clown Cried* appears to have transformed a tale of "horror, conceit, and finally, enlightenment and self-sacrifice . . . into a sentimental, Chaplinesque representation of his own confused sense of himself, his art, his charity work, and his persecution at the hands of critics" (380). Lewis himself regards the film as "a project that I know is going to leave its mark in the cinema community for the rest of my life. . . . [It is] the most sensitive work of my entire life" (Alpert 1977, 35). The logic of *The Day the Clown Cried* resembles the emotional dynamics of the telethon: Lewis abandons himself to the misfortunes of others but at the same time ensures that their suffering is rendered meaningful only through his own. Interviewed by Howard Schneider of the *Los Angeles Times* in 1973, he admitted that ultimately he found it difficult to tell "how much of it was selfish, how much is selfless" (Schneider 1973, 2:9). Overtly personalizing the horror of the holocaust, Lewis argues that the agony he endured while making the film qualifies him to speak of and for the millions who died in the concentration camps: "I lived through my whole Jewish heritage and what these people went through in the Nazi years" (Alpert 1977, 35).[29] The star-director has repeatedly stressed his determination that film will be distributed in his lifetime, but while it stays unreleased he is one of the few who can speak of it with any degree of authority. Accordingly, *The Day the Clown Cried* remains an intensely private vision that cannot be tested or challenged by the critical gaze of others.[30]

After the trials and tribulations of his holocaust story, Lewis retreated from the big screen for several years. The 1970s proved the low point of his career, the result of diminished work opportunities and a series of personal difficulties. In November 1978 Lewis announced to a Miami television interviewer that for the past thirteen years he had been addicted to the powerful drug Percodan, which he took to anesthetize the pain of a chipped spinal column sustained during a fall onstage (Jackson 1979, 1). Lewis confides that his desperation reached a head on the eve of his twenty-ninth wedding anniversary in 1973, when he almost ended his life with a .38-caliber revolver.[31] Contributing to Lewis's misery was the litigation he faced both from *The Day the Clown Cried* fiasco and from a $3 million civil fraud and antitrust suit that followed the collapse of the Jerry Lewis Network Cinema Corporation in 1973.[32] A few years later a further series of tortuous proceedings were brought against him by the producers of the disastrous 1977 revival of *Hellzapoppin'*, in which Lewis starred (Levy 1996a, 398-406). Such financial problems led him to file for bankruptcy in 1980, at the same time as he had to contend with the breakdown of his thirty-five-year marriage to Patti Lewis.[33]

Absent from cinema screens since his 1970 war comedy *Which Way to the Front?* Lewis railed at his exclusion from films by attacking the "garbage" produced in modern Hollywood. He told reporter Bart Mills in 1975, "You haven't been able to make a movie if you don't take your pants down or show a broad's tits. That never bothered me when it was for specialized theatres, but now it's in every theater. I've been writing. I've got projects. I've been holding. There's no point in putting out $2½ million of your own money and then seeing your movie go into a theater that's just finished showing *Deep Throat*" (8).

Lewis essayed a return to the cinema in the late 1970s, encouraged by the success of slapstick comedies like *Animal House* (1978) and Steve Martin's Lewisian debut *The Jerk* (1979). Promoter Joseph Ford Proctor showed him the script for *Hardly Working,* written by Michael Janover, and managed to obtain modest funding when Lewis agreed to direct and star in the movie (Jackson 1979, 1). Lewis rewrote the script and began shooting the film in Fort Lauderdale, Florida, in 1979. But when the project was completed Proctor and Lewis were unable to secure a U.S. distributor and it was first released in Europe in 1980. *Hardly Working* did good business in both Germany, where Lewis claims it took in $7.25 million over four weeks (Williams 1982), and France.[34] Eventually distributed in the United States by Twentieth Century Fox in 1981, Lewis's comeback movie was a surprise hit— aided by a $5 million TV promotional campaign (Pollock 1981, K5). *Variety* listed *Hardly Working* as the top-grossing release in the country during its opening week: playing in seven hundred theaters, it pulled in an astonishing $4.16 million over three days (Levy 1996a, 416).

The film begins by recalling Lewis's past successes, with a montage of clips from *Cinderfella, The Bellboy, The Errand Boy, Who's Minding the Store?* and *The Patsy*.[35] This is similar to the opening of John Wayne's final film, *The Shootist* (1976), which uses scenes from the star's earlier westerns to establish a framework of cinematic myth to contextualize his role as dying gunfighter John Books. Where *The Shootist* mourns the passing of an icon of the Hollywood West, *Hardly Working* celebrates the return of Jerry Lewis to screen comedy, doing so in a manner that underlines his estrangement from the glory days of his big-screen stardom. As in *The Family Jewels* and *The Day the Clown Cried,* the film draws upon the figure of the lost clown to articulate Lewis's relationship with his public role as an entertainer. Lewis plays Bo Hooper, a clown forced into the uncertainties of contemporary America when his circus is closed down by the bank. Cast adrift from his professional role, Hooper wanders from job to job as he tries to find a place in a modern world that no longer requires his talents. Hooper bungles every opportunity in characteristically Lewisian fashion, but he lacks the resilience of youth. As a middle-aged man with no prospects, Hooper is acutely aware of the economic constraints that delimit the possibilities for self-definition. Like earlier Lewis heroes, Hooper expresses a heartfelt desire to "be somebody," but his conception of self-transformation is more narrowly and more desperately materialist: "I want what I never realized I wanted—to be somebody. Not just anybody, but *somebody.* With a direction and a purpose. For as long as I can remember, I thought I was satisfied with this job, that job, any job. As long as I had 3 squares a day, and a place to put my head. But I think it's about time I dug some roots for myself—with a steady job, steady money."

Hardly Working generates a curiously jaded atmosphere as it piles one scene of maladaptation upon another. *People* magazine observed that "Lewis's once-manic energy is barely suggested in a few labored outbursts, and his lovable bewilderment is now more like bitterness. What was endearing in an innocent youth is plain wretchedness in a man [of] 55" (Neibaur and Okuda 1995, 222).[36] Jonathan Rosenbaum's review of the film for the *Soho Weekly News* offered a far more positive reading, calling it "the most politically honest film I've seen this year. . . . A key document of the Reagan era. . . . Unbearable, terrible, wonderful, stupid, brilliant, awful, shocking, inept, and even very funny. . . . Jerry Lewis is America, and both are hardly working" (Levy 1996a, 417). Lewis acknowledges that *Hardly Working* is a flawed film, describing the script as "the worst thing I've put pen to paper [*sic*]. . . . I had people in the theater, and the money was in the box office, but I was not proud of the work" (Neibaur and Okuda 1996, 223). Nevertheless, it marked an important step in his career because it reintroduced him to his favored medium after a troubled decade in which outlets for public exposure had severely contracted. With the decline of his film career from the mid-1960s, Lewis had dedicated himself progressively to one particular showcase, the annual telethon for the Muscular Dystrophy Association (MDA). The most gargantuan and controversial enterprise of his career, the telethon has provided Lewis with a regular mass-market celebrity platform for three decades.

TELETHON JERRY: MAN OR MESSIAH?

Watching Jerry Lewis run his Telethon is a nerve-wracking thrill, like watching an agitated schizophrenic conduct a heated group discussion in an empty room. He is many men in one, all of them demented. Much of the time, he looks like a sort of hoodlum priest—the Sage of Vegas.

—Mark Crispin Miller

Lewis has been closely and publicly involved with the Muscular Dystrophy Association since it was founded in 1950. Besides presenting the MDA Telethon regularly since 1966 he also serves the organization as a tireless campaigner, a national chairman, and a symbolic figurehead. Lewis's humanitarian activities have reaped over a billion dollars for the MDA cause, and they have brought the kind of acclamation denied him while he was merely an entertainer. In 1971 the March of Dimes charity named Lewis as their man of the year (Levy 1996a, 371). Six years later Lewis was nominated for a Nobel Peace Prize by Congressman Les Aspin of Wisconsin, who described him as "a man for all seasons, all people, all times. His name has, in the hearts of millions, become synonymous with peace, love and brotherhood."[37] In 1984 French president François Mitterand awarded Lewis the prestigious Légion d'Honneur medal in recognition of his work for charity. Lewis's grandstanding efforts on behalf of the MDA have also aroused suspicion and dissent, especially in the 1990s, when disability rights activists led highly public protests against his role in the telethon's spectacle of pity.

Lewis began his association with charitable causes at a precociously early age. His debut performance, as a six year old, was at a Fireman's Association benefit in the Catskills, and four years later he organized his own benefit for the Red Cross in Irvington, New Jersey (Levy 1996a, 15, 22). In April 1949 Martin and

Lewis were among the celebrities assembled for the very first telethon, in aid of the Damon Runyon Memorial Fund.[38] Transmitted on NBC, the show was a great success, generating $1.1 million in pledges and meeting with critical raves (ibid., 106–7). Through the 1950s the telethon was established as a popular television genre. Such shows not only raise funds for charitable causes but also provide valuable publicity for both the celebrities taking part and the television institution itself. These grandiose variety spectacles operate as potent propaganda for the medium of television, displaying its strengths in the provision of entertainment and promoting an idealized vision of its role as an agent of public service.[39]

As guest stars and masters of ceremony, Martin and Lewis were much in demand on charity telethons of the period.[40] In March 1952 they hosted a sixteen-and-a-half-hour fund-raising show for the New York Cardiac Hospital on New York's WNBT. *Variety* reporter Leonard Traube was greatly impressed: "By any kind of reckoning, it was one of the greatest show biz shows in TV history. . . . While smashing over for a great cause, it gave trade and public a new view of the comics. They not only worked themselves silly, staying on screen virtually all the way . . . but emerged as guys with considerable personality quite divorced from their 'in character' zaniness" ("Martin and Lewis Write Show Biz History in 16½-Hour Telethon," 19 March 1952).

A percentage of the revenues brought in by the 1952 program was earmarked for Martin and Lewis's favored charity, the MDA, for whom they hosted telethons in 1953 and 1956.[41] Lewis's autobiography claims that he first became aware of neuromuscular diseases in 1941, when he read that New York Yankees baseball hero Lou Gehrig had died from amyothropic lateral sclerosis (Lewis and Gluck 1982, 66–67). Paul Cohen, one of the MDA's founders, befriended Lewis in the late 1940s and enlisted his aid in promoting the organization and its cause.[42] From December 1950 Lewis regularly closed the *Colgate Comedy Hour* shows with a brief promo spot in which he asked viewers to send in money for the fight against muscular dystrophy (ibid., 218–22). These MDA announcements allowed Lewis to step from the guises of Idiot and entertainer to communicate with the audience in what Harry Shearer (1979) describes as a "strangely serious voice — all throat, no nose, an octave and a half lower than the one he'd been using for the past twenty-nine minutes [*sic*]" (37).

Lewis continued to work on behalf of various charities through the 1950s, but the MDA occupied a special place in his heart. After parting from Martin in 1956 he continued to do benefits for the MDA and speak for the cause on his television shows (Levy 1996a, 217, 229). He also hosted MDA telethons in 1957 and 1959 but was reluctant to make them a regular commitment. On *The Jerry*

Lewis MDA 1959 Thanksgiving Party he declared that this was to be his final telethon, though he would serve the MDA in other ways ("Jerry Lewis Big Click in Staging 4th & Final Telethon; 575G 'Take,'" *Variety,* 25 November 1959). He relented in 1961 but thereafter steered clear of these mammoth charity fests for several years. In 1966 Lewis agreed to the MDA's request that he host a telethon broadcast to the New York area during the Labor Day weekend, traditionally a slow period on television. The twenty-hour *Jerry Lewis Labor Day Telethon* show was the most successful one-off fund-raising event for humanitarian purposes to date (Lewis and Gluck 1982, 271). Raising $1,002,114 in pledges, this one program brought in more money than the MDA had solicited over the past five years (Levy 1996a, 346). Following the slide of his cinematic career, the show also represented a personal triumph for its star-presenter at a time when his confidence was at low ebb. It brought Lewis success in the medium that had seen his most wrenching creative disappointments: the barracking he received from the critics for his disastrous ABC show in 1963 had made him "gun-shy about going back into television" (Lewis and Gluck 1982, 268).[43]

With Lewis at the helm the Labor Day Telethon went from strength to strength, expanding both its earning power and its audience from year to year. As it grew as a televisual phenomenon, the program was responsible for bringing the MDA half its annual income (Shearer 1979, 35). The show raised $1.25 million in pledges in 1967, $1.4 million in 1968, $2.039 million in 1969, and a staggering $5.093 million in 1970.[44] The telethon was networked for the first time in 1968, when it was relayed across five stations, and the following year Lewis established the coast-to-coast hookup that he named the "Love Network." Comprising 20 stations in 1969, the network expanded to 140 in 1972 and 195 in 1975 (Levy 1996a, 371, 387). The telethon also occupied an increasingly important role in Lewis's career: in 1976 his manager Joey Stabile confided to Harry Shearer that "Jerry spends so much of the year on Muscular Dystrophy, that he's not developing film and TV projects like he should be doing" (Shearer 1979, 38).

Lewis's immersion in the MDA project may have been inspired by the constricting options he faced elsewhere. Over the past three decades the show has provided him with regular and extended exposure to North American audiences (Levy 1996a, 387, 389). For twenty or more hours over the Labor Day holiday weekend, Jerry Lewis is networked into potentially every domestic space in the United States and Canada. Moreover, his highly personal involvement with both the telethon and the MDA renders him the emotional and symbolic hub around which the fund-raising marathon revolves. As Carole Walters (1987) suggests, the telethon is a Lewisian meta-text that draws upon all phases and facets of his past celebrity: "All his successes, failures, and frustrations come out and take hold of him during the course of the Telethon. His whole life, his career, his family and friends, the betrayals and denials, are doled out in quirky spasms, so painful at times you have to leave the room. It takes a lot of guts for him to expose so much of himself over so long a time. And it takes a lot of guts to sit there for 20 hours and watch it" (48).

By forcefully manipulating his personality and his show-biz history, Telethon Jerry holds together a grandiose mixture of fund-raising campaign, variety spectacle, and corporate self-promotion.[45] A mature and passionately dedicated Lewis prowls in front of backgrounds dominated by Al Hirschfield's affectionate caricature sketch of the young, madcap entertainer. This pervasive image of Jerry the Kid does more than evoke nostalgia for Lewis's past, it also underlines the gulf that separates his earlier comic antics from the crusading man with a mission. One of Lewis's acquaintances interviewed by Harry Shearer in the 1970s remarked that "the character he played in his earlier pictures is a tremendous source of pain. He hated playing what he called the idiot" (Shearer 1979, 39). Lewis's earlier performative strategies still erupt through the melodramatic gravitas of the telethon host. As on the *Colgate Comedy Hour* shows Lewis interrupts the carefully rehearsed routines of his guests and rushes up to the camera to push his face into it. However, such characteristically Lewisian shtick is not allowed to upstage the philanthropic powerhouse from whom it springs. Telethon Jerry lays claim to the adult role his earlier misfits had either spurned or been excluded from. He cannot exorcise the spirit of the Kid because it is too integral a part of his public and personal history, but he exercises it on a leash. In his *Film Comment* article on the 1976 telethon Shearer observes caustically that

the small spark of an anarchic comic impulse still left inside Jerry Lewis . . . doesn't show up on camera very often, because it conflicts with Lewis's sense of what he's supposed to be doing now. When the manic Jerry does surface, its head has been held under the waters of passionate humanitarianism for so long it often comes up foaming with hostility, strangely vicious toward the people and things Lewis still feels safe in ridiculing. . . . Jerry Lewis is working very hard, trying his best to act like a grownup, suppressing that crazy kid except for those brief, startling outbursts. The Telethon is his chance to be an adult in public, talking nice to the men from the big companies. . . . If only his idea of being a grownup weren't so goddam unctuous, so full of unconscious flashbacks of the adults who used to give him a hard time. If only he were doing this caricature of a grownup as a bit, instead of as a life. (Shearer 1979, 39)

The evocations of his earlier comic style both humanize and deify him — they are a testimonial to the self-contained past the man-god "Jerry Lewis" has grown out of but not abandoned. As David Thompson (1981) puts it, "There are religious glimmerings throughout the telethon. The Love Network is an electronic hot gospel sparked by soap opera passion" (124). Televangelist Oral Roberts announced on the 1976 broadcast that he had instructed the students attending his self-founded university to "think of your love for crippled children. Think of your love for Jerry Lewis. Think of your love for God" (ibid., 46). Lewis is a humanitarian messiah who has ascended from the ranks of mere mortal celebrity, transubstantiating the money donated by the American public into the symbolic currency of atonement. And the most curious aspect of the telethon phenomenon concerns the credentials Lewis brings to his role as spokesman for the fight against disability. Having founded his career on a bodily simulation of disability and disadvantage, Lewis infuses the broadcast with complex and discomfiting resonances.

ORPHANS OF THE STORM

The Love Network carries a forceful message of love for "Jerry Lewis," bombarding him continually with onscreen eulogies from both sufferers of dystrophic disease and show-biz personalities. As Telethon Jerry, Lewis dedicates himself to serving the disabled but inevitably services his own celebrity at the same time: a point made by Lenny Bruce, who described muscular dystrophy as a disease invented by Lewis (Tolkin 1976, 116). Because of the intensity with which he has personalized the MDA cause, it is impossible to distinguish what Lewis does for others from what he does for himself. Thus he must continually justify his right to speak on behalf of both the disabled and their families. In an article he wrote for *Parade* in 1989, for example, Lewis reveals that his second wife recently lost the baby she was carrying. He then explores the relationship between his own bereavement and the suffering of parents with dystrophic children:

So who is better off—those who have the imperfect baby . . . or those of us who lost the baby? . . . Now I know how parents feel with a Duchenne child who doesn't make it. Now I know what I couldn't have ever known in 40 years about the loss of a child. Is there any difference? Only one small one. Those parents got to meet and suffer with theirs, and we didn't do either . . . except for the pain we felt. And pain and suffering are two different things. . . . After working at this for 40 years, I certainly feel qualified to write about what I saw, what I see, what I know—and I know for sure the loss of a child in the first two months of pregnancy cannot in any way compare or be put in the same category with a child who is born handicapped. But it's pretty close! (Lewis 1989, 5-6)

The Jerry Lewis Labor Day Telethon massages the nervous interface between self and selflessness by contextualizing Lewis's dominating presence through a forcefully articulated rhetoric of family. Lewis and his aides refer continually to the supportive family of presenters, production staff, performers, and sponsors who donate their time, talent, and money to the cause of the Muscular Dystrophy Association — an organization that has adopted the familial concept as corporate policy (its 1993 annual report includes within the "MDA family . . . all those who care about our mission").[46] The extended family comprises not simply the able-bodied presenters of the show and the disabled who form its pretext but also the telethon viewers, who are bonded to Lewis and the MDA through the Love Network. The familial discourse gains special force from its regular annual presence within the domestic spaces of the United States during a public holiday weekend. With his "family" encompassing potentially the whole of North America, the telethon in many ways represents the apotheosis of Lewis's self-willed trajectory of fame.

The relationship between Jerry Lewis and "Jerry's Kids" is pivotal to the telethon's family concept. Lewis is the father who rages, cries, pleads, and cajoles on behalf of the "children" he has seen struck down. The melodramatic scenario of the telethon pits the victim-child against the devastating villain of disease. It offers to the tearful audiences, watching from the comfort of their homes, an opportunity to intervene. Exchanged for dollars, their emotional responses will fund the search for a cure that will one day vanquish muscular dystrophy. Beth Haller (1994) suggests that the discourse of the telethon positions the audience "as a threatened family who must put its fear of affliction to work to help others" (143). On the 1992 broadcast Lewis warned parents, "Any one of your healthy children could be one of my kids tomorrow" (ibid., 146).[47] Arousing pity through its spectacle of childhood disability, the telethon assures able-bodied audiences that they can do something about the problem without needing to get too close to it. Its very nature as a televisual event makes it possible to substitute emotional proximity for physical closeness. As David Hevey argues, "Charity advertising sells fear, while commercial advertising sells desire. Charities promote a brand not to buy but to buy your distance from" (ibid.).

The rhetoric of "love" that suffuses the telethon knots together complex currents of meaning and emotion. As a mediating father, Jerry Lewis permits emotional release by translating guilt and fear into a love that dare not speak of gain, and he is rewarded by the love that is directed through him and to him, a love that insulates him against the hostility of the world. In a cynical yet nonetheless pertinent comment Harry Shearer (1979) observes that, with the telethon, Lewis "has devised a method of measuring America's love for him in its most heartfelt form — dollars — while appearing in the role of the selfless crusader. Only with the license granted by 'his kids' would he have the nerve to stand up and sing 'Can I have your love?' Only with the protection of those afflicted thousands, whose strength and courage he says he envies, can he be sure the audience is not yelling back at its sets, 'Sure, Jerry, you can have my love. Up a tube'" (41). In a similarly caustic account of the 1981 telethon for the *New Republic* Mark Crispin Miller remarks that the ubiquitous pronouncements of love operate as "a device to hide other, less comfortable feelings." Lewis, Miller declares, is

a man barely able to control his rage. All his mugging, wheedling, weeping, and pontificating seem only the expression of a vast, unquenchable resentment. He is a figure of immense self-pity, obviously seeing himself as a pathetic little schnook, despite his imposing presence, his years of success, the grateful millions. In other words, his role as friend to the sick is only another version of the maudlin role he played in most of his films: the little jerk, well meaning but unloved. While he poses as a father figure to the afflicted . . . he clearly identifies with them, sharing in their wretchedness, because they are so much more genuinely pitiable than he could ever be. His hostility demands many outlets, and he finds them on the Telethon. (Miller 1981, 28)[48]

Many of those who watch the show or appear on it are not troubled by Lewis's paternalistic dominance. In a television news profile transmitted shortly before the 1992 telethon airline executive Barry Goldberg, recently struck with a neuromuscular disease, staunchly defended Lewis's objectives. "The point about 'Jerry's Kids,'" he argued, "is not to make them children but to create a sense of family, with Lewis at the head. . . . There's just something special about it. I mean, he wants to help save lives. And if I could applaud, and I could stand up, I would give Jerry Lewis a standing ovation that would last for a year."[49] Defenders of Telethon Jerry, including Lewis himself, see his tireless work in raising funds and consciousness for the MDA as amply justifying his central role in the enterprise. In 1992 wheelchair-bound Shelley Obrand, a Jerry's Kid for eleven years, was one of many paraded before the TV cameras as both an encouraging example of individual perseverance and a testimonial to the worth of Lewis's MDA project. She declared emotively that Lewis is a suitable figurehead for the disabled because of the extent to which he believes in himself. Her eulogy concluded with the valedictory declaration: "We all need heroes."

The image of disability proffered through the telethon's highly charged emotionalism has provoked heated dissent in recent years. On a 1981 edition of the *Phil Donahue Show,* for example, Lewis was confronted with a barrage of accusations from the host and studio audience, who condemned the telethon for both its cross-promotional relations with corporate sponsors and its demeaning attitude toward the disabled (Levy 1996a, 425).[50] Two weeks later the *New York Times* published an article by Evan J. Kemp Jr., executive director of the Disability Rights Center, that blasted the telethon for its pity approach:

Many people in our society consider the disabled to be childlike, hopeless, nonfunctioning and noncontributory members of society.

The Jerry Lewis Muscular Dystrophy Association Telethon with its pity approach to fund-raising has contributed to these prejudices that create vast frustration and anger among the 36 million disabled people in this country. . . . The very human desire for cures for these diseases can never justify a television show that reinforces a stigma against disabled people. These prejudices create stereotypes that offend our self respect, harm our efforts to live independent lives and segregate us from mainstream society. (Kemp 1981, A19)

Kemp raises three specific objections to the telethon's ideology of disability, which have been echoed by many later protesters. First, he suggests that the prominence of children in the MDA campaign "seems to proclaim that the only socially acceptable status for disabled people is their early childhood. The handicapped child is appealing and huggable — the adolescent or mature adult is a cripple to be avoided." Second, he points out that the focus on "the desperate helplessness of the most severely disabled . . . reinforces the public's tendency to equate handicap with total hopelessness." Finally, Kemp complains that "the Telethon's critical stress on the need to find cures supports the damaging and common prejudice that handicapped people are 'sick'" (ibid.).

Disability rights activists have exerted increasing pressure on Lewis and the telethon in the 1990s. Groups such as Disabled in Action, Tune Jerry Out, and Jerry's Orphans have denounced the "pity mongering" approach of the show and Lewis's self-appointed role as hero and father figure to the disabled. The controversy was inflamed by an article he wrote for *Parade* magazine in 1990.[51] Imagining himself confined to a wheelchair by "this curse that attacks children of all ages," Lewis describes the daily "indignities" he would face — in the home, at school, in restaurants, on planes, in hotels (Lewis 1990b, 4). Everywhere he goes, trapped in his wheelchair, "that steel imprisonment that long has been deemed the dystrophic child's plight" (ibid.), he is subjected to the estranging stares of others: "You know what I'm talking about. There's something in the back of the mind of every healthy, walking human being that seems to trigger the need to stare at someone in a wheelchair. . . . I have a little trouble with people in public places whispering. No, I'm not paranoid. It's just that being in a wheelchair makes you feel like everyone is whispering about you" (Lewis 1990, 5). The emotively melodramatic exposé of the disability trauma climaxes with the following provocative statement: "When I sit back and think a little more rationally, I realize my life *is* half, so I must learn to do things halfway. I just have to learn to try to be good at being half a person . . . and get on with my life. I may be a full human being in my heart and soul, yet I am still half a person" (ibid.).

Lewis's article sparked widespread criticism from the disability community. Cris Matthews, one of the founders of Jerry's Orphans, told journalist Leslie Bennetts,

I used to think the telethon was harmless, until the *Parade* article. It was like running into a brick wall: all of a sudden we realized the harm it was doing. They have a spokesperson who thinks he's the god of disability, and he just totally misrepresented what we've spent our lives fighting for, which is the idea that our lives are worthwhile and that they could be functional. He painted the worst picture of disability you could paint. It was like "I would rather have my child dead than have dystrophy." My brother and I decided we had to do something about this. Jerry Lewis has to go. He has no right to do this to anybody's life. (Bennetts 1993, 32)

Consisting of erstwhile MDA poster children, the Chicago-based Jerry's Orphans overtly challenges Lewis's paternalistic dominion.[52] Matthews's brother Mike Ervin insists that the concept of Jerry's Kids "reinforces the childlike stereotype; it infantilizes and emasculates people with disability" (Bennetts 1993, 33). Accusations of "disability bigotry" have spurred Lewis to defend himself with a passionate anger that recalls his justification of total filmmaking: "I'm spitting my gut out. I'm coming from my *gut*. . . . I am so right because my heart and my gut steers me. I'm one of the luckiest men alive. I do very good work. No-one can tell me different" (Lewis 1992). Acting as a father betrayed by his children's ingratitude, Lewis claims that the means he uses are justified by the high profile he has earned for the MDA and by the fact that the telethon has generated more than a billion dollars for the cause. The telethon's modus operandi has been especially problematic since the Americans with Disabilities Act was introduced by the Bush administration in 1990. Extending civil rights protection to the forty-three million Americans with physical or mental disabilities, the act aimed to end discrimination against the disabled in such key areas as employment, housing, public accommodations, education, recreation, and health services.[53] In 1992 Deborah Kaplan, an executive of the World Institute on Disability, complained to the White House that the MDA was not in tune with the new climate promoted by the act because its "pity approach does not encourage 'mainstreaming' or civil rights for persons with disabilities" (Bennetts 1993, 35).[54]

In a recent article on the telethon's strategies Beth Haller argues that the show's presentation subordinates the disabled to Lewis's authority, allowing them only constrained opportunities to speak. She points to the fact that Lewis remains on his feet throughout the telethon, even when sharing the screen with the dystrophic interviewees. Not only does Lewis's imposing height visibly diminish their stature, but by retaining control over the microphone he also requires people in wheelchairs to gaze up at him in order to speak. When sports reporter and former poster child Matt Schuman talks to Lewis on the 1992 telethon he "must shift his eyes from direct address of the camera to look up at Lewis, who stands over him. Schuman shifts his eyes upward toward Lewis 10 times during his speech of less than one minute. The eye shifts give the impression of worship and raising eyes to a heavenly savior" (Haller 1994, 145). Lewis possesses the power not only to speak for the disabled but also to direct and contain their speech within the terms of the telethon's spectacle of pity. "We're going to give them a feeling of nobility," he told the audience on the 1992 telethon, "and we're going to help them be better people" (ibid., 144). The "we/them" dichotomy immediately locates the disabled as objects rather than not subjects of discourse, "othering" them within the telethon's circuitry of address.[55]

Lewis's messianic pretensions have also aroused lurid protestations from the tabloid press. On several occasions the sensationalist *National Enquirer* has allegedly exposed the "real life" Jerry Lewis as a monstrous inversion of the telethon humanitarian. In May 1989 it carried a cover feature entitled "Jerry Lewis Viciously Whipped His Kids," which portrayed him as a drug-addled abusive father. Lewis subsequently disowned his youngest son Joseph, the prime source of these unsavory revelations (Levy 1996a, 450-51). The following year the *National Enquirer* continued to subject Lewis to its frenzied populist outrage. On the front page pictures of an open-mouthed, seemingly furious Lewis accompany shrieking headlines such as "Jerry Lewis Goes Berserk—After He's Dumped as TV Telethon Boss" and "Jerry Lewis Attacked Me in My Wheelchair! . . . Charges Crippled Victim of Muscular Dystrophy."[56] In the stories to which these captions refer, Lewis is portrayed as an egomaniacal sadist who is capable of fearsome rage.[57] In the second of these articles, Doug Bady, "a crippled wheelchair-bound midget comedian" describes how Lewis "viciously" attacked him, "screamed obscenities," and threatened to kill him after he appeared in an anti-Jerry skit. A "witness" claimed that "Lewis was red-faced, like some wild beast. His eyes were bulging and he was spitting as he screamed at Doug" (Brenna 1990, 17). Lewis survived these scandal-fevered character assassinations, just as he outlasted numerous critical onslaughts in the past. No matter what dirt it found to throw at him, the *National Enquirer* was unable to stem the growing tide of public adoration that has been lapping at Lewis's feet through the 1990s. As the next chapter considers, recent years have produced a remarkable resurgence of interest in his life, work, and career—a renaissance that Lewis has done his best to nurture and direct.

COMING HOME

THE NUTTY NATIONAL TREASURE

Lewis was berated frequently through the 1960s and 1970s for his old-style vaudeville shtick. In the 1990s, however, the show-biz heritage that was once an embarrassing reminder of an unhip past has been reclaimed as a cultural treasure. A profile of Lewis that appeared in the *Washington Post* shortly before the 1997 MDA Telethon provides a neat illustration of the new eminence visited upon the former bête noire of American show business. Tom Shales's article begins with a revisionist proclamation of Lewis's talent that lays old critical controversies to rest:

What do you know, the French were right—Jerry Lewis is a genius after all. At least, a genius of sorts. He wants to be thought of as a great film director, but it's as a performer that he's earned his honors. He is a comic genius. He also has a genius for surviving and is thus, inevitably, a symbol of hope.

Who better to host the biggest telethon of the year?

Lewis was dismissed for years as a vulgar egomaniac and buffoon, but through the prism of time one can see how inspired much of his buffoonery was. Sight gags in his best movies are worthy of Buster Keaton or Charles Chaplin, critics' darlings. His riotous appearances on *The Colgate Comedy Hour* in the '50s with partner Dean Martin were masterpieces of controlled anarchy. . . . Jerry Lewis is more than one of the great clowns of the century. He's the Nutty National Treasure. (Shales 1997, D1, D5)

Passing over Lewis's hotly contested accomplishments as a total filmmaker, Shales redeems him as a performer who has, almost singlehandedly, preserved entertainment traditions threatened with extinction in the video age. Shales (1997) argues that the telethon is "Lewis's crowning achievement" because it operates as a living museum of variety specialisms. Besides its parade of former greats and Vegas washouts, the telethon provides a national showcase for the kind of small-scale acts—"tap-dancing kids or flip-flopping or people in tights juggling fire" (D5)—that have virtually disappeared from mainstream television since the glory days of Ed Sullivan, Arthur Godfrey, Perry Como, and Dinah Shore. "One of the last artifacts of the 1950s" (Jones 1991, A3), Lewis's fundraising gala hearkens back to the live aesthetic of early television, counterpoising an authenticity of presence to the lustrous surfaces of mainstream film and video fare. Journalist Lloyd Grove (1996) claims Lewis as a key icon of 1950s America, describing him "as important a piece of our collective identity as Ike, Joe McCarthy, Elvis, the Edsel, flying saucers, the atom bomb, Milton Berle and Marilyn Monroe." Speaking of Lewis's role in *Damn Yankees,* a musical first mounted in the 1955, Grove notes that he is "virtually the last performer of his generation left standing. Not only standing, but singing and dancing—the last breathing link to the bygone days of vaudeville, the entertainment tradition of his performing (and usually absent) parents" (D4).

Lewis's triumphant performance in the highly successful revival of *Damn Yankees* has played a crucial part in his contemporary reconfiguration as a grand old man of U.S. popular entertainment. The show ran on Broadway and in London's West End and toured across North America, garnering incredible publicity for Lewis in the mid-1990s. Several other factors have contributed to the resurgence of interest in this once-maligned entertainer. As I will consider below, his performance in Martin Scorsese's satire *The King of Comedy* (1983) had a substantial impact upon critical perceptions of the mature Lewis, demonstrating his potential as both a dramatic actor and an icon of show-biz culture. Although *Hardly Working* marked his return to filmmaking, Lewis was unable to reestablish his career as a director-comedian; his second self-directed project, *Smorgasbord* (*Cracking Up*) (1983), failed to repeat the success of his comeback film.[1] Though he may yearn for a more active role in his favored medium, since working with Scorsese Lewis has been offered key supporting roles in a range of ambitious and often left-field feature films: *Slapstick of Another Kind* (1984), *Cookie* (1989), *Arizona Dream* (1991), *Mr. Saturday Night* (1992), and *Funny Bones* (1995).[2]

Renewed interest in Lewis has also been prompted by the 1990s cycle of "dumb" body comedies (or "dumbedies," as the trade press tagged them), featuring performers such as Jim Carrey, Pauly Shore, Chris Farley, Adam Sandler,

Michael Myers, and Dana Carvey.[3] Sandler, Farley, Myers, and Carvey were regulars on NBC's *Saturday Night Live,* an influential showcase for comedians that previously had spawned Dan Ackroyd, John Belushi, Chevy Chase, and Eddie Murphy. Shore's breakthrough comedy *Encino Man* (1992) capitalized on his cult reputation with MTV's *Totally Pauly* show, and Carrey first achieved widespread exposure as the only white member in the cast of Fox's African American sketch show *In Living Color* (1990-92). The phenomenal success of many of these films, especially Carrey's 1994 hit *Dumb and Dumber,*[4] provoked alarm among cultural tastemakers, who seized upon them as barometers of the dumbing down of American popular culture. Asserting the preeminence of the gag above the values of narrative and character, these comedies revel in bodily indecorum and intellectual blockage: as one journalist put it, "In the dumbedy tradition, many of the movies have at their centers the inept, the insulting and the borderline idiotic" (Associated Press 1996). As such, they represent a concerted revival of the vaudeville aesthetic, which with few notable exceptions had been virtually abandoned by Hollywood since Lewis's heyday.[5] Lorne Michaels, producer of the Chris Farley comedy *Black Sheep,* insisted that the "entire purpose" of his film "is to make people laugh. It doesn't exist for any other purpose" (ibid.). Given the striking resemblance of this agenda to the "anything goes" ethos of Borscht Belt entertainment (Hill 1949, 2:5), it is not surprising that Lewis's name features repeatedly in discussions and reviews of the dumb comedies.

Jim Carrey, the most successful of the contemporary comedians, is routinely compared to the young Jerry Lewis.[6] In a 1996 article Shawn Levy notes, "It's easy to see in Carrey an echo of Lewis's curious combination of physical and psychological comedy. . . . Just as Jerry behaved as no grown man ever before an American audience, Carrey pushes the limits of propriety for us moderns." Levy argues that although his physical comedy shares Lewis's extremism, Carrey is far more aggressive: "Carrey's humor is inevitably debasing. . . . [He] humiliates his victims with lewdness, cruelty and excess. Like Jerry, he abuses himself, but he also abuses those around him, much of the humor in his films is rooted in the discomfort of his victims, not, as in Lewis's case, the desire of the comedian to connect with the world. If they're two sides of the same canned ham, Lewis represents by far the sweeter" (Levy 1996b). Levy's thesis is strikingly well illustrated by Carrey's most courageous, outrageous and financially unsuccessful film, *The Cable Guy,* a darkly comic same-sex variant of *Fatal Attraction* in which Carrey's psychotic loner launches a series of psychological and physical assaults upon Matthew Broderick's disoriented yuppie. Carrey's performance assimilates Lewis's physicality and facial grimaces, but he transforms the sentimental yearning to "be" and to "belong" into a relentlessly menacing drive to subjugate another within his fantasy of affection.

Lewis has also benefited from the high-profile revival of stand-up comedy that began in the 1980s. Numerous contemporary comedians — including David Letterman, Steve Martin, Howie Mandel, Martin Short, Robin Williams, Chevy Chase, and Eddie Murphy — have acknowledged his influence on their work. In 1986 Lewis's appearance on the first U.S. "Comic Relief" benefit for the homeless drew a standing ovation from a celebrity-studded audience (Levy 1996a, 444). Five years later he was presented with the Comic Life Achievement Award by the National Academy of Cable Programming and was inducted into the Broadcast Hall of Fame by the National Association of Broadcasters. Lewis received an even greater accolade in March 1998 when, in a glitzy ceremony broadcast live on the Fox channel, he received a Lifetime Achievement Award at the twelfth annual American Comedy Awards. It may be, as Shales suggests, that the awards have been heaped upon him because Lewis has maintained his public career for so long, surviving all manner of setbacks and brickbats. But at the same time, there is belated recognition for the audacity of the comic pathway he chose: "Jerry Lewis has had attitude and edge and continually pushed the envelope for more than six decades now" (Shales 1997, D5).

Lewis's status as symbolic godfather to the screen comedians of the 1990s was given a further boost by Eddie Murphy's 1996 remake of his best known film, *The Nutty Professor,* on which Lewis was credited as executive producer.[7] A longtime admirer of Lewis, Murphy had performed with the veteran star when the latter hosted an episode of *Saturday Night Live* in 1983 (Levy 1996a, 433). Directed by Tom Shadyac, whose first film was the 1994 Jim Carrey hit *Ace Ventura, Pet Detective, The Nutty Professor* marked Murphy's triumphant return to broad comedy after a series of disappointing screen outings.[8] According to Shadyac, Murphy saw *The Nutty Professor* as an opportunity to get back "to his roots: pure, foot-to-the-floor, let-loose comedy" (Afronet 1996). Whereas the original film transforms the geeky academic into a heartless Las Vegas swinger, Murphy came up with the idea of making the misfit professor grossly overweight. Producer Brian Grazer claims that "as the character developed, Eddie and I thought the film could be a way to explore contemporary culture's obsession with weight in a humorous context" (ibid.). The emphasis on physical maladaptation enables the Murphy version to incorporate many more body-oriented gags — including a much-debated fart scene — which align the film with the 1990s revival of physical comedy.

The remake retains the original's concern with the representation of the star image — but with a twist. Jonathan Romney (1996) argues that Murphy's version of *The Nutty Professor* is "all about the problems of the star persona": "Once again, we root for the underdog against the *Übermensch*. But where Lewis has us favoring his usual nerdy persona against the smoothie imposter, in the new version it's the familiar much-loved Eddie Murphy that's found wanting. The sleek motormouth of the eighties is revealed to be a harsh, callous dinosaur of a comic, whose aggressively self-congratulatory humor turns out to be a poor second to the simple knock-about jollity indulged in by the professor and his blubbery clan—mother, father, brother, grandma, all of them played by Murphy himself" (10).[9]

Sherman Klump, Murphy's nutty professor, is totally unlike his usual screen roles, whereas his alter ego Buddy Love is a close approximation of the star's familiar image. "So, for me, the acting challenge is just the opposite," Murphy noted. "For me, the change of pace is doing Professor Klump. Sherman is shy, he's sweet, he's really seriously cuddly. It was such a wonderful acting thing to do, and I was very excited about the possibilities" (Afronet 1996). With Klump, Murphy could play against—and distance himself from—his increasingly unsuccessful "cool" screen image, revitalizing his career in the process.[10] Lewis also benefited enormously from *The Nutty Professor*. He not only received a reported $1.4 million for the remake rights, but the film's theatrical success (more than $100 million) inspired a flurry of interest in Lewis's back catalogue. In 1997 Touchstone Pictures/Disney acquired the remake rights of *The Errand Boy* and MGM purchased *The Bellboy*.[11] There was also talk in 1998 of a new version of *Cinderfella* from New Line Cinema and a sequel to *The Nutty Professor*.[12]

Lewis has been keen to fan the flames of his new celebrity. His company, JAS Productions, made a series of five feature-length video programs documenting his career. The first three episodes, including substantial footage from Martin and Lewis's *Colgate Comedy Hour* shows and Lewis's solo NBC specials, were first transmitted on the Disney cable channel in 1992 (JAS Productions 1992a, 1992b, 1992c). The final two installments, first shown in 1993, focus on the Martin and Lewis film comedies and Lewis's experiences as a total filmmaker (JAS Productions 1993a, 1993b). Making extensive use of Lewis's painstakingly assembled archives, the series provided an outlet for material that had rarely been exposed to public view.[13] The programs also draw on exclusive interviews with the man himself and with a select coterie of his celebrity admirers. A few years later Lewis also cooperated with a reverential feature-length video biography put together by Soapbox Productions and broadcast on the Arts & Entertainment network. Entitled *Jerry Lewis: The Last American Clown,* the documentary defines him as "a national treasure" and "America's ambassador of comedy" (Soapbox Productions 1996).

Charles Derry (1985) closes his perceptive account of the comedian–director in the *International Dictionary of Films and Filmmakers* by suggesting that "perhaps only Lewis's death will allow any definitive evaluation of his substantial career" (331). Lewis's recent activities reveal that he is determined to stake his own claim to the memorialization that, with his demise, will pass into the hands of others. The consolidation of his reputation has been aided by the creation of the Official Jerry Lewis Comedy Museum and Store, a web site managed by his son Chris. Launched in 1997, this ambitious and handsomely designed Internet venture serves as both a myth-making platform and a merchandising outlet (offering such mementos as the red canes Lewis used in *Damn Yankees* and autographed copies of books, photographs, and posters). Providing an officially sanctioned memorial to his career, the web site demonstrates Lewis's continuing commitment to new technologies.[14] The museum section is adorned with photographs from all stages of his professional life, many of them showing him in the company of dignitaries such as Eleanor Roosevelt, Marilyn Monroe, Maurice Chevalier, Frank Sinatra, Robert Mitchum, and Queen Elizabeth II. Also included are pictures of Lewis's French Legion of Honor medal and his nomination for the Nobel Peace Prize. The web site's much-used chat line allows fans to exchange adoring comments about Lewis's past and present works.[15]

In conclusion, I will examine key texts from the final phase of Lewis's career as an American entertainer. Martin Scorsese's film *The King of Comedy* and the Broadway musical *Damn Yankees* draw knowingly upon his history and status as a public icon, but to very different effect. In *The King of Comedy* Lewis plays a television talk-show host who exemplifies the emptiness at the heart of the show-biz dream. Jerry Langford has "lost his soul" in the process of "making it" as a mass-culture celebrity. *Damn Yankees* presents a far more upbeat vision of American popular culture: cast as Applegate, a vaudevillian Mephistopheles, Lewis serves as the centerpiece of a flamboyant affirmation of U.S. entertainment traditions.

THE KING OF COMEDY?

Theatre is life. Film is art. Television is furniture.

—Jerry Lewis

The King of Comedy takes a scathingly satirical look at the strange obsessions nurtured by the media-fueled culture of celebrity.[16] The film centers on the fanatical drive of Rupert Pupkin (Robert De Niro) to make it as the new "king of comedy," an ambition that requires him to challenge the reigning monarch, Jerry Langford (Jerry Lewis). After rescuing the talk-show host from a mob of autograph hunters, Pupkin pesters him repeatedly for a guest shot on Langford's program. Several rebuffs later, it finally sinks through that Langford has no intention of gratifying his fantasy of instant stardom—and Pupkin resorts to more desperate measures to launch himself into the public eye. With the aid of another obsessive fan, Masha (Sandra Bernhard), Pupkin kidnaps Langford and uses him as a hostage to blackmail the network into taping and broadcasting his stand-up monologue. When the performance is transmitted to eighty-seven million homes in the United States, Pupkin happily faces imprisonment because, he says, it is "better to be king for a night than schmuck for a lifetime." The kidnapping makes Pupkin the subject of intensive media scrutiny: TV news programs eagerly devour his story, and his picture adorns the covers of *Time, Newsweek, People, Life,* and *Rolling Stone.* On his release from prison less than three years later, Rupert capitalizes on his notoriety with a best-selling autobiography, *King for a Night,* and achieves the public attention he always dreamed of. The film ends with Pupkin returning in front of the television cameras to the rapturous applause of a studio audience.

Reviewers who had responded enthusiastically to Scorsese's earlier films, especially his collaborations with actor Robert De Niro, were unsettled by this studied anticomedy.[17] David Denby (1983) of *New York* magazine described it as "a clever, sometimes brilliant movie, but ice-cold and not really likable" (74). Sheila Benson (1983) complained in the *Los Angeles Times* that the film is "so abrasive and debilitating that the last emotion you could come up with would be a laugh" (1).[18] As Vincent Canby (1983) argued in his review for the *New York Times,* the film does not lack laugh-grabbing moments so much as it undermines the security they generally bring: "One of the ways in which *The King of Comedy* works so effectively is in the viewer's uncertainty whether it's going to wind up as terrifyingly as is always possible. It's full of laughs, but under all of the comic situations is the awful suspicion that our laughter is going to be turned against us, like a gun" (C10). Besides handling the materials of comedy in an unconventional manner, the film also withholds the cinematic pyrotechnics expected from its director.[19] Compared with the restlessly energetic and cathartic camera work of *Mean Streets, Taxi Driver* and *Raging Bull, The King of Comedy* is a "hermetically sealed movie" (Gordon 1983, 81). Its "dry, academic style" (Rafferty 1983, 188) ensures that the tensions accumulated by its scenarios of obsession find no easy discharge.

In a lively review article for *Film Quarterly* Ed Sikov (1983) suggests that the film is remarkable not simply because of its comic treatment of obsession but also because of "its refusal to offer any explanation for its characters' behavior—any explanation, that is, outside of the domain of images and their effects" (17).

Pupkin belongs to the first generation to have grown up with television as a regular presence in the home (Houston 1984, 76-77). Far from considering it as a piece of furniture, he regards the medium as a "tube of plenty" that can compensate for the multitude of lacks and insufficiencies that have dogged his life.[20] His overwhelming compulsion to dissolve the glass screen separating the worlds of life and illusion is highlighted by the way he has transformed the basement of his home into a facsimile of the Langford set, complete with a wall-sized photograph of a studio audience. With the aid of life-sized cutouts of Jerry Langford and Liza Minnelli, Pupkin stages a mediatized family romance that permits him to escape into a simulation of television's own simulational promises of home and community.[21] The height of his ambition, Arthur Gordon (1983) observes, is "to swim in Jerry's onscreen world, to slap a guest on the knee, to laugh uproariously at someone else's jokes, to kiss Liza on the cheek, to be part of something—a fantasy—which will sustain him" (81).[22]

Pupkin is driven not by his creative aspirations as a comedian but by the imaginary plenitude of public visibility. In a telling maneuver the film prevents the spectator from judging the worth of his comic skills: when Rupert records an audition tape for Langford the soundtrack drowns his words beneath the laughter of an invisible audience.[23] Although Pupkin invests television with the power to confer meaning and identity, the film reveals that the medium has inspired within him a psychotic blurring of the boundaries between actuality and fantasy.[24] In one of his imagined scenes Rupert is invited to Langford's country home for the weekend, but he responds by taking his girlfriend Rita (Diahnne Abbott) there for real—with predictably embarrassing results.[25] Scorsese's film forces the spectator to share in Pupkin's perceptual derangement by strategically confusing the diegetic registers of wishing and reality. When the two men say goodbye after the rescue there is a direct cut to a scene in which they are dining in a restaurant—only retrospectively is this identified as one of Pupkin's fantasies. The film's ending presents an especially provocative representational conundrum, a suggestive equivocation that is highlighted by the contrasting positions articulated by Lewis and Scorsese:

Lewis: "I'd like to think that the audience believes that the ending is a fantasy. . . . Maybe while Rupert's in the slammer, he's thinking that. . . . I wish the fantasy quality of the ending was a little clearer."
Scorsese: "Nobody seems to want to understand that it's not a fantasy. . . . To this day, most people think it's a fantasy. They will not accept it." (Houston 1983, 91)

Lewis had a specific investment in the problem of celebrity stalkers that made him uneasy with the apparent triumph of the fanatic: "What is so ludicrous about the film's ending is that you don't glorify the actions of a madman—you don't have a fucking psychotic win. That's not good filmmaking" (Neibaur and Okuda 1995, 232). One of several stars interviewed in 1973 for a *Los Angeles Times* feature on obsessive fans, Lewis told David Shaw, "They don't bother you if they don't love you. But I get mad when they take the position that they own me. I will not allow anyone to impose on my home. When they come there, I become totally irrational" (Shaw 1973, 3).[26] Lewis argued that *The King of Comedy* required a tougher and more emphatic ending: "Rupert should have been Bickle. He should have blown someone away, and then they plant him somewhere in the cement, like in front of Grauman's. . . . The picture suffers because no one was hurt" (Houston 1983, 89).[27] As it stands, however, the ending does a highly effective job in undermining the conditions of its legibility. Does it constitute the last of Rupert's imaginary scenarios, or is it a real-life demonstration of the excesses of televisual culture? The question cannot be resolved because all meaning stops at the image in the media-saturated world depicted by *The King of Comedy*. If, as Sikov (1983) claims, Pupkin and Masha "are unable to reconcile their attraction toward images with the fact that images are not substantial" (19), the film's ending forces the spectator into a confrontation with the same problem.

Scorsese's unsettling exploration of the seductions and contaminations of media culture is intensified by Lewis's long and contested history as an entertainment icon and image-maker. The Langford role was first offered to Johnny Carson, longtime host of NBC's highly successful *Tonight Show*—the obvious template for Langford's program.[28] After Carson declined the offer, Scorsese thought about casting one of the Las Vegas Rat Pack—Frank Sinatra, Joey Bishop, Sammy Davis Jr., or Dean Martin (Thompson and Christie 1989, 90)— and this led him in turn to consider the complex signifying baggage Lewis would bring to the film. Whereas Carson was strongly identified with one particular medium, Lewis had "done everything in show biz, has more to draw from" (Rickey 1982, 69). Scorsese regarded Lewis as "the epitome of the Las Vegas entertainer" (Rafferty 1983, 191), but he also recognized in his work some of the problems he wished to explore in *The King of Comedy*: "Lewis is not only a stand-up comic and a director, but also a philanthropist, because of his incredible telethon for cerebral palsy [*sic*], which with its combination of money pouring in for charity, and its Vegas sensibility, seems at times to verge on nervous breakdown. Also the thin line between reality and drama seems to be shattered constantly during this telethon. Anyone who could conjure up and sustain this atmosphere is quite extraordinary" (Thompson and Christie 1989, 90).[29]

Lewis may have been a relatively late addition to the film, but it is hard to imagine it without him—not simply because of his striking performance but also, as Steve Jenkins (1982) points out, because the finished product is "shot through with Lewis-linked ideas" (151).[30] A notoriously passionate and obsessive cinéaste, Scorsese constructs his films as elaborate rearticulations of the images stored in his encyclopedic memory bank of film history.[31] *The King of Comedy* is no exception: the film reverberates with resonances from Lewis's career as a filmmaker and entertainer. It cuts abruptly from the opening credits of the *Jerry Langford Show* to the pack of autograph hunters waiting for Langford outside the studio. Flashbulbs explode violently when the star leaves the building, and the crazed fans swarm around him. This scene recalls the moment near the beginning of *The Patsy* when the Brandford retinue overwhelms Stanley Belt. As the crowd closes in upon him, Langford beseeches "Will you stop shoving please. Will you stop pushing." This echoes the harassed "Jerry Lewis" of *The Bellboy,* who keeps yelling "Hold it!" in a vain attempt to keep his entourage at bay. In all three films Lewis is located as a victim to the crowd, as a man who cannot escape the demands made upon him by faceless others.

Langford flees from the mob into the security of his waiting limousine, but even there he is not safe: Masha makes her first appearance in the film by throwing herself into his car and leaping upon the star in erotic abandon. As Pupkin steps to Langford's rescue by pulling him away from her, the film evokes *The Patsy* once more by interrupting the action midscene with a freeze frame. As in Lewis's film, the credits then begin. They are accompanied by Ray Charles's version of the much-recorded "Come Rain or Come Shine," a song that played a vital role in Lewis's career.[32] As he elaborates in his 1957 article "I've Always Been Scared," Lewis performed the number during his crucial post-Martin debut when he deputized for Judy Garland in Las Vegas: "As the act drew to a close, I didn't know how to get off. I leaned down and asked Judy, 'What do you sing in the act?' She mentioned a song called 'Come Rain or Come Shine.' I announced to the audience, 'You're going to hear Judy by proxy.' Then, while she whispered the words in my ear, I got down on my knees and belted out the song as I remember my hero, the great Al Jolson, doing it. It was the first time in my adult life that I had sung before an audience" (Lewis and Davidson 1957, 60).

The most sustained Lewisian inflection is the representation of Pupkin as a psychotic version of the star-struck Kid Lewis played in *Hollywood or Bust, The Errand Boy,* and *The Patsy.*[33] Like Morty Tashman and Stanley Belt, he is a nobody who yearns desperately to escape his status as an *Untermensch* through a fantasy of stardom.[34] For all three protagonists, being a somebody involves defining and consolidating the self through the public gaze.[35] But Pupkin has a much more extreme investment in the image, as Sikov argues when he compares *The King of Comedy* with the 1956 Martin and Lewis vehicle *Hollywood or*

Bust. In the latter film Lewis's Malcolm Smith is so enraptured by movie goddess Anita Ekberg that he is compelled to traverse the United States to see her in the flesh. Sikov (1983) elaborates that for Malcolm "the screen appearance of the star is merely an incomplete substitute. . . . The star exists above him, and the unsatisfying nature of the relationship he has with her by way of the movies is due, he thinks, to his own inadequacy." But whereas Malcolm is in awe of Ekberg, Rupert and Masha "see no qualitative difference between themselves and the star and therefore have no hesitation in approaching him. Since he has, after all, been in their homes every night for years, they see Langford as being no different from themselves" (19).[36]

Because the cinema invests its images with such an extraordinary allure, Lewis's youthful protagonists regard Hollywood as a fabulous realm of enchantment. Instead of seducing with the resplendent and transcendent otherness of the image, as cinema does, television compels by delivering the world to the realm of the everyday.[37] It is the very familiarization of the small-screen medium that entices Pupkin to lose sight of the border between reality and desire. In an intriguing reading of Scorsese's film Beverle Houston (1984) argues that, through Lewis, the contest between Langford and Pupkin is figured as a struggle between the contrasting image regimes of cinema and television. She suggests that "Lewis as Langford is a man of cinema who is subject of, but not subject to, television. . . . Past fifty, and played by Jerry Lewis rather than Johnny Carson, the Langford figure is a subject formed when cinema discourse dominated the visual image; he has been transplanted into television. Rupert Pupkin, on the other hand, is vulgar, noisy and without taste or control over himself or others. He is associated with electronics and photography-as-reproduction, rather than as a vehicle for creativity" (79, 81). Ironically, whereas Lewis was renowned for his struggle to gain creative control over his representation, Pupkin's sole desire is to transform himself into a commodified image—via a medium Lewis repeatedly derided.

By defining Langford as a hostage to his visibility, the film effectively undermines Pupkin's craving to escape anonymity through televisual fame.[38] Andrew Sarris (1983) commented in the *Village Voice* that "Langford's life, for all its creature comforts, is in some ways bleaker and lonelier than Rupert Pupkin's. Pupkin at least has his fantasies to keep him going. Langford must subsist entirely on a diet of reflex professionalism, instinctive suspiciousness, and galloping paranoia. . . . [Scorsese] turns the tables on the Lewis persona by making this often abrasive performer a remarkably stoical and jaded victim" (45).

The private spaces in which the star seeks sanctuary from the crowd are persistently violated: Masha invades his car, Rupert intrudes into his house. But it is the kidnapping itself that most clearly exemplifies Langford's sacrifice of self to the public gaze. The two crazed consumers literally appropriate him as a means by which they can enact their fantasies. Rupert wants to make it as a star (to *be* a somebody), but Masha aims to *make* the star (to *have* a somebody), and she launches a grotesquely one-sided seduction attempt on the defenseless entertainer. In a striking repression of the manic exuberance expected from Lewis, Langford is mummified in white tape, rendered mute and immobile. Sikov remarks that his "explosive persona is kept under such tight control that he becomes sinister — forbidden to scream, to roll his eyes, even to gesture wildly or contort, he becomes a sort of hollowed-out reproduction of himself, an image never able to do what is expected of it" (1983, 18).

As Sikov indicates, *The King of Comedy* strips Lewis of his most distinctive qualities as a cinematic icon. Scorsese explains that just as the film sidelines the question of Pupkin's comic skills it also refuses to show Lewis in action: "I shot a [Jerry Langford] monologue, but I took it out. If you show him performing, if you show any real comedy in the picture, you're testing what's funny to me and what's funny to you. I mean, I may find a Jerry Lewis monologue funny and the film audience may not, and that may take away from the validity of the main character, Rupert Pupkin, who idolizes this guy's comedy. The audience may say 'What do you want to be like him for? *We* don't like his jokes.' So I thought I'd take any chance of that away" (Rafferty 1983, 187).[39] The elision of comic performance highlights that what Langford *does* is by no means as important as what he *is:* a self-affirming celebrity sign. For Pupkin, Terrence Rafferty argues, all that matters is that "he's 'Jerry Langford,' a star, a fully achieved, self-contained rocklike identity" (ibid.). But for the film spectator Langford is also, inescapably, "Jerry Lewis."

Lewis's nuanced and disciplined character acting draws upon extensive insider knowledge of celebrity culture. As Richard Schickel (1983) observed in· *Time* magazine, "He has been around, and he knows exactly how to play a star. As Langford, he mimes warmth perfectly until you notice the deadness in the eyes, betraying the veteran public figure's inability to perceive any reality, even a menacing one, that exists outside his own ego" (80).[40] Because he brings such authority to the role of the embattled king of comedy it is tempting to read Lewis's performance as offering a privileged glimpse of the man behind the mask. Shawn Levy insists that

with the exception of Buddy Love, Jerry Langford was absolutely the closest thing he'd played to himself on screen. . . . Wearing his own clothes, sitting with his own dog, with a picture of his adolescent self on his mantle, Jerry Langford is very, very nearly

Jerry Lewis. He has a caricature of himself as the logo of his show and his company; he plays golf; he lives in a pristine, modernistic environment; he has an explosive, caustic temper; he feels compelled to display himself to the public (despite his celebrity, he walks the streets of Manhattan to go to work) yet simultaneously loathes it (he tells Rupert that if he becomes famous, "then you're gonna have idiots like you plaguing your life"). (Levy 1996a, 433–34)[41]

But just as the private individual Jerry Langford is forever a prisoner of his publicly circulated image, so too it is impossible to disentangle a real-life Jerry Lewis from the vortex of representations through which he is known to the world. This blurring of the boundaries between image and self was already a hallmark of Lewis's work, and in many respects *The King of Comedy* operates as a meta-Lewisian text that extends and reinterrogates the legacy of the films he directed films in the 1960s.

   Lewis's against-the-grain performance as the beleaguered celebrity drew accolades from a critical establishment that had vilified him for most of his career. Vincent Canby (1983) praised Lewis's "brilliant solemnity" (C10) and Jack Kroll (1983) of *Newsweek* congratulated him for capturing "something dark and disturbing as he projects the overweening ego, the exhaustion and vulnerability of the superstar who needs and fears the gigantic fix of the worshiping millions" (60). On the strength of his commandingly stoical character acting in *The King of Comedy,* Lewis was offered further dramatic roles. In 1987 he starred with Patty Duke in ABC's "disease of the week" telemovie *Fight for Life,* and the following year he landed a plum part in a five-episode story line of the prestigious CBS crime series *Wiseguy* (broadcast in December 1988 and January 1989). More recently, Lewis had a central role in *Funny Bones,* another film dealing with the desperation that lies in the shadow of comedy. In a part written especially for him by British writer-director Peter Chelsom, Lewis plays a Las Vegas entertainer whose success is built upon the misery of others.[42] Chelsom explains that Lewis was ideal for this "magical realist" dissertation on comedy and pain because "he is considered king of shtick, but he's got great weight as an actor, and there's a real dark side to him. When you see the mask being pulled away, you're aware of a man who has toiled and labored and been in combat with something all his life" (Romney 1995, 24).

SHOW-BIZ SATAN

On opening night, I was so emotional that I'd finally made Broadway. . . .
When I came on the [stage] elevator that first night, I heard my dad. I heard

his voice. He said, "Now you've got it, kid. You've got it!" And I had to contain myself from losing it emotionally. I almost couldn't turn around. I felt
in my bones him saying, "Now you've got it."

I could've lost it there, because of this explosion of love and appreciation. What I thought was, "It doesn't get better than this. I've come home."

—Jerry Lewis, 1995

The King of Comedy, Wiseguy, and *Funny Bones* may have brought Lewis critical
acclaim for his abilities as a "straight" actor but they were all targeted at non-
mainstream audiences. With the Broadway revival of *Damn Yankees* he found a
showcase that would garner both critical esteem and popular success. Tireless in
his efforts to promote the show, Lewis told a legion of interviewers that it
marked the culmination of his career.[43] As with *The King of Comedy,* Lewis was
not the first candidate for the *Damn Yankees* role. When the revival opened at
Broadway's Marquis Theater in March 1994 Applegate was played by forty-six-
year-old Vincent Garber in a performance that won him a Tony Award
(Richards 1994, C1). Although the show was a hit with audiences and critics,
producer Mitchell Maxwell gambled on a ploy designed to boost its Broadway
fortunes: in December he put *Damn Yankees* on hiatus for the lean theater season that traditionally follows the holiday season (McNeil 1994, C13).

The show was relaunched in February 1995 with Lewis replacing Garber—
in what was reputedly the highest deal ever offered to a performer on Broadway.[44] Maxwell outlined his strategy to Harry Haun in an article written for the
Marquis Theater's *Playbill:* "The thing we're most excited about is we're bringing a great star to Broadway. Other than Glenn Close, we don't have a great star
on Broadway—an international star where you say, 'You gotta see this guy'—
and Broadway *needs* grandeur. Apart from his performance and the fact he'll sell
tickets, I think he's going to bring an aura of star power back to Broadway"
(Haun 1995, 20). *Damn Yankees* was extensively repromoted to capitalize on
Lewis's name and was a hit all over again. After its Broadway run ended in August 1995, Lewis took the show on the road for two years, playing almost eight
hundred performances in more than fifty North American cities (Majendie
1997, 23).[45] The production arrived at the London's Adelphi Theatre in May
1997 for what was announced as the beginning of a world tour that would take
in Paris, Berlin, Canada, Australia and Japan (ibid.). Lewis declared that *Damn
Yankees* would play for more than a year in London (Johns 1997), but despite a
generally favorable press reception it closed at the end of the summer. There
were reports that the show would reopen at the Victoria Theatre, but this never

happened.[46] Lewis left after the curtailed London run, and the musical began the third year of its North American tour without him.

The original version of *Damn Yankees,* which opened in May 1955 with Ray Walston as Applegate, was a major success, playing more than one thousand performances on Broadway and touring the United States for sixteen months (Green 1985, 167).[47] For its 1990s revival the musical comedy was reconfigured as a period piece, a lovingly detailed memorial to an America of imaginary innocence.[48] The narrative ("book" in Broadway parlance) centers on a middle-aged estate agent who seeks liberation from the constraints of his small-town existence.[49] The opening number, "Six Months Out of Every Year," introduces Joe Boyd amid a group of middle-aged husbands gathered in front of the television. In mournful silence they watch the latest in a long line of humiliating defeats for their baseball team, the Washington Senators, whose failing fortunes parallel Joe's sense of personal deficiency. He fears that he has not made the most of his life, that his dreams of adventure have been smothered by domestication.[50]

The frustrated fifties husband strikes a bargain with the devil. In exchange for his soul he is allowed to trade the anonymity and stagnation of his life for the heroic arena of the baseball diamond. Transformed into the youthful sportsman "Shoeless" Joe Hardy, he not only helps the Senators reverse their losing streak but also achieves media renown as a sports celebrity. Once he has tasted the fruits of his Faustian pact Joe begins to pine for the home comforts he left behind. Sensing danger, Applegate aims to prevent Joe using the escape clause in their contract, which permits him to return to his former life, if he so chooses, on the day of the championship final. The devil dispatches a slinky female temptress to entice him into a sexual liaison, but Lola is so moved by Joe's steadfast loyalty to his wife, Meg, that she thwarts Applegate's scheme to snare his soul. She engages the devil in a performance of "Two Lost Souls," detaining him in the mist-shrouded realm of limbo while Joe leads the Senators to victory over the New York Yankees before the 9:00 P.M. deadline. After achieving his ambition Joe escapes from Applegate's clutches and returns home to embrace the life that had formerly oppressed him.

As an emissary of the pleasures of wishing and transgression, Applegate proposes a contending vision of 1950s America. But his role as a dissident voice is carefully negotiated: instead of fangs, this serpent in the suburban garden wields gags, ruses, and wheezes. The devil is rendered an agent of vaudevillian carnivalesque, a show-biz prankster whose disruptions are motivated by mischief rather than evil. Like Lola, Applegate may be estranged from the domestic ideal exalted by the book of *Damn Yankees,* but he has a crucial role to play in its success as a show. The devilish entertainer and the showgirl are licensed to deviate from the norm, enabling excess to be safely translated into entertainment. Lewis remains on the flanks of the affirmatory spectacle, underlining Applegate's opposition with archly performative asides that prick holes in its composure. When Joe Hardy declaims that "there are more important things in life than being a hero," show-biz hero Jerry Lewis mocks the domestic homily with a series of exaggerated faces. Jonathan Romney (1995) compares his performance to the professionalized disdain of a game-show host: "The rest of the cast duck and dive for all they're worth, but Jerry—lightning shooting from his fingertips—doesn't seem too impressed by any of it. He stands back with saturnine amusement, like a jaded casting agent who's not signing tonight. This is Lucifer as an unflappable game show host who can make anything possible, but who knows the star prize is a tawdry piece of work. There's a weight of cynicism in those pursy jowls" (22).

In the first act Lewis is offered a largely peripheral role and does not participate in any of the musical numbers. The second act permits him a showstopping display of vaudevillian tricks. Taking over the stage for a ten-minute solo version of "Those Were the Good Old Days," Lewis transforms Applegate's lament for the sinful days of yore into a vibrant resurrection of the vanished art of variety entertainment. Midway through the song the stage is evacuated of scenery and Lewis launches into a soft-shoe shuffle. Garbed in a salmon-hued approximation of the hoofer's traditional costume—straw hat, blazer, and cane—Lewis parades about the stage with limelight-hugging bravura.[51] This routine, which is lifted directly from his nightclub act, permits Lewis to make the most of his liberation from the narrative. Strips of garish red light frame the stage, Vegas style, and a succession of canes are pitched at Lewis from the wings: for every one he fails to catch he must come up with a gag.[52] Whenever a cane falls to the ground Lewis feigns an incompetence that is rapidly vanquished by a dazzlingly assured display of showmanship. Lloyd Rose's review of *Damn Yankees* for the *Washington Post* captures perfectly the frisson delivered by this remarkable performance:

Lewis never hurries, he never strains, he hardly seems to raise his voice—he knows he doesn't have to sweat, that he can make us come to him. This kind of supreme confidence is a form of performer's grace, and when Lewis finally gets to take over the show in the middle of Act 2, the grace becomes transcendent and we enter show-biz heaven. Singing and dancing "Those Were the Good Old Days," halting the show for a stand-up routine that's the best thing in it, he's just a trifle unearthly. He brings the mythical theatrical past with him, after all — his parents were vaudevillians, and he is one of the few remaining denizens of the old, vulgar, knockabout, hard-working, glitzy shameless tradition that used to epitomize American show business. (Rose 1996, C1)

Although Ray Walston had originated the concept of Applegate as a show-biz devil in the original version of *Damn Yankees* (Haun 1995, 22), Lewis brings with him the powerful legacy of a lifetime's history in American popular entertainment. References to his past were interpolated into the show. At one point in the first act Applegate emits a trademark Lewisian whine — "Is this your hose, *Lay-ay-dee?*" — that sparks an explosion of applause from the auditorium. When Meg Boyd's sister invites Joe Hardy to appear at a benefit for the Georgetown hospital, Lewis cracks that he can't stand charity — and pauses knowingly for the gag to strike home. The show concludes with the cast taking their bows in front of the same cartoon sketch of the young Jerry that is used as a backdrop on the telethon. Such evocations of his star image only underline the absence of the manic physical comedy associated with the early Lewis.[53] Vincent Canby (1995) notes that he takes to the stage with the assurance of a seasoned entertainer who knows exactly how to transform every public appearance into a star turn: "Over the years he seems to have acquired the laid-back Las Vegas body language I associate with Frank Sinatra and the great Jack Benny, though it's also the way Ed Sullivan used to hold himself: somewhat stiff-shouldered, almost pensive, a mannerism intended to persuade the other performers to play to him. . . . At this point in its run, *Damn Yankees* looks as if it could use a little more of the anarchic Lewis spirit" (C11).

Damn Yankees bypasses both the edgy unmapability of Lewis's star persona and the disorientating Id/iocy that brought him renown. By circumventing his singular and contested history as a public figure, the show is able to brandish Lewis as an exemplary American entertainer. As Canby (1995) declared in his *New York Times* review, with *Damn Yankees* "Jerry Lewis is legitimate at last" (C11). This comment was readily appropriated by the show's publicists, who used it as a banner quotation on posters, and Lewis himself seemed to adopt it as his personal manifesto. In numerous interviews he affiliated the cultural respectability bestowed upon him by the show with the resolution of his ambivalent relationship with Danny Lewis. "Broadway was my dad's dream," he asserted. "But it was his dream for me, never for himself" (Rader 1995, 6).[54] Danny Lewis had persistently scorned his son's considerable accomplishments by insisting that the Broadway stage was the only true measure of show-biz fame.[55] As Jerry tells it, *Damn Yankees* enabled him to square the symbolic debt he owed his father and, as a consequence, to reconcile himself with his own role as paterfamilias: "I think my dad has had his hand on me all these years, more steering than pulling me. But he doesn't need to steer me anymore, because he got me where he wanted me to be. I don't need to do anything anymore. I've got all the artist needs to last the rest of my life. Work well done. Acceptance. Each night . . . I run backstage and embrace my child, named after my dad, Dani, knowing she can be proud of all I've done" (ibid.).[56]

With consummate skill inherited from five decades lived as a media star, Lewis appropriated *Damn Yankees* as a grandiose showcase for his biographical legend. Portraying himself as a man revitalized by the outpouring of love from theater audiences and from his adopted daughter Danielle,[57] Lewis constructed the perfect happy ending to a life story of struggle and contestation — a resolution that sees the hero rewarded, at long last, with adulation and serenity. When he addressed his former journalistic adversaries at a National Press Club dinner in April 1995, Lewis avowed, "I need you as much as you need me. The angry man isn't there anymore" (Lewis 1995).[58] The intensely emotional standing ovation that greeted his Broadway debut signaled that this most embattled and confrontational of entertainers had finally been granted a chance to escape from the wilderness of disapproval. But Lewis was welcomed home not as the sacred monster of old but as a lovable old devil who had learned to relinquish the hubris that had formerly consumed him.

NOTES

INTRODUCTION

1. Gene Kelly and Stanley Donen, both dancer-choreographers from the Broadway stage, made their directorial debut with *On the Town* and subsequently worked together on *Singin' in the Rain* and *It's Always Fair Weather*. Betty Comden and Adolph Green, also Broadway veterans, scripted all three musicals. With several sequences shot on location in New York, *On the Town* was acclaimed for liberating the Hollywood musical from the confines of the sound stage. The film concerns a trio of sailor buddies on twenty-four-hour passes who transform the big city into their playground. The opening sequences of *It's Always Fair Weather* explicitly evoke the ebullient spirit of *On the Town*, especially when the three soldiers dance in the streets with trashcan lids on their feet.

2. Useful discussions of the "man in gray flannel suit" as an archetype of hegemonic masculinity can be found in Ehrenreich 1982, 29-41 and Cohan 1997, 34-78.

3. Contemporary executive-speak receives a similar parodic treatment in *Will Success Spoil Rock Hunter?* (1957), *The Apartment* (1960), and *How to Succeed in Business Without Really Trying* (1967).

4. As an instance of spontaneous self-expression through song and dance, the party sequence resembles the "Make 'Em Laugh" number performed by Cosmo Brown (Donald O'Connor) in *Singin' in the Rain*. In the latter sequence, as Jane Feuer (1986) suggests, "the impression of spontaneity . . . stems from a type of *bricolage;* the performers make use of props at hand—curtains, movie paraphernalia, umbrellas, furniture—to create the imaginary world of the musical performance" (332). Whereas the "Make 'Em Laugh" number is explicitly coded as *performance,* Doug

Hallerton's eruption constitutes a performative rebellion against the formal constraints that have imprisoned him within his role as "gray flannel man." Doug's potential as a creative *bricoleur* is first suggested in the scene in which the three buddies dance through the streets at the start of the film — it is he who comes up with the idea of dancing with the trashcan lids.

5. The term "monster from the id" comes from the 1956 science fiction film *Forbidden Planet.*

6. Lewis has been the subject of books published in France by Jean-Louis Leutrat and Paul Simonci (1965), Noël Simsolo (1969), Gérard Recasens (1970), Robert Benayoun (1972), and Pierre Etaix (1983). Two book-length studies of Lewis, by Giorgio Cremonini (1979) and Mauro Marchesini (1983), have been published in Italy, and another has been published in Sweden (Uppsala Studenters Filmstudio 1969).

7. Despite its subtitle *The Jerry Lewis Films: an Analytical Filmography of the Innovative Comic,* by James L. Neibaur and Ted Okuda (1995), is not especially analytic, relying largely on narrative description and value judgments as it takes a film-by-film tour through Lewis's cinematic achievements. Lewis cooperated with the authors, and his web site, the Jerry Lewis Museum and Comedy Store, officially endorses it.

8. Notable exceptions include Charles Derry (1985, 1997), Ephraim Katz (1986), David Thompson (1981, 1994), Raymond Durgnat (1969), Michael Stern (1975), Jean-Pierre Coursodon (1983), Dana Polan (1984a), Scott Bukatman (1988), Michael Selig (1990), Joanna E. Rapf (1993), Steve Shaviro (1993), Ed Sikov (1994), and Frank Krutnik (1994, 1995b).

9. The dismissive treatment of Lewis is not restricted to the United States. At a time of intensified anxieties about the relationship between the United Kingdom and Europe, journalists in Britain routinely flaunt a similar mockery of the French regard for Lewis. There were howls of indignation from the "quality" press, for example, when in 1995 Lewis's *Nutty Professor* was included within the BBC's *Cinema Century* season — a collection of one hundred masterpieces broadcast to commemorate the centenary of cinema.

10. Shales groups Lewis with Milton Berle and Red Skelton as entertainers whose broad comic styles and mass audience appeal alienated the arbiters of refined taste: "Nobody loves them but everybody else" (Shales 1997, D5).

11. Notable journalistic discussions of Lewis include Bill Davidson (1951), Daniel Farson (1952), Robert Kass (1953), Lewis and Davidson (1957), Isabella Taves (1958), Edward Linn (1963), John Russell Taylor (1965), Hollis Alpert (1966), Mark Peploe and Hercules Belville (1969), Charles Higham (1972), Howard Schneider (1973), Michael Tolkin (1976), Patrick McGilligan (1979), Harry Shearer (1979), Lynn Hirschberg (1982), Leslie Bennetts (1993), and Jonathan Romney (1995). Television profiles include the Disney series *Martin and Lewis: Their Golden Age of Comedy,* made by Lewis's company JAS Productions (1992a, 1992b, 1992c, 1993a, 1993b), and the biographical documentary feature *Jerry Lewis: The Last American Clown* (Soapbox Productions 1996). Other television profiles are listed in the appendix. Representative of the tabloid witch-hunting of Lewis are the *National Enquirer* articles written by Tony Brenna (1990) and Tony Brenna, Richard Taylor, Patricia Towle, and Steve Herz (1990).

12. For example, Richard Dyer's extensive work on stardom (1981, 1987), explores how the star functions as a semiotic process that cannot be owned or authorized by the in-

dividual performer. Jeremy Butler provides a useful summary of Dyer's work on this topic: "Central to Dyer's approach, and to that of many subsequent star studies, is the semiotics notion that stars should be studied as clusters of signs, as systems of signifies or texts that communicate meaning to the spectator. These star texts are, of course, grounded in the lives of real human beings. There is no doubt that Mel Gibson and Demi Moore really exist. But Dyer stresses that these images are highly manipulated texts that have been fabricated, intentionally and unintentionally, through the work of the star, his or her representatives, and other cultural workers (*e.g.* gossip columnists, talk show hosts, and so on). Moreover, since there is no way to know a star except through media artifacts such as magazine articles and news reports, it is fruitless to search for the star's true identity 'behind' or 'beneath' the media-constructed facade. Few of us will ever meet Gibson or Moore in person, and even if we did there is little chance that we would penetrate their media shells and glimpse their 'true' identities. In so far as the viewer-analyst is concerned, the star's identity is his or her facade—our knowledge of him or her is always filtered through media accounts. Consequently, it is impossible to know the star in any other way. The study of stars, therefore, does not aim to reveal the truth behind a star's image—as is often the false claim of TV and magazine journalists—but rather seeks to bring out the meanings within a star's image and to contextualize them within larger discursive structures" (Butler 1998, 343).

13. As Bennetts suggests, on the annual telethon for the Muscular Dystrophy Association, which he has hosted for more than thirty years, Lewis wields a melodramatized persona that "has always included a large measure of hostility, if not outright malice" (Bennetts 1993, 28).

14. Lewis's answering-machine message has been incorporated into the ambient song "Jerry Lewis (Please Call)," written and performed by the band Moosegow in 1999. An MPEG version of the song is available from the Moosegow web site: http://home.freeuk.net/moosegow.

15. The 1976 unabridged edition of *Webster's Third New International Dictionary* defines "deformation" as "1: the action of deforming or the state or being deformed 2: change for the worse . . . 3a: the process whereby rocks are folded . . . b: the result of the process 4: change in either shape or size of a material body or of a geometrical figure." Under "deform," the dictionary has "to spoil the shape or form of . . . to spoil the looks of: DISFIGURE, DEFACE . . . make offensive," etc. What Lewis read to me over the phone was closer to the meanings cited for "deformed": "2: distorted or unshapely in form: misshapen esp. in body or limbs: MONSTROUS, LOATHSOME."

16. Admittedly, the *Film Quarterly* article does not stop at this meaning but points to the uncomfortable connection between the formal and corporeal deformations of Lewis's early work and his role as champion of the disabled, a paradox discussed by many earlier commentators.

17. A scene in *The Ladies Man* (1961) provides a neat illustration of Lewis thinking with his body. Attempting to pacify a tearful woman, Lewis's character tells her, "Gee whiz, I don't want you should cry. Let me . . . let me *think* a minute." He then tilts his head to the side and pulls a grotesquely strained face. Getting nowhere, he tells himself, "I gotta think harder" and comes with an even more agonized expression of painful exertion.

18. For examples of how Bakhtin's work on carnival has influenced writers on film comedy, see the books by William Paul (1994) and Kathleen Rowe (1995) and many of the essays in the collection *Comedy / Cinema / Theory* edited by Andrew Horton (1991).

19. Elaborating on the liberatory logic of carnival, Bakhtin suggests that it generated "an extremely rich idiom that expressed the unique yet complex carnival experience of the people. This experience, opposed to all that was readymade and completed, to all pretense at immutability, sought a dynamic expression; it demanded ever changing, playful, undefined forms. All the symbols of the carnival idiom are filled with this pathos of change and renewal, with the sense of the gay relativity of prevailing truths and authorities. We find here a characteristic logic, the peculiar logic of the 'inside out' . . . of the 'turnabout,' of a continual shifting from top to bottom, from front to rear, of numerous parodies and travesties, humiliations, profanations, comic crownings and uncrownings" (Bakhtin 1984, 10-11).

20. Bakhtin continues: "The stress is laid on those parts of the body that are open to the outside world, that is the parts through which the world enters the body or emerges from it, or through which the body itself goes out to meet the world" (Bakhtin 1984, 26). Lewis's extravagant open-mouthed gestures constitute prominent examples of such orificial carnivalesque—and one of his 1960s films was even entitled *The Big Mouth*.

21. This does not mean that the folk dynamic is absent from contemporary popular culture, but it certainly is dispersed and displaced.

22. As Thomas Doherty considers, the "teenager" emerged as an economically, culturally, and socially defined identity after World War II: "In postwar America and in 'Americanized' foreign countries, the teen years became a unique transitional phase between childhood and adulthood, in some senses an autonomous and in most cases a privileged period in an individual's life. . . . Truth to tell, '50s teenagers *were* strange creatures, set apart from previous generations of American young people in numbers, affluence, and self-consciousness. There were more of them, they had more money, and they were more aware of themselves as teenagers" (Doherty 1988, 44-45).

23. The relationship between the carnivalesque modes of comedy and horror is most explicit in Lewis's 1963 film *The Nutty Professor,* which transforms Robert Louis Stevenson's *Strange Case of Dr. Jekyll and Mr. Hyde* into a distinctly Lewisian exploration of the dual-personality theme.

24. In one of the key scenes in *Funny Bones* (1995) George Fawkes (Lewis) tells his son Tommy (Oliver Platt) that "there are two types of comedian. There's a 'funny bones' comedian and a non-'funny bones' comedian. They're both funny. One *is* funny, the other *tells* funny." Lewis's readiness to appropriate these words for his own philosophy of comedy is characteristic of the blurring between fiction and autobiography he routinely encourages.

25. For example, in a 1963 profile in the *Saturday Evening Post,* Edward Linn observes, "Jerry believes firmly that he can separate himself from the character he portrays. And, professionally, sometimes he can make the division. Watching the daily rushes, he is cool and merciless. The man on the screen is always him, never me. 'I get him in too much here, I got to cut some footage. He's funny here. . . . No, he's lying

there. . . . No, this is a force job. . . . Look in his eyes there: he's lying. Lose that.' But whatever he may think, he does drift back and forth between *him* and *me,* not only in his actions but in his language" (Linn 1963, 83–84). Further instances will be discussed below.

1. AN EMBARRASSMENT TO THE ORDER

1. Lewis was made a Commander of the Order of Arts and Letters at a ceremony at the French Ministry of Culture in 1984.
2. For example, a recent travel guide to France published by the Australian company Lonely Planet includes the following consideration of French humor within a section entitled "Facts about the Country": "Though it may come as a surprise to some people, French people do like to laugh. . . . Inexplicably, the moronic American comedian Jerry Lewis is immensely popular in France" (Fallon, Robinson, and Nebesky 1997, 47).
3. Partially as a result of the widespread dissemination of television, France and other European countries experienced a drastic decline in cinema attendance in the late 1950s. In this context high-budget studio productions were no longer such a secure option. The emergence of the *nouvelle vague* was also stimulated by government subsidies that created new opportunities for entry into the film industry. In 1953 money was made available for new directors to make short films, and 1959 saw the introduction of the *avance sur recettes* scheme, which provided funding for first-time directors of feature films. Besides these institutional factors, the emergence of the new French cinema was also influenced by broader social transformations. Aided by the Marshall Plan for European economic recovery, France underwent a rapid process of industrial modernization after World War II. Increased national prosperity was not accompanied by political stability, however: the country came close to civil war in May 1958, when officers in the French army mounted a coup in the colony of Algeria. The crisis brought down the government of the Fourth Republic, founded in 1946, and led to General de Gaulle's return to power as president. The *nouvelle vague* phenomenon coincided with the start of the de Gaulle's Fifth Republic.
4. Emerging in French cinema during the same period was a rival group, known as the *Rive Gauche* (Left Bank) filmmakers (most notably, Alain Resnais, Agnès Varda, and Marguerite Duras), whose films reveal an explicit allegiance to the experiments of literary high modernism.
5. Other *Cahiers du Cinéma* writers who turned to directing included Jacques Rivette, Eric Rohmer, Pierre Kast, Jacques Doniol-Valcroze, Roger Leenhardt, and Luc Moullet.
6. Thompson and Bordwell (1994) sketch an evocative picture of the heightened film culture that flourished after the war: "The atmosphere of *cinéphilie* ('love of cinema') must have been heady. The *ciné-club* movement was revived, and by 1954 there were 200 clubs with approximately 100,000 members. The Catholic Church's lay group on public education formed an agency that arranged screenings for millions of viewers. University courses began to teach cinema, and an academic discipline called 'Filmology' was elaborated. Several film journals were launched, most notably

L'Écran Français (published secretly during the occupation, openly in 1945), *La Revue du cinéma* (founded 1946), *Cahiers du Cinéma* (1951), and *Positif* (1952). Soon after the war's end, publishers had brought out film histories by Georges Sadoul and theoretical works by André Bazin, Jean Epstein, André Malraux, and Claude-Edmonde Magny. . . . Postwar French film culture has long served as the paradigm case of intellectual ferment around the cinema. The ideas explored by several brilliant thinkers have permanently shaped the direction of film studies and filmmaking. Out of the debates in *ciné-clubs,* the screenings of esoteric classics and recent Hollywood products, and the articles in *Cahiers du Cinéma* and *Positif,* the New Wave of the 1950s would be born" (436).

7. In a 1962 interview Godard professed that "all of us at *Cahiers* thought of ourselves as future directors. Frequenting *ciné-clubs* and the Cinémathèque was already a way of thinking cinema and thinking about cinema. Writing was already a way of making films, for the difference between writing and directing is quantitative not qualitative" (Hillier 1985, 13). Truffaut (1968) similarly acknowledged that he learned to think cinematically as a result of his regular work as a film reviewer for the weekly papers *Arts:* "This rich period was the equivalent for me, I suppose, of the training of a scriptwriter. It led me to see more clearly and evolve my tastes, my predilections, my biases. I came to dissect films so much that during my last year on *Arts* I was no longer writing criticism proper, I was speaking as a director" (87).

8. The most influential French film critic since 1920s avant-garde filmmaker and theorist Louis Delluc, André Bazin was something of a godfather to the New Wave critics/directors (Williams 1992, 307). Long before the advent of *Cahiers du Cinéma* Bazin involved himself fervently in the shaping of the new French ciné-culture. During the occupation he wrote passionate criticism about the cinema for the Resistance journal *L'Écran Français* and helped to revive the ciné-club movement after its virtual demise in the early 1930s (ibid., 308). After the liberation Bazin continued as an organizer of film societies, a lecturer, and a critic, writing increasingly ambitious articles for *L'Écran Français* and *La Revue du Cinéma* as well as daily reviews for *Le Parisien Libéré.* Dudley Andrew (1882) argues that Bazin's activities during the postwar years played a pivotal role in the shaping of the new critical approaches to film and cinema that would flourish with New Wave criticism and filmmaking (14-16).

9. Discussion of the filmic auteur could be found in *Cahiers du Cinéma* before Truffaut's article, and in its predecessor, *La Revue du Cinéma* (Caughie 1981, 35-36; Hillier 1985, 2-3). An important influence upon the *Cahiers* brand of auteurism was Alexandre Astruc's article "The Birth of a New *Avant-Garde: La Caméra-Stylo,*" published in *L'Écran Français* in 1948 (Buscombe 1981, 24; Hayward 1993, 141). From early on, Jim Hillier (1985) indicates, there was a great deal of imprecision in the use of the term "auteur." Truffaut, for example, employs it to refer to both the hyphenate director-writer and, more generally, "the creator whose authentic personality is felt in the work." Hillier observes: "Since the basic concept in the *politique* was the director's control of, and hence responsibility for, his work, despite collaboration with others and despite industrial constraints, primarily through the process of directing itself, through the *mise-en-scène,* the two senses did not need to go together" (75). As Susan Hayward (1993) elaborates, "The *auteur* was distinctive for his style and not necessar-

ily for his subject matter *per se*. Thus the *auteur* no longer needed to be the 'totality' of the film (*i.e.*, scriptwriter, editor, etc.). This shift in the meaning of *auteur* was largely due to the avid attention which *Cahiers* paid to American cinema where, it must be remembered, a director had little or no say over any of the production. The only space for creativity was with *mise-en-scène,* which became the expressive tool at the filmmaker's disposal, and it was through the reading of that *mise-en-scène. . . that* a critic could determine the specificity of the cinematographic work and decipher the film's text and subtext" (141). See also Hillier 1985, 10, 222.

10. For example, *L'Écran Français* faced a split between a Marxist core that viewed Hollywood films as insidious products of the U.S. culture industry and a faction (which included Bazin) that argued that certain American films embodied new possibilities for cinema because they connected with the "everyday" (Andrew 1982, 15–16). For a detailed consideration of the political, economic, and ideological complexities of French relations with the United States after World War II, see Kuisel 1996.

11. Matters were made worse by a 1946 trade agreement, negotiated by Léon Blum of the French government and U.S. secretary of commerce James Byrnes, that "imposed quotas on the screening of French films within France as part of the price of American economic aid" (Reader 1993). For further consideration of the Blum-Byrnes accord, see Crisp 1993, 74–77.

12. "The Tradition of Quality continued the political, moral, and artistic concerns of occupation filmmaking, while more and more of its audience was living in a greatly transformed postwar France. Quality productions routinely took traditional Left potshots at the clergy, at a time when the old conflict between clericalism and anticlericalism finally had begun to seem outdated, at least to younger French citizens. And social analysis in the tradition of 1930s Marxism, such as informs *Le Rouge et le noir* and many other works, seemed equally a thing of the past for young people finding their way in the increasingly Americanized postwar European culture" (Williams 1992, 281–82).

13. French intellectuals had long been fascinated by American culture. Before World War II, for example, American genre films attracted the French surrealists (Naremore 1995–96, 18), and modern American writers such as William Faulkner, Ernest Hemingway, John Dos Passos, John Steinbeck, and Dashiell Hammett similarly met with an enthusiastic reception. Translations of hard-boiled American crime fiction (*série noir*) were extremely popular after the war, when the liberation paved the way for a generally favorable reception of U.S. cultural forms (Elsaesser 1973, 207–10).

14. "The *nouvelle vague* bequeathed to later French cinema a fascination with the details and small rituals of everyday life: lighting cigarettes, shopping, conversing in cafes, walking in the streets. The theatricalized, socially neutral speech which dominated the Tradition of Quality disappeared. New characters spoke again with the accents, vocabulary, and rhythms of the world in which most film spectators lived" (Williams 1992, 338).

15. For example, Chabrol, Truffaut, and Godard all turned their hands to American-style thrillers—with, respectively, *Un Double Tour/Web of Passion/Leda* (1959), *Tirez sur le pianiste* (*Shoot the Piano Player*) (1960), and *À bout de souffle* (which even bore a dedication to the Hollywood B-movie studio Monogram Pictures). Chabrol coauthored a critical book on Alfred Hitchcock, and his own films have frequently adapted

Hitchcockian strategies to French bourgeois settings. Godard's 1960s films play with a wide range of Hollywood genres: the musical in *Une Femme est une femme* (*A Woman Is a Woman*) (1961), the melodrama in *Le Mépris* (*Contempt*) (1963), the outlaw couple story in both *À bout de souffle* and *Pierrot Le Fou* (1965), the science fiction film in *Alphaville* (1965), the road movie in *Weekend* (1967), and the western in *Vent d'Est* (*Wind from the East*) (1969).

16. Alan Williams (1992) sees the height of the New Wave as the 1958-62 period, after which *nouvelle vague* techniques had lost their shock value and become a standardized part of the cinematic vocabulary (328-38). David A. Cook (1996) argues that the French New Wave "can be credited with almost singlehandedly revitalizing the stagnant British and American cinemas during the sixties, and it produced similar chain reactions in Italy, West Germany, Eastern Europe, and indeed around the world" (567). Since the 1960s numerous American directors—including Arthur Penn, Robert Altman, Mike Nichols, Martin Scorsese, Francis Ford Coppola, and, more recently, Quentin Tarantino—have reworked conventional generic projects through *nouvelle vague* stylistics.

17. Hillier (1985) notes that their major auteurs were non-American—for example, Roberto Rossellini, Robert Bresson, Jean Renoir, F. W. Murnau, and Sergei Eisenstein—and that their main aim was to challenge the priorities of French cinema (73).

18. As Richard Maltby and Ian Craven (1995) note, outside the United States "the American culture that Hollywood offered was an alternative to national culture, and could be adopted as a gesture of local resistance to 'official' culture" (168).

19. In *Distinction: A Social Critique of the Judgment of Taste* Pierre Bourdieu distinguishes three hierarchical "zones of taste" that correspond roughly to educational levels and social classes: legitimate taste, middlebrow taste, and popular taste (Bourdieu 1986, 16).

20. As Richard Maltby (1998) observes, "As cultural Other, American culture has appeared dangerous to elites because it is radically democratic; at a variety of levels, it challenges hierarchies of discrimination, taste and class. To a significant extent, this danger is contained by being classified as 'entertainment,' and the interchangeability of the terms 'entertainment,' 'popular culture' and 'American culture' indicates the ways in which ideas of aesthetic distinction have been intertwined with elite definitions of nationalism in the perception that 'Americanization' involved a process of 'leveling down' moral and aesthetic standards" (106).

21. In 1957 Jacques Doniol-Valcroze summarized the views of his fellow auteurists in a pithy comment: "We've reached a point where the cinema is a medium of expression for saying something. And the staggering thing is that the cinema in France has nothing to say, and that French film says nothing" (Hillier 1985, 38). Bazin's reading of the significance of American films was anticipated by Soviet filmmaker Lev Kuleshov, who in 1922 spoke admiringly of American genre cinema: "The success of American films lies in their maximum degree of cinema specificity, in the maximum amount of movement, in primitive heroism, in an organic link with contemporary life" (Taylor and Christie 1988, 73).

22. Dudley Andrew (1982) quotes a line from Bazin's wartime criticism that neatly encapsulates his views on the relations between the aesthetic and the social: "The cinema esthetic will be social, or cinema will have to do without an esthetic" (14).

23. Apart from the lone voice of Marxist writer-filmmaker Pierre Kast, the *Cahier*ist polemic was aesthetically but not politically radical. By contrast, *Positif* considered cinema from an avowedly left-wing perspective. However, the uncertain political climate provoked by the war in Indochina and the Cold War had severely decreased public support for leftist politics, and *Positif* represented a minority voice in French film culture — the pro-communist *L'Écran Français* had folded in 1953, a year after *Positif* was launched. Colin Crisp (1993) suggests that *Positif* managed to secure regular financial backing only after it moderated its initial hard-left sentiments (248-49). Susan Hayward (1993) argues that the *Cahier*ist valuation of American cinema was especially suited to the apolitical context of 1950s France because in American films "social problems were addressed socially and not politically" (143-44).

24. For further consideration of *Cahiers du Cinéma* in the late 1960s and early 1970s, see Browne 1990.

25. Houston (1960) plows the same furrow for so long she risks a premature burial: "The weakness of the *Cahiers du Cinéma* school, both in its own country and among its exponents here, seems to be that it barely admits of experience which does not take place in the cinema. Its criticism too easily becomes shop talk for the initiated; its enthusiasms are self-limiting; it turns inward upon itself, so that a film's validity is assessed not in relation to the society from which it draws its material but in relation to other cinematic experiences. It is all a bit hermetic, as though its practitioners had chosen to live in the dark, emerging to blink, mole-like, at the cruel light, to sniff the chilly air, before ducking back into the darkness of another cinema" (164).

26. In the first issue of *Motion,* a university-based film journal launched in the summer of 1961, Peter Armitage describes a period of critical warfare in contemporary intellectual film culture. The institutional position of *Sight and Sound,* "a dedicated literary magazine," faced challenges from younger critics writing for several small university-based journals, such as *Oxford Opinion, Universities and Left Review, Definition,* and *Motion* itself. Along with Lindsay Anderson, Gavin Lambert, and Peter Ericsson, Houston had earlier written for the pioneering Oxford journal *Sequence* (1947-52), which also defined itself against the "deadly respectability" of *Sight and Sound.* Lambert took over the editorship of the British Film Institute journal and Houston succeeded him (Armitage 1961, 4-5)

27. Bazin concludes his 1957 article "On the *politique des auteurs*" with the following emphasis: "*Auteur,* yes, but what *of?*" (Bazin 1985, 258).

28. Houston tries to cover herself on this front, pointing out that her generation of Oxford intellectuals made the critical discovery of director Nicholas Ray, one of *Cahiers*' hottest directors (Houston 1960, 164). However, it is clear from the rest of her argument that he stands no chance in competition with the ethno-humanism of Satyajit Ray.

29. Roud is more accommodating, albeit selectively so. Like Hoveyda, he can see merit in Nicholas Ray's gangster film *Party Girl* (1958), though he takes pains to distinguish his reasoned appraisal of the film from Hoveyda's rhapsodic eulogy to the spellbinding power of mise-en-scène (cf. Hoveyda 1985).

30. To substantiate their case against the new film criticism, Roud and Houston parade numerous rabble-rousing assertions from selected France and British extremists.

31. *Film Culture* first appeared in January 1955, and Sarris contributed to its second issue.

He was soon being credited as an associate editor. From 1960 he also contributed to the similarly fringe arts/culture journal the *Village Voice*.

32. To counter Sarris, the next issue of *Film Culture* was devoted to directors from the independent avant-garde sector.

33. In his 1968 book Sarris conceded that auteurist criticism had a flamboyantly anti-Establishment agenda: "The notion that a nonliterary director can be the author of his films is difficult to grasp in America. Since most American film critics are either literary or journalistic types with no aspirations or even fantasies of becoming film directors, the so called *auteur* theory has had rough sledding indeed. Truffaut's greatest heresy, however, was not in his ennobling direction as a form of creation, but in his ascribing authorship to Hollywood directors hitherto tagged with the deadly epithets of commercialism. This was Truffaut's major contribution to the anti-Establishment ferment in England and America" (Sarris 1968, 27–28). Sarris's account of his uneasy relations with Mekas and the advocates of the American avant-garde can be found in his *Village Voice* article "*Avant-Garde* Films Are More Boring than Ever" (Sarris 1977). Mekas responded in *Soho Weekly News* with "Sarris in the Palace, or After the Coup" (Mekas 1977).

34. Dwight Macdonald, also opposed to Sarris's auteurism, suggested that Kael "is obsessed with other critics, using their opinions too often as a springboard for her own performance and almost always quoting them adversely, and often unfairly" (Murray 1975, 219).

35. As a further illustration of the circular nature of the debates about auteurism, compare Kael's words with the following remark by Benayoun: "If [the New Wave filmmakers] turn their nose up at what they call 'big themes,' it is because they are still clinging to the ataxia of pubescent mental defectives, and see themselves threatened by the specter of culture as though by some omniscient father figure, at once a philosopher and a poet" (Benayoun 1968, 167).

36. Sarris shifted his terms, probably in response to Kael's critique. By 1968 he describes auteurism more loosely: "Ultimately, the *auteur* theory is not so much a theory as an attitude, a table of values that converts film history into directorial autobiography. . . . The *auteur* theory is merely a system of tentative priorities, a pattern theory in constant flux" (Sarris 1968, 30, 34). Kael's conception of film criticism rejects theory explicitly: "It is very difficult to explain to such people [Sarris and others] that criticism is exciting just because there is no formula to apply, just because you must use everything you are and everything you know that is relevant, and that film criticism is particularly exciting just because of the multiplicity of elements in film art" (Kael 1966, 309–10).

37. After the success of the New Wave films Kael can issue guarded praise for French auteurism, noting that it helped "to liberate the energies of the French critics" (Kael 1966, 311). But she will not allow such a positive role for the Anglo-American importations, accusing Sarris and the *Movie* writers of deploying a perverse and regressive critical program that rides roughshod over sensible criteria of artistic excellent and intellectual integrity. Quite clearly, Kael does not view her own critical premises as requiring such liberation. Reading Kael's article three decades on, she seems astonishingly blind to the impact that auteurism would have. For example, she sneers repeatedly at the claims made for director Alfred Hitchcock, subsequently to become one of the securely canonized directors of all time.

38. Polan quotes a 1960 comment by Jean-Pierre Coursodon: "Jerry Lewis seems to us to represent the lowest degree of physical, moral and intellectual debasement that a comic actor can reach. The majority of his films are physically close to intolerable, even the least bad ones like *Artists and Models*" (Polan 1984a, 44).

39. Truffaut remained resistant to Lewis's appeal, even at the height of the Lewis cult among French critics.

40. Benayoun's book *Bonjour Monsieur Lewis* was published in 1972. It formed the basis for his six-part profile of the same name broadcast on French television in 1982.

41. For example, Robert Benayoun credits Lewis with supplying script material to fifteen of the twenty-two films he made before his first stint as a director in 1960 (Benayoun 1972, 338).

42. Seven of Lewis's self-directed films featured in *Cahiers du Cinéma*'s annual listings of best films from 1961 to 1967, and the journal voted him best director of the year on two occasions (Hillier 1986, 330-33). Lewis also won best director of the year awards in Italy, Belgium, Germany, Spain, and the Netherlands.

43. Where the auteurist controversy had united Anglo-American critics in defense of their professional values, British critics did not regard the French claims for Lewis with the same hostility as their U.S. counterparts. In 1964 the *Times Educational Supplement* carried a glowing appraisal of *The Nutty Professor:* "There is a genius at work, largely unheeded. And that genius, ladies and gentlemen—no, don't laugh right away—is Jerry Lewis" (Alpert 1966, 77). The following year Lewis received a highly favorable notice from Kenneth Tynan in the *Observer:* "Jerry Lewis could well be a stray, black-sheep member of J. D. Salinger's Glass family. . . . Watch the electric spontaneity of his response to events, how totally he abandons himself to each leap, swerve, shriek or gurgle—this is exemplary Zen behavior, in the finest tradition of the Glass menagerie" (Alpert 1966, 77). That same year, *Sight and Sound* published John Russell Taylor's warmly responsive account of his achievements as a filmmaker (Taylor 1966).

44. Shawn Levy (1996a) suggests that physical comedy had long been taken more seriously in France than in the United States: "A country capable of producing and appreciating a [Jacques] Tati was obviously a place where the comic film was respected as a style of moviemaking with a heritage and grammar all its own" (331). Daniel Royot (1978) points to the phenomenal popularity of Laurel and Hardy and W. C. Fields in postwar France. He also suggests that Jacques Tati was influenced more by Hollywood silent comedy than French vaudeville traditions (129-30).

45. *Cahiers du Cinéma* 197 (December 1967/January 1968).

46. Domarchi views Lewis as an intuitive artist and social critic: "The one I prefer above the others is *The Nutty Professor*. Ah, that is a magnificent picture—so inventive, so profound. For me it is not necessary that Lewis be fully conscious of his profundity. Nor does it take away from the significance of the films, which can be taken as reflecting problems of contemporary American civilization" (Alpert 1966, 74).

47. Sarris similarly vulgarizes the audiences for the comedian's films. In a snobbish comment evoking Pauline Kael's description of the debased fans of Hollywood action movie Sarris asserts that "Lewis appeals to unsophisticated audiences in the sticks and to ungenteel audiences in the urban slums" (Sarris 1966, 64).

48. From the moment sixteen-year-old Joseph Levitch appropriated his parents' Amer-

icanized stage name to embark upon a career as an entertainer, "Jerry Lewis" has remained an identity born of show-biz fabrication. Shawn Levy (1996a) opens his biography with the revelation that although Lewis has always claimed that he was born Joseph Levitch, his birth certificate identifies him as "Jerome." Levy comments: "The matter of Jerry Lewis's real name is no earth-shattering revelation, but it does raise the slippery question of personal identity in this life of shifting guises" (1).

2. THE COMIC BONDAGE OF DEAN MARTIN AND JERRY LEWIS

1. The following account of Lewis's early career draws extensively from Levy 1996a, 8–157. As Levy indicates throughout his biography, Lewis's history has been headily mythologized, by publicists, by journalists, and by Lewis himself.
2. For most of the first fifteen years of his life, Joey Levitch was raised by his grandmother, Sarah Rothberg, and saw very little of his parents (Soapbox Productions 1996).
3. Although Lewis did not realize it at the time, such "record acts" were already a staple form in vaudeville (Levy 1996a, 29).
4. Lewis also claims that from the age of fourteen he was writing material for Borscht Belt comedians such as Jack Carter (Alpert 1977, 46; Kantor et al. 1970, 271).
5. Lewis was helped by the fact that the wartime draft had depleted the stock of available entertainers (Levy 1996a, 35–45).
6. Accounts vary as to how the two men actually met and teamed up. Most of the details here are drawn from Tosches 1992, 84–139.
7. A residency at the Riobamba nightclub in late 1943 drew favorable responses from audiences and the trade press, and Martin subsequently found regular work in nightclubs and hotels and did several radio broadcasts (Tosches 1992, 97–100).
8. Lewis likes to give an extremely colorful account of their reteaming, claiming that he and Martin were pressurized by the mobster who ran the 500 Club into reprising their Havana-Madrid stuff (Levy 1996a, 67; Lewis and Gluck 1982, 140–41; JAS Productions 1992a).
9. Greshler himself would later be ousted. In 1950 MCA (the Music Corporation of America), the most powerful talent brokers in the country, seduced Martin and Lewis away from Greshler. A series of protracted and messy wrangles followed: Martin and Lewis sued Greshler for financial irregularities, but Greshler filed a countersuit against the team and MCA. MCA eventually bought Greshler's silence with a handsome settlement (Tosches 1992, 218–24; Levy 1996a, 123–26).
10. Evans worked for the team until his death in 1950, after which they passed into the hands of his West Coast partner, Jack Keller—who would remain with Lewis after his split from Martin (Tosches 1992, 145, 215).
11. For example, a 1951 article by Bill Davidson depicts Martin and Lewis as compulsive and unrestrained: "When the Messrs. Martin and Lewis ride in New York's glass-topped taxis, they stand up, their heads poking through the roof, playing gin rummy on the sliding top. At rehearsals for their television show, they chase the cameras about the stage, holding censorable pictures in front of the lens. On movie sets they climb into the rafters to bind and gag such necessary personages as the chief electri-

cian. And between shows at night clubs, it is not uncommon for them to pursue each other through the crowded customers on the dance floor, clad in nothing more than socks and undershorts" (Davidson 1951, 31).

12. Wallis quit his post as Warner Brothers' production chief to go into partnership with lawyer Hazen in 1944 (Levy 1996a, 88). The Wallis-Hazen deal with Paramount allowed them use of the studio's extensive facilities.

13. Martin and Lewis starred in five films for York Pictures: *At War with the Army, The Caddy, Living It Up, You're Never Too Young,* and *Pardners.* The company was formed in 1949 with Martin, Lewis, and Greshler as co-owners and Greshler as president and executive producer (Levy 1996a, 115). Greshler was bought out in 1952, and Paramount acquired Martin and Lewis's interests in York after the dissolution of the partnership. The company subsequently continued as a branch of Paramount Pictures, coproducing several of Lewis's solo ventures in the 1960s (*It's Only Money, The Disorderly Orderly, Who's Minding the Store,* and *Boeing Boeing*) (ibid., 275).

14. The team had already played live support to several Manhattan movie premieres. In January 1947 they did five or six shows a day to accompany *The Jolson Story,* and later they would provide a similar service for *The Naked City, Dear Brat,* and *Give My Regards to Broadway* (Levy 1996a, 77-83). Like many other New York premieres, *My Friend Irma* was supported by a condensed variety revue. Martin and Lewis were featured onstage for about thirty-five minutes, with the remaining twenty minutes filled by dancing team the Four Step Brothers, singer Carolyn Grey, and the Dick Stabile Orchestra ("Paramount, N.Y.," *Variety,* 5 October 1949, 6).

15. DC Comics published forty issues of *The Adventures of Dean Martin and Jerry Lewis* from 1952 to late 1957. In November 1957 the magazine was renamed *The Adventures of Jerry Lewis* and ran until 1971. During the same period the company also published *The Adventures of Bob Hope* (Daniels 1995, 97).

16. In a review of one of those stints at the Copacabana in 1949 *Variety* observed that "they have polished, refined and retailed their buffoonery in a manner which makes them the hottest comedy act in the saloons. . . . The result is a double-feature, two-ply parlay that appeals to the heps and the squares alike" ("Copacabana, N.Y.," 27 April 1949, 53).

17. As Hill recognizes, Martin and Lewis renewed the performative dynamism of variety entertainment, a popular tradition encompassing forms like the minstrel show, burlesque, and vaudeville. Variety shows were structured in accordance not with the representational protocols of drama but with "an aesthetic based on heterogeneity, affective immediacy, and performance" (Jenkins 1992, 278). Henry Jenkins (1990) notes that the audiences' response to vaudeville or burlesque comedy "did not involve the quick perception of subtle incongruity or any specialized knowledge and background; it required merely a visceral reaction to crude shock, intense stimulation and immediate sensation" (6). Aiming to provoke instant and intense responses from their audiences, variety entertainments combined a range of performative attractions—singing, dancing, juggling, joke-telling, physical routines—within the context of a structured bill, or program, designed to provide both diversity and cumulative impact (Karnick and Jenkins 1995, 154).

18. See also Marx 1975, 37.

19. Eighteen episodes of Martin and Lewis's NBC radio shows are collected on CD and

audio cassette, available from the nostalgia company Radio Spirits, Inc. (Martin and Lewis 1995).

20. *Jouessance:* a neologism. The noun *jouissance,* popularized in critical theory by French revisionist psychoanalysis, can mean both "orgasm" and more generalized "pleasure" or "enjoyment." Its root verb, *jouir,* "to enjoy," is also fortuitously close to *jouer,* "to play."

21. The Hope and Crosby films of the 1940s were *The Road to Singapore* (1940), *The Road to Zanzibar* (1941), *The Road to Morocco* (1942), *The Road to Utopia* (1946), and *The Road to Rio* (1948). Douglas Gomery points out that Hope and Crosby were the most consistently successful star teaming in 1940s Hollywood and that the series grossed more than any other during the studio era (Gomery 1986, 43). The screen partnership was revived with *The Road to Bali* (1953) and *The Road to Hong Kong* (1962).

22. According to Allan Bérubé, mass mobilization not only led to the entry of a large number of gay men and women into the armed services but also brought people who regarded themselves as heterosexual into intense emotional, and sometimes sexual, relations with members of the same sex: "Veterans of all kinds describe the love they felt for each other with a passion, romance, and sentimentality that often rivaled gay men's expressions of their love for other men and made gay affections seem less out of place" (Bérubé 1990, 186). Informally, and sometimes officially, the army encouraged a "buddy system" of close male friendships. "Buddy relationships," comments Bérubé, "easily slipped into romantic and even sexual intimacies between men that they themselves often did not perceive to be 'queer.' 'You'd get a buddy,' explained Maxwell Gordon, who served in the South Pacific on a Navy carrier, 'and you'd look out for each other and pretty soon you started exchanging clothes. And you ate together, usually bunked close together, went down to the head and showered together, and shared everything together. . . . A lot of friendships became intense and men were getting closer and closer. People ended up lovers. The ship was crawling with them. It was an accepted thing.'" (ibid., 188–89).

23. A former New Orleans beauty queen, Lamour worked as a singer before she was signed to Paramount. Her first film, *The Jungle Princess* (1936), established the screen persona for which she would become famous — the exotic native girl, natural and unsophisticated. Subsequent roles of this kind included *The Hurricane* (1937), *Her Jungle Love* (1938), and *Moon over Burma* (1940).

24. Drawing upon Bérubé's history of gays and lesbians in the U.S. military, Cohan provides an intriguing reading of Hope's 1940s comic persona as a feminized male: "The Hope persona condensed and revalued what amounted to the Forties discursive construction of 'queerness' as a gender disorder, particularly within the institutionalized framework of the military during the war. Let me quote from Bérubé once again: 'Military psychiatrists . . . identified what they considered to be the three major traits of the homosexual personality — effeminacy, a sense of superiority, and fear. Effeminacy was by far the most common characteristic psychiatrists attributed to the typical homosexual. At a time when national survival depended on aggressive masculinity, military psychiatrists paid special attention to effeminacy as a sign of homosexuality, expressing on hospital wards the same interest in gender characteristics that their colleagues had shown at induction stations. Researchers described their gay male patients as womanly in their bodies, mannerisms, emotional make-up, and interests.' The very traits celebrated through the considerable popularity of Bob Hope's screen

persona in hit after hit—his boasting and self-conscious bravado, his recurring cowardice and passivity, his effeminacy and sexual ambiguity, not to mention the way he could turn any costume into a drag performance or, for that matter, the occasions when Crosby joked about Hope's rear end—all served to identify, in another but more official context, the homosexual personality for military psychiatrists at the moment in the early forties when the ban against homosexual soldiers was first instituted as national policy" (Cohan 1993, 9).

25. "As families were reunited and struggled to put their lives back together after the war, articles, books, advertisements, and the media promoted idealized versions of the nuclear family, heterosexuality, and traditional gender roles in home and the workplace. Accompanying this preoccupation with conformity was a fearful scapegoating of those who deviated from a narrowing ideal of the nuclear family and the American way of life" (Bérubé 1990, 258).

26. Molly Haskell (1974) suggests that the male comedy duos exclude heterosexuality for a latently homosexual "union of opposites (tall/short, thin/fat, straight/comic) who, like husband and wife, combine to make a whole" (66).

27. The *Variety* reviewer of one of Lewis's 1956 solo shows at the Sands Hotel, Las Vegas, was similarly affronted by his hardcore effeminacy: "He's not only doing a panz, but doing it overly broad and too often. It goes beyond the laugh stage; it gets to the shock point. Lewis gets going with the homo stuff very early . . . on 'Sometimes I'm Happy,' during which Lewis starts making passes at the choristers, stretching the gestures and mouth contortions far beyond reasonable bounds" ("Jerry Lewis," 5 December 1956, 73).

28. A good example of Lewis's shifts between these forms of "deviance" occurs in the longest of the stage performances in *The Stooge*. Martin is on stage singing "Give Me Just One More Chance" when Lewis heckles him; the crooner then invites him to come onto the stage to see if he can do any better. Lewis immediately does an impression of a monkey and later attempts to disrupt Martin further by slipping on a dress and set of pigtails.

29. In the 1955 book *Television Program Production* Carroll O'Meara made a similar point about the antithetical regimes of the big city nightclub and television: "What is acceptable to broad-minded night club audiences in Manhattan, Hollywood, or Las Vegas is rarely apt to be fare for admission in homes in any city or town. . . . Jaded and liquored celebrants in a night club will accept as sophisticated humor and wit what is actually nothing but smut. . . . What many entertainers fail to realize, actually, is that the areas containing the bistros, night spots and bright lights are only a minute segment of America. And yet, somehow, they insist on broadcasting to the entire nation comic and other material which is definitely not acceptable in the average American home. . . . Our nation consists of 160 million citizens, most of whom live in small towns, go to church on Sunday, attempt to bring up their children decently, and do not regard burlesque shows as the ultimate in theater" (Boddy 1993, 102).

30. For example, there was a large-scale migration from the metropolitan centers to suburbia, and a general reduction of the working week released more time for leisure activities. The increase in disposable income was matched by a boom in the availability of consumer durables, including labor-saving appliances such as vacuum cleaners, washing machines, and refrigerators (Balio 1990, 3; Belton 1992, 70-74).

31. Lynn Spigel's study of the way that television was represented in U.S. women's magazines of the late 1940s and early 1950s highlights the extent to which it was promoted as an agent of familial unification during this period: "The magazines included television as a staple home fixture before most Americans could even receive a TV signal much less consider purchasing the expensive item. These media discourses did not so much reflect social reality; instead, they preceded it. The home magazines helped to construct television as a household object, one which belonged to the family space. More surprisingly, however, in the span of roughly four years, television itself became *the* central figure in images of the American home; it became the cultural symbol par excellence of family life. . . . In its capacity as a unifying agent, television fit well with the more general postwar hopes for a return to domestic values. It was seen as a kind of household cement which promised to reassemble the splintered lives of families who had been separated during the war. It was also meant to reinforce the new suburban family unit which had left most of its extended family behind in the city" (Spigel 1990, 76). For further consideration of the role played by home and family in postwar America, see May 1990, 20–36.

32. Through the 1950s television progressively displaced the cinema as "the focus for media consumption and consumption promoted by media" (Allen 1980, 492). In terms of advertising revenues it overtook radio in 1952 and the print media in 1955 (Boddy 1993, 155).

33. For example, between 1948 and 1953 most of the television stations in the United States were NBC affiliates (Balio 1990, 18).

34. Early 1950s television — the era of liveness — is often regarded nostalgically as a "Golden Age" of aesthetic innovations that was killed off by the shift of the production base from New York to Hollywood and by the displacement of liveness by the telefilm. William Boddy argues that this account was disseminated and consolidated by a group of powerful New York television critics — including Gilbert Seldes, Jack Gould, and John Crosby — who were hostile to Hollywood entertainment and devoted to New York theater. Their arguments were subsequently appropriated by the networks themselves as a means of defending their hegemony over broadcasting when faced with the threat of low-budget Hollywood telefilm series: "The comparison of film versus live program formats became the central element in the highly prescriptive critical discourse of television's Golden Age. Critics seized on weaknesses of the cheap, genre-based thirty-minute telefilms, comparing them to the big-budget sixty-minute network spectaculars to support claims of television as an essentially live medium" (Boddy 1993, 73). These critics were most concerned to champion the virtues of anthology drama series — such as the *Ford Television Theater, Kraft Television Theater, Armstrong Circle Theater, Studio One, Playhouse 90,* and the *U.S. Steel Hour*—whose liveness made them akin more to the respectable modes of New York drama than to Hollywood's alien populist entertainments (ibid., 74). The upmarket television critics felt betrayed by the networks' embrace of telefilm drama at the expense of live drama: by 1959 there was only one live dramatic program on U.S. television (ibid., 76, 188).

35. As Barry Putterman considers, the variety show had virtually played itself out as a mainstream television form by the early 1960s: "The gradual shift in production

techniques from live shows broadcast from New York to videotaped shows from Hollywood drained much of the vitality from the format without substituting a new aesthetic that could take advantage of those changing conditions. . . . By the end of the 1960s, a new wave of variety shows like *Rowan and Martin's Laugh-In* and the second *Andy Williams Show* had developed new strategies for using videotape to their comedic advantage" (Putterman 1995, 20-21). The ratings for *Texaco Star Theater* and *The Colgate Comedy Hour,* NBC's two major variety shows, weakened from 1952 as competing forms — telefilm series such as *I Love Lucy* (1951) and *Dragnet* (1952) and quiz shows such as *The $64,000 Question* (1955) — took off in popularity (Boddy 1990b, 76).

36. Arthur Wertheim (1983) ascribes Berle's phenomenal success to the fact that the television audience was largely urban until 1952. After coaxial cable brought television to small-town and rural areas, Berle's slick urban vaudeville style lost favor and his ratings began to drop rapidly (56, 69-70).

37. Until electronic videotape was available from 1957, rebroadcasting of live transmissions was only possible with the aid of low-quality kinescopes — 16mm copies that were filmed by pointing a camera directly at a cathode ray tube (Barnouw 1975, 205, 212).

38. Unless otherwise noted, citations from television reviews in *Variety* and *Daily Variety* are taken from the multivolume collection of *Variety* television reviews (Prouty 1989-96), which do not contain the original page numbers. The trade journals minimized the importance of individual writers, identifying them only by means of a brief coded tag (e.g., "Abel," "Newt," "Kahn," "Jose"). Given the journals' stress on institutional authorship, I will likewise treat the reviewers as a consistent voice, as spokespersons of the magazines rather than individual contributors.

39. Retitled *The Ed Sullivan Show* in 1955, *Toast of the Town* proved one of the most successful and long-lasting variety shows: it had a twenty-three-year run as a Sunday-night fixture on CBS and was a premier venue for new talent. As Tim Brooks and Earle Marsh (1985a) note, Sullivan strenuously objected to the "vaudeo" tag because the show's diversity of performing attractions was far more ambitious than the repertoire of vaudeville: "There was grand opera and the latest rock stars, classical ballet and leggy Broadway showgirls, slapstick comedy and recitations from great dramatic writings, often juxtaposed on a single telecast" (63).

40. Martin and Lewis had been guests on Bob Hope's radio shows and television specials in 1948 and 1949. They also traded guest shots in one another's films: Martin and Lewis appeared for a gag appearance in the 1952 film *The Road to Bali,* and the following year Hope and Crosby repaid the favor by stepping in for the closing gag of *Scared Stiff.* (Excerpts from Martin and Lewis's appearance on the Hope and Crosby telethon are included in JAS Productions 1993b, and a longer version of the show is available on videotape.)

41. Although Crosby himself ran a successful telefilm production company (Anderson 1994, 57), he was nervous about making the move to television and may have been pressurized into the move by his commercial sponsors. According to *Daily Variety* ("Hope-Crosby Olympics Telethon Grabs $1,000,000 Plus Some TV Firsts," 23 June 1952), Crosby wanted to concentrate on radio, but Coca-Cola insisted that he represent them on TV as well. Crosby was contracted to CBS, Hope to NBC, and the re-

combination of this popular film partnership was seen by the networks as a prime video opportunity to promote these flagship stars ("Bing & Bob's Olympic Telethon Doubles Goal, Exceeds $1,000,000," *Variety*, 25 June 1952). Crosby's telethon appearance was a tryout for a more regular showcase.

42. But coincidentally—and I kid you not!—at this point a huge moth decides to fly into the view of the camera and lands on Bob Hope's jacket. Hope is not aware of this new embarrassment, but the production team seems to be, as there is a quick cut to another camera, with a tighter framing of the comedian that excludes the moth. Another source of embarrassment may underlie the spectacle: Shawn Levy ascribes Crosby's retreat from the scene to his fear that Lewis would topple his toupee (Levy 1996a, 153).

43. Subsequent hosts included Donald O'Connor, Abbott and Costello, Bob Hope, Spike Jones, Phil Silvers, Jimmy Durante, and Gordon McCrae. From the 1952-53 season, the format was broadened to include special presentations based on Broadway shows—such as *Anything Goes* and *Oklahoma!*—and broadcasts from a variety of locations across the United States. The show was both lavish and adventurous: in September 1951 it became the first network show to originate from Hollywood, and in November 1953 the program included the first network color telecast. The title was amended to *The Colgate Variety Hour* in 1955, when production of the Martin and Lewis component was taken over by York Pictures (Brooks and Marsh 1985b, 48; Tosches 1992, 280). Colgate-Palmolive decided to end its sponsorship of the show in December 1955, but in a move that makes plain the stars' continuing bankability, NBC offered them $7.5 million for four television specials per year for five years. When the team folded the NBC deal was renegotiated as two separate contracts for Dean Martin and Jerry Lewis (Levy 1996a, 201).

44. For example, Milton Berle faced a punishing schedule on the *Texaco Star Theater*, having to mount a live weekly show for thirty-nine consecutive weeks. Another comedy revue, launched in 1950, used rotating hosts: the *Four Star Revue* (a.k.a. *All-Star Revue*) alternated Ed Wynn, Danny Thomas, Jack Carson, and Jimmy Durante (Wertheim 1983, 62, 71).

45. In the night clubs Martin and Lewis's two-man showcase was incorporated within a broader revue context. At the top-flight clubs, these could be elaborate affairs. For example, at the Copacabana in April 1949 they topped a bill that included dancer Ramona Lang, male comedy-music group the Vagabonds, two bands, vocalists Jack Cassidy and Penny Carroll, and eight Copa showgirls ("costumes adorn them in brilliant and sometimes quite Ziegfeldian splendor," noted *Variety*). Martin and Lewis themselves were onstage for over an hour ("Copacabana, N.Y.," 27 April 1949).

46. By 1951 the network of coaxial cable and microwave linking East and West Coasts had been completed, enabling television stations across the country—in cities, suburbs, and backwaters—to connect to the major commercial broadcasting services. The wonders of television had already penetrated 40 percent of U.S. homes, and the rest would follow shortly (Belton 1994, 258).

47. In a study of the ethnic profiles of Hollywood stars of the early 1930s to early 1950s Ian Jarvie (1991) reports that "it is unclear whether in his Martin and Lewis days Lewis was recognizably Jewish to his audience" (89). In his ghosted 1982 biography Lewis more confidently proclaims his Jewishness. For example, he discusses his ex-

periences in the Catskills, his problems with the racist German American Bund in 1930s Irvington, and the familial problems he encountered when he married the Catholic Patti Palmer (who, like Joey Levitch, Americanized her name from the more ethnically marked Esther Calonico). Lewis's paternal grandfather was a rabbi, and although Danny Lewis was well aware of the compromises required in American show business he did not approve of his son's cross-faith marriage. Patti was initiated into the Jewish faith through a second wedding ceremony, three months before the birth of her first child (Lewis and Gluck 1982, 124-28).

48. As John DiMeglio suggests, mainstream variety entertainment mirrored the American ideologies of the melting pot and the success ethic: "The very nature of vaudeville . . . was representative of the American mystique. The expansiveness of vaudeville, as well, where novelty acts, animal acts, impersonators, acrobats, variety acts, magicians, soloists, monologists, comedy teams, drama sketches, dancers, and even chasers, all got billing and did their separate, highly individual parts, yet all somehow integrating into the whole, served as symbol of Americanism" (Scheurer 1985, 318).

49. David Marc (1990) claims that after World War II "the Jew returned to American popular-culture cosmology with a vengeance," as comedians such as Milton Berle, Sid Caesar, George Burns, Jack Benny, and Phil Silvers were given their own starring shows (43). However, they did not assert their ethnicity in a manner that would necessarily have been read in these terms by all audiences across the United States. Marc cites a Sid Caesar sketch, written by Carl Reiner and Mel Brooks, which featured characters with Yiddish-derived names. Although Gantze Mishpuckeh, Gehackte Liebe, and Shmateh (respectively, "the whole big family," "chopped liver," and "rag") may have been greeted with the laughter of recognition by New York audiences, it is likely that midwesterners read them more simply as comically abstruse nonsense. Significantly, Lewis played his two most explicitly Jewish roles in the television dramas *The Jazz Singer* (1958) and *Fight for Life* (1987).

50. In this sense Lewis resembled the pioneering Jewish entertainer Lew Fields (né Schoenfeld), whose career ran from the late 1870s to the early 1940s. In their fascinating study of Fields's career in show biz, Armond Fields and L. Marc Fields (1993) note that although ethnic comedy was the lifeblood of popular variety theater in the late nineteenth century, Jews—who in the 1870s constituted almost 10 percent of the city's population—remained virtually unrepresented on the New York stage until the 1890s (31-32). In the 1880s Fields and his partner Joe Weber shrewdly accommodated their repertoire to whatever ethnic style happened to be in vogue—blackface, Irish, or "Dutch" (i.e., *deutsch,* "German") (ibid., 45): "Growing up in a world of sharply defined ethnic categories, Lew Fields attempted to blur or conceal the distinguishing characteristics of his own background: his nationality, even his name. It is as if this pioneer of ethnic humor had to purge himself of his own ethnic identity to create the characters that would make him famous. Offstage, he made himself ethnically 'neutral,' a living *tabula rasa,* awaiting the character delineation that came with blacking up, donning green knee-pants or the Dutchman's chin whiskers and flat derby. He became the primed canvas on which the Bowery audiences would paint their grotesque self-portraits" (ibid., 52-53).

51. For example, during approximately 25 percent of the *Colgate Variety Hour* telecast on 11 November 1955 Lewis does a bucktooth impersonation of a Japanese film star.

Lewis more or less reprised this material on several of his solo TV shows ("Ribbing of orientals," *Variety* noted, "has become a major specialty for Lewis" ["*The Jerry Lewis Show*," 12 June 1957]). Many of the films he made with Martin feature Lewis's exaggerated ethnic impersonations: he does a Hawaiian native near the end of *Sailor Beware;* a French barber near the opening of *You're Never Too Young;* and French, Austrian, and Chinese doctors in one scene in *Living It Up.* Lewis's comedy also carries a further, little discussed ethnic subtext. In an interview for the 1996 *Frontline* documentary *Secret Daughter* (PBS, and WGBH Educational Foundation 1996) he acknowledged that black performers were a vital influence on his own comedy. In the 1940s Lewis regularly attended shows at Harlem's Apollo Theater to catch the acts of black comedians such as the Stump and Stumpy team. As Lewis admits, because these performers were rarely exposed to white audiences, it was easy to "pirate" their material: "The black community, they loved the clown. They knew of what I took from their culture, which was their comic sense of timing, their ability for self-deprecating humor, which is everything I used, their rhythm in comic timing. I mean, I learned from some pretty good people. . . . You see, when a performer's influenced by greatness, you don't know that you are because comics are thieves. They thieve" (PBS, and WGBH Educational Foundation 1996, 12-13). However, black comedian Jimmy Cross, a great influence on Lewis, stresses that a two-way process of cultural exchange was involved. His own act borrowed licks from white artists: "And the whole beginning of me, James Cross—I loved Charles Chaplin, Joe Penner. I had a very, very good liking for Milton Berle. And then I love me because I conglomerated all of them and dropped them into a chocolate drop and made them me" (ibid., 13).

52. Charles Musser (1991) notes that the early 1930s comedies of Eddie Cantor and the Marx Brothers "base their humor on role-playing and the conjunction of diverse ethnicities. . . . Ethnicity is shown to be a constraint—and a construction—from which characters and audiences can be at least temporarily liberated. Role-playing, which was necessary and typically alienating, could become pleasurable, subversive, and affirming of self" (43).

53. Putterman makes it clear, though, that in practice a more mobile set of relations existed between the performer and the sponsor, In dramatic shows, for example, "the commercials never became part of the storyline. In fact, the commercial presentation tended to underline the multiple roles of the actors as commercial spokespeople, fictional characters, and private citizens, thus ensuring a distanced and ambivalent message for the audience. The ways that commercial messages were structured into live variety shows not only varied in style, but were used by the performers as another strategy to define their relationship to the audience" (Putterman 1995, 9).

54. For example, at NBC Pat Weaver used a policy of big-budget spectaculars as a means of pricing the cost of production beyond the reach of individual sponsors, thus encouraging a model of participating sponsorship that strengthened the power of the networks as brokers for commercial airtime (Anderson 1994, 86-87). By the late 1950s multiple-sponsor participation had displaced the single sponsor as the norm of television advertising (Boddy 1993, 159).

55. Arthur Godfrey's easygoing TV persona, which replicated the conditions of radio intimacy, enabled the promos to be integrated within the show in a similar manner: "Godfrey not only handled his own commercial spots for Lipton soup and tea but

treated them as particularly special moments during which he could share quality time with the audience" (Putterman 1995, 14).

56. Later in the decade the nervous companionship of entertainment and promotion erupted into major scandals: the radio payola controversies that laid waste to Alan Freed and the exposé of rigged questions on the television quiz show *The $64,000 Question* (dramatized in Robert Redford's 1994 film *Quiz Show*) (Boddy 1990a, 98–116).

57. For an influential discussion of the utopian ethos of American popular entertainment, see Richard Dyer's article "Entertainment and Utopia" (Dyer 1981). The Martin and Lewis film *The Stooge* features a scene that neatly illustrates the importance of this ethos. Martin's aggressive and drunken crooner Bill Miller is jealous of the extent to which his success in vaudeville relies upon the contribution of his stooge, Ted Rogers (Lewis), and he decides to terminate the relationship. Ted reminds him they have a show scheduled for that night, and Bill mutters to himself, "You bet I got a show to do, I'll show everybody." The pun on the word "show" makes plain the degree to which the selfishness of Martin's character is polluting the other-directed and communalizing promise of show-biz utopianism.

58. *Variety*'s review of the *Colgate Variety Hour* (*Martin & Lewis Show,* 21 September 1955) complains about the flagrant plug for their film *You're Never Too Young.* The review of the show telecast on 25 June 1951 takes umbrage at their plug for *That's My Boy* ("Tele Follow-Up Comment," *Variety,* 27 June 1951). A *Daily Variety* review (31 December 1951) similarly notes a heavy promo for *Sailor Beware.* Lewis persisted with such tactics after his split with Martin; for example, in its review of his first solo TV special *Variety* complained that "in one respect, Lewis hasn't changed. He's still handing out lotsa cuffola plugs, on this occasion for mags with his phizz on the cover" ("*The Jerry Lewis Show,*" 23 January 1957). Similar criticism greeted his subsequent solo shows.

59. The *Variety* reviewers were fond of mentioning the contributions of writers to the *Comedy Hour* show. In part this mirrors the prestige accorded the writer-as-author by quality television in their discourse on the merits of the live teleplay. For a consideration of the valuation of the writer in TV drama of the Golden Age, see Boddy 1993, 85–90.

60. Ed Simmons subsequently established himself as a respected television writer and also produced *The Carol Burnett Show* from the late 1960s. Norman Lear emerged in the 1970s as one of the major creative forces in U.S. situation comedy: he formed a writing-producing-directing partnership with Bud Yorkin (a *Comedy Hour* director) that was responsible for such 1970s successes as *All in the Family, Sanford and Son,* and *Maude* (Marx 1975, 132).

61. A similar complaint had been made the previous year: "The Martin & Lewis comedy formula seldom strays from the loud, the raucous and the pratfall school. Several times during the melee, ribtickling comic gems emerged but for the most part it was the same old M&L knockabout pattern" ("Tele Follow-Up Comment," *Variety,* 13 January 1954).

62. Prop gags became increasingly important to their television shows, and similar misfires proved solid laugh-getters. For example, in one sketch an automatic towel-puller needed for a gag falls off the wall, and Lewis rushes off camera to brings on a prop man to fix it (*Colgate Comedy Hour,* 10 January 1954).

63. In *Damn Yankees* the number is performed by the temptress Lola and the devil Applegate. Martin and Lewis's version pointedly de-heterosexualizes the song.

64. An earlier show contains a sketch that operates in a similar fashion. Martin is a music shop employee who is fired because of the havoc wreaked by Lewis's customer: the two men pal up and conclude with a rendition of "We Belong Together" (*Colgate Comedy Hour*, 2 May 1954). Other displays of this principle of creative disruption can be found in a sketch broadcast on 4 February 1951 that casts them as guests at formal wedding and a sketch broadcast on 24 June 1951 that features Lewis running amok in a high-society club house.

65. Showcasing routines like this, which evoke the "pure" performance of their nightclub act, recur throughout the Martin and Lewis films. Examples include "The Donkey Serenade" sequence in *My Friend Irma*, the "Singing a Vagabond Song" number in *My Friend Irma Goes West*, "The Old Calliope" sequence in *Sailor Beware*, the "Give Me Just One More Chance" stage performance in *The Stooge*, and the nightclub routine in *Scared Stiff*.

3. PHOTOCHEMISTRY

1. *That's My Boy, At War with the Army, Sailor Beware, Jumping Jacks, The Caddy, Scared Stiff, The Stooge,* and *Living It Up.*

2. For example, the films Martin and Lewis made for their own company, York Pictures, also relied heavily upon remakes: *Pardners* was a loose revision of Bing Crosby's *Rhythm on the Range* (1936), *Living It Up* reworked the screwball film *Nothing Sacred* (1937), and *You're Never Too Young* revisited the 1942 Billy Wilder-Ginger Rogers comedy *The Major and the Minor.*

3. For a consideration of the history and dynamics of the comedian-comedy genre, see Seidman 1981 and Krutnik 1995a, 17-38.

4. In the musical film, another genre dedicated to entertainment spectacle, the fit between star and role is often "legitimized" by casting the star within a diegetic context of performance (the world of theater, for example). In comedian comedies the star is occasionally cast as a professional entertainer, as in the Hope and Crosby films; Danny Kaye's *Knock on Wood* (1954); Martin and Lewis's *Jumping Jacks, The Stooge,* and *The Caddy;* and Lewis's *The Geisha Boy* and *The Patsy.* However, this is by no means essential.

5. This is made clear by the Hope and Crosby films. The simple plot of the series— from *The Road to Singapore* (1940) to *The Road to Hong Kong* (1962)—was "always this: the boys are in a jam, as many jams as possible, and they have to clown their way out" (Faith 1983, 142). Crosby claimed, "The jams are plotted in the script and although they're bogus situations and on the incredible side, they are important because they hold the story together and provide a framework for our monkeyshines. Gags can't be played against gags; they have to be played against something serious even though the serious stuff is melodramatic. Hope and I invent many of these gags from predicaments as we go along" (ibid.).

6. Hal Wallis has taken credit for *That's My Boy,* one of the most commercially successful and highly regarded of the Martin and Lewis films: "We [Wallis and writer Cy

Howard] felt that the earlier Martin and Lewis pictures were essentially excuses for gags, but this time we made the characters more interesting, even complex, and the two boys played them beautifully" (Wallis and Higham 1980, 142).

7. Lewis plays similarly sickly neurotics in *Sailor Beware, The Caddy,* and numerous *Comedy Hour* sketches.

8. *The Caddy* returns to the Paramount Theater, and to the self-reflexive mode, for the closing scene. Booked to follow Anthony and Miller at the venue, Martin and Lewis appear backstage and are mistaken for the fictional team by the latter's girlfriends. In a process shot Anthony and Miller then confront Martin and Lewis and take the women away.

9. Furthermore, as Nick Tosches suggests, the film is "strangely evocative of the Martin-and-Lewis story itself, whose future it uncannily seemed to presage — in mirrored reverse." The difference from the real-life Martin-Lewis story is that in *The Stooge* it is Martin's character, not Lewis, who represents the corruptions of egomania. Suggestively enough, this unusual Martin-Lewis vehicle was actually made in 1951 but its release was held back for two years. Tosches ascribes the delay to Hal Wallis's misgivings about the film, conjecturing that "there was something about it, that faint undertow of reality, that he did not like" (Tosches 1992, 235).

10. Arthur Marx describes one of their 1946 shows at the Havana-Madrid:

During Dean's last number, he [Lewis] appeared among the tables dressed as a busboy, precariously balancing a large tray of dishes on one hand raised over his head. As he wove his way through the tables, he suddenly appeared to lose control of his heavy load, and the whole tray of dishes went crashing to the floor.

"Oh, sorry, kind sir," apologized Jerry, as Dino stopped his song in midlyric and fixed his twinkling black eyes on the mock busboy. "I hope I didn't interrupt anything."

"No, I was getting pretty tired of that song, anyway," responded the quick-thinking Dino.

The audience roared as Jerry got down on his knees and started picking up the broken crockery piece by piece, and Dino came off the stage to help him. All the while, the two of them continued their ad libs.

At the next show, Jerry repeated the stunt, and the two of them expanded the bit by throwing in a few more lines and pieces of business. (Marx 1975, 47)

A further variation on this routine appeared on the *Colgate Comedy Hour* telecast of 3 June 1951.

11. *At War with the Army* is even more unusual because Lewis's character is married.

12. The film is actually based on *Hazel Flagg,* the 1953 Broadway musical adaptation of *Nothing Sacred,* featuring songs by Jule Styne and Bob Hilliard (Jasen 1990, 251). Ben Hecht, the original screenwriter of *Nothing Sacred,* also wrote the book for the Broadway show, which began a run of 190 performances at the Mark Hellinger Theater on 11 February 1953.

13. By taking over Carole Lombard's role, Lewis is cast as the "feminine" eccentric, but his "difference" is more explicitly contextualized as childlike deviance. As Catherine Irene Johnson notes, "Lewis whines, hangs his head, slumps into pouts, and other-

wise observes the conventions signaling childhood. . . . All the men Lewis encounters . . . are either considerably older (the old geezer at the gas pumps, the waiter at
the Boulevard Room), or they are in positions of authority: his boss, his doctor, the
army, the newspaper editor, the ambulance drivers, the specialists in radiation poisoning" (Johnson 1981, 128). Everywhere he goes, Homer is a pampered center of
attention, and his wildest eccentricities are excused as signs of his illness.

14. Steve sings to and dances with Wally during a special Homer Flagg Night at the
Wonderland Ballroom. Homer is plied with alcohol by a tearfully sympathetic waiter
and then takes to the floor for a jitterbug contest. Homer's frenetic dance with guest
star Sheree North provides a marked contrast to the decorous ballroom smooching
of Steve and Wally. After this spectacular display of bodily excess Homer collapses.

15. With Betsy, Hap is incapable of asserting a masculine perspective. Although dressed
in the uniform of a man, he is clearly more of a boy: toward the end of their opening song, Betsy consoles Hap by embracing him affectionately, like a mother. This
maternal domination marks both their stage performance and their offstage interaction; she instructs the smitten Hap that their relationship will remain purely professional ("We do a swell act on stage. Let's just keep it that way, huh?"). Kissing him on
the forehead, she tells him he's just about the nicest boy she knows. Whereas the
civilian, heterosexual world is associated with frustration and restraint, Hap's reluctant immersion in the army enables a creative liberation: he becomes a star instead of
a stooge. Several other Martin and Lewis films play out their scenarios of male unification in contexts in which close relationships between men can be readily legitimized: in the world of sport (*That's My Boy* and *The Caddy*), the entertainment business (*The Stooge, The Caddy, Three Ring Circus*), the masculine world of the Wild
West (*Pardners*), and, in particular, the armed services (*At War with the Army, Sailor Beware,* the beginning of *Three Ring Circus*).

16. When Hap is ordered to help the men pack parachutes — a teamwork procedure —
he manages to get the strings all knotted together. He sorts the mess out by cutting
the strings, which, in a childlike way, is the 'logical' solution to the immediate problem! Hap is a willful misfit, but the male group pulls together to protect him (Chick
has the damaged parachute replaced in the nick of time) because they are reliant
upon his skills as entertainer, comedian, and sanctioned misfit.

17. The original script for *Jumping Jacks* dates from the same period as the Hope and
Kaye films. Robert Lees and Fred Rinaldo, who also scripted several Abbott and
Costello films, wrote *Jumping Jacks* sometime between 1941 and 1943, but Paramount
did not succeed in finding suitable stars for the project (Neibaur and Okuda 1995,
51–53).

18. In his 1942 book *A Generation of Vipers* Philip Wylie portrayed the American mother
as a sinister, castrating figure who exerted total domination over the helpless male:
"Mom is everywhere and everything and damned near everybody, and on her de-
pends all the rest of the U.S. Disguised as good old mom, dear old mom, sweet old
mom, your loving mom, and so on, she is the bride at every funeral and the corpse
at every wedding. Men live for her and die for her, dote upon her and whisper her
name as they pass away" (Kaplan 1992, 116). Betty Friedan credits the 1946 book *Their
Mother's Sons*—by Dr. Edward Strecker, a consultant to the surgeon general of the
army and navy — with the consolidation of the misogynist mystique of Momism. She

cites the following definition by Strecker: "A mom is a woman whose maternal behavior is motivated by the seeking of emotional recompense for the buffets which life
has dealt her own ego. In her relationship with her children, every deed and almost
every breath are designed unconsciously but exclusively to absorb her children emotionally and to bind them to her securely. In order to achieve this purpose, she must
stamp a pattern of immature behavior on her children. . . . Being immature herself,
she breeds immaturity in her children and, by and large, they are doomed to lives of
personal and social insufficiency and unhappiness" (Friedan 1965, 167-69).

19. Some further indicative examples: (*a*) In *Sailor Beware* Martin teaches Lewis how to
box in preparation for a contest: the scene provides an excuse for a physical "clinch"
between the two men; (*b*) in *You're Never Too Young* the two first meet when Martin
visits Lewis's incompetent trainee barber: Lewis manhandles the elevating swivel
chair on which Martin sits, and as it rises into the air Lewis sits astride the handsome
man in a manner that is strikingly suggestive of coitus; (*c*) in a sketch on the *Colgate
Comedy Hour* (4 May 1954) Lewis and Martin are pressed into facial contact as they
squeeze into a crowded closet, their lips meeting in what is, to all intents and purposes, a screen kiss (this sketch is included in JAS Productions 1992a).

20. For a nuanced teasing-out of the logic of absurdity in gag comedy, see Palmer 1987,
39-58.

21. It is worth noting how the emotional complexities of this sequence are dealt with
subsequently. Harvey waits impatiently for Joe to return, and when a cab pulls up
outside the cabin he mistakes the inebriated husband it disgorges for his buddy. Harvey grabs the stranger and hustles him inside the cabin. He pushes him onto the bed
and begins to take off his shoes and trousers. It is only when the man on the bed addresses him as "Emma" that Harvey realizes his mistake; Harvey shows him outside,
where the formidable Emma waits in the doorway of a neighboring cabin. This
scene extends the Lewis-as-wife equation established earlier but displaces it into a
more safely comic mode by replacing Joe with an actual husband. According to
Arthur Marx it was Lewis himself who was responsible for this "homosexual" material (Marx 1975, 141).

4. ONE MAN ALONE

1. General details of the Martin and Lewis breakup are drawn from Gehman 1964,
136-50; Marx 1975, 126-98; Lewis and Gluck 1982, 3-6, 189-205; Tosches 1992,
269-72; and Levy 1996a, 178-211. For a detailed account of the Byzantine intrigues
surrounding the production of *Three Ring Circus,* see Levy 1996a, 178-85.

2. Three months later Martin let him down again, when he refused to participate for a
benefit Lewis had organized at the Shrine Auditorium; once more Lewis had to deliver a solo show (Lewis and Gluck 1982, 198-99).

3. Initially featured in the *Colgate Comedy Hour* show broadcast on 18 September 1955,
the sketch was subsequently included in the second installment of *Martin and Lewis:
Their Golden Age of Comedy* (JAS Productions 1992b).

4. Martin and Lewis returned to live performance after a fourteen-month hiatus, playing the Sands Hotel, Las Vegas, in March 1956. The documentary *Jerry Lewis — the*

Last American Clown features a telling moment from the show in which Lewis speaks "seriously" to the audience about the recent troubles experienced by the two men while Martin stands to one side and mocks his earnestness (Soapbox Productions 1996).

5. Lewis admits that he behaved extremely badly during the production of *Hollywood or Bust:* at one point Frank Tashlin even banished him from the set (Lewis and Gluck, 200–201).

6. On occasions Lewis has claimed that he and Martin did not speak with one another for twenty years, when Frank Sinatra brought the crooner onstage for Lewis's 1976 Telethon broadcast. However, they crossed paths several times in the intervening years. For example, Bing Crosby briefly brought Martin onstage during Lewis's appearance on an Eddie Fisher television show in September 1958 (Tosches 1992, 416). Two years later Martin invited his former partner onstage when he spotted him in the audience at the Sands Hotel, and the two improvised their way through a comic version of "Come Back to Me" (Levy 1996a, 249). A few days later Martin took over from Lewis when the comic was too fatigued to perform one of his own shows at the Sands (ibid.). Generally, however, they seem to have avoided one another's company as much as possible.

7. Nick Tosches's fascinating bio-fiction of Dean Martin portrays the crooner as a seductive incarnation of masculine cool. While he was a key figure in Sinatra's show-biz clan, the Rat Pack, Martin never succumbed fully to the group ethos but preserved his own space within their elitist self-containment (Tosches 1992, 313). For a lively overview of Sinatra's gang, see Shawn Levy's book *Rat Pack Confidential* (Levy 1998).

8. The first version of *The Dean Martin Show* was aired by NBC from 1957 to 1961. For several years Martin resisted the network's offers for other series because he was tired of the medium, although he continued to appear as a guest on variety programs hosted by others (Tosches 1992, 334). The Matt Helm films were *The Silencers* (1966), *Murderer's Row* (1966), *The Ambushers* (1967), and *The Wrecking Crew* (1969).

9. Lewis had hosted the twenty-eighth annual Academy Awards in March 1956 while he was still in partnership with Martin. Although the two men performed one number together, the event was largely a one-man show—for which Lewis received highly appreciative critical notices. *Daily Variety* wrote, "It was a triumphant evening for Hollywood's emcee, Jerry Lewis, who gagged and quipped with presenters and winners and made it an evening of high carnival" ("50,000,000 Watch Oscar Parade Winners Prance on TV," 22 March 1956). Lewis hosted subsequent Oscar ceremonies in 1957 and 1959.

10. The Martin and Lewis releases comprised the single "The Money Song" / "That Certain Party" (1948), "Ev'ry Street's a Boulevard (in Old New York)" (1954), and "Pardners" (1956).

11. Danny Kaye's influence is especially apparent on numbers like "I Can't Carry a Tune" (1952), in which Lewis displays a range of comically exaggerated voices, and especially on "I'm a Little Busybody" (1950), in which he attempts a breakneck vocal delivery similar to Kaye's song "Tchaikovsky." The use of sound effects on recordings such as "I Love a Murder Mystery" (1949) and "Y-Y-Y-Y-Yup" (1953) also suggest the influence of Spike Jones and His City Slickers. All songs cited can be found on the 1990 compact disc "Capitol Collector's Series—Jerry Lewis" (Lewis 1990a). Be-

sides these generalized novelty numbers Lewis also recorded material explicitly for children, including the story discs "The Nagger" and "The Puppy Dog Dream" (both for Capitol records) and the 1960 Decca album *Big Songs for Little People.*

12. Information about Lewis's solo activities in 1956 and 1957 is drawn from Levy 1996a, 217–31.

13. Lewis produced the NBC shows and codirected a couple of them. Extracts from the TV specials are included in JAS Productions 1992c.

14. In 1959 Cecil Smith of the *Los Angeles Times* described Lewis as "a man who runs with such ferocity that he makes Sammy Glick seem like a cigar store Indian—he continually sets up goals to prove himself; he must prove things over and over and over again" (Levy 1996a, 241).

15. Lewis reprised his sabotage of Eddie Fisher when the latter made a guest appearance on his show in May 1960. When Fisher came on for his second song, Lewis once more reached "the height of professional discourtesy"—he "shouted and bellowed throughout the entire rendition" (*"The Jerry Lewis Show,"* *Daily Variety,* 23 May 1960).

16. Lewis reprised his definition of comedy as a man in trouble on numerous occasions; see, for example, Madsen 1966, 29; Lewis 1969, 3; and Peploe and Belville 1969.

17. According to Arthur Marx (1975), "Typical of what Jerry wanted to do—and did do—was a TV skit on *The Colgate Comedy Hour* in which he played a poor slob of a fellow who joined a 'friendship club.' He tried so hard to make friends that everybody went out to the refreshment stand and left him alone. For the blackout, Jerry ended up dancing with a mannequin. Dean hated that bit. He kept saying to Jerry, 'Why don't you cut out this sad stuff and just be funny!'" (173).

18. *The Band Wagon* drew from the catalogue of songs by Schwartz and Dietz. "By Myself" was initially featured in a 1938 Broadway revue called *Between the Devil* (Fordin 1986, 8).

19. Intriguingly, Judy Garland—the archetypal troubled movie star—renders a highly emotional version of "By Myself" in her final film *I Could Go On Singing* (1963), and the song was also a regular feature of her concerts (Dyer 1987, 189).

20. Shawn Levy argues that the accounts of Lewis's life presented by Gehman 1964, Marx 1975, and Benayoun 1973 are heavily indebted to the Lewis-Davidson article (Levy 1996a, 2).

21. Similar depictions of Lewis's early life can be found in Lewis and Gluck 1982, Rader 1995, and Soapbox Productions 1996.

22. In 1977 Lewis told an audience at the American Film Institute that the bounteous plenitude of the Martin and Lewis days was supplanted by a wilderness of self-doubt: "I was frightened at what might happen. I was really intimidated by the fear of not being accepted. In the last year of the relationship, it was totally apparent to me that without Dean I'd be nothing, because he made that very clear to me. He didn't mean that, but in our anger and our distress with one another a lot of things came out. . . . So I worked so desperately, and I was so driven that I couldn't now in all honesty tell you what I was doing. I only know that I worked hard and tried everything I could because I was more concerned with acceptance than with what I was doing" (Alpert 1977, 47).

23. Patti and Jerry Lewis had five sons of their own—Gary (born 1945), Scott (1956),

Chris (1957), Anthony (1959), and Joseph (1964)—and adopted another, Ronald, in 1950.

24. Danny Lewis had also appeared on a *Comedy Hour* show in March 1952, where he performed two Jolson numbers.

25. For example, the tone of the *Look* articles differs substantially from the breezy confidence and wisecracking tomfoolery of the three-part "autobiography" of Martin and Lewis published by the fan magazine *Picturegoer* in 1953 (Martin and Lewis 1953a, 1953b, 1953c).

26. However, the review also draws attention to the inconsistency and forwardness of his arguments: "Lewis is a man of strong opinion, as was evident in his show, some not entirely supported by the logic of the situation, and some were even contradictory to previously stated opinions. However, he did show a more mature side and a great respect for himself" ("*Youth Wants to Know*," *Variety*, 7 October 1959).

27. Raphaelson's original 1922 short story, "The Day of Atonement," was itself inspired by an Al Jolson performance he witnessed in 1917. Raphaelson's play, *The Jazz Singer*, opened on Broadway in September 1925, with George Jessel in the lead role. It was a massive popular success (Carringer 1979, 11–12). Jolson himself was memorialized in the postwar era through two hugely successful Hollywood biopics, *The Jolson Story* (1946) and *Jolson Sings Again* (1949); and Martin and Lewis performed shows in support of the former in 1947. Hollywood remade *The Jazz Singer* twice: in 1952 (with Danny Thomas) and in 1980 (with Neil Diamond).

28. Describing *The Jazz Singer* as "one of Jerry's most personal and heartfelt undertakings," Levy notes that Lewis also changed the name of Joey's mother to Sarah, after the grandmother he idolized (Levy 1996a, 241).

29. However, the *New York Times* reviewer described Lewis performance as having "the virtue of simplicity and direction," noting that "he survived last night's interesting experiment far more successfully than might have been the case" (Carringer 1979, 32).

30. The *Daily Variety* critic also complained that Lewis's "minute and shaky singing voice" required substantial studio enhancement ("*The Jazz Singer*," 15 October 1959).

31. A two-minute extract from NBC's *The Jazz Singer* was included in Robert Benayoun's 1982 French teleseries *Bonjour Monsieur Lewis*.

5. DELICATE/DELINQUENT

1. Lewis named his home movie company Garron Productions-USA, after his sons Gary and Ronnie. Other Garron films included *The Reinforcer*, *Watch on the Lime*, *Fairfax Avenue*, *Son of Spellbound*, *Streetcar Named Repulsive*, *A Spot in the Shade*, *Melvin's Revenge*, *The Whistler*, *I Should Have Stood in Bedlam*, and *Come Back Little Shiksa* (Neibaur and Okuda 1995, 258).

2. During the 1996 documentary "Jerry Lewis: The Last American Clown" Lewis says that when it came to comedy Wallis "had a sense of humor like a menstrual period" (Soapbox Productions 1996). Even so, the films Martin and Lewis made for York Pictures Corporation are not significantly different from the Wallis productions, and even used the same directors (Hal Walker and Norman Taurog).

3. Ernest Glucksman, producer of Martin and Lewis's *Colgate Comedy Hour* shows, testifies to Lewis's astuteness a businessman. Glucksman recalls that when he first met Lewis to discuss the programs, "he was to the point, he was businesslike, he showed me that he had every bit of information about every appearance he had ever made, every bill he had ever played on, carefully documented and bound. He even knew dates, salaries, scripts, everything. He was possibly twenty-two years old, but he already was big business, and by the time I left him that night I knew why he was big business. He was organized" (Gehman 1964, 136). Bandleader Lou Brown concurs: "He acted 9, but he was always 57. He was always very sharp — if you know what I mean" (Soapbox Productions 1996).

4. "Independents produced around 20 percent of the 234 pictures released by the eight majors in 1949; in 1957, the majors released 291 productions, of which 170 (58 percent) were produced by independents" (Balio 1990, 10).

5. These packages were put together not just by the major studios but also by ambitious talent agencies such as MCA, which began to exert significant control in Hollywood production just as they had on network television (Balio 1990, 10).

6. "The star provides the studio with a tangible attraction, with an image that could be advertised and marketed, offsetting the less tangible qualities of the story, direction, acting, art direction, costume design, and overall studio style. Though these latter elements could be marketed as well, they rarely achieved the identifiability of the star and could not, in themselves, guarantee that a film would make a profit" (Belton 1994, 85).

7. For further consideration of Chaplin's career, see Maland 1991 and Robinson 1986. A remarkable insight into Chaplin's production methods is provided by the three-part television documentary series *The Unknown Chaplin* (Brownlow and Gill 1983). See Staiger 1985 for a useful account of the role of the continuity script in Hollywood studio filmmaking.

8. Through the late 1950s Paramount was regarded as one of the most conservative and overly cautious of the Hollywood majors — reportedly, its major asset besides Lewis was the late Cecil B. DeMille's much reissued 1956 blockbuster *The Ten Commandments* (Schumach 1959, 32).

9. After he signed the Paramount deal Jerry Lewis Productions, Inc. spawned a bewildering proliferation of subsidiary enterprises: Jerry Lewis Pictures Corporation; Patti Enterprises, Inc.; Jerry Lewis Enterprises, Inc.; and the Garron Pictures Corporation (Levy 1996a, 250).

10. Toward the end of the Martin and Lewis partnership Wallis was considering a number of other projects for the troubled team, including *The Pajama Game* (later filmed with Doris Day), *Teahouse of the August Moon* (later filmed with Marlon Brando), and an original project entitled *The Martin and Lewis Story* (Levy 1996a, 199).

11. Damon and Pythias (a.k.a. Phintias) were philosophers living in Syracuse in the fourth century B.C. When Pythias was condemned to death for treason, his loyal friend Damon agreed to put forth his own life as bail so that Pythias could set his private affairs in order before the execution. Pythias's return was delayed, and he arrived back in Syracuse as Damon was on the verge of being executed. The ruler, Dionysius, was sufficiently moved by the devotion of the two men that he rescinded Pythias's death sentence. Two of the most influential literary articulations of the story

were a sixteenth-century English play by Richard Edwards and an eighteenth-century ballad by Friedrich von Schiller. When Martin and Lewis appeared on *Person to Person* in June 1954 to dispel rumors of their split, Lewis told presenter Ed Murrow, "So few people realize that Dean and I have had probably one of the greatest Damon and Pythias relationships that any two men ever had" (Soapbox Productions 1996).

12. In a 1957 *Positif* article, "Simple Simon, ou l'anti James Dean," Robert Benayoun compared Lewis to the performers trained in Lee Strasberg's Actors Studio, the Mecca of method acting in the United States. Benayoun argues that Lewis deals with the same kind of projective psychological impulses as method performers such as Marlon Brando and James Dean: "In one sense, Jerry Lewis is the triumph of the era of schizophrenia inaugurated by Elia Kazan and Lee Strasberg in dramatic performance: as we know, the Actors Studio represented for the beat generation a veritable form of therapy, in the sense that it moved forward the interpretation of paranoia in the direction of schizophrenia, and spared the psychiatrist a whole generation of unstable hipsters, crucified in their isolation, curled up in a cool version of the maternal womb. Joseph Levitch has no need for the Actors Studio. Jerry provides him with his own personal safety valve. . . . Jerry's mimicry, a psychological progression from the surrealist game of 'one person inside another,' allows him to cast out (like poison) in successive sketches key roles such as those of Harpo Marx, Humphrey Bogart, or Elvis Presley. In the first solo part which he wrote for himself (Dean Martin having returned to his golf clubs), Jerry attempts in *The Delicate Delinquent* to create a hysterical telescopic version of *Rebel Without a Cause* and *East of Eden;* on a very concrete level he can be seen as the authentic anti-James Dean" (Benayoun 1972, 23) (privately translated by Barry Redhead).

13. Lewis makes explicit the relationship between his own life and the scenario of his first solo film: "Years later, I remembered those conversations with Grandma Sarah. I wrote them down and they became the basis for my new movie, *The Delicate Delinquent*" (Lewis and Davidson 1957, 52).

14. Tashlin also held Lewis in high esteem. In 1964 he told Robert Benayoun, "I have great confidence in him. He is a genius" (Benayoun 1994, 128).

15. Tashlin worked at the Schlesinger unit as a director of animated shorts from 1936 to 1938 and from 1942 to 1944. He was also employed in the story department at Walt Disney Studios (1939-41) and worked for Screen Gems (1941-42). A list of Tashlin's cartoon work can be found in Prouty 1994, 197-210.

16. This is especially evident in *Hollywood or Bust,* in which Martin and Lewis embark on a drive "across a landscape exclusively populated with the sorts of females found in service station calendars in the United States. . . . It's clear that for Tashlin, Hollywood is less a place than a state of sexual excitation" (Ehrenstein 1994b, 168).

17. The recurring obsessions of these 1950s comedies are neatly encapsulated in the opening scene of *Artists and Models*. Dean Martin's Rick Todd is working on a massive billboard advertisement for "Trim Maid" cigarettes, painting color into the lips of a woman's ecstatic open-mouthed face. He pokes his head into the gaping mouth to ask Lewis's Eugene Fullstack to start the machine that is supposed to pump puffs of smoke between the lips. Eugene is so engrossed in his cherished *Bat Lady* comics, however, that he fails to see that the tube from the smoke machine is not actually connected to the mouth; as a result, the device sucks up his comics and then his own

body. When Eugene and Rick finally get the smoke machine to work, it spews shredded comic books into the street. Eugene then panics and knocks over three cans of paint, which end up splattering the advertising men and the policeman who wait below. The scene concludes with Eugene escaping censure by crawling back through the painted mouth. As Ed Sikov (1994) comments, in this scene "Tashlin sets up a 1955 America constituted almost entirely by artifice and violently distorted sexuality. . . . The billboard, treated as a bizarre distortion of human desire, takes oral gratification to an extreme" (194).

18. Clayton is resistant to the sexual advances of Carla's sister Sandy (Connie Stevens), who throws herself at him continually, because he is blinded by his images of Carla. In similar fashion Eugene Fullstack in *Artists and Models* only responds to Bessie Sparrowbush (Shirley MacLaine) when she dons the costume of the phantasmic comic book character the Bat Lady.

19. When Clayton's parental diligence causes him to collapse from exhaustion, he is advised by Mr. Wright (Hans Conried)—his employer, attorney, and chairman of the city council—that "women are built to take such punishment, but not men. . . . Take care of yourself, mother."

20. A further difficulty with Fischer's article is that she dehistoricizes the films she considers. For example, the situational comedies *Mr. Mom* (1983) and *Three Men and a Baby* (1987) and the melodrama *Kramer vs. Kramer* (1979) were produced in an era that had witnessed the ascendancy of feminism and the decaying credibility of the traditional familial ideal. The male appropriation of motherhood achieves a very different significance in this context than it does in *Their First Mistake* and *The Kid*.

21. Clayton's achievements as a "mother" stand in sharp contrast to the grotesque female impersonations of the Martin and Lewis films, for example, Lewis's drag routines in *At War with the Army* and *The Stooge* and his Carmen Miranda impression in *Scared Stiff*.

22. Tashlin and Lewis virtually replay the scene in the 1963 film *Who's Minding the Store?* in a sequence in which Lewis's harassed department store clerk demonstrates a vacuum cleaner to a demanding female customer. In Lewis's hands the vacuum cleaner proceeds to suck up everything in sight, including the woman's yapping dog.

23. Sikita is played by veteran Japanese actor Sessue Hayakawa, recently cast as the prison-camp commander in the war epic *The Bridge on the River Kwai* (1957). When Wooley first encounters him, Sikita is in full military dress, supervising the construction of a bridge across the pond in his garden. As the soundtrack breaks into a snatch of the "Colonel Bogey" theme, the film presents a cutaway shot of Alec Guinness in a scene from *River Kwai*.

24. Besides serving as the agent of many of the film's cartoonlike irruptions, the rabbit is also a knowingly eccentric substitute for Dean Martin. In one of their numerous intimate exchanges Wooley tells his partner, "Now remember, Harry, we're friends and we're buddies, and we're supposed to stick together—so you shouldn't try to run away from me."

25. Bernard Eisenschitz (1994b) complains about the film's "blatant mawkishness," which he ascribes to Lewis as a means of preserving his valuation of Tashlin (171). Lewis, however, claims that the film "was Tashlin's complete creative work. And I didn't contribute any more to it than I did to any film, but it didn't need a lot of help. The

material was on the paper. I produced the picture because I knew Frank had written a marvelous story" (Neibaur and Okuda 1995, 136).

26. In this regard the film operates as a strange variant of the contemporary East-West romantic melodramas *Love Is a Many Splendored Thing* (1955) and *Sayonara* (1957).

6. MAN WITH A MOVIE CAMERA

1. Unless otherwise noted, information on the production of *The Bellboy* is drawn from Lewis and Gluck 1982, 224–26.

2. A sixty-five-minute version of the film was completed by April, but Lewis reshot several scenes at the Paramount studios in May after disappointing feedback from a preview audience. A seventy-two-minute version, completed by 1 June 1960, was released on 20 July (Levy 1996a, 248–49).

3. For an influential example of the Golden Age thesis, see James Agee's 1949 essay "Comedy's Greatest Era" (Agee 1967).

4. In order to promote their sound-film systems in the mid-1920s—and to illustrate the new entertainment territories that could be colonized by films with sound, speech, and music—the Vitaphone Corporation (formed by Warner Brothers and electrical trust Western Electric) showcased name performers from vaudeville and Broadway. The second exhibition of Vitaphone's sound-on-disc system, in October 1926, climaxed with an hour-long collection of shorts that was described by one critic as proceeding "almost precisely as the most extravagant booker would build a show for his vaudevillle house" (Barrios 1995, 26). The highlight of the show was a short in which Al Jolson gave an energetic performance of three of his most popular hits—a year before his appearance in *The Jazz Singer* propelled the Hollywood sound-film into mainstream acceptance, opening the way for a torrent of talking and singing pictures (ibid., 27).

5. As Jenkins (1992) points out, Hollywood cinema entered the sound era by appealing fervently to "Broadwayness" in the drive to build urban audiences (160).

6. Nolan (1994) suggests that from the early 1930s Broadway shows also faced intense competition from nightclubs and cabaret restaurants (195).

7. Earlier in his essay Benjamin (1992) quotes the following passage from a novel, written in the presound era, by Luigi Pirandello: "The film actor feels as if in exile—exiled not only from the stage but also from himself. With a vague sense of discomfort he feels inexplicable emptiness: his body loses its corporeality, it evaporates, it is deprived of reality, life, voice, and the noises caused by his moving about, in order to be changed into a mute image, flickering an instant on the screen, then vanishing into silence. . . . The projector will play with his shadow before the public, and he himself must be content to play before the camera" (672).

8. Although he argues that the age of mechanical reproduction brings with it a destruction of the singularity of the artwork, Benjamin also posits that the shriveling of aura has a liberatory potential. The emancipation of the work of art from its "parasitical dependence" on ritual "democratizes" ownership of both texts and textual meanings. This can bring into play a cathartic "liquidation of the traditional value of

the cultural heritage" (Benjamin 1992, 668) that makes possible new forms of expression and new relationships to existing forms.

9. In traditional Hollywood practice scenes are filmed out of sequence and the recorded sounds and images can thereafter be subject to extensive manipulation and recombination. The fullness and plenitude that typifies the classical Hollywood style rests upon a highly crafted effacement of the fragmentation and discontinuity that characterizes the work of production. The cinema screen thus functions both as a surface upon which the totalizing illusion is presented and as a barrier that conceals the processes through which the illusion is constructed.

10. In 1966 Arthur Knight, head of film studies at the University of Southern California, invited Lewis to lecture to his class. The event was such a success that Lewis was recruited as an adjunct professor of film studies and allowed to take a weekly class for two academic years; among those attending were future directors George Lucas, Peter Bogdanovich, and Steven Spielberg (Levy 1996a, 364, 377). The audio recordings of these lectures formed the basis of *The Total Film-Maker,* an idiosyncratic collage of thoughts about the medium in which Lewis's passion for every aspect of filmmaking shimmers on the page.

11. In another interview Lewis noted, "The material on the [film] stage is basic. That's ABC or one-two-three or you have to get it. It must be made in the editing because your principal photography will take eight weeks. I spend six months cutting" (Kantor et al. 1970, 290). Lewis also told the AFI audience of his fascination for dubbing, another activity that involves a play of division and totality: "When I arrived at Paramount it was the summer of 1948, and they could never find me. The first stop for me was dubbing. I had to see that. The camera department was second. I had to know what a BNC looked like ripped, and I had to know how to put it together again" (Alpert 1977, 37).

12. In a discussion of silent-era slapstick, for example, Henry Jenkins (1997) refers to "the uncertainties and ambivalence a vaudevillian must have felt toward this new medium. News reports described vaudevillians as confused and agitated when they stepped onto a film set, uncertain what audience to address, directing jokes toward the cameramen and thereby 'spoiling' takes, looking into the camera and violating Hollywood's edicts against direct address. Vaudevillians had difficulty grasping the temporal and spacial separation between performer and audience as well as the need to reproduce the performance the same way for each take" (49).

13. Lewis's remarks echo a comment made by Pierre Kast in a discussion with his colleagues at *Cahiers du Cinéma* in 1957: "When [Roger] Vadim makes a film or [Alexandre] Astruc makes a film, whatever the film is like or whatever reservations you may have about it, it's something quite different from a film made by two people—a scriptwriter and a director" (Bazin et al. 1985, 38).

14. When he was interviewed by Cashin, Lewis was in England for location work on the first film he directed but did not star in: the Sammy Davis-Peter Lawford buddy comedy *One More Time,* a sequel to their earlier Rat Pack-style vanity project *Salt and Pepper.*

15. Around the same time Bernard F. Kantor, Irwin R. Blacker, and Anne Kramer interviewed Lewis for a book on contemporary U.S. directors. They noted that "on

the wall facing him where he sat on a sofa was a large painting of Jerry Lewis in clown makeup and costume. Several times during the interview he pointed to the clown and referred to 'him' as though he were someone else" (Kantor et al. 1970, 267).

16. Lewis continued to use video monitoring on subsequent films and tried in vain to convince Paramount to adopt the system as a regular production tool; as the "video-assist" or "videocom" it would eventually become a standardized feature of main-stream filmmaking (Levy 1996a, 247-48). In recognition of his work in devising the video assist Lewis was awarded a Golden Light Technical Achievement Award in 1966 (Alpert 1977, 43). In a useful appendix to their book on Lewis's films Neibaur and Okuda include a section from a Paramount report—written by technical super-visor Bruce Denny in 1960—that describes Lewis's use of the closed-circuit video system during the production of *The Bellboy* (Neibaur and Okuda 1995, 271-75). For further information on the video assist, see Geuens 1996.

17. In a 1963 profile of Lewis for *Saturday Evening Post* Edward Linn claims that "every performance he has given has also been recorded and filed away, complete with the date, the place, his salary, the cast and his own rating of the show. He now has three rooms full of tapes, all neatly catalogued and virtually ignored" (Linn 1963, 87). Ob-serving the leather-bound scrapbook collection that dominates Lewis's study, Richard Gehman (1964) pondered, "It is as though Lewis is compulsively determined to record, photographically or in print, every breath drawn by his family and himself" (45). Lewis told Judith Simons in 1975, "Each of my sons, as he grows older, takes over the job of keeping the library up to date. . . . All my photographs, interviews, television shows" (Simons 1975, 8). Harry Shearer and Michael Tolkin both suggest that Lewis also records his phone calls (Shearer 1979, 39; Tolkin 1976, 117).

18. Gary Lewis and the Playboys topped the *Billboard* charts with "This Diamond Ring" in January 1965. The band also shows up later in the film for a brief gag appearance, playing inside a storage cupboard on an aircraft.

19. Another son, Scott, comments, "We always 'did' Christmas day as a family. Dad al-ways had the camera rolling to record our reactions to the presents we opened. He would yell at us when we wouldn't face the camera, and then my mom would yell at my dad that it was Christmas" (Lewis and Coleman 1993, 60).

20. The Claude Ollier quotation is in Hillier, *Cahiers du Cinéma* (1986), 196-209; origi-nally in Jean-Louis Comolli, Jean-André Fieschi, Gérard Guégan, Michel Mardore, Claude Ollier, and André Téchiné, "Twenty Years On: A Discussion about Ameri-can Cinema and the *politique des auteurs*," *Cahiers du Cinéma* 172 (November 1965).

21. In a consideration of the moral panic provoked in the United States by the aggres-sively populist forms of "New Humor" Henry Jenkins examines the ideological function served by the canonization of restraint as an integral criterion of comedy. From the 1890s to the 1910s there was "a massive proliferation of comic materials, a large-scale commodification of the joke" purveyed through joke books, mass-market newspapers and magazines, variety entertainments, and the cinema (38). Resisting the socially leveling energy of this new humor, literate bourgeois critics propagandized for a laughter that was thoughtful, purposeful, and refined. As Jenkins observes, "Such 'refinement' was possible only where individuals could remove themselves from the immediacy of their environment and achieve a degree of mental distance from popular thought and follies." Jenkins suggests that the hysterical opposition to

the new humor was fed by anxieties about the threat posed to white middle-class cultural hegemony by ethnic diversity, urbanization, and industrialization (Jenkins 1992, 38, 28, 41–43).

22. This gag is lifted from the ending of the 1941 Ole Olsen and Chic Johnson comedy *Hellzapoppin'*.

23. A typical Lewisian body gag from *Rock-a-Bye Baby* is also worth noting. After being woken up by the triplets Clayton stumbles sleepily into the kitchen to heat some milk for them. He lights the gas stove but at the same time ignites his finger. Clayton stares dozily at the burning finger and then douses it under the tap; only when the flame is extinguished does he shriek with pain. The gag is inherited from a routine in *Way out West* (1937), in which, much to the amazement of Oliver Hardy, Stan Laurel magically snaps his finger to transform it into a flaming torch. Like Harpo Marx, Laurel consciously controls the deformation of his body, whereas Clayton is shocked by it.

24. Brian Henderson (1991, 153–73) explores this point in detail in an essay comparing the comic styles of Tashlin and Preston Sturges.

25. Shawn Levy (1996a) observes that *The Geisha Boy* "is structured less in a point-counterpoint fashion, with each episode featuring Jerry and his plot line balanced by one focused on a contrasting plot line, than in a block-by-block fashion, with chunks of material utterly unrelated to the plot being dispersed throughout the story as comic relief. Its straightforward narrative borders on melodrama, but it incorporates material wholly independent of the narrative throughout: a Los Angeles Dodgers exhibition game in Tokyo, a montage of botched performances at military posts, subplots concerning the jealousy of a hulking Japanese first baseman and the vanity of an American movie actress. The formula allowed both star and director to indulge in his specialty. Jerry could break away from the story to sing, do impressions, cavort in block comedy scenes; Tashlin could stop the plot at any moment for a gag. It became a working formula, the basis of the four films Jerry and Tashlin were to make together between 1958 and 1964 and the germ of the movies Jerry hoped to direct on his own" (230–31).

26. Chuck Derry (1985) follows Coursodon in his account of Lewis in *The International Dictionary of Films and Filmmakers,* citing "his interest in surrealism; his experimentalism and fascination with self-conscious stylistic devices; his movement away from conventional gags towards structures apparently purposely deformed; his interest in plotlessness and ellipsis; the reflexivity of his narrative; his studied use of extended silence and gibberish in a sound cinema; the ambiguous sexual subtext of his work; and finally, his use of film as personal revelation in a tradition which ultimately recalls Maya Deren and Stan Brakhage more than Chaplin and Keaton" (331).

27. Raymond Durgnat (1969) remarks of the gags in *The Ladies' Man*, "Part of a gag is a *non sequitur* from the previous gag and *non sequiturs* are indispensable links in the causal chain within each gag. Many gags are shaggy dog gags, or partly shaggy dog gags, or shaggy dogs in sheep's clothing. Or they are played down to become incredulous titters rather than belly-laughs, that is, to create a mood of liberation and alienation rather than of howling hilarity" (236).

28. Coursodon (1983) continues in more skeptical vein: "They may have a point, yet what Lewis is doing is reminiscent of the story about the comedians' convention

where they gave well-known jokes numbers and called out the numbers instead of telling the jokes. Very clever, but wouldn't you rather hear a new joke told?" (197).

29. "What is most disturbing," Shaviro (1993) argues, "is that the comic destruction of norms becomes the source of a judgement not against the norm, but against the self. Lewis's characters cannot assert themselves as individuals in opposition to society, for it is only in the stereotypical, hegemonic terms of social order that they can conceive of themselves as individuals at all. This is why Lewis's humor continually threatens to give way, first of all to sentimentality and pathos, but even more to an embarrassing orgy of humiliation and abjection" (113).

30. The Lewisian misfit's incapacity to deal with the logistics of hierarchy is especially well illustrated by two scenes from *The Patsy* in which Stanley Belt is forced to receive rather than provide service. In the first sequence Stanley is seated in a barber's chair and subjected to an all-purpose makeover by a swarm of attendants. Following a haircut, a manicure, and a pedicure, Stanley gives himself over to an irrepressibly enthusiastic shoeshine boy (Scatman Crothers). The latter works to the accompaniment of a feverish vocal scat rhythm, which both he and Stanley get so caught up in that they neglect the business at hand—or, rather, at foot. When the shoeshine boy completes his job, he looks down to see that he has covered Stanley's naked foot in black polish. Out of the two, it is Stanley who seems most unsettled by the experience. In a later scene Stanley finally plucks up courage to invite Ellen Betts (Ina Balin) to dine out in a fancy restaurant. Unable to make the adjustment from server to client, Stanley guiltily gives away all his money to the waiters and musicians who prey upon his table. In an overpowering desire to rid himself of the symbolic currency of authority Stanley hands over the last of his money to a posse of thirteen violinists when they surround his table.

31. Shaviro (1993) describes the typical process of the unraveling: "Each incident of disorder is one more thing the Idiot is responsible for, one more cause for him to make endless apologies and excuses, and one more reason these apologies are never sufficient. He reaches a point at which he is forced to acknowledge his own incompetence, but this self-consciousness only makes him all the more unable to function. Such a feedback mechanism is a mainstay of Lewis's comedy: he ties himself into verbal knots, or finds his speech breaking down altogether, as he tries to explain and compensate for his well-meaning but pragmatically disastrous action" (112).

32. This applies also to the Brandford team at the beginning of *The Patsy*: the film emphasizes how the authority of their gaze causes Stanley to disintegrate, but it also makes it clear that Lewis's spectacular abasement blocks their own immediate response to the situation. Like Bob, all they can do is just stand and stare.

7. A BIG NIGHT IN HOLLYWOOD

1. For a consideration of the standardized comedian comedies of the sound era, see Krutnik 1995a, 21–36.

2. Designed by Morris Lapidus, "the Father of the Modern Retail Store," the Fontainebleau opened in December 1954. Lapidus said that "every part of the hotel was a stage setting—the gardens, the huge pool deck with its hundreds of cabanas, the foun-

tained entrance driveway[,] . . . the regal dining room, the intimate cocktail lounge, even the corridors and the guest rooms and luxury suites" (Hoberman 1993, 109, 111).

3. As in Chaplin comedies such as *The Floorwalker* (1916) and *The Cure* (1917), for example, the film's coherence derives from setting rather than story line. Lewis pays direct homage to *The Floorwalker* in a brief gag in which he runs up a down escalator.

4. When the two Stanleys meet in *The Bellboy* they share an unspoken bond of mutual recognition, underscored by the way "Stan Laurel" appropriates the bellboy's trademark whistling. After he finished shooting *The Bellboy* Lewis was introduced to Laurel, whom he regarded as "the only comedian I would put in the same category as Chaplin. He was a consummate genius." Lewis wanted the veteran screen comic for a lucrative job as a comic consultant, but Laurel declined to accept the offer (Neibaur and Okuda 1995, 270, 146).

5. Lewis wrote the scenes with the help of his friend and drummer Bill Richmond, who became his regular scriptwriting collaborator (Neibaur and Okuda 1995, 10). Although he did not receive credit for *The Bellboy*, Richmond is acknowledged as the coscreenwriter of *The Ladies' Man*, *The Errand Boy*, *The Nutty Professor*, *The Patsy*, *The Family Jewels*, *The Big Mouth*, and the 1983 film *Cracking Up*. Lewis has elaborated on their working procedures: "Bill Richmond, whom I trained and who was my apprentice, wrote a few films with me. I would write the storyline and the bulk of the film and I'd give him sections. Meet me there. He's very good; he's getting better and better. And I would give him, oh, maybe a twenty-page section or three seven-page sections. And then I could depend on him a little more and I could let him meet me deeper" (Kantor, Blacker, and Kramer 1970, 285).

6. The gags that derive from these situations frequently involve Stanley's inability to carry out these jobs properly. For example, when ordered to take the contents of a Volkswagen's trunk up to its owner's room, he dutifully rips out the engine and delivers it into the arms of the bewildered guest.

7. The voice-over of Jack Emulsion returns at this point, to create a formal sense of closure: "So you see, there was no story. But there is a moral. And a simple one. You'll never know the next guy's story — unless you ask him."

8. As Lewis confessed years later, "My feeling is that the camera belongs within four walls" (McGilligan 1979, 65).

9. As Neibaur and Okuda (1995) observe, "Lewis created a huge set that was essentially a replica of the actual Hollywood Studio Club. The set was 177 feet long, 154 feet wide, and several rooms deep with individual lighting and sound for each room. It stood before the viewer like a stage, allowing Lewis to capture simultaneous interrelated action with a natural flow of spontaneity. Whereas separate sequences in the various rooms needed more intimate camera work, those done in long shot to reveal the whole set and allow one scene to build into another displayed an especially impressive directorial technique for someone who was being credited for only his second time as director" (154).

10. The film conveys Herbert's panic through a notable special-effects trick whereby Lewis is splintered into multiple images of a man in flight.

11. The prominent scar Gainsborough carries on his face further aligns him with Raft.

12. As Rapf (1993, 196) points out, the issue of sexual duality is foregrounded through the Lewis-figure's very name —*Herbert H. He'bert*.

13. In a later scene that develops these maternal connotations Katie forces Herbert into a baby's high chair and spoonfeeds him.

14. The Kelly-Charisse dance is featured in *Singin' in the Rain*'s extravagant "Broadway Melody" production sequence. Kelly's hoofer first meets Charisse, a femme fatale, in a low-life nightclub populated by gangsters who engage repeatedly in the coin-tossing action popularized by George Raft — also, of course, borrowed by *The Ladies' Man*.

15. As J. Hoberman (1993, 111) points out, this cartoon logic is also a key feature of *The Bellboy*, in which "the cartoon structure belies the movie's black-and-white documentary quality, a look rendered all the more hyperreal by the noonday Florida sun."

16. The film's black-and-white cinematography also signals a shift away from the sumptuous colorfest of *The Ladies' Man*. The decision to revisit the rough-hewn documentary look of *The Bellboy* effectively deglamorizes the allure of Hollywood's factory of illusion.

17. Similar scenes of imaginative conjuring recur through Lewis's films. For example, in *The Bellboy* Stanley conducts an invisible orchestra in the hotel ballroom, in *Cinderfella* the beleaguered protagonist does an animated impersonation of the Count Basie Orchestra as one of their records plays on the kitchen radio, and in *Who's Minding the Store* Norman Phiffier plays an imaginary typewriter as if it were a musical instrument.

18. This stroke of Lewisian multiplicity is anticipated when Morty/Lewis is first introduced into the film: he is shown putting up a poster that features the words "Jerry Lewis." The film's credits then begin, played against caricature sketches of Lewis that depict him in a variety of roles — as performer, writer, and filmmaker.

19. This term is borrowed from Yvonne Tasker, who uses it to describe "the physical definition of masculinity in terms of a developed musculature." Tasker herself is concerned with the "musculinization" of such contemporary action heroines as Ripley (Sigourney Weaver) in the *Alien* series and Sarah Connor (Linda Hamilton) in the *Terminator* films (Tasker 1993, 3).

20. In a 1976 profile of Lewis, Michael Tolkin offers an elegant account of the complex Lewisian connotations carried by Love and Kelp: "One can view *The Nutty Professor* as allegory. Julius Sumner Kelp is the early Jerry Lewis, the developmental deviant, crybaby, demicripple, schlemiel. There's something wrong with that man. Kelp extends the Jerry Lewis tic — that sudden interruption of gracefulness with the bobbing tongue, squelched voice, frozen spine — into a character of organized helplessness. Kelp is very much like Jerry from the Martin and Lewis days. In this light, Buddy Love is the sideman that got away, the self assured Dean Martin. And Buddy Love looks just like the Jerry Lewis of the telethons. Television marathon man" (Tolkin 1976, 116).

21. Levy (1996a) also comments, "The cigarettes, the tyrannical outbursts, the overdone wardrobe, the fondness for brassy big-band swing, the hipster's lingo, and the unctuous manner with the ladies were all attributes of Jerry's private personality. Indeed, insofar as the "real" man he conveyed to his audience on TV shows, on nightclub stages, and in the press was itself a role, Buddy Love was very nearly that character: loud, arrogant, abrasive, abusive, and conceited" (293).

22. Kelp's confessional has a significant precursor in a scene from *The Stooge,* considered in chapter 3, in which Bill Miller (Dean Martin) delivers a repentant speech to the audience apologizing for the failure of his solo act.

23. In a manner reminiscent of the finale of *The Geisha Boy* the epilogue is introduced via a written title—"That's *Not* All Folks"—which invokes the magical world of Warner Brothers' Looney Tunes shorts.

24. The scene also implies that Stella yearns for something more than the humble Julius Kelp, and that the potion will allow her to control the type of masculinity *she* desires.

25. *Son of Bellboy* was the working title of *The Patsy* (Neibaur and Okuda 1995, 177). Besides returning to the central figure of Lewis's first self-directed film, *The Patsy* also echoes *The Errand Boy* in its exploration of the entertainment business.

26. Because he never actually appears in the film, the audience is unable to judge Wally's merits for themselves. However, the members of his retinue speak of the deceased star as a talented and totalizing individual who seems yet a further variant of Jerry Lewis.

27. Not only does the audience greet Stanley's act with open hostility but the sequence concludes with a fantasy shot in which he imagines the Brandford team as a firing squad lined up in front of him.

28. For example, a flashing light bulb is superimposed on the kid's head when he hits upon the idea of transmuting his street clothes into evening dress.

29. In this sense Lewis differs emphatically from Chaplin, who often presents his scenes of comic virtuosity through long takes that display the integrity of his performance (a good example being the shop window sequence in *City Lights*).

30. When Ed Sullivan introduces the sketch, for example, he announces that Stanley Belt is following in the illustrious footsteps of such former guests as Richard Burton, Audrey Hepburn, the Beatles, . . . and Martin and Lewis.

31. The sketch was featured in *The Jerry Lewis Show* (NBC) on 27 December 1957. In the live television version Lewis's self-transformation is presented in real time and thus works as a less "compromised" demonstration of the performer's ingenuity. This sketch is included in "Jerry . . . Alone at the Top," the third part of *Martin and Lewis: Their Golden Age of Comedy,* shown on the Disney cable channel in 1992 (JAS Productions 1992c). Lewis subsequently recycled the "Big Night in Hollywood" routine on one of his NBC shows in 1967 (Levy 1996a, 353). Another example of recycled comic business is the typewriter number in his 1963 film *Who's Minding the Store?* It appeared both in his 1957 shows at the Palace Theater and on *The Jerry Lewis Show* broadcast of 8 June 1957.

32. As he addresses his former masters, Stanley wears neither the red jacket of the bellboy nor the shiny gray apparel of the star (both of which mark his servitude) but a black business suit.

8. KID ON THE RUN

1. Barney Balaban remained with Paramount until 1966, when he retired at the age of seventy-six.

2. Other mergers followed: in 1967 United Artists was taken over by the Transamerica Corporation, in 1969 Warner Brothers became a subsidiary of Kinney National Services, and in 1969 MGM was acquired by Kirk Kerkorian's hotel and leisure corporation. The conglomerates exemplified the practices of advanced multinational enterprise, operating multiple profit centers and a diversified portfolio of interests.

Even those Hollywood majors that were not acquired by conglomerates followed a similar practice of diversification, investing their profits in a range of related fields of entertainment—such as TV stations, video companies, pinball manufacturing, holiday resorts, and Coca-Cola bottling plants (Balio 1985, 439).

3. Neibaur and Okuda (1995) list the following reissues of Lewis's films: 1957, *Sailor Beware* and *Jumping Jacks;* 1958, *Jumping Jacks* and *Scared Stiff;* 1962, *The Delicate Delinquent, The Sad Sack, Rock-a-Bye Baby,* and *Don't Give Up the Ship;* 1964, *The Caddy* and *You're Never Too Young;* 1966, *Visit to a Small Planet* and *The Bellboy;* 1965, *Living It Up* and *Pardners;* 1967, *Cinderfella, The Errand Boy, The Nutty Professor,* and *The Patsy;* 1968, *Sailor Beware;* 1978, *Three Ring Circus* (rereleased as *Jerrico the Wonder Clown*).

4. Although *The Bellboy* was a smash hit, *Cinderfella, The Ladies Man,* and *The Errand Boy* were far less successful—the former two owing to high production costs (Taylor 1965, 85). *The Nutty Professor* was helped on its way to a glorious box office by an extensive seven-week tour of personal appearances that Lewis undertook to promote the film (Levy 1996a, 285–91).

5. As Levy (1996a, 325–26) points out, Lewis actually left Paramount before Gulf and Western completed its acquisition of the studio. Nevertheless, the company was indeed in the grip of administrative chaos during the period he speaks of.

6. For Columbia Lewis directed both *Three on a Couch* (1966) and *The Big Mouth* (1967) and starred in *Don't Raise the Bridge, Lower the River* (1968) and *Hook, Line and Sinker* (1969). *The Big Mouth* was a modest success, but the other Columbia films were low achievers at the U.S. box office. Concerned about Lewis's commercial viability, Columbia followed Paramount in pressurizing Lewis to forsake direction—and, as a result, he broke off relations with the studio in February 1969 (Levy 1996a, 354, 360). He took the next Jerry Lewis production—*Which Way to the Front?*—to Warner Brothers but the company had little faith in the film and allowed it only a tokenistic release in the United States.

7. Others studio-era stars who found themselves casualties of the new Hollywood were Bob Hope, Bing Crosby, Frank Sinatra, Doris Day, Audrey Hepburn, Rock Hudson, Burt Lancaster, Kirk Douglas, John Wayne, Lana Turner, Charlton Heston, Henry Fonda, Gregory Peck, Dean Martin, William Holden, Jack Lemmon, Marlon Brando, and James Stewart.

8. The new wave of film actors included Jack Nicholson, Al Pacino, Dustin Hoffman, Gene Hackman, Barbara Streisand, Robert Redford, Robert DeNiro, Warren Beatty, Clint Eastwood, and Woody Allen.

9. In his autobiography (Lewis and Gluck 1982, 242), published almost two decades later, Lewis acknowledges responsibility for the debacle:

Then it was time to face my peers. After all the hoopla—the press, magazines, television interviews and so forth—that Hollywood and the rest of the public had heard about for months on end, how was I to tell them that I blew it? Blame ABC? Hardly! Blame the crew, staff, technicians and writers? Of course not! I simply took out a full-page ad in all the theatrical periodicals. Only one word appeared:
"OOPS!!"
jerry lewis"

10. Shawn Levy (1996a) suggests that Lewis conceived of the series as a return to the interwar entertainment culture he had grown up with: "With the elaborate, customized theater, the live audience, the shifting guest roster, and the box seats just off the stage, it had all the trappings, once again, of Casino Night in a Catskills Hotel. Just as he had with the Gar-Ron Playhouse and the productions of *The Bellboy* and *The Ladies' Man,* Jerry took a major new step in his career by harkening back to the favorite show-biz model of his youth" (298).

11. As I have not been able to see the show, I rely upon Shawn Levy's (1996a, 336) description in his biography of Lewis.

12. The Treniers—comprising the brothers Claude, Clifford, Buddy, and Milt Trenier—were formed in 1951. Claude and Clifford had previously worked as vocalists for Jimmy Lunceford's dance band before forming The Trenier Twins in the late 1940s. The band were renowned for their pumping horn-driven rhythms, scat singing and comic routines (Scott and Ennis 1993, 278). They also made a guest appearance in Frank Tashlin's 1956 rock and roll satire, *The Girl Can't Help It.*

13. In 1960 Lewis appeared on the top U.S. pop show *American Bandstand* for a lesson in how to do the Twist provided by singer JoAnn Campbell (Dawson 1995, 44).

14. One of Lewis's Las Vegas shows, recorded in the Congo Room of the Sahara Hotel on 13 October 1984 is available as the videotape *Jerry Lewis Live* (JAS Productions 1984). There are several gags about male genitalia: at one point he walks close to the front of the stage, looks down at the woman sitting in front of him, and cracks, "This is known as the crotch shot (laughter). I'll back off so there's no pressure." Another gag features Lewis dropping a microphone against his crotch and making a pained facial expression. Later in the show he puts his hand in his pocket and makes a face suggesting pleasure from masturbation. He also throws out one-liners about women's breasts. This sex-grounded adult comedy coexists with more familiar Lewisian moments, including an Al Jolson medley, pantomime sequences, a comic tap dance, an impression of a five-year-old boy, and Lewis's interaction with the onstage band. The most striking feature of the performance is Lewis's rapid and commanding verbal style, a professionalized machine-gun patter generally excluded from his film work. Overall, Lewis does not seem at ease with the need to maintain a balance between *interacting* with the audience and *delivering* material to them.

15. Ironically, Hal Wallis had initially designed the film as a vehicle for Dean Martin (Levy 1996a, 323).

16. In 1965 rising star Woody Allen, a great admirer of Lewis's work, asked him to direct *Take the Money and Run* (Madsen 1966, 31). Lewis considered the offer but ultimately declined, and Allen directed the film himself. He also approached Lewis to direct his next film, *Bananas* (Levy 1996a, 340).

17. Lewis has also directed television dramas—episodes of *Ben Casey* in 1964 and *The Bold Ones* in 1970—and an eight-minute segment of the humanitarian portmanteau film *How Are the Kids?* (1990).

18. An example of the Rosenbloom routine can be found in the changing-room sequence prior to the boxing match in *Sailor Beware.*

19. Two years later, Lewis reused both the gangster and Julius Kelp characterizations in *The Big Mouth.*

20. Stern (1975) suggests that in playing the six uncles Lewis "has created six alternative personalities, each providing a comic resonance or thematic thrust that may be read as Willard's alter-egos. . . . Each 'uncle' is allowed to do what Willard—who must remain responsible in order to get the girl—never can do. That is, they can let loose, go crazy; they can be wildly and unreservedly Jerry Lewis-like" (12).

21. Particularly suggestive of the altered significance attached to multiplicity in this film is Lewis's odd decision to abandon standard production procedures by shooting the film in sequence: "The problem, directorially speaking, was that I tried to shoot the picture in continuity, and I was in different outfits as different characters. . . . I found, after it was over, that we would have been better off 'blocking' that production shoot—in other words, shooting all the scenes with the photographer at one time, then all the scenes with the gangster, then all the scenes with the clown, and so on. And I would have eliminated the old-man character (James Peyton) entirely. Instead, I went back and forth, and I didn't know who I was at what point in time" (Neibaur and Okuda 1995, 188).

22. In a 1909 essay Sigmund Freud discusses the family romance as a mode of fantasy in which a child rearranges its familial origins, effectively displacing its real parents with the parents of its desire (Freud [1909] 1977). The term is used more generally to refer to fictional structures that pivot around familial reorderings. Sylvain Godet (1966) proposes that by acting as Donna's guide, and moving her from uncle to uncle, Willard effectively controls the masquerade: "Willard disguises himself and plays the six characters; he 'does cinema' for Donna, in this way staging an entire spectacle, whose mechanism is given us to see" (35).

23. The clown makeup was designed by Lewis for his first filmic performance as a clown in *Three Ring Circus* and was reused in *Hardly Working* (Neibaur and Okuda 1995, 91).

24. In this sense the clown figure of *The Family Jewels* collapses together the roles played by Lewis and Dean Martin in *Three Ring Circus*. In the latter Lewis incarnates an ideal of the clown as a selfless bringer of joy whereas his buddy always goes for himself alone—until a final conversion to the comic spirit.

25. Unless otherwise noted, details of the production history of *The Day the Clown Cried* are drawn from Shawn Levy's biography (Levy 1996a, 377–82).

26. Lewis kept hold of the negative of the material shot for the film's ending, as a guarantee that the film cannot be released without his cooperation (Lewis and Gluck 1982, 283).

27. Lewis told Howard Schneider in 1973 that his desire to make this film was partially inspired by Gary Lewis's shattering experiences in the Vietnam war (Schneider 1973, 2:9).

28. In the 1990s a copy of the script became available "on an underground basis only" and received a sarcastic review from Scott Rodgers (1995) for the right-wing Ape-O-Naut web site. Rodgers describes it as a "monster epic [that] weighs in at over 160 pages, no small film by any stretch of the imagination (each page of a screenplay equals one minute, so most movies are 90-120 pages long). . . . Virtually each and every page is crammed top to bottom with ponderous dialogue and over-complicated, impossible to show on-film, directions." Rodgers quotes the following description of the screenplay's final scene: "[Helmut's] face is pressed against the steel door. He fights the panic within him. Then, he quickly wipes his eyes and turns back

towards the children. Slowly he takes the three chunks of stale bread from his coat pocket and begins juggling them, at the same time waggling his head from side to side, slowly at first, then more gaily. From deep inside him comes a tiny, tiny laugh. The CAMERA PULLS BACK SLOWLY to reveal the children in the f.g. [foreground]. Suddenly, Helmut tosses the pieces of bread high, high into the air and stretches out his arms to encompass all of the children. As they gather around him, they take up his soft laugh, timidly at first, then more assuredly until the chamber resounds with gentle laughter."

29. Lewis's justification resembles a notorious statement made by Francis Ford Coppola during the 1979 Cannes Film Festival, where his film *Apocalypse Now* was awarded a prize: "My film is not a movie; it's not about Vietnam. It *is* Vietnam. It's what it was really like; it was crazy. The way we made it was very much like the way the Americans were in Vietnam. We were in the jungle, there were too many of us, we had access to too much money, too much equipment; and little by little, we went insane. I think you can see it in the film. As it goes up the river, you can see the photography going a little crazy, and the directors and the actors going a little crazy. After a while, I realized I was a little frightened, because I was getting deeper in debt and no longer recognized the kind of movie I was making. I thought I was making a kind of war film, and it was no longer a war film. Then, as Marlon [Brando] (as Kurtz) says, 'it struck me like a diamond bullet in my head' that I wasn't making the film. The film was making itself; the jungle was making the film, and all I did was do my best" (Chown 1988, 126).

30. Levy reports that there have been several subsequent attempts to make a film from the O'Brien and Denton script, which all fell through. A version was announced in 1980, in which Richard Burton was considered for the lead; two versions were mooted in 1991, one to be made in the Soviet Union, the other to star Robin Williams; and a further plan to bring the story to the screen was declared in 1994, with William Hurt considered for the central role (Levy 1996a, 381).

31. "Jerry Lewis Death Bid," *Evening Standard,* 4 December 1978, in British Film Institute library clippings file, "Jerry Lewis." The incident was first reported in *People* magazine that same month.

32. Through the 1960s Lewis was a forthright spokesman for the values of wholesome family entertainment: in 1969 *Showguide* described him as "a family man working for family audiences. He makes no bones about it, visualizing no reason for departing from his route; 'the family is the biggest and least cultivated audience'" (*Showguide* 1969). That same year he took a practical step to support and disseminate family movies by entering into arrangements with the Network Cinema Corporation to establish an international franchise chain of automated mini-cinemas bearing his endorsement (Levy 1996a, 365). Jerry Lewis Cinemas opened in the United States, Canada, France Italy, Germany, and Britain but were hampered by a shortage of suitable films: "I got killed by product immediately. . . . There wasn't any: what existed wasn't what I was building the theaters for. I wasn't going to run R's and X's. I was going to run whatever product would come along as long as it came in the PG rating for families" (Alpert 1977, 35–36). Nevertheless, the Jerry Lewis Cinema that opened in Corby, England, in 1973 booked such adult fare as *The Godfather* and *Cabaret* (Williamson 1973, 8). The company went bust in 1973, snarling Lewis in litigation that persisted into the 1980s.

33. "Jerry Lewis Files Chapter 13, Stays '73 Suit," *Variety,* 22 October 1980; "Jerry Lewis Gives Court His Earnings Outlook for '81–'82," *Variety,* 4 February 1981.

34. *Which Way to the Front?* had also done extremely well at the box office in both countries, despite the lack of confidence that Warner Brothers had in the film's commercial potential (Levy 1996a, 411–12).

35. The cast also includes performers who featured in Lewis's 1960s movies—Buddy Lester, Susan Oliver, Harold J. Stone, and Leonard Stone (Neibaur and Okuda 1995, 221).

36. Gary Arnold of the *Washington Post* observes that "in his prime Lewis could usually construct a whole feature around the chaos his character created trying to master a single occupation: draftee, rookie cop, errand boy, bellhop, domestic, hospital orderly, academician. In *Hardly Working* he keeps breaking down after each situation is exploited for a clumsy gag or two underlining Bo's heedlessness" (Arnold 1981, C3).

37. Unless otherwise noted, details of Lewis's honors are taken from the biography page of the Official Jerry Lewis Comedy Museum and Store web site (http://www.jerrylewiscomedy.com). Numerous other awards are listed: in 1971 he was presented with the Murray-Green Award for Community Services by the AFL-CIO; in 1976 the U.S. Senate adopted a resolution praising his "outstanding contribution in the fight against muscular dystrophy"; in 1978 he was awarded the National Association of Television Program Executives' Award of the Year for his work on the MDA Telethon; that same year he received the Jefferson Award for "Greatest Public Service Benefiting the Disadvantaged"; in 1980 he was presented with the Hubert H. Humphrey Humanitarian Award by the Touchdown Club of Washington, D.C.; in 1984 he received the Neal Pike Prize for Service to the Handicapped from Boston University's School of Law; in 1985 he received the Department of Defense Medal for Distinguished Public Service; in 1987 Mercy College made him an honorary doctor of humane letters for being, as the college president declared, "a shining example for people everywhere that one person can have an impact on society and change the world"; and in 1988 he was presented with the Award of Professionalism and Achievement by the Eterna Watch Corporation for his dedication to humanitarian causes.

38. The event was masterminded by influential columnist Walter Winchell, who set up the fund in 1947 to raise money for research into throat cancer, from which his friend Runyon had died. Winchell persuaded Milton Berle to host the celebrity-packed fund-raising gala, which was carried by fifteen stations. Winchell was influenced by the celebrity fundraising events staged by Basil O'Connor's March of Dimes campaign to raise money for polio research; however, where the "March of Dimes" made use of radio and the theater, Winchell grasped the possibilities afforded by the fledgling medium of broadcast television. (Levy 1996a, 106).

39. For example, *Variety* described a 1950 benefit show in aid of cerebral palsy sufferers as "one of the lushest variety shows presented to date" ("*Show of the Year*," 14 June 1950). In 1951 the trade journal suggested that the very slickness of these "carefully rehearsed super productions" did not always make for sparkling viewing ("Royal Flush" [review of NBC telethon for the Damon Runyon Cancer Fund], 13 June 1951).

40. In June 1950 Martin and Lewis performed on *Show of the Year,* a 150-minute NBC telethon for cerebral palsy sufferers hosted by Milton Berle ("*Show of the Year*," *Va-*

riety, 14 June 1950). In June 1951 they did an acclaimed fifteen-minute set on another show for the Runyon Cancer Fund telethon hosted by Berle ("Royal Flush," *Variety*, June 13, 1951). In June 1952 the team appeared on an Olympics telethon hosted by Bob Hope and Bing Crosby.

41. The two-hour *Martin and Lewis Thanksgiving Party* was telecast from Hollywood by ABC-TV in November 1953 and broadcast simultaneously on radio ("*The Martin and Lewis Thanksgiving Party*," *Variety*, 2 December 1953). The twenty-one-hour 1956 MDA Telethon, staged at Carnegie Hall and carried by the DuMont network, was their final television appearance as a team ("*Martin and Lewis Telethon*," *Variety*, 4 July 1956).

42. Lewis is generally reluctant to expand upon his reasons for embracing the MDA cause so fervently. He became further acquainted with neuromuscular disease through Bud Yorkin, stage manager of *The Colgate Comedy Hour*, whose nephew was struck by the illness (Levy 1996a, 139). In a teasingly enigmatic section of his autobiography he says that it was something else that happened shortly afterward that made him adopt the search for a cure to dystrophic diseases as his personal crusade: "Then something disastrous happened, something very personal. The effect almost wiped me off the face of the earth. My mind still can't escape from that experience. There's only one way out. One exit. It's the day we find a cure for muscular dystrophy" (Lewis and Gluck 1982, 219). In a 1975 interview with Dave Smith of the *Los Angeles Times* Lewis provided a similarly mysterious "explanation" of what impelled his involvement with the MDA: "This is my one secret. . . . I'll tell you this much — and it's more than I usually say. If I told you, it could easily backfire. And it would be my kids who would suffer. So it's my secret and I'm gonna keep it" (Smith 1975, 1). A year later, he dished out more of the same to Michael Tolkin of the *Village Voice*: "It's something that happened, very personal, and I decided I had to do something. In the 26 years I've devoted myself to this my wife has never asked why. No one knows. Until the time that someone tells me that it's vital to announce it, and it'll be productive. . . . But until that time it's my very own. . . . It's not important why. The fact is, that I do" (Tolkin 1976, 116).

43. Apart from the telethons, and his appearances as substitute for Johnny Carson on the *Tonight* show, Lewis has had a precarious career as a television entertainer since the 1950s. He told Charles Higham that his experiences on the ABC series illustrated the institutional limitations of the medium: "I hated the endless hypocrisy and lying, the crap, the stop-watch. My funny bone has no time for statistics. I couldn't bear the clock dictating when I would start and finish a joke. And the censorship — network censors are stupid, anti-creative men. What those stupid morons don't understand is that if you're given freedom you don't abuse it" (Higham 1972, 18). Significantly, one of Lewis's most critically acclaimed television appearances was his straight acting role in the CBS crime series *Wiseguy* (1988–89).

44. Apart from a temporary slowdown in the early 1980s, each telethon continued to outdo its predecessor: raising $9.2 million in 1972, $12.4 million in 1973, $18.8 million in 1975, $21,723,813 in 1976, and more than $31 million in 1981 (Levy 1996a, 387ff).

45. In 1973 the show moved from New York to Las Vegas, featuring contributions from Los Angeles, New York, and the local stations that relayed the event. As Levy (1996a)

comments, the telethon's "emphasis on money, gaudiness, broad emotionalism, and lounge-style entertainment all glittered with the vulgarity the casino city represented" (388). The casino hotels provide a refuge for show-biz values excluded from the cultural hegemony exerted by the entertainment centers of Los Angeles and New York. Faded stars, names with an exalted past, can still exult in the Las Vegas time capsule — a theme-park of adult rebelliousness where anarchic excesses (gambling, drink, sex) are simultaneously available and contained. Shawn Levy (1996a) suggests that during the 1970s the telethon became synonymous with the "tackiness and glitz" of Vegas culture, embodying "a kind of showbusiness excess that previous generations had unthinkingly supported but that seemed self-parodic in the age of punk rock and *Saturday Night Live*. It regularly featured such performers as Charo, Don Rickles, Tony Orlando and Dawn, Norm Crosby, Steve and Eydie, Sammy Davis, Jr., Vic Damone — exemplars of a waning era of showmanship and entertainment" (388).

46. "Muscular Dystrophy Association — 1993 Annual Report," obtained from the Internet Nonprofit Center web site at http://nonprofits.org/gallery/alpha/mda.

47. A traditional feature of the MDA Telethon is a spot where Lewis walks into the audience to pick up a healthy child who exemplifies the ideal the MDA is striving for. During the 1992 broadcast he selected the six-and-a-half-month-old Danielle Lewis, the daughter he adopted with his second wife, SanDee (also known as Sandra and Sam) Pitnick. Parading the radiant Danielle as the kind of child desired by every parent, Lewis proceeded to sing a specially written song, which warns that the tragedy of disease can strike anyone at any time. The song concludes: "I hate to beg for money, but please give all you can give / We need it, we take it, so my kids can make it — and live." Lewis met the twenty-nine-year-old Pitnick when he cast her in a small role in *Hardly Working* and began a relationship with her while still married to Patti (Levy 1996a, 409-14). After a messy divorce Lewis wed SanDee in 1983. The 1992 telethon does not acknowledge that his new familial bliss arose from the rupture of his old family, but this is not the point: in the evangelical rhetoric of the telethon, the surrogate family of Lewis's public overrides the claims of real life.

48. Miller is especially offended by the telethon's evangelism, noting that Lewis "conducted this 'love-in' with the sort of paranoid rancor that you'd expect from a Moony congress rather than a charitable fundraiser" (Miller 1981, 28).

49. *Prime Time Live,* ABC, September 1992.

50. Donahue accused: "The charity enterprise and structure in this country is a competitive, rancor-filled, inefficient system that does not speak equitably to the various difficulties that afflict not only young people but older people as well. To make it worse, we have a bunch of greedy, bottom-line companies coming in here, and their motive has more to do with selling merchandise than with helping the kids" (Levy 1996a, 425-26). Founded in the early 1950s by a handful of people who were either disabled themselves or had disabled children, the MDA has grown into a large-scale enterprise. In 1998 it had 186 district offices in the United States besides its headquarters in Tucson. It operates 230 hospital-affiliated clinics and supports nearly 400 international research projects (MDA web site: http://www.mdausa.org). Leslie Bennetts (1993) describes the MDA as "a big-business behemoth" that requires substantial funding to maintain its administrative infrastructure and executive salaries

(34–35). In itself a corporate entity, the organization ostentatiously courts the support of American big business. On the 1981 telethon, for example, Lewis declared that the corporate sponsors "are *friends,* on a very *emotional* and very *caring* level" (Miller 1981, 29). Commercial sponsors are keen to involve themselves with the telethon because its humanitarian agenda provides a valuable publicity boost for their business. A public relations executive for McDonald's expanded on the telethon's feel-good cachet: "I've got no research on this, it's just gut-level, . . . but to the extent that this replaces sales efforts, its effect on consumers is just as positive as if they were seeing a McDonald's commercial. You know, people don't mind feeling good about corporations. And where the product and the price choice are similar, people will be influenced by—and I hate to use this word—the image of the company. When the question comes down to Big Mac or Whopper, Jerry's kids can swing the undecideds." Harry Shearer reports that in 1976 corporate sponsors donated more than $6 million to the telethon and spent another $5 million promoting it (Shearer 1979, 40).

51. *Parade* is a weekly magazine distributed as a supplement with Sunday papers across the United States. For many years it has printed articles on the MDA just before the annual telethon, many of them bearing Lewis's name.

52. Setting themselves in opposition to the Lewisian telethon rather than the MDA itself, Jerry's Orphans tried to convince corporate sponsors to circumvent the telethon by donating money directly to the charity organization (Haller 1994, 149). This strategy ignores the fact that the prime attraction for the sponsors lies in the telethon's profile as a promotional showcase.

53. A copy of the Americans with Disabilities Act of 1990 can be found on the web at http://www2.wcoil.com/~mkaugie/ada.html. Further information can be found at Americans with Disabilities Act Questions and Answers, a web page published by the Kraut and Kraut Law Firm (http://www.kraut-law/em1.html).

54. Levy (1996a) reports that the MDA responded to such protests by reconfiguring the show "to include lengthy informational spots about adults with neuromuscular disease who had families and careers; more time was spent discussing the MDA's work with people stricken by nonpediatric strains of the disease" (464).

55. Writing in the early 1980s Mark Crispin Miller (1981) described the telethon as "an ugly circus," arguing that "whatever good they may accomplish in the short run, these television shows dehumanize the sick, reducing them to pitiable objects" (29).

56. *National Enquirer,* 15 May 1990, 1; *National Enquirer,* 10 July 1990, 1.

57. According to Leslie Bennets (1993), Lewis warned a reporter investigating charity fund-raising, "If you do anything to hurt my kids, I'll have you killed, you understand. I'll have you killed. I'll have you killed!" (26).

9. COMING HOME

1. Under the title *Smorgasbord,* the film was shown theatrically in France in 1983. The film's U.S. distributors, Warner Brothers, lost confidence in the movie after disappointing preview screenings and released it—as *Cracking Up*—directly to the video and home cable markets (Neibaur and Okuda 1995, 233). A more confident return to Lewis's earlier self-directed project, *Smorgasbord* was recognized by Lewis enthusi-

ast J. Hoberman as having "the aesthetic, abstract quality that one associates with *auteurs* in the moody twilight of their obsessions" (Levy 1996a, 432). Lewis's sole directorial effort since the early 1980s is *Boy,* his highly regarded and award-winning contribution to the portmanteau film *How Are the Kids?* (1990), which Jonathan Rosenbaum describes "an odd, moving fable about racism" (Neibaur and Okuda 1995, 249).

2. In 1984 Lewis also starred in two French farces (*Retenez moi . . . où je fais un malheur* and *Par où t'es rentré? On t'a pas vue sortir*), which have never been released in the United States.

3. Pauly Shore appeared in *Encino Man* (1992), *Son in Law* (1993), *In the Army Now* (1994), *Bio-Dome* (1996), *Jury Duty* (1995), and *Kingpin* (1996). The late Chris Farley made *Airheads* (1994), *Tommy Boy* (1995), *Black Sheep* (1996), and *Almost Heroes* (1998); and Adam Sandler starred in *Shakes the Clown* (1991), *Airheads, Billy Madison* (1995), *Happy Gilmore* (1996), and two hugely successful 1998 films, *The Wedding Singer* and *The Waterboy.* Michael Myers and Dana Carvey appeared together in the two *Wayne's World* films (1992, 1993), based on their popular *Saturday Night Live* sketch, and Myers also starred in *So I Married an Axe Murderer* (1993) and two *Austin Powers* films (*Man of Mystery* [1997] and *The Spy Who Shagged Me* [1999]). Jim Carrey rocketed to cinematic success with three films released in 1994—*Ace Ventura, Pet Detective, Dumb and Dumber,* and *The Mask* and subsequently starred in *Ace Ventura: When Nature Calls* (1995), *Batman Forever* (1995), *The Cable Guy* (1996), *Liar Liar* (1997), and *The Truman Show* (1998). Other notable dumb comedies with their roots in television include *Beavis and Butthead Do America* (1996) and *Rocket Man* (1997), featuring Harland Williams from the TV show *Simon*). As the deliriously eccentric child-man Pee-Wee Herman, comedian Paul Reubens made two significant precursors to the current cycle of dumb comedies—*Pee-Wee's Big Adventure* (1985) and *Big Top Pee-Wee* (1988).

4. *Dumb and Dumber,* made by the writing-directing team of Peter and Bobby Farrelly and costing a modest $14 million, grossed almost $300 million worldwide. The dumb comedies are especially attractive to the Hollywood industry because their generally low production costs virtually guarantee that they will turn a profit (Associated Press 1996). In 1998 the Farrelly brothers had another monumental box-office hit with *There's Something about Mary.*

5. Comedian comedy was one of the most visible casualties of the dismantling of the studio system. Until he left Paramount in the mid-1960s Lewis was the last of the Hollywood clowns working regularly for a major film company. Slapstick comedy persevered, but in a form that displaced the centrality of the specialized solo comedian—most notably with the grandiose chase spectacles *It's a Mad Mad Mad Mad World* (1963), *The Great Race* (1965), *Those Magnificent Men in Their Flying Machines* (Britain, 1965) and *Monte Carlo or Bust/ Those Magnificent Men in Their Jaunty Jalopies* (Britain-France-Italy, 1969). These lavish comedy epics feature a range of performers who literally compete for the central focus: including comedians such as Lewis, Peter Cook and Dudley Moore, the Three Stooges, Milton Berle, and Phil Silvers; situational-comedy performers such as Jack Lemmon, Tony Curtis, and Terry-Thomas; and such straight actors as Spencer Tracy, George Macready, and Stuart Whitman. The sustaining principle in these films is the competition between diverse

modes of performance and spectacle. The dispersal of the centralizing star personality is also manifested by the team-based films of the *National Lampoon* (nine films from 1978 to 1997) and *Police Academy* (seven films from 1984 to 1994) series, and the scattershot generic burlesques of the writer-producer-director team of Jim Abrahams, Jerry Zucker, and David Zucker—*The Kentucky Fried Movie* (1977), *Airplane!* (1980), *Top Secret!* (1984), the *Naked Gun* films (1988, 1991, 1994), and Abrahams's *Hot Shots!* (1991) and *Hot Shots! Part Deux* (1993). Leslie Nielsen, the pivotal figure of the *Naked Gun* series, is not a comedian so much as a perpetually befuddled straight man. The most prominent screen comedians since the 1960s—for example, Woody Allen, Steve Martin, Eddie Murphy, and Robin Williams—have resisted restricting themselves to slapstick vehicles. Performer, director, producer, and writer Mel Brooks, however, has kept faith with the protocols of "low" physical comedy in a series of old-style generic parodies, including *Blazing Saddles* (1974), *Young Frankenstein* (1974), *Silent Movie* (1976), *High Anxiety* (1977), *Spaceballs* (1987), *Robin Hood: Men in Tights* (1993), and *Dracula: Dead and Loving It* (1995).

6. After the phenomenal box-office totals of *Dumb and Dumber* Carrey was able to command a $20 million fee for starring in *The Cable Guy.*

7. Lewis had been interested in the idea of making a sequel to *The Nutty Professor* for some time, and through the 1980s there were rumors that such a film would soon materialize (Levy 1996a, 474–75).

8. Murphy shot to fame as a result of his appearances on *Saturday Night Live* from 1980 to 1984. He became the leading black cinema star in the 1980s as a result of films such as *Trading Places* (1983) and the action comedies *48 Hours* (1982) and *Beverly Hills Cop* (1984). Thereafter Murphy had mixed fortunes at the box office, owing to several ill-chosen screen vehicles (including a sequel to *48 Hours* and two further replays of *Beverly Hills Cop*). In the early 1990s he attempted to reinvigorate his film career with the more restrained comic persona he displayed in *Boomerang* and *The Distinguished Gentleman* (both 1992). In 1998 Murphy followed *The Nutty Professor* with *Dr. Doolittle,* another intriguing and highly profitable remake. Despite the waywardness of his cinematic career from the mid-1980s, Eddie Murphy's success made it possible for other black comedians—including Damon and Keenan Ivory Wayans, Robert Townsend, Martin Lawrence, and Will Smith—to gain acceptance as screen performers.

9. As Romney suggests, in a distinctively Lewisian inflection Murphy plays not only Klump and Love but also the professor's similarly oversized relatives. Murphy had earlier taken on multiple roles in his 1988 film *Coming to America.*

10. Romney (1996) points out that "at bottom, the film is little to do with body image, and everything to do with Murphy reappraising his career and realizing that he's best, and most unfettered, when he dumps his self-regarding 'real self' and goes full out as a ribald black Dick Emery" (10). (Emery was a British television comedian who specialized in broad character impersonations.)

11. Lewis was scheduled to serve as executive producer on the remake of *The Errand Boy.* In May 1997 Elizabeth Johns reported that Lewis intended to perform in the film, but not in the central role: "In the updated version, the new Morty will become the actual Lewis's comic rival at the studio" (Johns 1997). Lewis's contract with MGM also permits him a degree of involvement in their proposed remake of *The Bellboy,*

which will be filmed in the MGM Grand Hotel in Las Vegas (Fleming 1997). Lewis also intimated on several occasions that he would appear in a big-screen version of *Damn Yankees* (Louden 1997).

12. Interest in Lewis has been building on another front: in 1998 Martin Scorsese was announced as the director of a Dean Martin biofilm based on the Nick Tosches book, rumored to feature Tom Hanks as Dean Martin, John Travolta as Frank Sinatra, and Jim Carrey as Lewis.

13. In 1988 Lewis had also provided many select items from his personal collection for a month-long tribute to his film and television work held at the American Museum of the Moving Image, New York (Hoberman 1988, 47, 61).

14. The web site's biography page subscribes to Lewis's revisionist account of his history by excluding any mention of his estranged son Joseph. Levy (1996a) quotes Lewis's rapturous vision of the new horizons opened to filmmakers since the 1960s: "I'd give my balls to be able to remake a couple of films with today's technology. DAT recording, Steadycams, Lumicranes, digital graphics. . . . The gags that I had to create with practical actual materials because that's the way it was. . . . I couldn't wait eight weeks for a process house to show me a little mouse sitting on a window. I'd shoot the joke myself. I'd have the art department build me a mouse, put a battery up his ass and move it." (461).

15. On several occasions he has also participated in online question-and-answer sessions with his virtual community of fans. One of the 1997 sessions took place while Lewis was playing in *Damn Yankees* at the Adelphi Theatre, London. The "liveness" of his dialogue was underlined by the fact that Lewis's responses were keyed in during breaks from the stage. The London premiere of *Damn Yankees* was also broadcast live over the Internet, one of a series of experimental cybercasts organized by Vancouver-based computer company ITV Technologies (Chen 1997, 8). In 1998 and 1999 the Jerry Lewis MDA Telethon was also carried live on the Internet.

16. Paul D. Zimmerman, formerly a film critic for *Newsweek* magazine, wrote the script for *The King of Comedy* in the early 1970s. He attracted the interest of Czech director Milos Forman, who spent some time developing the project for Paramount. By 1974 Forman had still not succeeded in securing financial backing, and Zimmerman sent the script to Martin Scorsese — who, in turn, gave it to Robert De Niro. The actor was extremely excited by Zimmerman's work and planned to film the project with Michael Cimino, his director on *The Deer Hunter* (1978). Cimino abandoned the idea when he was caught up in extravagant production schedule of *Heaven's Gate* (1980), and De Niro then convinced Scorsese to take it over. (Details from Rickey 1982, 72–73.)

17. Scorsese and De Niro worked together on *Mean Streets* (1973), *Taxi Driver* (1975), *New York, New York* (1977), and *Raging Bull* (1980). They were subsequently reunited for *Goodfellas* (1990), *Cape Fear* (1991), and *Casino* (1995).

18. Janet Maslin (1983) of the *New York Times* likewise noted the disengaging effect of the film: "It tells a story in which the audience can't really become involved and toward which both director and star demonstrate a certain detachment themselves" (19). A good indication of the film's strategic frustration of character identification is the deliberate avoidance of close-ups (Thompson and Christie 1989, 88).

19. Steve Jenkins (1983) suggests that the "concentration on performance-as-display

seems to have had the effect of keeping Scorsese's camera, for the most part, uncharacteristically immobile" (151). Scorsese explains that with *The King of Comedy* he sought to depart from his customary cinematic flourishes with a minimalist style, which he admits he found difficult to accomplish: "I tried to be restrained through the whole picture—not to move the camera—I tried to be very simple. I tried to be almost like television for some reason. You have to think like television and I couldn't do that. Couldn't get too close. I had to be a certain way. Couldn't look in the eyes a certain way. I just couldn't" (Houston 1984, 87). Unlike Scorsese's other work, Terrence Rafferty (1983) notes, *The King of Comedy* has "an almost classical *mise-en-scène,* cut to the stately editing rhythms of the traditional American narrative film" (186).

20. The phrase is borrowed from Eric Barnouw's famous study, *Tube of Plenty: The Evolution of American Television* (Barnouw 1975).

21. Rupert situates Langford and Minnelli as the adoring parents of his imagination. His real-life mother is displaced outside the visible boundaries of the frame, represented exclusively as a chiding off-screen voice.

22. Pupkin's inability to distinguish fantasy from reality reveals his kinship to Travis Bickle, the alienated protagonist of *Taxi Driver*. Both men accomplish desperate acts of aggression to bring meaning to their lives—and both reap the ironic rewards of a media glory that obscures the perversity of their motives. Bickle first attempts to assassinate a political candidate, but when thwarted he automatically transfers his attentions to rescuing the child prostitute Iris (Jodie Foster) from her "captors." The rescue allows Travis to enact a devastating bloodbath through which the ostensible object of his quest is subordinated to a gun-defined fantasy of masculine assertion. Like Pupkin, Bickle's thinking about the relations between self and the world is highly mediated: he is propelled by generic visions of movie heroism, by pornography, by the daytime soap operas he blankly devours. *Taxi Driver* emphasizes Bickle's disconnection from the world he moves by foregrounding the screens he observes it through (television, cinema, the windshield and rear-view mirror of his taxicab).

23. Pupkin's performance is shown only when his monologue is broadcast on the Langford show after the kidnapping. The act comprises a string of slickly professionalized gags that repackage the desperate frustrations of his life into absurdly comic vignettes that deal with poverty, neglect, brutalization, . . . and even the kidnapping of Jerry Langford! (In a blatant example of wish fulfillment, Rupert even kills off his domineering mother in one of the gags.) It is also crucial that he savors his moment of public glory as a *spectator:* he watches the monologue on television in the bar where Rita works.

24. The film is punctuated with a series of fantasy sequences in which Pupkin imagines himself schmoozing with the glitterati of the small screen, finding in their company an acceptance and purposefulness that elude him elsewhere. In the first of these sequences Langford confides that he no longer enjoys his work and begs Pupkin to take over for him. In a later scene Langford once more regales the wanna-be comedian with excessive praise: "I envy you. I hate you but I envy you. Because it's purity, it's marvelous, it's humor based on you. Nobody else could do it but you." The joke is that the film consistently portrays Pupkin as a sad, misguided "anorak" who has very little to offer apart from his delusions.

25. Rita, the woman Rupert has adored from afar since childhood, plays a key role in the articulation of his fantasy. Early in the film Pupkin outlines his dream of show-biz stardom to her, saying that his meeting with Langford will lead to a spot on the talk show, which will in turn springboard him into the comedy circuit . . . and eventually onto a network showcase of his own. Although Pupkin invites Rita to share in his success — because "every king needs a queen" — a later sequence makes it plain that the erotic components of his desire are both subordinated to and codified through his rapture with television. In one imagined sequence Pupkin marries Rita on the Langford show, in a ceremony officiated by George Kapp, the principal of Pupkin's former high school. During the wedding Kapp apologizes on behalf of everyone who failed to recognize and encourage Rupert's immense talent, and then thanks him for the meaning he has brought to people's lives. A mute presence throughout this public testimonial, Rita operates as both status symbol (attractive, black, statuesque) and witness (a metaphor for the audience "out there"). She *signifies* but does not embody the true prize, the value of which is measured in the currency of renown.

26. Lewis continues to attract the unwelcome attention of celebrity stalkers. In 1995 Gary Benson, formerly the husband of Lewis's housekeeper, pleaded guilty to a felony charge of aggravated stalking. Benson, a schizophrenic, was sentenced to five years' probation but this was revoked three years later because he failed to comply with the condition that he kept away from Lewis (Mr. Showbiz 1998).

27. Lewis claims that he devised a different ending, which Scorsese was keen on shooting but which De Niro rejected: "In my finish, Jerry Langford escapes from the kidnapping and gets to the television studio. We hear the sounds of the studio just before the show goes on the air; we pan the audience, and there are two nuns, a priest, Bobby [De Niro], and another nun. The reason for the nuns and the priest was so that Bobby was glaringly spotted among those black outfits. Then we cut to the band as they're playing the fanfare, and you hear the announcer say, 'From New York, the Jerry Langford Show, and here's the star of our show, Jerry Langford.' So I come out onstage, then there's a swish pan to the audience just as you hear a gunshot. You hear screams and the camera tilts down; we see the two nuns, the priest, an empty seat, and the other nun. And you know damn well that Bobby shot Langford. *That* should have been the finish" (Neibaur and Okuda 1995, 232).

28. *The Tonight Show* was first broadcast in 1954, hosted by Steve Allen, who was succeeded by Jack Paar in 1957. Lewis has served as guest host on several occasions. In 1962, before Johnny Carson took over as Paar's replacement, Lewis helmed the program for two weeks. His assured performance encouraged ABC to sign him for the ill-fated series he mounted the following year (Levy 1996s, 278–79). For further information on *The Tonight Show*, see Bianculli 1997, 336–43.

29. Scorsese has fond childhood memories of Lewis's irreverent attitude to the television medium: "One time he walked on and just put his mouth on the lens. Ate the camera. It was bad. Vulgar. But the surrealism of it . . . it just worked. It was total anarchy. It destroyed television as we know it, and that's the interesting thing about Lewis" (Houston 1984, 85).

30. Before shooting started Lewis consulted with Scorsese, De Niro, and Zimmerman, sharing with them his knowledge of celebrity: "They don't know celebrity. They

only know anonymity. You could walk by Bobby de Niro today, you wouldn't know him. It's just the way he is. . . . They needed me to tell them about celebrity. And we wrote together. Paul Zimmerman and Marty and myself, we wrote the things they had never heard about" (Levy 1996a, 420). Lewis also reports that Scorsese and De Niro were both "very knowledgeable about my film work, and they showed me a great deal of respect" (Neibaur and Okuda 1995, 231).

31. Scorsese's account of how he arrived at the visual atmosphere of *Taxi Driver* provides an especially clear example of his "cannibalization" of earlier films: "We looked at Hitchcock's *The Wrong Man* for the moves when Henry Fonda goes into the insurance office and the shifting points of view of the people behind the counter. That was the kind of paranoia that I wanted to employ. And the way Francesco Rosi used black and white in *Salvatore Giuliano* was the way I wanted *Taxi Driver* to look in color. We also studied Jack Hazan's *A Bigger Splash* for the head-on framing, such as the shot of the grocery store before Travis Bickle shoots the black guy. Each sequence begins with a shot like that, so before any moves you're presented with an image like a painting" (Thompson and Christie 1989, 60).

32. "Come Rain or Come Shine" was written by Johnny Mercer and Harold Arlen for the 1946 film *St Louis Woman* (Jasen 1990, 233). Lewis himself recorded the song for his Decca album *Jerry Lewis Just Sings*.

33. In a review of the film Michael Buckley (1983) also reads Sandra Bernhard as a twisted reworking of the Lewisian Kid, suggesting that she "resembles the 1950s Lewis in drag" (301). Another nod to Lewis's films is the fact that Pupkin, like Morty Tashman, has a low-status job as an errand boy for a film company.

34. In *The Errand Boy* and *The Patsy* Lewis's Kid ultimately triumphs over the corruptions of the entertainment business owing to his natural talent and goodness of heart. Where Lewis had once propagandized for entertainment that comes from the heart or the gut, in *The King of Comedy* he plays a cynically professional emissary of a corporate entertainment culture that affords little space for creativity and enthusiasm. The advice Langford offers Pupkin near the start of the film, for example, stands in stark contrast to the method director's passionate vision of the unique individual in *The Errand Boy:* "This is a crazy business, but it's not unlike any other business. There are ground rules. And you don't just walk onto a network show without experience. Now I know it's an old hackneyed expression, but it happens to be the truth—you got to start at the bottom. . . . It looks so simple to the viewer at home. Those things that come so easily, that are so relaxed and look like it's a matter of just taking another breath. It takes years and years and years of honing that and working it."

35. Paul Zimmerman points out that his screenplay for *The King of Comedy* originally opened with the words "Are you Somebody?" (Rickey 1982, 73).

36. David Shaw suggests that television celebrities are more likely than movie stars to attract stalkers because they seem so instantly "approachable": "A television performer, particularly the star of a series, comes into your home every week. If he's on the late-night talk shows, he's practically in bed with you. That breeds a certain familiarity and intimacy that makes them seem like one of the family. Movie stars seem more distant: they're on that huge screen, larger than life, and most fans are more in awe of them, less likely to walk up and slap them on the back in public" (Shaw 1973, 35). Beverle Houston follows a similar line of argument: "It is cinema that produces

plenitude, the stars we truly love; television's talk show host, himself not a figure of ecstatic desire, provides access to them. The identity of the host is somewhere between that of a star and a family member—one who knows the stars and is known by them, one whom they allow to mediate between their imagined location of pure desire and the living room where television delivers them to the domestic world" (Houston 1984, 78).

37. Lewis told Charles Higham that television had been "one of the most destructive forces in our society" because it "destroys dreams, it makes everything real" (Higham 1972, 18). Although he was a high-profile performer in both media, Lewis repeatedly aligned himself with cinema rather than television. In a chaotic sequence in which an outside broadcast is conducted from the Wellenmellen house *The Ladies' Man* represents television as inferior to the magical possibilities of cinema. In *The Patsy* Stanley becomes a star after his performance on Ed Sullivan's television variety show but the sketch he enacts is both explicitly concerned with cinematic desire and receives a distinctively filmic articulation.

38. David Denby (1983) observed that "one of the sarcastic ironies in this movie is that what Rupert wants isn't worth having—being a big star looks like misery. Scorsese has induced Jerry Lewis to give a rather malignant performance. His Jerry Langford is a heavy, bored, put-upon celebrity, a man who never cracks a joke off-camera, a man always alone, always angry. . . . Jerry Langford is as big a failure as a human being as he is a success in the great world" (74).

39. Steve Jenkins (1983) also makes the point that there is no room in this film for a Jerry Lewis performance because "as a physical presence, he functions almost entirely as a passive cipher through which Rupert and Masha can work out their fantasies" (151).

40. In her 1983 review of the film for the *New Yorker* Pauline Kael wrote that "Jerry Lewis is the only real thing here; his performance has the weight of authenticity—we can feel Langford's physical need for solitude. . . . There's something believable here: it's in Jerry Lewis's bullying face and his solid slab of a body—you feel he has reserves of rage to draw on. With a minimum of dialogue, Lewis lets us understand that Langford believes he earns his peace and isolation. Lewis doesn't try to make the off-camera Langford likable; the performance says that what the off-camera star feels is his own damn business" (Kael 1987, 459).

41. In 1993 Lewis told Graham Fuller, "When I did *The King of Comedy* I had the hardest fucking time maintaining Jerry Langford because that character was so close to my breast; he lived a lifestyle not unlike mine, with all the stalkers and bullshit that disrupts your life" (Fuller 1993, 115).

42. Like *The King of Comedy*, *Funny Bones* uses Lewis as a contested icon of American show business. Although his character, George Fawkes, exemplifies the slickness and glitz of Las Vegas entertainment, the film reveals that his fame is built upon the "folkloric" variety traditions he discovered in Blackpool, England—and shamelessly pirated. Fawkes's professional malfeasance is compounded by personal treachery: he engages in an adulterous relationship with the wife of the man whose act he steals. The illicit union produces a prodigiously gifted but psychologically disturbed son, Jack Parker (Lee Evans), whose virtuoso physical comedy recalls the early performances of Lewis himself.

43. When he was interviewed in London shortly after the show transferred there, Lewis

declared, "I call my body of work throughout all these years as the huge white cake. And *Damn Yankees* is the cherry" (*Kaleidoscope* 1997). Variations on this theme pop up frequently in newspaper interviews and profiles of Lewis in the late 1990s. In 1995 he told Harry Haun, "I'm very focussed on the responsibility of Broadway — more than ever in my career — because I'm finally getting to that place I've been dreaming about. . . . With a body of work like mine, then all of a sudden — hey, Broadway! This just doesn't happen to a guy in the autumn of his life. To have done as much as I've done and still get a shot at something that I've never done — I mean, it's really incredible!" (Haun 1995, 22).

44. Lewis had already been lined up for the touring version of the show, which was scheduled to follow its Broadway run.

45. *Damn Yankees* began its first year of touring on 22 September 1995 at the Eisenhower Hall in West Point. After a layoff in August 1996, while Lewis was busy with preparations for the MDA Telethon, the show kicked off its second annual tour in San Francisco.

46. In August 1997 *Damn Yankees* closed at the Adelphi Theatre for a few weeks so Lewis could work on the telethon. According to a report posted on the Mr. Showbiz web site, the promised transfer to the Victoria Theatre was unexpectedly canceled because producer Mitchell Maxwell no longer found the show a profitable enterprise — a problem exacerbated by declining ticket sales and by Lewis's weekly $100,000 pay check (Mr. Showbiz 1997). In subsequent months Lewis kept remarkably quiet about the circumstances surrounding his departure from the show, and for several months there were ongoing rumors that he would yet rejoin the production at some stage of its international tour. (Information posted between 20 September 1997 and 3 April 1998 in Damn Yankees News at the Applegate's Apartment web site, which is no longer active).

47. *Damn Yankees* was based on Douglass Wallop's 1955 novel *The Year the Yankees Lost the Pennant.* Wallop collaborated on the book for the show with veteran writer-director George Abbott. Richard Adler and Jerry Ross provided the songs, and the choreographer was Bob Fosse. Opening at New Haven's Shubert Theater in April 1955, the show transferred to Broadway a month later. Gwen Verdon and Ray Walston reprised their roles in 1958 film adaptation by Warner Brothers. On 13 November 1955 Martin and Lewis duetted one of the songs from the musical, "Two Lost Souls," on *The Colgate Variety Hour.*

48. Kathleen Rhames of the *Daily Bruin* suggests that few features of the original show were altered in the revival, with the exception of the updated choreography and the additional of new musical number such as the "Blooper Ballet," danced by the Senators (Rhames 1996). Lloyd Rose (1996) points out the male sports reporter of the original show was transformed into a woman and that "the story has somehow metamorphosed into a tale about a guy who really loves his unglamorous wife" (C1). Whereas the original show was actually set in 1950s America, the revival looks back on this era with the hindsight of four decades. The 1990s version of *Damn Yankees* pays nostalgic tribute to the Eisenhower era, with a treatment that oscillates between the cute and the kitsch.

49. The ensuing discussion of *Damn Yankees* is based on viewings of the show at the Marquis Theater, New York, in March 1995 and the Adelphi Theatre, London, in

June 1997. There were some differences between the two performances—especially in Lewis's rendition of "Those Were the Good Old Days"—but I combine the two occasions as a singular "text."

50. In this respect Joe resembles George Bailey (James Stewart), the frustrated protagonist of Frank Capra's small-town epic *It's a Wonderful Life* (1946), which, as Applegate correctly guesses, is his favorite movie.

51. The differences between Joe and Applegate are underlined by their contrasting responses to public attention. The more Joe is exposed to the public gaze, the more he retreats into a longing for the small-town anonymity he has forsaken. Applegate is a performer who flourishes before an audience.

52. An earlier version of the cane routine can be found in the videotape recording of Lewis's 1984 performance at the Sahara Hotel, Las Vegas (JAS Productions 1984). As in the Vegas show Lewis peppers his *Damn Yankees* spot with sex-theme gags and jokes about Catholics and Jews.

53. One impressive exception occurs at the end of the first act when Applegate takes Lola to task for failing to seduce Joe: Lewis does a high-kicking parody of her earlier showy performance of "Whatever Lola Wants (Lola Gets)."

54. During the *Damn Yankees* publicity spree Lewis spoke effusively of his father's heroic talents: "Anything you ever saw me do, my father did—only better. He molded me. I watched every performance my father did except when he was in burlesque or on the road. My father was absolutely the most versatile man I've ever seen. He danced as good as Astaire, he played instruments, he did mime, he conducted the orchestra. He was my hero. He should have been the biggest star in the world" (*Iran News* 1996). The invocation of Danny Lewis also serves to parade Jerry's own connection to the "authentic" vaudeville culture of the pre–World War II era, legitimizing his role as a torchbearer for "traditional" values of American entertainment.

55. Lewis made his first stab at Broadway with a revival of the 1938 Ole Olsen and Chic Johnson show *Hellzapoppin'*, a madcap collage of comedy-variety routines that ran for more than eleven hundred performances (Maltin 1970, 246). The show was filmed by Universal in 1941 as a much more conventional Hollywood comedy. In the mid-1970s Alexander H. Cohan decided to produce an updated version of the *Hellzapoppin'* "razzle-dazzle fun house" concept, building it around Lewis's central presence (Levy 1996a, 398). In pre-Broadway tryouts in Baltimore, Washington, D.C., and Boston the show was plagued by "technical and artistic difficulties" (Lewis and Gluck 1982, 298). Drawing scornful reviews and lackluster attendances, *Hellzapoppin'* closed in Boston in January 1977—a few weeks before its scheduled opening in New York's theaterland (Levy 1996a, 400-404). As usual much of the blame for the show's failure was heaped on Lewis's shoulders, with newspapers gleefully reporting his wrangles with both the producer and costar Lynn Redgrave.

56. Lewis elaborated upon the intergenerational dynamic in a 1997 interview. He proposed that the uplifting impact of *Damn Yankees* derives to a significant degree from the mutual accommodation between the veteran showman and his young supporting cast: "The wonderful thing about this is . . . what I see happening in the theater every night. Our audiences are like a bunch of people watching a Beatles concert. They get totally into it, and I've figured out why. First, the show and the music are wonderful. It's about love and hope and deception and revenge—a whole spectrum of

emotions that really stir an audience. And, second, the company is busting its ass for the old man, and the old man adores the young kids. The audience can feel that. They stand and cheer at the end of the show and, as I've been told a thousand times on this tour, walk out saying 'that's the best night we've spent in the theater ever!'" (Louden 1997).

57. This interview extract is typical: "Danny is my center. . . . She's part of my second lifetime. For me, she is what I didn't have at 18. At that time, I was so busy with myself, so enamored with what was happening to my career, that I didn't really meet my sons until they were 4 or 5 years old. We eventually bonded and became very close, but I missed their beginnings. Now with Danny, since the day she was born, she's mine every morning for two hours" (*Iran News* 1995).

58. The benignly conciliatory tone he adopted was shared by the many reviewers and interviewers who paid court to Lewis in the mid-1990s. Believing they were dealing with a man reborn, journalists were keen to affirm how surprisingly fit and youthful Lewis seemed. To prepare for *Damn Yankees* he put himself on a rigorous exercise program, losing a much-publicized thirty-five pounds, and delighted in proclaiming himself sixty-nine years going on nine.

APPENDIX

LEWISOGRAPHY

During his prolific career as an American entertainer Jerry Lewis conquered a formidable array of media territories. He has courted public attention with such unashamed promiscuity that it would be foolish to attempt a definitive record of his output. What follows, then, is a comprehensively *indicative* catalogue of his most significant achievements in cinema, radio, television, phonographic recording, and cabaret. A complete list of Lewis's film releases is provided, but it is much more difficult to find reliable information on other areas — especially his prodigious activities as a television and live performer. With Lewis's television work I have tried to suggest the range of different capacities in which he has served the medium. With live appearances I have restricted myself to charting pivotal dates in the progression of his career. To compile this appendix I have drawn extensively on the books by Shawn Levy, Nick Tosches, James Neibaur and Ted Okuda, and Robert Benayoun (especially the biography compiled by Simon Mizrahi), as well as the anonymous entry on Lewis in the magazine *Film Dope* (1986, 16–19) and the trade magazines *Variety* and *Daily Variety*.

FILMS WITH DEAN MARTIN

1949
My Friend Irma (Wallis-Hazen / Paramount Pictures)
Produced by Hal B. Wallis. Directed by George Marshall. Screenplay by Cy Howard and Parke Levy. Based on the CBS radio series *My Friend Irma*. Starring John Lund, Diana Lynn, Don DeFore, Marie Wilson, Hans Conried, Dean Martin, and Jerry Lewis. U.S. release: August 1949.

1950
At War with the Army (York Pictures–Screen Associates / Paramount Pictures)
Produced by Fred F. Finklehoff. Directed by Hal Walker. Screenplay by Fred F. Finklehoff. Based on a play by James B. Allardice. Starring Dean Martin, Jerry Lewis, Mike Kellin, Jimmie Dundee, and Dick Stabile. Filmed in 1949. U.S. release: December 1950.

My Friend Irma Goes West (Wallis–Hazen / Paramount Pictures)
Produced by Hal B. Wallis. Directed by Hal Walker. Screenplay by Cy Howard and Parke Levy. Based on the CBS radio series *My Friend Irma*. Starring John Lund, Corinne Calvet, Diana Lynn, Marie Wilson, Dean Martin, and Jerry Lewis. U.S. release: May 1950.

1951
Sailor Beware (Wallis–Hazen / Paramount Pictures)
Produced by Hal B. Wallis. Directed by Hal Walker. Screenplay by James Allardice and Martin Rackin. Based on a play by Kenyon Nicholson and Charles Robinson. Adaptation by Elwood Ullman, with additional dialogue by John Grant. Starring Dean Martin, Jerry Lewis, Corinne Calvet, Marion Marshall, Robert Strauss, Leif Erickson, Don Wilson, and Skip Homeier. U.S. release: February 1952. Previously filmed as *Lady Be Careful* (1936) and *The Fleet's In* (1942).

That's My Boy (Wallis–Hazen / Paramount Pictures)
Produced by Hal B. Wallis. Directed by Hal Walker. Screenplay by Cy Howard. Based on a screen story by Cy Howard. Starring Dean Martin, Jerry Lewis, Ruth Hussey, Eddie Mayehoff, Marion Marshall, and Polly Bergen. U.S. release: May 1951.

1952
Jumping Jacks (Wallis–Hazen / Paramount Pictures)
Produced by Hal B. Wallis. Directed by Norman Taurog. Screenplay by Robert Lees, Fred Rinaldo, and Herbert Baker, with additional dialogue by James Allardice and Richard Weil. Based on a screen story by Brian Marlow. Starring Dean Martin, Jerry Lewis, Mona Freeman, Don DeFore, Robert Strauss, Dick Erdman, Ray Teal, and Marcy McGuire. U.S. release: June 1952.

1953
The Caddy (York Pictures / Paramount Pictures)
Produced by Paul Jones. Directed by Norman Taurog. Screenplay by Edmund Hartmann and Danny Arnold, with additional dialogue by Ken Englund. Based on a screen story by Danny Arnold. Starring Dean Martin, Jerry Lewis, Donna Reed, Barbara Bates, Joseph Calleia, and Fred Clark. U.S. release: August 1953.

Money from Home (Wallis–Hazen / Paramount Pictures)
Produced by Hal B. Wallis. Directed by George Marshall. Screenplay by Hal Kanter. Based on a story by Damon Runyon; adaptation by James Allardice and Hal Kanter. Starring Dean Martin, Jerry Lewis, Marjie Millar, Pat Crowley, Richard Haydn, Robert Strauss, Gerald Mohr, and Sheldon Leonard. U.S. release: February 1954. Martin and Lewis's first film in Technicolor; also produced in 3-D. Lewis received screen credit for staging material in song sequences.

Scared Stiff (Wallis–Hazen / Paramount Pictures)
Produced by Hal B. Wallis. Directed by George Marshall. Screenplay by Herbert Baker and Walter DeLeon, with additional dialogue by Ed Simmons and Norman Lear. Based on a play by Paul Dickey and Charles W. Goddard. Previously filmed as *The Ghost Breakers* (1940). Starring Dean Martin, Jerry Lewis, Lizabeth Scott, Carmen Miranda, George Dolenz, and Dorothy Malone, with guest appearances by Bob Hope and Bing Crosby. U.S. release: April 1953.

The Stooge (Wallis–Hazen / Paramount Pictures)
Produced by Hal B. Wallis. Directed by Norman Taurog. Screenplay by Fred F. Finklehoff and Martin Rackin, with additional dialogue by Edwood Ullman. Based on a screen story by Fred F. Finklehoff and Sid Silvers. Starring Dean Martin, Jerry Lewis, Eddie Mayehoff, Marion Marshall, and Polly Bergen. Filmed in 1951. U.S. release: February 1953.

1954
Living It Up (York Pictures / Paramount Pictures)
Produced by Paul Jones. Directed by Norman Taurog. Screenplay by Jack Rose and Melville Shavelson. Based on the musical comedy *Hazel Flagg;* adapted from the 1937 film *Nothing Sacred;* and scripted by Ben Hecht. Starring Dean Martin, Jerry Lewis, Janet Leigh, Edward Arnold, Fred Clark, Sheree North, and Sig Ruman. U.S. release: July 1954.

Three Ring Circus (Wallis–Hazen / Paramount Pictures)
Produced by Hal B. Wallis. Directed by Joseph Pevney. Screenplay by Don McGuire. Based on a screen story by Don McGuire. Starring Dean Martin, Jerry Lewis, Joanne Dru, Zsa Zsa Gabor, Wallace Ford, Elsa Lanchester, Sig Ruman, Gene Sheldon, and Nick Cravat. U.S. release: December 1954. Martin and Lewis's first film in VistaVision.

1955
Artists and Models (Wallis–Hazen / Paramount Pictures)
Produced by Hal B. Wallis. Directed by Frank Tashlin. Screenplay by Frank Tashlin, Hal Kanter, and Herbert Baker. Based on a play by Michael Davidson and Norman Lessing; adaptation by Don McGuire. Starring Dean Martin, Jerry Lewis, Shirley MacLaine, Dorothy Malone, Eddie Mayehoff, Eva Gabor, Anita Ekberg, George Winslow, and Jack Elam. U.S. release: December 1955.

You're Never Too Young (York Pictures / Paramount Pictures)
Produced by Paul Jones. Directed by Norman Taurog. Screenplay by Sidney Sheldon. Based on a story by Fannie Kilbourne, suggested by Edward Childs Carpenter's play *Connie Goes Home*. Previously filmed as *The Major and the Minor* (1942). Starring Dean Martin, Jerry Lewis, Diana Lynn, Nina Foch, Raymond Burr, Mitzi McCall, and Veda Ann Borg. U.S. release: August 1955.

1956
Hollywood or Bust (Wallis–Hazen / Paramount Pictures)
Produced by Hal B. Wallis. Directed by Frank Tashlin. Screenplay by Erna Lazarus. Starring Dean Martin, Jerry Lewis, Anita Ekberg, Pat Crowley, Maxie Rosenbloom, and Mr. Bascom. U.S. release: December 1956.

Pardners (York Pictures / Paramount Pictures)
Produced by Paul Jones. Directed by Norman Taurog. Screenplay by Sidney Sheldon. Based on a screen story by Jerry Davis, based on a story by Mervin J. Houser. Previously filmed as *Rhythm on the Range* (1936). Starring Dean Martin, Jerry Lewis, Lori Nelson, Jeff Morrow, Jackie Loughery, Jack Baragrey, Agnes Moorehead, Lon Chaney Jr., and Lee Van Cleef. U.S. release: July 1956.

SOLO FILMS

1957
The Delicate Delinquent (York Pictures / Paramount Pictures)
Produced by Jerry Lewis. Directed by Don McGuire. Screenplay by Don McGuire. Based on a screen story by Don McGuire. Starring Jerry Lewis, Darren McGavin, Martha Hyer, Robert Ivers, and Horace McMahon. U.S. release: June 1957.

The Sad Sack (Wallis-Hazen / Paramount Pictures)
Produced by Hal B. Wallis. Directed by George Marshall. Screenplay by Edmund Beloin and Nate Monaster. Based on a comic strip created by George Baker. Starring Jerry Lewis, David Wayne, Phyllis Kirk, Peter Lorre, Jone Mantell, Gene Evans, and George Dolenz. U.S. release: November 1957.

1958
The Geisha Boy (York Pictures / Paramount Pictures)
Produced by Jerry Lewis. Directed by Frank Tashlin. Screenplay by Frank Tashlin. Based on a screen story by Rudy Makoul. Starring Jerry Lewis, Marie McDonald, Sessue Hayakawa, Barton MacLane, Suzanne Pleshette, Nubo McCarthy, Robert Hirano, Ryuzo Demura, and Harry Hare. U.S. release: December 1958.

Rock-a-Bye Baby (York Pictures / Paramount Pictures)
Produced by Jerry Lewis. Directed by Frank Tashlin. Screenplay by Frank Tashlin. Based on a screen story by Frank Tashlin, based on Preston Sturges's film *The Miracle of Morgan's Creek* (1944). Starring Jerry Lewis, Marilyn Maxwell, Connie Stevens, Salvatore Baccaloni, Reginald Gardiner, Hans Conried, Isobel Elsom, and Gary Lewis. U.S. release: July 1958.

1959
Don't Give Up the Ship (Wallis-Hazen / Paramount Pictures)
Produced by Hal B. Wallis. Directed by Norman Taurog. Screenplay by Herbert Baker, Edmund Beloin, and Harry Garson. Based on a story by Ellis Kadison. Starring Jerry Lewis, Dina Merrill, Diana Spencer, Mickey Shaughnessy, Robert Middleton, Gale Gordon, and Claude Akins. U.S. release: July 1959.

1960
The Bellboy (Jerry Lewis Productions / Paramount Pictures)
Produced by Jerry Lewis. Directed by Jerry Lewis. Screenplay by Jerry Lewis. Starring Jerry Lewis, Alex Garry, Bob Clayton, Herkie Styles, Sonny Sands, Eddie Shaeffer, David Landfield, Bill Richmond, Jack Kruschen, and Milton Berle. U.S. release: July 1960.

Cinderfella (Jerry Lewis Pictures Corporation / Paramount Pictures)
Produced by Jerry Lewis. Directed by Frank Tashlin. Screenplay by Frank Tashlin. Based on "Cinderella" by Charles Perrault. Starring Jerry Lewis, Ed Wynn, Judith Anderson, Anna Maria Alberghetti, Henry Silva, Robert Hutton, and Count Basie and his orchestra. Filmed in 1959. U.S. release: December 1960.

Visit to a Small Planet (Wallis-Hazen / Paramount Pictures)
Produced by Hal B. Wallis. Directed by Norman Taurog. Screenplay by Edmund Beloin, Henry Garson. Based on a play by Gore Vidal. Starring Jerry Lewis, Joan Blackman, Earl Holliman, Fred Clark, Lee Patrick, Gale Gordon, Jerome Cowan, and John Williams. U.S. release: February 1960.

1961
The Errand Boy (Jerry Lewis Productions / Paramount Pictures)
Produced by Ernest D. Glucksman. Directed by Jerry Lewis. Screenplay by Jerry Lewis and Bill Richmond. Starring Jerry Lewis, Brian Donlevy, Dick Wesson, Howard McNear, Kathleen Freeman, Isobel Elsom, Fritz Feld, Sig Ruman, Iris Adrian, Benny Rubin, Del Moore, Snub Pollard, Robert Ivers, and Joe Besser. U.S. release: September 1961.

The Ladies' Man (York Pictures / Jerry Lewis Productions / Paramount Pictures)
Produced by Jerry Lewis. Directed by Jerry Lewis. Screenplay by Jerry Lewis and Bill Richmond. Starring Jerry Lewis, Helen Traubel, Kathleen Freeman, Pat Stanley, Buddy Lester, Sylvia Lewis, George Raft, Harry James and his band, Jack Kruschen, and Fritz Feld. U.S. release: June 1961.

1962
It's Only Money (York Pictures / Jerry Lewis Productions / Paramount Pictures)
Produced by Paul Jones. Directed by Frank Tashlin. Screenplay by John Fenton Murray. Starring Jerry Lewis, Zachary Scott, Joan O'Brien, Mae Questel, Jesse White, Jack Weston, and Pat Dahl. U.S. release: November 1962.

1963
The Nutty Professor (Jerry Lewis Productions / Paramount Pictures)
Produced by Ernest D. Glucksman. Directed by Jerry Lewis. Screenplay by Jerry Lewis and Bill Richmond. Starring Jerry Lewis, Stella Stevens, Del Moore, Kathleen Freeman, Med Flory, Howard Morris, Elvia Allman, Milton Frome, and Buddy Lester. U.S. release: June 1963.

Who's Minding the Store? (York Pictures / Jerry Lewis Productions / Paramount Pictures)
Produced by Paul Jones. Directed by Frank Tashlin. Screenplay by Frank Tashlin and Harry Tugend. Based on a screen story by Harry Tugend. Starring Jerry Lewis, Jill St. John, Agnes Moorehead, John McGiver, Ray Walston, Francesca Bellini, and Nancy Kulp. U.S. release: November 1963.

1964
The Disorderly Orderly (York Pictures / Jerry Lewis Productions / Paramount Pictures)
Produced by Paul Jones. Executive producer, Jerry Lewis. Directed by Frank Tashlin. Screenplay by Frank Tashlin. Based on a screen story by Norm Liebmann and Ed Haas. Starring Jerry Lewis, Susan Oliver, Glenda Farrell, Everett Sloane, Karen Sharpe, Kath-

leen Freeman, Del Moore, Jack E. Leonard, and Alice Pearce. U.S. release: December 1964.

The Patsy (Jerry Lewis Productions / Patti Enterprises / Paramount Pictures)
Produced by Ernest D. Glucksman. Directed by Jerry Lewis. Screenplay by Jerry Lewis and Bill Richmond. Starring Jerry Lewis, Everett Sloane, Ina Balin, Keenan Wynn, Peter Lorre, John Carradine, Phil Harris, Hans Conried, George Raft, Hedda Hopper, and the Step Brothers. U.S. release: August 1964.

1965
Boeing Boeing (Wallis-Hazen / Paramount Pictures)
Produced by Hal B. Wallis. Directed by John Rich. Screenplay by Edward Anhalt. Based on a play by Marc Camoletti. Starring Jerry Lewis, Tony Curtis, Dany Saval, Christiane Schmidtmer, Suzanna Leigh, and Thelma Ritter. U.S. release: December 1965.

The Family Jewels (Jerry Lewis Productions / Paramount Pictures)
Produced by Jerry Lewis. Directed by Jerry Lewis. Screenplay by Jerry Lewis and Bill Richmond. Starring Jerry Lewis, Donna Butterworth, Sebastian Cabot, Neil Hamilton, Jay Adler, Robert Strauss, Gene Baylos, Milton Frome, and Benny Rubin. U.S. release: July 1965.

1966
Three on a Couch (Jerry Lewis Productions / Columbia Pictures)
Produced by Jerry Lewis. Directed by Jerry Lewis. Screenplay by Bob Ross and Samuel L. Taylor. Based on a story by Arne Sultan and Marvin Worth. Starring Jerry Lewis, Janet Leigh, James Best, Mary Ann Mobley, Gila Golan, Leslie Parrish, Kathleen Freeman, Buddy Lester, and Fritz Feld. U.S. release: July 1966.

Way . . . Way Out (Jerry Lewis Productions / Coldwater Productions / Way Out / Twentieth Century Fox)
Produced by Malcolm Stuart. Directed by Gordon Douglas. Screenplay by William Bowers and Laslo Vadnay. Starring Jerry Lewis, Connie Stevens, Robert Morley, Dick Shawn, Anita Ekberg, Dennis Weaver, Howard Morris, Brian Keith, and Sig Ruman. U.S. release: October 1966.

1967
The Big Mouth (Jerry Lewis Productions / Columbia Pictures)
Produced by Jerry Lewis. Directed by Jerry Lewis. Screenplay by Jerry Lewis and Bill Richmond. Based on a screen story by Bill Richmond. Starring Jerry Lewis, Harold J. Stone, Susan Bay, Buddy Lester, Del Moore, Paul Lambert, Jeannine Riley, Leonard Stone, and Charlie Callas. U.S. release: July 1967.

1968
Don't Raise the Bridge, Lower the River (Jerry Lewis Productions / Walter Shenson / Columbia Pictures)
Produced by Walter Shenson. Directed by Jerry Paris. Screenplay by Max Wilk. Based on a novel by Max Wilk. Starring Jerry Lewis, Terry-Thomas, Jacqueline Pearce, Bernard Cribbins, Patricia Routledge, Nicholas Parsons, Michael Bates, and John Bluthal. U.S. release: July 1968.

1969
Hook, Line and Sinker (Jerry Lewis Productions / Columbia Pictures)
Produced by Jerry Lewis. Directed by George Marshall. Screenplay by Rod Amateau.
Based on a story by Rod Amateau and David Davis. Starring Jerry Lewis, Peter Lawford,
Anne Francis, Pedro Gonzalez-Gonzalez, Jimmy Miller, Jennifer Edwards, and Kathleen
Freeman. U.S. release: June 1969.

1970
One More Time (Chrislaw / Trace-Mark Productions / United Artists)
Produced by Milton Ebbins. Directed by Jerry Lewis. Screenplay by Michael Pertwee.
Starring Sammy Davis Jr., Peter Lawford, Maggie Wright, Leslie Sands, John Wood,
Sydney Arnold, Edward Evans, Percy Herbert, and Bill Maynard. U.S. release: May 1970.

Which Way to the Front? (Jerry Lewis Productions / Warners-7 Arts)
Produced by Jerry Lewis. Directed by Jerry Lewis. Screenplay by Gerald Gardner and
Dee Caruso. Based on a screen story by Gerald Gardner, Dee Caruso, and Richard
Miller. Starring Jerry Lewis, Jan Murray, John Wood, Steve Franken, Dack Rambo,
Willie Davis, Robert Middleton, Kaye Ballard, Harold J. Stone, and Kathleen Freeman.
U.S. release: July 1970. Released in Britain under the title *Ja! Ja! Mein General! But Which
Way to the Front?*

1981
Hardly Working (Hardly Working / Twentieth Century Fox)
Produced by James J. McNamara and Igo Kantor. Directed by Jerry Lewis. Screenplay
by Michael Janover and Jerry Lewis. Based on a screen story by Michael Janover. Star-
ring Jerry Lewis, Susan Oliver, Roger C. Carmel, Deanna Lund, Harold J. Stone, Steve
Franken, and Buddy Lester. Filmed in 1979. U.S. release: April 1981.

1983
Cracking Up / Smorgasbord (Orgolini-Nelson Productions / Warner Brothers)
Produced by Arnold Orgolini and Peter Nelson. Directed by Jerry Lewis. Screenplay by
Jerry Lewis and Bill Richmond. Starring Jerry Lewis, Herb Edelman, Zane Buzby, Foster Brooks, Buddy Lester, Milton Berle, and Sammy Davis Jr. Film was released in France
in 1983 but went straight to videotape that same year in the United States. U.S. theatrical premiere (as *Smorgasbord*) in May 1985.

The King of Comedy (Embassy International / Twentieth Century Fox)
Produced by Arnold Milchan. Directed by Martin Scorsese. Screenplay by Paul D. Zim-
merman. Starring Robert DeNiro, Jerry Lewis, Diahnne Abbott, Sandra Bernhard, Ed
Herlihy, Shelley Hack, Fred De Cordova, and Tony Randall. U.S. release: February 1983.

1984
Par où t'es rentré? On t'a pas vue sortir (Carthago Films) (France)
Produced by Tarak Ben Ammar. Directed by Philippe Clair. Screenplay by Philippe
Clair, Daniel Saint-Hamont, and Bruno Tardon. Based on a screen story by Philippe
Clair. Starring Jerry Lewis, Philippe Clair, Marthe Villalonga, Philippe Castelli, and
Anne Berger. No U.S. release.

Retenez-moi . . . où je fais un malheur (Imacite-Coline) (France)
Produced by Pierre Kalfon and Michel Gérard. Directed by Michel Gérard. Screenplay by Michel Gérard, David Milhaud, and Jean-François Navarre. Starring Jerry Lewis, Michel Blanc, Charlotte de Turckheim, and Laura Betti. No U.S. release.

Slapstick (of Another Kind) (S. Paul / Serendipity Entertainment Releasing / International Film Marketing)
Produced by Steven Paul. Directed by Steven Paul. Screenplay by Steven Paul. Based on a novel by Kurt Vonnegut. Starring Jerry Lewis, Madeline Kahn, Marty Feldman, John Abbott, Jim Backus, Samuel Fuller, Merv Griffin, and Orson Welles. Filmed in 1982. U.S. release: March 1984.

1990
How Are the Kids? (C91 Communications)
Lewis wrote and directed an eight-minute segment of this portmanteau film, entitled *Boy,* which starred Isaac Lidsky. Released in Europe in 1990, it premiered in the United States in December 1993.

1992
Arizona Dream (Union Generale Cinématographique / Constellation Productions / Hachette Premiere / Arrowtooth Productions / Canal+ Productions) (France/United States)
Produced by Claudie Ossard and Yves Marmion. Directed by Emir Kusturica. Screenplay by David Atkins and Emir Kusturica. Starring Johnny Depp, Jerry Lewis, Faye Dunaway, and Vincent Gallo. Short version premiered in the United States at the 1994 Telluride Film Festival and had limited release from Warner Brothers (which quickly consigned it to video). "Director's cut" version released to art circuit in 1995 by Kit Parker Films.

1995
Funny Bones (Hollywood Pictures) (Great Britain)
Produced by Simon Fields and Peter Chelsom. Directed by Peter Chelsom. Screenplay by Peter Chelsom. Starring Jerry Lewis, Oliver Platt, Lee Evans, Leslie Caron, and Oliver Reed. U.S. release: March 1995.

1996
The Nutty Professor (Imagine Entertainment)
Produced by Brian Grazer and Russell Simmons. Executive producers, Jerry Lewis, Karen Kehela, and Mark Lipsky. Directed by Tom Shadyac. Screenplay by David Sheffield, Barry W. Blaustein, Tom Shadyac, and Steve Oedekerk. Based on a 1963 film written by Jerry Lewis and Bill Richmond. Starring Eddie Murphy, Jada Pinkett, James Coburn, and Larry Miller. U.S. release: June 1996.

CAMEO APPEARANCES

1950
The Milkman
Directed by Charles T. Barton. Starring Donald O'Connor, Jimmy Durante, and Piper Laurie.

1952
The Road to Bali
Directed by Hal Walker. Starring Bob Hope, Bing Crosby, and Dorothy Lamour.

1959
Li'l Abner
Directed by Melvin Frank. Starring Peter Palmer, Leslie Parrish, Stubby Kaye, Julie Newmar, and Stella Stevens.

1963
It's a Mad Mad Mad Mad World
Directed by Stanley Kramer. Starring Spencer Tracy, Milton Berle, Sid Caesar, Ethel Merman, the Three Stooges, and others.

1989
Cookie
Directed by Susan Seidelman. Starring Peter Falk, Dianne Wiest, and Emily Lloyd.

1992
Mr. Saturday Night
Directed by Billy Crystal. Starring Billy Crystal, David Paymer, Julie Warner, and Helen Hunt.

16MM AMATEUR

Late 1940s–Early 1950s
Watch on the Lime, a parody of *Watch on the Rhine*

Son of Lifeboat, a parody of *Lifeboat*

Son of Spellbound, a parody of *Spellbound*

How to Smuggle a Hernia across the Border

Fairfax Avenue, a parody of *Sunset Boulevard*

The Reinforcer, a parody of *The Enforcer*

A Spot in the Shade, a parody of *A Place in the Sun*

A Streetcar Named Repulsive, a parody of *A Streetcar Named Desire*

Come Back, Little Shicksa, a parody of *Come Back, Little Sheba*

I Should Have Stood in Bedlam, a parody of *From Here to Eternity*

Melvin's Revenge

The Whistler, a parody of the radio series *Flapper's Party*

UNRELEASED
1972
The Day the Clown Cried / Le jour où le clown pleura (France/Sweden)
Scripted, directed by, and starring Lewis.

FORTHCOMING
The Bellboy (MGM), a remake of Lewis's 1960 film.

The Errand Boy (Caravan Pictures / Jacobson Company / Touchstone Pictures), a remake of Lewis's 1961 film.

Cinderfella (New Line Cinema), a remake of Lewis's 1960 film.

The Nutty Professor 2 (Imagine Entertainment / Universal Pictures), a sequel to Eddie Murphy's 1996 film.

UNREALIZED PROJECTS
1953
We Three
Starring Martin and Lewis.

Mid-1950s
The Pajama Game
Hal Wallis tried to obtain the film rights to the Broadway show for Martin and Lewis.

Teahouse of the August Moon
Hal Wallis tried to obtain the film rights to the Broadway play for Martin and Lewis.

1956
Damon and Pythias
Proposed Martin and Lewis version of a Don McGuire script that Lewis later filmed as *The Delicate Delinquent.*

1957
The Martin and Lewis Story
Produced by Hal Wallis. Starring Martin and Lewis.

1959
Some Like It Hot
Jack Lemmon's role was initially offered to Lewis

Mid-1960s
Robinson Crusoe
Directed by Frank Tashlin. Starring Jerry Lewis and Sammy Davis Jr.

1960s
Waldorf
Starring Jackie Gleason.

1966
Take the Money and Run
Woody Allen invited Lewis to direct this film, which Allen later made himself.

1967
The Silent Treatment
Unfinished nondialogue feature. Directed by Ralph Andrews. Starring Jerry Lewis, George Raft, Milton Berle, and Gene Autry.

1970s
International House
Starring Lewis and Cantinflas.

1971
Bananas
Woody Allen invited Lewis to direct this film, which Allen later made himself.

1978
Lévy s'envolé / Levy Flies Away
Directed by Alex Joffé. Starring Jerry Lewis, Marina Vlady, and Klaus Kinski. Filming never commenced.

1979
That's Life
Directed and co-scripted by Jerry Lewis. Starring Molly Picon. Folded after six days of shooting.

1980s
Untitled film
Peter Bogdanovich contemplated a cinematic reunion of Martin and Lewis.
On several occasions Lewis declared his interest in making sequels to *That's My Boy* and *The Nutty Professor*. Among the more fanciful film projects announced by Lewis were *Leatherneck*, *Operation Madhouse*, *Son of Lifeboat*, *H-Bomb Beach Party*, *The Worst Robber that Ever Lived (and We Don't Mean Maybe)*, and *The Kicking Rabbi*.

OTHER

1950
The Goldbergs (a.k.a. *Molly*) (Paramount)
Directed by Walter Hart. Starring Gertrude Berg, Philip Loeb, and Eli Mintz. Guest appearance by Lewis in promotional trailer for this film adaptation of the popular radio and television show.

1951
Hollywood at Play (Columbia)
September. Entry in "Screen Snapshots" series of short films, featuring Martin and Lewis.

1958
Film short
Lewis appeared in a short film for the National Association of Mental Health campaign.

1960
Raymie (Allied Artists)
Feature film directed by Frank McDonald. Starring David Ladd, Julie Adams, and John Agar. Title song performed by Lewis.

1965-1967
Film shorts
Lewis guest-directed three short films for Film Industry Workshops, Inc., a nonprofit workshop for film actors and directors based at Columbia Pictures.

1966
Man in Motion (Columbia)
Directed by Robert Quinn. Short film about the production of *Three on a Couch*.

1984
Jerry Lewis Live
Directed by Arthur Forrest. Record of Lewis's show in the Sahara Hotel's Congo Room, Las Vegas, 13 October. Videocassette.

1985
Hollywood Clowns (PBS)
Television comedy compilation on videocassette, narrated by Glenn Ford. Includes scenes featuring Martin and Lewis, Buster Keaton, W. C. Fields, Charles Chaplin, the Marx Brothers, Bob Hope, and others.

1986
The Best of Comic Relief
Featuring Lewis, Whoopi Goldberg, Robin Williams, Billy Crystal, Sid Caesar, Steve Allen, and others. Videocassette.

1950s-1990s
MDA promotional trailers
Lewis has appeared in numerous promotional trailers for the Muscular Dystrophy Association.

RADIO WITH DEAN MARTIN

1948-1949
The Bob Hope Show (NBC)
26 October 1948, 23 November 1948, 29 March 1949, and 12 April 1949. Martin and Lewis were guests.

1949
Elgin Holiday Star Time (NBC)
25 November. Martin and Lewis were among the guests on this Thanksgiving variety special.

1949–1952
The Martin and Lewis Show (NBC)
3 April 1949–1952.

1950–1951
The Big Show (NBC)
17 December 1950 (with Bob Hope, Phil Harris, Louis Armstrong, and Deborah Kerr) and 11 February 1951 (with Groucho Marx and Judy Garland). Martin and Lewis were guests on this variety program hosted by Tallulah Bankhead.

TELEVISION WITH DEAN MARTIN

INTERVIEW, COMEDY, AND VARIETY
1948
Welcome Aboard (NBC)
3 October, hosted by Phil Silvers; 10 October, hosted by Russ Morgan; and 17 October, hosted by Russ Morgan.

1948–1949
Toast of the Town (CBS)
20 June 1948 and October 1949. Hosted by Ed Sullivan.

1948–1950
Texaco Star Theater (NBC)
3 August 1948, hosted by Morey Amsterdam; 18 October 1949, hosted by Milton Berle; 15 April 1950, hosted by Rudy Vallee; and 13 June 1950, hosted by Milton Berle.

1950
Broadway Open House (NBC)
3 June. Hosted by Morey Amsterdam.

Saturday Night Revue (NBC)
17 April. Hosted by Jack Carter.

1953
The Abbott and Costello Show (*The Colgate Comedy Hour*)
1 November.

1954
The Bob Hope Show (CBS)
3 May. Hosted by Bob Hope.

Person to Person (CBS)
2 July. Hosted by Ed Murrow.

1955
The Colgate Variety Hour (NBC)
16 October. Tribute to Rodgers and Hammerstein.

The Milton Berle Show (NBC)
27 September and 20 December. Hosted by Milton Berle.

SERIES
1950–1955
The Dean Martin and Jerry Lewis Show (*The Colgate Comedy Hour*) (NBC)
September 1950-December 1955. Twenty-eight programs.

TELETHONS
1949
Damon Runyon Memorial Fund (NBC)
9 April. Guests on this twenty-four-hour telethon hosted by Milton Berle.

1950
Show of the Year (NBC)
June. Guests on this 150-minute fund-raiser for cerebral palsy sufferers hosted by Milton Berle.

1951
Damon Runyon Cancer Fund (NBC)
9–10 June. Guests on this fund-raiser hosted by Milton Berle.

1952
New York Cardiac Hospital (WNBT, New York)
15–16 March. Hosts of this sixteen-and-a-half-hour telethon.

U.S. Olympic Fund (NBC/CBS)
21–22 June. Guests on fourteen-and-a-half-hour telethon for the U.S. Olympics fund hosted by Bob Hope and Bing Crosby.

1953
Martin and Lewis's Thanksgiving Party (ABC)
25 November. Hosts of this two-hour fund-raiser for the Muscular Dystrophy Association.

1956
Martin and Lewis Telethon (DuMont)
29–30 June. Hosts of this twenty-one-hour fund-raiser for the Muscular Dystrophy Association.

SOLO TELEVISION

SERIES
1963
The Jerry Lewis Show (ABC)
21 September–21 December. Blighted two-hour talk-variety series.

1967–1969
The Jerry Lewis Show (NBC)
12 September 1967–26 May 1969. Weekly sixty-minute variety show that ran for two seasons.

1970–1972
Will the Real Jerry Lewis Please Sit Down (ABC)
12 September 1970–2 September 1972. Seventeen-episode, thirty-minute animated cartoon series from Filmation Productions. The concept was created by Lewis, and he also scripted several episodes.

1984
The Jerry Lewis Show (Metromedia/Fox)
11–15 June. Five sixty-minute pilot episodes for a celebrity interview series.

SPECIALS

1957–1960
The Jerry Lewis Show (NBC)
January 1957–May 1960. Fifteen one-hour programs.

1962
The Wacky World of Jerry Lewis (ABC)
29 May. Sixty-minute special.

1971
The Friars Roast Jerry Lewis (NBC)
With Johnny Carson, Milton Berle, and Don Rickles.

Jerry Lewis à L'Olympia (ORTF2, France)
27 December.

1988
HBO Comedy Hour: An Evening with Sammy Davis Jr. and Jerry Lewis (HBO)
Performance recorded at Bally's Hotel, Las Vegas, 1988.

GUEST APPEARANCES ON SPECIALS

1965
A Salute to Stan Laurel (CBS)
23 November. Benefit for the Motion Picture Relief Fund, featuring Lewis, Bob Hope, Buster Keaton, Jimmy Durante, and Lucille Ball.

The Wonderful World of Burlesque (NBC)
8 December.

1970
The Klowns (ABC)
15 November. Circus-based variety show hosted by Lewis, Sammy Davis Jr., and Charlie Callas.

1971
Gala de l'Union des Artistes (ORTF1, France)
5 June. Star-packed variety spectacular featuring Lewis as a clown.

1986
Comic Relief (HBO)
29 March. With Robin Williams, Whoopi Goldberg, and Billy Crystal.

GUEST HOST

1956
Person to Person (CBS)
9 November.

1962, 1965, 1971, 1973
The Tonight Show (NBC)
25 June-6 July 1962, 11-15 July 1965, 1971, February 1973, and July 1973.

1965
Hullabaloo (NBC)
September. With Gary Lewis.

1966
The Sammy Davis Jr. Show (NBC)
4 February.

1970, 1974, 1977, 1978
The Mike Douglas Show (syndicated)
1970, February 1974, 1977, and December 1978.

1979
Circus of the Stars (CBS)
20 June.

1983
Saturday Night Live (NBC)
19 November.

1995
Live with Regis and Kathie Lee (ABC)
16 March.

AWARDS CEREMONIES

1956
28th Academy of Motion Picture Arts and Sciences Award Ceremony (NBC)
21 March. Hosted by Lewis.

1957
29th Academy of Motion Picture Arts and Sciences Award Ceremony (NBC)
27 March. Hosted by Lewis.

1959
31st Academy of Motion Picture Arts and Sciences Award Ceremony (NBC)
6 April. Hosted by Lewis.

1998
The American Comedy Awards (Fox)
17 March. Lewis was awarded a Lifetime Achievement Award.

MISCELLANEOUS GUEST APPEARANCES

The Steve Allen Show (NBC), 1956; *The Arthur Murray Party* (NBC), 1957; *The Eddie Fisher Show* (NBC), 1 October 1958, 14 October 1958, 24 December 1958; *The Jack Paar Show* (NBC), 1958, 1960; *Louis Jourdan Presents the Timex Show* (NBC), 1959; *Here's Hollywood* (NBC), 1960; *American Bandstand* (ABC), 1960; *The Ed Sullivan Show* (CBS), 6 December 1960, 1961, 1962, 6 December 1964; *The Gary Moore Show* (CBS) 1961; *I've Got a Secret* (CBS), 1961; *High Hopes* (syndicated), 1961; *Stump the Stars* (CBS), 1962; *The Joey Bishop Show: Joey Goes to CBS* (CBS), 1964; *The Andy Williams Show* (NBC), 15 March 1965; *Jack Benny Special* (CBS); *Rowan and Martin's Laugh-In* (NBC); *The Tonight Show* (NBC), 1968, 1973, 1984; *The Merv Griffin Show* (syndicated), 11 June 1970, 22 March 1984; *The David Frost Show* (syndicated), 1970; *The Englebert Humperdinck Show* (ABC), 1970; *The Red Skelton Show* (NBC), September 1970; *The Dick Cavett Show* (ABC), 1972, 1973; *NBC Follies* (NBC), 1973; *Celebrity Sportsmen,* February 1974; *Dinah!* (syndicated), 1975; *Oral Roberts' "Christmas Is Love"* (syndicated), 1975; *The Phil Donahue Show* (NBC) 1977, January 1982, 1997; *Donny and Marie* (ABC), 1978; *20/20* (ABC), 9 April 1981; *Late Night with David Letterman* (NBC), 1982, 30 March 1984, 1993, 1995; *Good Morning America* (ABC), November 1988; *Lifestyles of the Rich and Famous* (syndicated); *The Arsenio Hall Show* (syndicated), 12 May 1989, 1990; *The Whoopi Goldberg Show* (syndicated), 12 October 1992; *Later with Bob Costas* (NBC), 1993; *The Late Late Show with Tom Snyder* (CBS), 15 March 1995; *Politically Incorrect* (ABC), 9 November 1998.

CAMEOS

1966
Batman (ABC)
21 April. Episode titled "While Gotham City Burns."

Sheriff Who (NBC)
September. Lewis as guest star in a thirty-minute pilot directed by Jerry Paris, starring Dick Shawn and John Astin.

1967
Run for Your Life (NBC)
Episode titled "Down with Willie Hatch." Lewis provided the voice for Don Rickles's impersonation of "Jerry Lewis."

1987
Brothers (Showtime)
18 September.

1993
Mad About You (NBC)
20 February. Episode titled "The Billionaire." Lewis made a guest appearance as himself.

OTHER

1954-1955
That's My Boy (CBS)
24 September 1954-1 January 1955. Thirty-minute sitcom based on a Martin and Lewis film of the same name. With Eddie Mayehoff as Jarring Jack Jackson, Rochelle Hudson as Alice Jackson, and Gil Stratton Jr. as Junior Jackson.

1981
Rascal Dazzle (HBO)
Documentary profile of the "Our Gang" series, directed by Edward Glass, with narration by Lewis.

1994
Coca-Cola commercials
Lewis donned his Julius Kelp guise for this series of Spanish-language commercials.

1996
Frontline: Secret Daughter (WGBH Educational Foundation)
26 November. Lewis was interviewed on June Cross's documentary program, broadcast on PBS.

DRAMATIC PERFORMANCES

1959
The Jazz Singer (NBC)
13 October. Sixty-minute drama in the *Ford Startime* series directed by Ralph Nelson, starring Lewis as "Joey Robbins."

1987
Fight for Life (ABC)
23 March. Based-on-fact television movie directed by Elliot Silverstein, starring Lewis, Patty Duke, Morgan Freeman, and Barry Morse.

1988-1989
Wiseguy (CBS)
December 1988-January 1989. Lewis costarred in a five-episode story arc.

AS DIRECTOR

1965
Ben Casey (ABC)
8 March. Episode titled "A Little Fun to Match the Sorrow." Lewis directed and acted in this episode of the popular medical drama.

1971
The Bold Ones: The Doctors (NBC)
Episide titled "In Dreams They Run." Lewis directed this episode devoted to the subject of muscular dystrophy.

Caroselli (Italy)
December. Episode titled "L'uomo d'oro." Lewis performed in, scripted, and directed fifteen two-minute sketches for this episode of the Italian television series.

INTERVIEWS

1956
Today (NBC)
26 June. With Dean Martin.

1957 and 1959
Youth Wants to Know (NBC)
28 July 1957 and 28 September 1959.

1958
Person to Person (CBS)
28 September.

1965
Open End (WPIX, New York)
7 and 14 November. Two-part interview with Lewis by David Susskind.

1971
L'invité du dimanche: Jerry Lewis (ORTF2, France)
2 May. Presented by Robert Benayoun.

1983
Tom Cottle Up Close (syndicated)

1987
CBS Morning Show (CBS)
1-4 September.

1988
Speaking of Everything (ABC)
13 March. Hosted by Howard Cosell.

1991
Larry King TNT Extra (TNT)
21 October.

1999
Inside the Actors' Studio (Bravo)
11 September.

PROFILES AND DOCUMENTARIES

1955
Hollywood Panorama
Thirty-minute account of the career of Martin and Lewis.

1967
The Movies: Great Directors of Our Time (BBC)
Three-part profile/interview by Paul Mayersberg.

1968
Cinéastes de notre temps: Jerry Lewis (ORTF2, France)
23 December. Directed by Robert Benayoun.

1971
Cinéastes de notre temps: Jerry Lewis (ORTF2, France)
22 October. Directed by André S. Labarthe.

1982
Bonjour Monsieur Lewis (Films Number One/Antenne 2/Jerry Lewis Films, France)
Six-hour series directed by Robert Benayoun.

1992
Martin and Lewis: Their Golden Age of Comedy. Part 1, *The Birth of the Team* (JAS Productions)
Shown on the Disney Channel.

Martin and Lewis: Their Golden Age of Comedy. Part 2, *The Kings of Comedy.* (JAS Productions)
Shown on the Disney Channel.

Martin and Lewis: Their Golden Age of Comedy. Part 3, *Jerry . . . Alone at the Top.* (JAS Productions)
Shown on the Disney Channel.

1993
Martin and Lewis: Their Golden Age of Comedy. Part 4, *Dean and Jerry at the Movies.* (JAS Productions)
Shown on the Disney Channel.

Martin and Lewis: Their Golden Age of Comedy. Part 5, *Jerry Lewis, Total Film-Maker.* (JAS Productions)
Shown on the Disney Channel.

1996
Jerry Lewis: The Last American Clown (Soapbox Productions)
Documentary broadcast as part of the *Biography* series on the United States' Arts & Entertainment network.

1998
In Profile: Jerry Lewis (CNBC)
9 September.

1999
Larry King Live (CNN)
26 August. Lewis's first television appearance after his recovery from viral meningitis.

TELETHONS
1957
Muscular Dystrophy Telethon (WABD, New York)
31 November–1 December.

1959
The Jerry Lewis 1959 Thanksgiving Party (WNEW, New York)
21–22 November.

1961
Muscular Dystrophy Telethon
New York.

1966
The Jerry Lewis Muscular Dystrophy Association Labor Day Telethon (syndicated)
1966–72, broadcast from New York; 1973–89 and 1991–94, broadcast from Las Vegas; and
1990 and 1995–98, broadcast from Los Angeles. Lewis performs on the first French MDA
Telethon in December 1987.

AUDIO RECORDINGS WITH DEAN MARTIN

1948
"The Money Song" / "That Certain Party" (Capitol 45 rpm)
"Ev'ry Street's a Boulevard (in Old New York)" (Capitol)
Song included on Dean Martin's EP.

1956
Pardners (Capitol EP)

SOLO AUDIO RECORDINGS

1949
"Are You for Real" / "I Love a Murder Mystery" (Capitol 45 rpm)

1950
"Sunday Driving" / "I'm a Little Busybody" (Capitol 45 rpm)

1951
"I Like It—I Like It" / "I'll Tell a Policeman on You" (Capitol 45 rpm)
"Lay Somethin' on the Bar (Besides Your Elbow)" / "I Love Girls" (Capitol 45 rpm)
"Pa-Pa-Pa-Pa-Polka" (Capitol 45 rpm)

1952
"I Can't Carry a Tune / "Crazy Words—Crazy Tune (Do-Do-De-O)" (Capitol 45 rpm)
"I've Had a Very Merry Christmas" / "Strictly for the Birds" (Capitol 45 rpm)
"The Noisy Eater" (Capitol 45 rpm)
"North Dakota, South Dakota" / "The Book Was So Much Better than the Picture"
    (Capitol 45 rpm)
"They Go Wild, Simply Wild over Me" / "I Keep Her Picture Hanging Upside Down"
    (Capitol 45 rpm)

1953
"The Nagger," part 1 / "The Nagger," part 2 (Capitol 45 rpm)

"Never Smile at a Crocodile" / "Follow the Leader" (Capitol 45 rpm)
"The Puppy Dog Dream" (Capitol 45 rpm)
"Y-Y-Y-Y-Yup" (Capitol 45 rpm)

1954
"Candelabra Boogie" (Capitol 45 rpm)

1956
"Rock-a-Bye Your Baby (With a Dixie Melody)" (Decca 45 rpm)

1957
The Birth of the Blues (Decca EP)
"By Myself" / "No One" (Decca 45 rpm)
Come Rain or Come Shine (Decca EP)
Jerry Lewis Just Sings (Decca LP)
"Let Me Sing and I'm Happy" (Decca 45 rpm)
The Sad Sack (Decca 45 rpm)

1958
The Geisha Boy (Jubilee LP)
More Jerry Lewis (Decca LP)

1960
Big Songs for Little People (Decca LP)
Cinderfella (Dot Records LP)
"Kids" / "Witchcraft" (Liberty 45 rpm)

1965
Yesterday and Other Folk-Rock Hits (Dot Records LP)
By the Jerry Lewis Singers.

SELECTED LIVE PERFORMANCES

1932
Lewis's stage debut at a benefit for the Fireman's Association, Swan Lake, New York.

1938
Lewis-organized benefit for the Red Cross, Rex Theater, Irvington, New Jersey.

1939
Lewis first performs his record act in the Catskills, with Lonnie Brown.

1941
Lewis's first paid performance at the Cozy Corner, Loch Sheldrake, New York.

1942
Lewis's first performances as a full-time professional, Loew's and RKO Theaters in New York state and New Jersey.

September. Lewis's first gig under the management of Abbey Greshler, the Palace Theater, Buffalo, New York. Commences period in burlesque.

1944
August. Lewis on the same bill with Dean Martin, the Glass Hat Club, New York.

1946
March. Lewis and Martin develop after-piece routine at the Havana-Madrid Club, New York.
July–August. Lewis and Martin develop act at the 500 Club, Atlantic City.

September. Official teaming of Martin and Lewis at the Latin Casino, Philadelphia, Pennsylvania.

1947
January. Martin and Lewis play shows in support of *The Jolson Story* at Loew's State Theater, New York.

1948
April. Martin and Lewis play the Copacabana, New York.

August. Martin and Lewis's first West Coast gig at Slapsie Maxie's Café, Los Angeles.

1949
September. Martin and Lewis's first Las Vegas gig, Flamingo Hotel.

September. Martin and Lewis play shows in support of *My Friend Irma,* Paramount Theater, New York.

1951
July. Martin and Lewis's record-breaking performance at the Paramount Theater, New York. Streets mobbed by thousands of fans.

1953
June. Martin and Lewis play the Palladium, London, their first overseas gig.

June. Martin and Lewis tour U.S. bases in France.

1955
June. Lewis does solo performance at the Browns Hotel in the Catskills after Martin withdraws from opening of *You're Never Too Young.*

1956
July. Martin and Lewis's final performances as a team, during a two-week residency at the Copacabana, New York.

August. Lewis deputizes for Judy Garland at the Frontier Hotel, Las Vegas. His first solo performance after the split with Martin.

December. Lewis stars in revue at the Sands Hotel, Las Vegas.

1957
February. Lewis plays for four weeks at the Palace Theater, New York.

1971
April. Lewis plays the Olympia music hall, Paris, as first stage of world tour.

1972–1973
Lewis's second world tour.

1983
April. Lewis returns to live performance after double-bypass heart surgery.

1986
29 March. Lewis plays first *Comic Relief* benefit. Hosted by Billy Crystal and Whoopi Goldberg.
Summer. Lewis performs at Just for Laughs Festival, Montreal, Canada.

1987–1988
Winter. Lewis tours in show with Sammy Davis Jr.

1991.
Summer. Lewis performs at Just for Laughs Festival, Montreal, Canada.

1993–1994
Fall–spring. *Jerry Lewis . . . Unlimited,* a two-hour show, toured across the United States.

1998–1999
1–5 June and 12–16 February. Lewis played highly successful engagements at the Crown Casino, Melbourne, Australia.

1999
August. Lewis begins second tour of Australia but cancels most dates when he is struck with viral meningitis.

THEATER

1976–1977
Hellzapoppin'
November 1976–January 1977. Baltimore, Washington, D.C., and Boston.

1995
Damn Yankees
February. Lewis makes his Broadway debut, replacing Vincent Garber as Applegate.

Damn Yankees
September. Lewis begins first year of his North American tour with the show in West Point.

1996
Damn Yankees
September. Lewis begins second year of his North American tour with the show in San Francisco.

1997
Damn Yankees
March–August. Lewis stars in the production in London's West End.

BOOKS

The Jerry Lewis Book of Tricks and Magic. By James Blackman. Random House, 1962. Lewis wrote the foreword.

Instruction Book for Being a Person. By Jerry Lewis. 1963. Privately published collection of Lewis's reflections on life.

Jerry Lewis in Person. By Jerry Lewis and Herb Gluck. Atheneum, 1983. An autobiography cowritten with Gluck.
The Total Film-Maker. By Jerry Lewis. Random House, 1971.

COMIC BOOKS

The Adventures of Dean Martin and Jerry Lewis. DC Comics. July–August 1952 (number 1) to October 1957 (number 40).

The Adventures of Jerry Lewis. DC Comics. November 1957 (number 41) to May–June 1971 (number 124).

WORKS CITED

BOOKS AND ARTICLES

Afronet. 1996. *The Nutty Professor.* Afronet web site. Http://www.afronet.com/NUT-TYPROF.

Agee, James. 1967. "Comedy's Greatest Era." In *Agee on Film,* by James Agee, 1–19. 1949. London: Peter Owen.

Allen, Jeanne. 1980. "The Film Viewer as Consumer." *Quarterly Review of Film and Video* 5, no. 4 (Fall): 481–99.

Alpert, Hollis. 1966. "France Is Mad for . . . Jerry Lewis? 'Le Roi du Crazy.'" *New York Times Magazine,* 27 February, sec. 6, pp. 28–29, 74–78.

———. 1977. "Dialogue on Film." *American Film* 2, no. 10 (September): 33–48.

Anderson, Christopher. 1994. *Hollywood TV: The Studio System in the Fifties.* Austin: University of Texas Press.

Andrew, Dudley. 1982. "Cinematic Politics in Postwar France: Bazin Before *Cahiers.*" *Cinéaste* 12, no. 1:13–16.

Archer, Eugene. 1964. "Paramount Sees the Big Picture." *New York Times,* 2 July, p. 41.

———. 1965. "*Cahiers:* An In Word that Means Out." *New York Times,* 23 May, sec. 2, p. 9.

Armitage, Peter. 1961. "The War of the Cults." *Motion: The University Film Magazine* (Great Britain) 1 (Summer): 4–6.

Arnold, Gary. 1981. "Slapstick Shambles: Lewis in *Hardly Working.*" *Washington Post,* 6 April, sec. C, pp. 1, 3.

Associated Press. 1996. "Dumb-Comedy Earns Money, Tops Drama." *Kansas State Colle-*

gian, 9 February. Http://collegian.ksu.edu/issues/v100/spln90/ap-a-e-reeldumb-movies.html.

Astruc, Alexandre. 1968. "The Birth of a New *Avant-Garde: La caméra-stylo.*" In Graham, *New Wave,* 17-21. Originally in *L'Écran Français* 148.

Aumont, Jacques, Jean-Louis Comolli, André Labarthe, Jean Narboni, and Sylvie Pierre. 1973. "A Concise Lexicon of Lewisian Terms." In Johnston and Willemen, *Frank Tashlin,* 89-115. Originally in *Cahiers du Cinéma* 197 (December 1967/January 1968).

Bakhtin, Mikhail. 1984. *Rabelais and His World,* Bloomington: Indiana University Press.

Balio, Tino, ed. 1985. *The American Film Industry: Revised Edition.* Madison: University of Wisconsin Press.

————, ed. 1990. *Hollywood in the Age of Television.* London: Unwin-Hyman.

Barnouw, Erik. 1975. *Tube of Plenty: The Evolution of American Television.* New York: Oxford University Press.

Barr, Charles. 1985. "A Letter from Charles Barr." *Velvet Light Trap* 21:5-7.

Barrios, Richard. 1995. *A Song in the Dark: The Birth of the Musical Film.* New York: Oxford University Press.

Bazin, André. 1985. "On the *Politique des Auteurs.*" In Hillier, *Cahiers du Cinéma* (1985), 248-59. Originally in *Cahiers du Cinéma* 70 (April 1957).

Bazin, André, Jacques Doniol-Valcroze, Pierre Kast, Roger Leenhardt, Jacques Rivette, and Eric Rohmer. 1985. "Six Characters in Search of *Auteurs:* A Discussion about the French Cinema." In Hillier, *Cahiers du Cinéma* (1985), 31-46. Originally in *Cahiers du Cinéma* 71 (May 1957).

Belton, John. 1992. *Widescreen Cinema.* Cambridge: Harvard University Press.

————. 1994. *American Cinema/American Culture.* New York: McGraw-Hill.

Benayoun, Robert. 1968. "The King Is Naked." In Graham, *New Wave,* 157-80. Originally in *Positif* 46 (June 1962).

————. 1972. "Simple Simon, ou l'anti James Dean." In Benayoun, *Bonjour Monsieur Lewis,* 19-25. Privately translated by Barry Redhead. Originally in *Positif* 29 (May 1958).

————. 1994. "The Raymond Chandler of Slapstick." In Garcia and Eisenschitz, *Frank Tashlin,* 125-29. Originally in *Positif* 69 (May 1965).

Benjamin, Walter. [1935] 1992. "The Work of Art in the Age of Mechanical Reproduction." In *Film Theory and Criticism: Introductory Readings, Fourth Edition,* edited by Gerald Mast, Marshall Cohen, and Leo Braudy, 665-81. New York: Oxford University Press.

Bennetts, Leslie. 1993. "Letter from Las Vegas: Jerry vs. the Kids." *Vanity Fair,* September, 26-37.

Benson, Sheila. 1983. Review of *The King of Comedy. Los Angeles Times/Calendar,* 18 February, p. 1.

Bérubé, Allan. 1990. *Coming Out under Fire: The History of Gay Men and Women in World War Two.* New York: Free Press, Macmillan.

Bianculli, David. 1997. *Dictionary of Teleliteracy: Television's 500 Biggest Hits, Misses and Events.* New York: Continuum.

Bingham, Dennis. 1994. *Acting Male: Masculinities in the Films of James Stewart, Jack Nicholson, and Clint Eastwood.* New Brunswick, N.J.: Rutgers University Press.

Boddy, William. 1990a. "The Seven Dwarfs and the Money Grubbers: The Public Relations Crisis of U.S. Television in the Late 1950's." In Mellancamp, *Logics of Television*, 98-116.

————. 1990b. "Building the World's Largest Advertising Medium: CBS and Television, 1940-60." In Balio, *Hollywood in the Age of Television*, 63-60.

————. 1993. *Fifties Television: The Industry and Its Critics*. Urbana: University of Illinois Press.

Bordwell, David, Janet Staiger, and Kristin Thompson. 1988. *The Classical Hollywood Cinema: Film Style and Mode of Production to 1960*. London: Routledge.

Bourdieu, Pierre. 1986. *Distinction: A Social Critique of the Judgement of Taste*. London: Routledge.

Brenna, Tony. 1990. "Crippled Midget with Muscular Dystrophy Charges . . . Jerry Lewis Roughed Me Up and Threatened to Kill Me." *National Enquirer*, 10 July, 17.

Brenna, Tony, Richard Taylor, Patricia Towle, and Steve Herz. 1990. "'I'll Quit!'—Jerry Lewis Goes Bananas as Telethon Topples Him from Throne." *National Enquirer*, 15 May, 40.

Brooks, Tim, and Erle Marsh. 1985a. *TV in the 1960s*. New York: Ballantine Books.

————. 1985b. *TV's Greatest Hits: The 150 Most Popular TV Shows of All Time*. New York: Ballantine Books.

Browne, Nick, ed. 1990. *Cahiers du Cinéma 1969–1972: The Politics of Representation*. Cambridge: Harvard University Press.

Brownlow, Kevin, and David Gill. 1983. *The Unknown Chaplin*, episodes 1-3. Television program, Thames Television.

Buckley, Michael. 1983. Review of *The King of Comedy*. *Films in Review*, May, 301.

Bukatman, Scott. 1988. "Paralysis in Motion: Jerry Lewis's Life as a Man." *Camera Obscura* 17 (Fall): 194-205. Expanded version in Horton, *Comedy/Cinema/Theory*, 188-205.

Buscombe, Edward. 1981. "Ideas of authorship." In Caughie, *Theories of Authorship*, 22-34. Originally in *Screen* 14, no. 3.

Butler, Jeremy G. 1998. "The Star System and Hollywood." In *The Oxford Guide to Film Studies*, edited by John Hill and Pamela Church Gibson, 342-53. Oxford: Oxford University Press.

Camper, Fred. 1971. "Essays in Visual Style No. 2: Jerry Lewis, *The Nutty Professor*." *Cinema* (Great Britain) 8:32-34.

Canby, Vincent. 1983. "Unusual Kidnapping: *The King of Comedy*." *New York Times*, 18 February 1983, sec. C, p. 10.

————. 1995. "Finally, Jerry Lewis Is on Broadway." *New York Times*, 13 March 1995, sec. C, pp. 11, 19.

Carringer, Robert L., ed. 1979. *The Jazz Singer*. Madison: University of Wisconsin Press.

Cashin, Fergus. 1969. "There Was This Director Who Said: 'Jerry Lewis Is a Cross-eyed, Yelping Lunatic. He's Putty and I Don't Like Him.'" *Daily Sketch*, 30 May 1969, 8.

Caughie, John, ed. 1981. *Theories of Authorship*. London: RKP, BFI.

Chen, David W. 1997. "Party in Cyberspace Is First for Broadway." *New York Times*, 26 March, sec. B, p. 8.

Chown, Jeffrey. 1988. *Hollywood Auteur*. New York: Praeger.

Clarity, James F. 1976. "*C'est Vrai*: Jerry Lewis Wows the French." *New York Times*, 31 May, p. 17.

Cohan, Steve. 1993. "Queering the Deal: On the Road with Hope and Crosby." Paper presented at the Society for Cinema Studies annual conference, New Orleans. Revised version published in *Out Takes: Essays on Queer Theory and Film,* edited by Ellis Hanson, 23-45. Durham, N.C.: Duke University Press, 1999.

————. 1997. *Masked Men: Masculinity and Movies in the Fifties.* Bloomington: Indiana University Press.

Cook, David A. 1996. *A History of Narrative Film.* 3d ed. New York: W. W. Norton.

Cook, Pam, ed. 1985. *The Cinema Book.* London: BFI.

Corrigan, Timothy. 1992. *A Cinema Without Walls: Movies and Culture after Vietnam.* London: Routledge.

Coursodon, Jean-Pierre. 1983. "Jerry Lewis." In *American Directors,* vol. 2, edited by Jean-Pierre Coursodon and Pierre Sauvage, 189-202. New York: McGraw-Hill.

Cremonini, Giorgio. 1979. *Jerry Lewis.* Florence: Il castoro cinema, La Nuova Italy.

Cripps, Thomas. 1983. "*Amos 'n' Andy* and the Debate over American Racial Integration." In O'Connor, *American History/American Television,* 33-54.

Crisp, Colin. 1993. *The Classic French Cinema, 1930–1960.* Bloomington: Indiana University Press.

Crowther, Bosley. 1949. Review of *My Friend Irma. New York Times,* 29 September, p. 39.

————. 1952. Review of *Jumping Jacks. New York Times,* 24 July, 30.

————. 1953. Review of *The Caddy. New York Times,* 18 September, p. 16.

————. 1954. Review of *Money from Home. New York Times,* 27 February, p. 11.

————. 1957. Review of *The Delicate Delinquent. New York Times,* 4 July, p. 16.

Curtis, James L. 1984. *Between Flops: A Biography of Preston Sturges.* New York: Limelight Editions.

Daney, Serge. 1966. "A Nothing on a Ground of Soft Music." *Cahiers du Cinéma in English* 4:33.

Daniels, Les. 1995. *DC Comics: Sixty Years of the World's Favorite Comic Book Heroes.* London: Virgin Books.

Davidson, Bill. 1951. "Anything for a Laugh." *Colliers,* 10 February, 30-31, 65.

Dawson, Jim. 1995. *The Twist: The Story of the Song and Dance that Changed the World.* Boston: Faber & Faber.

Denby, David. 1983. Review of *The King of Comedy. New York,* 21 February, 74.

Derry, Charles. 1985. "Jerry Lewis." In *The International Dictionary of Films and Filmmakers.* Vol. 2, *Directors/Filmmakers,* edited by Christopher Lyon, 331-34. Chicago: St. James Press.

————. 1997. "Jerry Lewis." In *The International Dictionary of Films and Filmmakers.* Vol. 2, *Directors,* 3d ed., edited by Laurie Collier Hillstrom, 602-6. Detroit: St. James Press.

Dixon, Winston Wheeler, ed. 1993. *The Early Film Criticism of François Truffaut.* Bloomington: Indiana University Press.

Doherty, Thomas. 1988. *Teenagers and Teenpics: The Juvenilization of American Movies in the 1950's.* London: Unwin-Hyman.

Durgnat, Raymond. 1969. *The Crazy Mirror: Hollywood Comedy and the American Image.* London: Faber & Faber.

Dyer, Richard. 1979. *Stars.* London: BFI.

————. 1981. "Entertainment and Utopia." In *Genre: The Musical,* edited by Rick Altman, 175-89. London: RKP, BFI.

————. 1987. *Heavenly Bodies: Film Stars and Society.* London: Macmillan, BFI.

———. 1991. "*A Star Is Born* and the Construction of Authenticity." In Gledhill, *Stardom*, 132–39.

Ehrenreich, Barbara. 1982. *The Hearts of Men: American Dreams and the Flight from Commitment.* London: Pluto Press.

Ehrenstein, David. 1994a. "Frank Tashlin and Jerry Lewis." In Garcia and Eisenschitz, *Frank Tashlin,* 43–47.

———. 1994b. "*Hollywood or Bust.*" In Garcia and Eisenschitz, *Frank Tashlin,* 167–68.

Eisenschitz, Bernard. 1994a. "Pardon My French." In Garcia and Eisenschitz, *Frank Tashlin,* 103–9.

———. 1994b. "*The Geisha Boy.*" In Garcia and Eisenschitz, *Frank Tashlin,* 170–71.

Ellis, John. 1992. *Visible Fictions: Cinema, Television, Video.* Rev. ed. London: Routledge.

Elsaesser, Thomas. 1975. "Two Decades in Another Country: Hollywood and the Cinephiles." In *Superculture: American Popular Culture and Europe,* edited by C. W. E. Bigsby, 199–216. Bowling Green, Ohio: Bowling Green University Popular Press.

Etaix, Pierre. 1983. *Croquis de Jerry Lewis.* Paris: Gilbert Salachas Éditeur.

Ewen, Stuart. 1977. *Captains of Consciousness: Advertising and the Social Roots of Consumer Culture.* New York: McGraw-Hill.

Faith, William R. 1983. *Bob Hope: A Life in Comedy.* London: Granada.

Fallon, Steve, Daniel Robinson, and Richard Nebesky. 1997. *France: A Lonely Planet Travel Survival Kit.* Hawthorn, Victoria: Lonely Planet Publications.

Farson, Daniel. 1952. "They Made Me a Myth: Funny Men Dean Martin and Jerry Lewis." *Sight and Sound* 22, no. 1 (July–September): 30–31.

Feuer, Jane. 1986. "The Self-Reflexive Musical and the Myth of Entertainment." In *Film Genre Reader,* edited by Barry K. Grant, 329–43. Austin: University of Texas Press.

Fields, Armond, and L. Marc Fields. 1993. *From the Bowery to Broadway: Lew Fields and the Roots of American Popular Theater.* New York: Oxford University Press.

Film Dope. 1986. "Jerry Lewis" (entry 975). *Film Dope* 35 (September): 16–18.

Fischer, Lucy. 1991. "Sometimes I Feel Like a Motherless Child: Comedy and Matricide." In Horton, *Comedy/Cinema/Theory,* 60–78.

Fleming, Michael. 1997. "Lewis's *Bellboy* Gets Redo at MGM." *Yahoo! News—Reuters,* 21 November 1997. Http://ww5.yahoo.com/headlines/971121/entertainment/stories/film_bellboy_1.html.

Fordin, Hugh. 1986. "Introduction" to *The Band Wagon,* edited by Betty Comden and Adolph Green. London: Lorrimer Publishing.

Freedland, Michael. 1984. *Dino: The Dean Martin Story.* London: W. H. Allen.

Freud, Sigmund. [1909] 1977. "Family Romances." In *On Sexuality,* by Sigmund Freud. Harmondsworth: Penguin.

Friedan, Betty. 1965. *The Feminine Mystique,* Harmondsworth: Penguin Books.

Friedman, Lester D., ed. 1991. *Unspeakable Images: Ethnicity and the American Cinema.* Urbana: University of Illinois Press.

Fuller, Graham. 1993. "Thank You Jerry Much." *Interview,* April, 92–93, 115.

Garcia, Roger, and Bernard Eisenschitz, eds. 1994. *Frank Tashlin.* London: Éditions du Festival International du film de Locarno/Éditions Yellow Now/BFI.

Gehman, Richard. 1964. *That Kid: The Story of Jerry Lewis.* New York: Avon Books.

Geuens, Jean-Pierre. 1996. "Through the Looking Glasses: From the Camera Obscura to Video Assist." *Film Quarterly* 49, no. 3 (Spring): 16–26.

Gledhill, Christine, ed. 1991. *Stardom: Industry of Desire*. London: Routledge.

Godard, Jean-Luc. 1986. "Struggling on Two Fronts." Interview with Jacques Bontemps, Jean-Louis Comolli, Michel Delahaye, and Jean Narboni. In Hillier, *Cahiers du Cinéma* (1986), 294–99. Originally in *Cahiers du Cinéma,* October 1967.

Godet, Sylvain. 1966. "Little Divagation." *Cahiers du Cinéma in English* 4:35.

Gomery, Douglas. 1986. *The Hollywood Studio System*. London: Macmillan.

Gordon, Arthur. 1983. "Ballad of a Funny Man: *The King of Comedy.*" *Stills* 7 (July/August): 81.

Gozlan, Gérard. 1968. "In Praise of André Bazin." In Graham, *New Wave,* 52–71. Originally in *Positif* 45 (May 1962).

Graham, Peter, ed. 1968. *The New Wave: Critical Landmarks*. London: Secker & Warburg (Cinema One).

Green, Abel. 1957. "Jerry Lewis' Dual-Role at Palace—Today's B.O. & Preview of Tomorrow." *Variety,* 13 February, 14.

Green, Stanley. 1985. *Broadway Musicals: Show by Show.* London: Faber & Faber.

Grove, Lloyd. 1996. "Jerry Lewis, Seriously Funny." *Washington Post,* 11 September, sec. D, pp. 1, 4.

Haller, Beth. 1994. "The Misfit and Muscular Dystrophy." *Journal of Popular Film and Television* 21, no. 4 (Winter): 142–49.

Hammel, William, ed. 1977. *The Popular Arts in America: A Reader*. New York: Harcourt Brace Jovanovich.

Haskell, Molly. 1974. *From Reverence to Rape: The Treatment of Women in the Movies*. London: New England Library.

Haun, Harry. 1995. "The Devil in Jerry Lewis." In the playbill for the Marquis Theatre, February, 20, 22.

Hayward, Susan. 1993. *French National Cinema*. London: Routledge.

Hebdige, Dick. 1988. *Hiding in the Light: On Images and Things*. London: Comedia, Routledge.

Henderson, Brian. 1991. "Cartoon and Narrative in the Films of Frank Tashlin and Preston Sturges." In Horton, *Comedy/Cinema/Theory,* 153–73.

Higham, Charles. 1972. "Jerry Isn't Just Clowning Around Now." *New York Times,* 30 July, sec. 2, pp. 9, 18.

Hill, Gladwyn. 1949. "The Borscht Belt's Latest Gift to the Movies." *New York Times,* 18 September, sec. 2, p. 5.

Hillier, Jim, ed. 1985. *Cahiers du Cinéma: The 1950s—Neo-Realism, Hollywood, New Wave*. Cambridge: Harvard University Press.

———. 1986. *Cahiers du Cinéma: The 1960s—New Wave, New Cinema, Reevaluating Hollywood*. Cambridge: Harvard University Press.

Hirschberg, Lynn. 1982. "What's So Funny about Jerry Lewis?" *Rolling Stone,* 28 October, 33–35, 78.

Hoberman, J. 1988. "The Nutty Retrospective." *Village Voice,* 15 December, 47, 61.

———. 1993. "Rubberface." *Interview* 23 (February): 109–10.

———. 1994. "Frank Tashlin: Vulgar Modernist." In Garcia and Eisenschitz, *Frank Tashlin,* 89–94.

Horton, Andrew, ed. 1991. *Comedy/Cinema/Theory*. Berkeley: University of California Press.

Houston, Beverle. 1984. "*King of Comedy:* A Crisis of Substitution." *Framework* 24 (Spring): 74–92.

Houston, Penelope. 1960. "The Critical Question." *Sight and Sound* 29, no. 4 (Autumn): 160–65.

Hoveyda, Fereydoun. 1985. "Nicholas Ray's Reply: *Party Girl.*" In Hillier, *Cahiers du Cinéma* (1985), 122–31.

Iran News. 1995. "Comedian Jerry Lewis Finally Makes It to Broadway." *Iran News* web site. Http://www.netiran.com.

Jackson, Nancy Beth. 1979. "Jerry Lewis Tries a Film Comeback." *New York Times,* 29 April, sec. 2, pp. 1–2.

Jackson-Willies, Jody. 1996. "Jerry Lewis: The Devil in the Everglades." J.J. Talks web site. Http://www.hpmetro.com/0408/jjtalk09.html.

Jarvie, Ian C. 1991. "Stars and Ethnicity: Hollywood and the United States, 1932–1951." In Friedman, *Unspeakable Images,* 82–111.

Jasen, David A. 1990. *Tin Pan Alley: The Composers, the Songs, the Performers and their Times.* London: Omnibus Press.

JAS Productions, Inc. 1989. *Jerry Lewis Live* (video tape), MSD Video Ltd., Great Britain, 1989. VHS 92452.

———. 1992a. *Martin and Lewis: Their Golden Age of Comedy.* Pt. 1, *The Birth of the Team.* First broadcast on the Disney Channel, 1992.

———. 1992b. *Martin and Lewis: Their Golden Age of Comedy.* Pt. 2, *The Kings of Comedy.* First broadcast on the Disney Channel, 1992.

———. 1992c. *Martin and Lewis: Their Golden Age of Comedy.* Pt. 3, *Jerry . . . Alone at the Top.* First broadcast on the Disney Channel, 1992.

———. 1993a. *Martin and Lewis: Their Golden Age of Comedy.* Pt. 4, *Dean and Jerry at the Movies.* First broadcast on the Disney Channel, 1993.

———. 1993b. *Martin and Lewis: Their Golden Age of Comedy.* Pt. 5, *Jerry Lewis, Total Film Maker.* First broadcast on the Disney Channel, 1993.

Jenkins, Henry. 1990. "'Fifi Was My Mother's Name': Anarchistic Comedy, the Vaudeville Aesthetic, and *Diplomaniacs.*" *Velvet Light Trap* 26 (Fall): 3–27.

———. 1992. *What Made Pistachio Nuts? Early Sound Comedy and the Vaudeville Aesthetic.* New York: Columbia University Press.

———. 1997. "'This Fellow Keaton Seems to Be the Whole Show': Buster Keaton, Interrupted Performance, and the Vaudeville Aesthetic." In *Buster Keaton's Sherlock Jr.,* edited by Andrew Horton, 29–66. Cambridge: Cambridge University Press.

Jenkins, Steve. 1983. "*The King of Comedy.*" *Monthly Film Bulletin* 50, no. 593 (June): 150–51.

Johns, Elizabeth. 1997. "Jerry Lewis Remakes *Errand Boy.*" E! Online web site, 1 May. Http://www.eonline.com/News/Items/0,1,1055,00.html.

Johnson, Catherine Irene. 1981. *Contradiction in 1950s Comedy and Ideology.* Ann Arbor, Mich.: UMI Research Press.

Johnston, Claire, and Paul Willemen, eds. 1973. *Frank Tashlin.* Edinburgh: Edinburgh Film Festival/*Screen.*

Jones, Robert A. 1991. "Jerry's Kids: It's a Pity but It Works." *Los Angeles Times,* 4 September, sec. A, p. 3.

Kael, Pauline. 1966. "Circles and Squares: Joys and Sarris." In *I Lost It at the Movies,* by

Pauline Kael, 292-319. London: Jonathan Cape. Originally in *Film Quarterly* 16, no. 3 (Spring 1963).

———. 1987. "Jokers." In *Taking It All In: Film Writings 1980–1983,* by Pauline Kael, 456-63. New York: A Williams Abrahams Book/Holt, Rinehart & Winston.

Kaleidoscope. 1997. Review of *Damn Yankees. Kaleidoscope,* BBC Radio 4, 5 June.

Kantor, Bernard F, Irwin R. Blacker, and Anne Kramer. 1970. *Directors at Work: Interviews with American Film Makers.* New York: Funk & Wagnalls.

Kaplan, E. Ann. 1992. *Motherhood and Representation: the Mother in Popular Culture and Melodrama.* London: Routledge.

Karnick, Kristine B., and Henry Jenkins, eds. 1995. *Classical Hollywood Comedy.* New York: Routledge.

Kass, Robert. 1953. "Jerry Lewis Analyzed." *Films in Review* 4, no. 3 (March): 119-23.

Katz, Ephraim. 1986. "Jerry Lewis." In *The International Film Encyclopaedia,* 718. London: Macmillan.

Kelley, Kitty. 1986. *His Way: The Unauthorized Biography of Frank Sinatra.* London: Bantam Books.

Kemp, Evan, Jr. 1981. "Aiding the Disabled: No Pity, Please." *New York Times,* 3 September, sec. A, p. 19.

Kepley, Vance. 1990. "From 'Frontal Lobes' to the 'Bob-and-Bob' Show: NBC Management and Programming Strategies, 1949-65." In Balio, *Hollywood in the Age of Television,* 63-89.

Krohn, Bill. 1994. "The Outsider: Joe Dante on Tashlin." In Garcia and Eisenschitz, *Frank Tashlin,* 135-37.

Kroll, Jack. 1983. Review of *The King of Comedy. Newsweek,* 21 February, 60.

Krutnik, Frank. 1994. "Jerry Lewis: The Deformation of the Comic." *Film Quarterly* 48, no. 4 (Fall): 12-26.

———. 1995a. "A Spanner in the Works? Genre, Narrative and the Hollywood Comedian." In Karnick and Jenkins, *Classical Hollywood Comedy,* 17-38.

———. 1995b. "The Handsome Man and His Monkey: the Comic Bondage of Dean Martin and Jerry Lewis." *Journal of Popular Film and Television* 23, no. 1 (Spring): 16-25.

Kuisel, Richard. 1996. *Seducing the French: The Dilemma of Americanization.* Berkeley: University of California Press.

Labarthe, André S. 1962. "Lewis au pays de Carroll." *Cahiers du Cinéma* 132 (June): 1-7.

Leutrat, Jean-Louis, and Paul Simonci. 1965. *Jerry Lewis.* Lyon: Serdoc/Premier Plan no. 36.

Levy, Shawn. 1994. "The Nutty Professor, Emeritus, Returns." *New York Times,* 4 March, sec. 2, p. 28.

———. 1996a. *King of Comedy: The Life and Art of Jerry Lewis.* New York: St Martin's Press.

———. 1996b. "Jim Carrey: The Jerry Lewis Connection." *Oregonian* web site. Http://www.bsc.nodak.edu/English/webgeist/Levy.htm.

———. 1998. *Rat Pack Confidential.* London: Fourth Estate.

Lewis, Jerry. 1969. Interview by John Deighton. *Today's Cinema* 9685 (16 June 1969): 2-3.

———. 1973. *The Total Film-Maker.* 1971. Reprint, New York: Warner Paperback Library.

———. 1990a. *Collector's Series: Jerry Lewis.* Capitol Records compact disc CDP 7 93196 2.

———. 1990b. "'If I Had Muscular Dystrophy.'" *Parade,* 2 September, 4-5.

———. 1992. Interview with Chris Wallace on *Prime Time Live.* NBC, 3 September.

————. 1995. "Jerry Lewis, National Press Club." Http://town.hall.org/Archives/radio/IMS/Club/950417_club_00_ITH.html.

Lewis, Jerry, and Bill Davidson. 1957. "I've Always Been Scared." *Look* 21, no. 3 (5 February): 51–61. The byline reads "Jerry Lewis, as told to Bill Davidson."

Lewis, Jerry, and Herb Gluck. 1982. *Jerry Lewis in Person.* Atheneum: New York.

Lewis, Jonathan R. 1983. "The Comedy Films of Jerry Lewis and Marilyn Monroe: A Narratological Study and an Introduction to the Social/Ideological Project." Ph.d. diss., University of California.

Lewis, Patti, with Sarah Anne Coleman. 1993. *I Laffed Till I Cried: Thirty-Six Years of Marriage to Jerry Lewis.* Waco, Tex.: WRS Publishing.

Linn, Edward. 1963. "The Search for Jerry Lewis." *Saturday Evening Post* 236, no. 3 (12 October): 83–87.

Lipsitz, George. 1990. *Time Passages: Collective Memory and American Popular Culture.* Minneapolis: University of Minnesota Press.

Louden, Christopher. 1997. "Devil May Care." In the playbill for the Hummingbird Theatre, Toronto, Ontario. Playbill on line at http://www.jerrylewiscomedy.com/devil.htm.

Madsen, Axel. 1966. "America's Uncle: Interview with Jerry Lewis." *Cahiers du Cinéma in English* 4:27–31.

Majendie, Paul. 1997. "Lewis in London." *Buffalo News,* 23 May, p. 23.

Maland, Charles. 1991. *Chaplin and American Culture: The Evolution of a Star Image.* Princeton, N.J.: Princeton University Press.

Maltby, Richard. 1998. "'D' for Disgusting: American Culture and English Criticism." In *Hollywood and Europe: Economics, Culture, National Identity, 1945–95,* edited by Geoffrey Nowell-Smith and Steven Ricci, 104–15. London: BFI.

Maltby, Richard, and Ian Craven. 1995. *Hollywood Cinema,* Oxford: Blackwell.

Maltin, Leonard. 1970. *Movie Comedy Teams.* New York: Signet.

————. 1978. *The Great Movie Comedians.* New York: Crown Publishers.

Marc, David. 1989. *Comic Visions: Television Comedy and American Culture.* Boston: Unwin-Hyman.

Marchesini, Mauro. 1983. *Jerry Lewis: Un comico a Perdere.* Verona: Casa Editrice Mazziana.

Marling, Karal Ann. 1994. *As Seen on TV: the Visual Culture of Everyday Life in the 1950s,* Cambridge: Harvard University Press.

Martin, Dean, and Jerry Lewis. 1953a. "Anything for a Laugh." *Picturegoer* 25, no. 944 (6 June): 14, 15, 19.

————. 1953b. "We Get Our First Break." *Picturegoer* 25, no. 945 (13 June): 14–15.

————. 1953c. "We Think We're Tops." *Picturegoer* 25, no. 946 (20 June): 15, 21.

————. 1995. *The Martin and Lewis Show.* Radio Spirits, Inc. Nine-CD box set of their NBC radio shows.

Maslin, Janet. 1983. "*The King of Comedy* Delivers a Passionless Sting." *New York Times,* 20 February, sec. 2, p. 19.

Marx, Arthur. 1975. *Everybody Loves Somebody Sometime (Especially Himself): The Story of Dean Martin and Jerry Lewis.* London: W. H. Allen.

May, Elaine Tyler. 1988. *Homeward Bound: American Families and the Cold War Era.* New York: Basic Books.

Mayersberg, Paul. 1967. "Jerry Lewis." Transcript of an interview for the BBC television progam *The Movies*. Job no. 5626/0490, 12 May. British Film Institute Library, London.

McGilligan, Patrick. 1979. "Recycling Jerry Lewis." *American Film* 4, no. 10 (September): 62–65.

McNeil, Donald G., Jr. 1994. "*Yankees* Plans 7th-Inning Stretch." *New York Times*, 8 December, pp. C13, C16.

Meisel, Myron, ed. 1972. "'Comedy Is the Mirror We Hold Up to Life . . .': Jerry Lewis, an Interview." *Focus* (Chicago) 7 (Spring): 4–8, 39.

Mekas, Jonas. 1977. "Sarris in the Palace, or After the Coup." In Hammel, *Popular Arts in America*, 178–86. Originally in *Soho Weekly News*, 20 May 1976.

Mellancamp, Patricia, ed. 1990. *Logics of Television: Essays in Cultural Criticism*. London: BFI.

Miller, Mark Crispin. 1981. "Sickness on TV: The Jerry Lewis Labor Day Telethon." *New Republic*, 7 October, 27–29.

Mills, Bart. 1975. "Lewis Fun." *Guardian* (Great Britain), 7 July, p. 8.

———. 1981. "Mature Is the Man Yelling that There's a Lot of the Little Boy in Him." *Guardian*, 29 October, p. 15.

Milne, Tom, ed. 1986. *Godard on Godard*. New York: Da Capo Press.

Mr. Showbiz. 1997. "*Damn Yankees:* Damn Expensive, Shuts Down." Mr. Showbiz web site, 6 October. Http://www.mrshowbiz.com/news/todays_stories/971003/yankees102_content.html.

———. 1998. "Jerry Lewis Stalker Put Away." Mr. Showbiz web site, 8 July. Http://www.mrshowbiz.com/news/todays_stories/980708/lewis070898_content.html.

Murray, Edward. 1975. *Nine American Film Critics: A Study of Theory and Practice*. New York: Frederick Ungar.

Musser, Charles. 1991. "Ethnicity, Role-playing, and American Film Comedy: From *Chinese Laundry Scene* to *Whoopee* (1894–1930)." In Friedman, *Unspeakable Images*, 39–81.

Naremore, James. 1995-96. "American *Film Noir:* The History of an Idea." *Film Quarterly* 49, no. 2 (Winter): 12–28.

Neale, Steve, and Frank Krutnik. 1990. *Popular Film and Television Comedy*. London: Routledge.

Neibaur, James L., and Ted Okuda. 1995. *The Jerry Lewis Films: An Analytical Filmography of the Innovative Comic*. Jefferson, N.C.: McFarland.

Nichols, Bill, ed. 1976. *Movies and Methods*. Vol. 1. Berkeley: University of California Press.

Noames, Jean-Louis. 1965. "Le discours de la méthode." *Cahiers du Cinéma* 16, no. 2 (January): 146–47. Privately translated by Corinna Russell.

Nolan, Frederick. 1994. *Lorenz Hart: A Poet on Broadway*. New York: Oxford University Press.

O'Connor, J. E., ed. 1983. *American History/American Television: Interpreting the Video Past*. New York: Frederick Ungar.

Palmer, Jerry. 1987. *The Logic of the Absurd: On Film and Television Comedy*. London: BFI.

Paul, William. 1994. *Laughing, Screaming: Modern Hollywood Horror and Comedy*. New York: Columbia University Press.

PBS, and WGBH Educational Foundation. 1996. "Secret Daughter." Documentary produced and presented by June Cross for the *Frontline* series. First broadcast on 26 November 1996. Transcript obtained from the WGBH Educational Foundation web site. Http://pbs.org/wgbh.

Peploe, Mark, and Hercules Belville. 1969. "Comedy Is a Man in Trouble." *Sunday Times Magazine,* 16 November, 83, 85.

Philippe, Claude-Jean. 1966. "Indifference and Terror." *Cahiers du Cinéma in English* 4:39.

Polan, Dana. 1984a. "Being and Nuttiness: Jerry Lewis and the French." *Journal of Popular Film and Television* 12, no. 1 (Spring): 42-46.

———. 1984b. *"The Nutty Professor."* In *The Macmillan Dictionary of Films and Filmmakers.* Vol. 1, *Films,* 333-34. London: Macmillan.

Pollock, Dale. 1981. "The Clown Prince's Hollywood Comeback." *Washington Post,* 5 April, sec. K, pp. 1, 5.

Prouty, Howard. 1994. "Documentation." In Garcia and Eisenschitz, *Frank Tashlin,* 185-240.

———, ed. 1989-96. *The Variety and Daily Variety Television Reviews, 1946–1994.* Vols. 1-23. New York: Garland Publishing.

Pryor, Thomas M. 1958. "Film Stars Now Corporate Galaxy." *New York Times,* 6 January, p. 121.

Putterman, Barry. 1995. *On Television and Comedy: Essays on Style, Theme, Performer and Writer,* Jefferson, N.C.: McFarland.

Rafferty, Terrence. 1983. "Martin Scorsese's Still Life." *Sight and Sound* 52, no. 3 (Summer): 186-92.

Rapf, Joanna E. 1993. "Comic Theory from a Feminist Perspective: A Look at Jerry Lewis." *Journal of Popular Culture* 27, no. 1 (Summer): 191-203.

Reader, Keith. 1993. "French Cinema Since 1945." In *French Culture since 1945,* edited by Malcolm Cook, 78-98. London: Longman.

Recasens, Gérard. 1970. *Jerry Lewis.* Paris: Seghers/Cinema d'Aujord'hui no. 59.

Rhames, Kathleen. 1996. "Satan Takes the stage." *Daily Bruin,* 21 October. *Daily Bruin* web site. Http://www.dailybruin.ucla.edu.

Richards, David. 1994. "A Faustian Fable from the Era of Eisenhower: *Damn Yankees."* *New York Times,* 4 March, sec. C, pp. 1, 28.

Rickey, Carrie. 1982. "Marty." *American Film* 8, no. 2:66-73.

Robinson, David. 1986. *Chaplin, His Life and Art.* London: Paladin.

Rodgers, Scott. 1995. "That's Infotainment: The Greatest Movie You've Never Seen." Ape-O-Naut web site. Http://www.westworld.com/~apenaut/infotain.htm.

Romney, Jonathan. 1995. "The Monkey's New Tricks." *Guardian Weekend* (Great Britain), 16 September, pp. 22-24.

———. 1996. "Why Tavernier Is Wrong about *The Nutty Professor." Guardian* (Great Britain), 4 October, p. 10.

———. 1997. "Jerry Lewis, the King of Comedy, Has Something to Tell You: That He Is a Very, Very Happy Man." *Guardian* (Great Britain), 31 May, p. 6.

Rose, Lloyd. 1996. "Devilishly Good Jerry Lewis in *Damn Yankees." Washington Post,* 12 December, sec. C, p. 1.

Rosenbaum, Jonathan. 1973. "Paris Journal." *Film Comment* 9, no. 1 (March-April): 2-6.

Roud, Richard. 1960. "The French Line." *Sight and Sound* 29, no. 4 (Autumn): 166-71.

Rowe, Kathleen. 1995. *The Unruly Woman: Gender and the Genres of Laughter.* Austin: University of Texas Press.

Royot, Daniel. 1979. "American Humor and the French Psyche." In *American Humor in France: Two Centuries of French Criticism of the Comic Spirit in American Literature,* edited by J. C. Austin. Ames: Iowa State University Press.

Said, Edward. 1978. *Orientalism: Western Conceptions of the Orient.* Harmondsworth: Penguin Books.

Sarris, Andrew. 1959. "The Seventh Seal." *Film Culture* 19:51-61.

———. 1962-63. "Notes on the *Auteur* Theory in 1962." *Film Culture* 27 (Winter): 1-8.

———. 1963a. "The American Cinema." *Film Culture* 28 (Spring): 1-51.

———. 1963b. "Directorial Chronology 1915-1962." *Film Culture* 28 (Spring): 52-68.

———. 1966. "Editor's Eyrie." *Cahiers du Cinéma in English* 4:64-66.

———. 1968. *The American Cinema: Directors and Directions, 1929-1968.* New York: E. P. Dutton.

———. 1977. "*Avant-Garde* Films Are More Boring than Ever." In Hammel, *Popular Arts in America,* 167-77. Originally in *Village Voice,* 17 May 1976.

———. 1983. "The King of Comedy." *Village Voice,* 15 February, 45.

———. 1995. "Notes of an Accidental *Auteurist*." *Film History* 7, no. 4:358-61.

Scheurer, Timothy. 1985. "The Variety Show." In *TV Genres: A Handbook and Reference Guide,* edited by B. G. Rose, 307-26. Westport, Conn.: Greenwood Press.

Schickel, Richard. 1983. Review of *The King of Comedy. Time,* 14 February, 80.

Schneider, Howard. 1973. "Lewis: The Clown and His Conscience." *Los Angeles Times,* sec, 2, p. 9.

Schumach, Murray. 1959. "$10,000,000 Pact for Jerry Lewis." *New York Times,* 8 June, p. 32.

Scott, Frank, and Al Ennis. 1993. *The Roots and Rhythm Guide to Rock.* Pennington, N.J.: a capella books.

Sedgwick, Eve Kosofsky. 1985. *Between Men: English Literature and Male Homosocial Desire.* New York: Columbia University Press.

Seidman, Steve. 1981. *Comedian Comedy: A Tradition in Hollywood Film.* Ann Arbor, Mich.: UMI Research Press.

Selig, Michael. 1990. "*The Nutty Professor:* A 'Problem' in Film Scholarship." *Velvet Light Trap* 26 (Fall): 42-56.

Shales, Tom. 1997. "Send in the Clowns: Jerry Lewis's Labor Day of Love." *Washington Post,* 30 August, sec. D, pp. 1, 5.

Shaviro, Steve. 1993. *The Cinematic Body.* Minneapolis: University of Minnesota Press.

Shaw, David. 1973. "Celebrities Act in Many Ways to Gain Privacy." *Los Angeles Times,* 5 September, pp. 1, 3, 34, 35, 36.

Shearer, Harry. 1979. "Midsection: Telethon." *Film Comment* 15, no. 3 (May-June): 33-48.

Showguide. 1969. "Merry Jerry—20 Years Later." *Showguide,* May. "Jerry Lewis" clippings file. British Film Institute Library, London.

Sikov, Ed. 1983. "*The King of Comedy*." *Film Quarterly* 36, no. 4 (Summer): 17-21.

———. 1994. *Laughing Hysterically: American Screen Comedy of the 1950s.* New York: Columbia University Press.

Simons, Judith. 1975. "It's Crossing His Eyes that Makes Jerry Look So Young." *Daily Express,* 7 July, p. 8.

Simpson, Mark. 1994. "The Straight Men of Comedy." *Attitude,* December, 64-68.

Simsolo, Nöel. 1969. *Le Monde de Jerry Lewis.* Paris: Éditions du Cerf.

Sklar, Robert. 1994. "Taking Tashlin Seriously." In Garcia and Eisenschitz, *Frank Tashlin,* 97-102.

Smith, Dave. 1975. "Jerry Lewis's Passion: A Telethon for 'His' Kids." *Los Angeles Times,* 24 August, pp. 1, 8-9.

Snowden, Lynn. 1992. "Fifty Ways to Kill an Insect by an Ex-Junkie Exterminator." *Guardian* (Great Britian), 25 April, p. 25. Originally published in *Esquire,* February 1992.

Soapbox Productions, Inc. 1996. *Jerry Lewis: The Last American Clown.* Documentary broadcast in the *Biography* series on the U.S. Arts & Entertainment network.

Spigel, Lynn. 1990. "Television in the Family Circle: The Popular Reception of a New Medium." In Mellancamp, *Logics of Television,* 73-97.

Staiger, Janet. 1985. "Blueprints for Feature Films: Hollywood's Continuity Scripts." In Balio, *American Film Industry,* 173-92.

Steinberg, Corbett. 1981. *Reel Facts: The Movie Book of Records,* Harmondsworth: Penguin.

Stern, Lesley. 1995. *The Scorsese Connection.* London: BFI.

Stern, Michael. 1975. "Jerry Lewis b. Joseph Levitch, Newark, New Jersey, 1926 res. Hollywood." *Bright Lights* 1, no. 3 (Summer): 4-14.

Tailleur, Roger. 1958. "Anything Goes." In Johnston and Willemen, *Frank Tashlin,* 17-31. Originally in *Positif* 29 (Fall 1958).

Tasker, Yvonne. 1993. *Spectacular Bodies: Genre, Gender and the Action Film.* London: Routledge.

Taves, Isabella. 1958. "Always in a Crowd—Always Alone." *Look,* 23 December, 83-84, 86, 87-88, 91.

Taylor, John Russell. 1965. "Jerry Lewis." *Sight and Sound* 34, no. 2 (Spring): 82-85.

Taylor, Richard, and Ian Christie, eds. 1988. *The Film Factory: Russian and Soviet Cinema in Documents 1896–1939.* Cambridge: Harvard University Press.

Thompson, Bob. 1997. "Taking Notes on *Nutty Professor.*" Canoe (Canadian Online Explorer) web site. Http://www.canoe.com/JamMoviesArtistsL2Q/lewis_jerry.html.

Thompson, David. 1981. "The Pied Piper of the Las Vegas Sahara." In *Overexposures: The Crisis in American Filmmaking,* by David Thompson, 123-33. New York: William Morrow.

———. 1994. *A Biographical Dictionary of Film.* London: Andre Deutsch.

Thompson, David, and Ian Christie, eds. 1989. *Scorsese on Scorsese.* London: Faber & Faber.

Thompson, Kristin, and David Bordwell. 1994. *Film History: An Introduction.* New York: McGraw-Hill.

Tiger Television/BBC. 1992. *Funny Business.* Pt. 3, "Let There Be Love." First broadcast on BBC2, 6 December.

Tolkin, Michael. 1976. "Jerry Lewis Is a 50-Year-Old Kid." *Village Voice,* 27 September, 116-17.

Tosches, Nick. 1992. *Dino: Living High in the Dirty Business of Dreams.* New York: Doubleday.

Truffaut, François. 1968. "Interview with François Truffaut." In Graham, *New Wave,* 9-15, 85-113. Originally in *Cahiers du Cinéma* 138 (December 1962).

―――. 1976. "A Certain Tendency of the French Cinema." In Nichols, *Movies and Methods*, 224-36. Originally in *Cahiers du Cinéma* 31 (January 1954).

―――. 1993. "*Un Pitre au pensionnat/You're Never Too Young.*" In Dixon, *Early Film Criticism of François Truffaut*, 66-68. Originally in *Arts* 601 (9-15 January 1957).

Uppsala Studenters Filmstudio. 1969. *Jerry Lewis*. Uppsala: Uppsala Studenters Filmstudio.

Variety. 1983-97. *Variety Film Reviews, 1907-1996*. Edited by Mike Kaplan. 24 vols. New Providence, N.J.: R. R. Bowker.

Vasey, Ruth. 1997. *The World According to Hollywood, 1918-1939*. Exeter: University of Exeter Press.

Wallis, Hal, and Charles Higham. 1980. *Starmaker: The Autobiography of Hal B. Wallis*. New York: Macmillan.

Walters, Carole. 1987. "The Compleat Jerry Lewis Telethon Guide." *Village Voice*, 1 September, 47-48.

Webster. 1976. *Webster's Third New International Dictionary of the English Language, Unabridged*. Vol. 1, *A to G*. Chicago: G. & C. Merriam.

Wertheim, Arthur F. 1983. "The Rise and Fall of Milton Berle." In O'Connor, *American History/American Television*, 55-78.

Wilk, Max. 1989. *The Golden Age of Television*. Mount Kisco, N.Y.: Moyer Bell.

Williams, Alan. 1992. *Republic of Images: A History of French Filmmaking*. Cambridge: Harvard University Press.

Williams, Christian. 1982. "What He Did for Love: Jerry Lewis Will Fall Down to Get His Audiences to Stand Up and Cheer." *Washington Post*, 24 October. "Jerry Lewis" clippings file. British Film Institute Library, London.

Williams, Linda. 1991. "Film Bodies: Gender, Genre, and Excess." *Film Quarterly* 44, no. 1 (Summer): 2-13.

Williamson, C. H. B. 1973. "Jerry Lewis Makes His Mark in the Midlands." *CinemaTV Today*, 14 April, 4-7.

Wolff, Craig. 1993. "Joys and Regrets and All in a Day: At Home with Jerry Lewis." *New York Times*, 5 August, sec. C, pp. 1, 8.

Wood, Robin. 1981. *Howard Hawks*. Rev. ed. London: BFI.

Zimmer, Christian. 1962. "Réalisateur du *Dingue du Palace* et du *Tombeur de ces Dames*. Jerry Lewis: Est-il un auteur de films?" *Télérama*, 1 July. Privately translated by Corinna Russell.

WEB SITES

The American Disabilities Act of 1990. Mike Augsburger web site. Http://www2.wcoil.com/~mkaugie/ada.html.

The Americans with Disabilities Act: Questions and Answers. Kraut & Kraut law firm web site. Http://www.kraut-law/em1.html.

Applegate's Apartment. Http://www.angelfire.com/ca/ApplegatesApartment/DYnews.html.

Le Burlesque réflexif de Jerry Lewis (par Emmanuel Dreux). Http://www.imaginet.fr/secav/bibliotheque/jlewis.

Damn Yankees. Http://www.damnyankees.com.

Dino's Lodge. Http://www.ualberta.ca/~mma/owan/dino/dino_index.html.

The Disability Rag. Http://www.inform.umd/EdRes/Topic/Disability/Journals/ News/Rag.

The King of Comedy: The Site Dedicated to Jerry Lewis. Http://www.angelfire.com/ ok/kingofcomedy.

Mr. Showbiz. Http://www.mrshowbiz.com.

Muscular Dystrophy Association. Http://www.mdausa.org.

The Official Jerry Lewis Comedy Museum and Store. Http://www.jerrylewiscomedy.com.

INDEX